A Devotional Experience of

THE PSALMS

A Devotional Experience of

THE PSALMS

Enjoying the Riches of God's Treasure Chest

Gerard Chrispin

A Devotional Experience of the Psalms
Enjoying the Riches of God's Treasure Chest

119 Press (www.119press.com)

Paperback ISBN 9798376559673
Hardcover ISBN 9798376717608
(Amazon Kindle version also available)

Cover design: www.greatwriting.org
Book layout and design: www.greatwriting.org

Today all over the world people are confused, worried and—most of all—lost.

The Book of Psalms shows God's readily available answer to each person, whether Christian or not, in each situation, who individually will trust God through His written Word.

Please read it regularly and ask God to speak to you and guide you. He will if you do!

This devotional will be a blessing to the person who wonders whether poems and songs written thousands of years ago and thousands of miles away have anything to say to them today. Gerard helps the reader to understand some of the context of each psalm and points the reader to its fulfilment in Jesus Christ. This is not a technical commentary directed at the mind. Instead, it is an accessible and heart-warming encouragement to the reader to place their trust in the crucified, risen and ascended Jesus Christ.
REV PHIL CHADDER, Anglican Minister

This book on the Psalms is a *treasure chest* from which we can pluck out spiritual gems to enrich our Christian life, a *war chest* from which we can withdraw reserves to aid us in our daily spiritual battle, and a *medicine chest* full of remedies with which we can treat our various ailments. I would heartily prescribe a daily dose! It is ideal to use for daily 'Quiet Times' whether we have been on the Christian path five days or fifty years, and is food for the soul which comes in helpful, digestible portions. Gerard Chrispin is not only a trustworthy, insightful Bible teacher, but he has the heart of an evangelist so never misses a gospel opportunity—the cross is never far away! I look forward greatly to using it in my own devotions.
MIKE MELLOR: Evangelist, Pastor, and Author

When it comes to the Old Testament there are few books more popular than the Psalms. The Psalms are known as the songbook of the Bible and for thousands of years, God's people have sung them, said them, prayed them and preached them. There are 150 Psalms covering the whole range of human emotions from exuberant joy to extreme sorrow and everything in between. In 'A Devotional Experience of the Psalms' Gerard Chrispin has given a helpful title and provided a short summary of each of the Psalms. Each reading summarises the main points and unique character of each Psalm. This helps the reader to quickly grasp the essential message of each Psalm, in the context of the gospel of Christ and of Him crucified and risen again.

While Genesis to Deuteronomy provide the foundation for all of Scripture, and Proverbs and Ecclesiastes give us wisdom for living, it is the Psalms that capture the heartbeat and heart-cry of the great Shepherd Himself, the Lord Jesus Christ. He is clearly seen here, and Gerard Chrispin captures that loving heartbeat as he takes us through the Psalms one by one. We will get to know the good Shepherd Himself in a deeper way as we walk through the green pastures of the Psalms.

PROF STEVE TAYLOR, B.Sc(ACGI), M.Eng, FIEE, FInstPhys, DSc(DIC), Professor of Electrical Engineering and Electronics

John Calvin called the Psalter 'An Anatomy of the Soul'. By this he meant that in the Psalms we find all the griefs, sorrows, fears, doubts, hopes, cares, and perplexities which we humans face. The Psalms not only provide the expression to these experiences but also the comfort to our cares. In this book Gerard, as a physician of the soul, skilfully applies both the sharp sword of God's Word and the balm of the Gospel to our hearts. Each chapter is full of helpful insights as well as insightful questions; substantive enough to delve deeply into the treasures of God's word, and yet short enough to be used in daily devotions. I heartily commend this book to you.

JAMIE SOUTHCOMBE, BA, AKC, DChA, MDiv, Pastor and Bible Teacher

A word from the author

Thank you to Phil Chadder, Mike Mellor, Jamie Southcombe and Steve Taylor for each commenting on *A Devotional Experience of the Psalms*. Better to have the objective view of these four respected Christian leaders than to offer my own opinion!

Phil is a much-loved Anglican minister whom I met during my prison ministry with Christian Prison Resources. Mike is a popular evangelist and pastor who also writes very readable books. Jamie is a former accountant and a highly respected preacher and teacher who now pastors a flourishing Baptist Church. Steve is a multi-talented university professor of electrical engineering and electronics who takes leading roles in both his church and in interdenominational work, including Young Life, United Beach Missions, Missions Vacances and Christian Answer.

I also extend my thanks to David Harding for his background help and support, as well as Jim Holmes of Great Writing Services.

So my comments are now strictly limited to suggesting how best to use this book, which started life as weekly messages printed off and delivered to prisoners on Sunday mornings.

First, obviously it can act as a reference book as it contains a commentary on every psalm, though the comments on Psalm 119 are more by way of summary.

Second, if the Book of Psalms is already included in your devotional Bible reading scheme (if you have one) just follow your scheme and consider the comments in this book, too. Hopefully your enjoyment of the psalms in your reading scheme will be enriched by considering this commentary.

Third, if you do not operate a Bible reading scheme, or one that now or soon includes Psalms, why not set yourself to read and consider one psalm each day (a few extra days for Psalm 119), and get into the daily habit of reading both the rest of the Bible and one psalm each day?

May God bless you as you read the psalms themselves—a key part of God's written Word—and as you mull over the thoughts expressed in this book.

Psalm 119:30 says, 'The entrance of Your words gives light; It gives understanding to the simple.'

GERARD CHRISPIN

Psalm 1—What really is 'blessing'?

The Way of the Righteous and the End of the Ungodly

1Blessed is the man
Who walks not in the counsel of the ungodly,
Nor stands in the path of sinners,
Nor sits in the seat of the scornful;
2But his delight is in the law of the LORD,
And in His law he meditates day and night.
3He shall be like a tree
Planted by the rivers of water,
That brings forth its fruit in its season,
Whose leaf also shall not wither;
And whatever he does shall prosper.

4The ungodly are not so,
But are like the chaff which the wind drives away.
5Therefore the ungodly shall not stand in the judgment,
Nor sinners in the congregation of the righteous.

6For the LORD knows the way of the righteous,
But the way of the ungodly shall perish.

❖

(VERSES 1-2) The first word in the Book of Psalms and in Psalm 1 itself is '*Blessed*'. It means 'Happy' or 'To be envied'. Most greetings at anniversaries, Christmas, Easter and birthdays start with 'Happy'. We all want to be 'Happy'. Many in our sad world do envy truly happy people. So, how does God, in Psalm 1, tell us we can become 'happy' and 'to be envied'? The starting point is always to turn from sin and trust Jesus as your Saviour: you then begin to know that the '*joy of the LORD is your strength*' (Nehemiah 8:10). Carry on being 'blessed' by not doing three things but by continually doing one thing each day.

The three things not to do are:

- First, refuse to walk in the sinful ways of others.
- Second, avoid spending unnecessary time with those who will lead you astray.
- And third, when possible, do not invest your time sitting with them as if you are their closest pals 'at home' with them.

The one thing to do each day is to read His Word, the Bible, having prayed that God will speak to you through it, and make it your delight as you meditate on it in the day ahead. Get to know it. Then ask keen older Christians about which books to read.

(VERSE 3) Put God first, as just described, to thrive personally and spiritually, and be like a leafy, well-watered tree planted by streams. Your life will be fruitful, and you will stay fresh and very much 'alive'. Your personality will prosper in God's strength. You will start to live in a new way that pleases both God and you! This spiritual prosperity is nothing to do with physical wealth: it grows from living close to the Lord. God also promises to always watch over you. He is a loving and caring God.

(VERSES 4-5) This new way of living for God is so different from those who will not go God's way. God calls them '*ungodly*'. That does not mean they all are 'mega-sinners'. We are all '*ungodly*', or sinful, in God's sight because of our sin. The lives of all who refuse to repent and trust in Jesus are like chaff which is finally blown away. They will fall and perish on God's Judgment Day. The saddest thing is that if even the world's most sinful man would turn from his sin and believe that Jesus loved him so much as to bear his sin and its penalty on the cross, to save him from eternal judgment, God would gladly pardon him. Jesus would answer his prayer to be forgiven and enter his heart through God's Holy Spirit. He would change him from within. As well as God's forgiving and blessing him, others who have received Christ would welcome him, too! He really would be at home '*in the congregation of the righteous*' (meaning other forgiven sinners now counted as '*righteous*' by God). He should be warmly welcomed at Sunday services and weekday Bible studies of any Bible-trusting church or fellowship group! He should find close friends with such folk.

(VERSE 6) Either God counts you as righteous, welcomes you in Heaven after death, and watches over you now—or—'*perish*' in eternal judgment (John 3:16 and 36).

Psalm 2—Rebels against God defy reason

The Messiah's Triumph and Kingdom
1Why do the nations rage,
And the people plot a vain thing?
2The kings of the earth set themselves,
And the rulers take counsel together,
Against the LORD and against His Anointed, saying,
3"Let us break Their bonds in pieces
And cast away Their cords from us."

4He who sits in the heavens shall laugh;
The LORD shall hold them in derision.
5Then He shall speak to them in His wrath,
And distress them in His deep displeasure:
6"Yet I have set My King
On My holy hill of Zion."

7"I will declare the decree:
The LORD has said to Me,
'You are My Son,
Today I have begotten You.
8Ask of Me, and I will give You
The nations for Your inheritance,
And the ends of the earth for Your possession.
9You shall break them with a rod of iron;
You shall dash them to pieces like a potter's vessel.' "

10Now therefore, be wise, O kings;
Be instructed, you judges of the earth.
11Serve the LORD with fear,
And rejoice with trembling.
12Kiss the Son, lest He be angry,
And you perish in the way,
When His wrath is kindled but a little.
Blessed are all those who put their trust in Him.

(VERSES 1-3) I heard a former atheist saying something like, 'When I thought I was shaking my fist in the face of God I realised I was only shaking it at a tiny part of his toenail.' Psalm 2 is all about attitudes against God like his was before he came to Christ. How stupid it is to go against '*the LORD*' and '*His Anointed One*' (namely the Lord Jesus Christ). Many of earth's rulers with big plans have tried and failed before. Here they want to break free of His '*bonds*' and '*cords*'. Ironically, they have this upside down: it is our sin that enslaves us, and repenting of it and turning to Jesus sets us free! Jesus said, '*Whoever commits sin is a slave to sin*' but '*If the Son*

makes you free, you shall be free indeed'. He breaks the bonds and cords of the sin that enslaves us when we ask Him to be our Saviour.

(VERSES 4-8) show it is laughable for puny men to resist God. He scoffs at them from Heaven. When they grasp that He rebukes them in anger and great wrath, they are terrified and realise that the King of kings, the holy Lord Jesus Christ, is in Heaven. This joint rule of God the Father and God the Son (and God the Holy Spirit, though not mentioned here) is eternal. And God hates all sin. God the Father reminds them that He has gifted the nations to His Son who inherits the nations and all the earth.

(VERSE 9) In His holiness and justice, Jesus will rule rightly but with '*a rod of iron*'. His grace and love for us took Him to the cross to bear our sins and be punished for us in our place. He cleanses and pardons every sinner who turns from sin to receive Him in his life. He leads and guides in a new way those trusting Him as Saviour. He provides a home for ever in Heaven for them. But Jesus will be Judge of those who refuse to repent, trust and follow Him. He is the King of Heaven, but also the all-knowing Judge in charge of Judgment.

(VERSES 10-12a) That is why the kings and rulers are very seriously warned and told to '*be wise*'. They are told to approach God with godly fear. If they do trust Jesus as Saviour and so rejoice in sins forgiven, peace with God, and a home in Heaven, their rejoicing should also reflect their trembling at the eternal fate they have escaped through coming to Jesus. Though God the Son will accept them with their signs of affection, they know that, when His righteous anger and wrath is kindled on those who refuse to turn from sins and trust Him, they will be judged.

(VERSE 12b) The Psalm's final message of hope and blessing, having wisely stressed judgment, is that '*all those who put their trust in Him*' not only will be '*blessed*' eternally but are '*blessed*' from that very moment of trust. They are '*happy and to be envied*' as Psalm 1 teaches. Is that you?

Psalm 3—Kept by God in the hard times

A Psalm of David when he fled from Absalom his son.
LORD, how they have increased who trouble me!
Many are they who rise up against me.
2Many are they who say of me,
"There is no help for him in God." Selah

3But You, O LORD, are a shield for me,
My glory and the One who lifts up my head.
4I cried to the Lord with my voice,
And He heard me from His holy hill. Selah

5I lay down and slept;
I awoke, for the LORD sustained me.
6I will not be afraid of ten thousands of people
Who have set themselves against me all around.

7Arise, O LORD;
Save me, O my God!
For You have struck all my enemies on the cheekbone;
You have broken the teeth of the ungodly.
8Salvation belongs to the LORD.
Your blessing is upon Your people. Selah

❖

(VERSES 1-4) Three times (after verses 3, 4 and 8), and often in the psalms, we are told to stop and think about what is said. The Hebrew word, *Selah*, means, 'stop and think', so do ask 'Why stop and think?' King David reminds us that many foes rise up against him. Many say that God will not help him against his foes. His own son, Absalom, leads a big rebellion against his own father to try to take David's throne. That must hurt David's father heart. But does it discourage him? No. Why not? He counts on God as a shield around him and the One who lifts up his head and gives and is, to David, what '*glory*' he knows as king.

David now responds by crying out loud to God in prayer. It is a wonderful privilege to know God and to also know you can pray to Him. But David goes further: he knows, too, that God hears and answers his prayers. He is not a dumb god, such as the idol worshippers follow. God sees, hears, knows and answers. He is living, loving, all-powerful, and shows mercy and kindness to all who turn from sin to Him. He still does if you receive Jesus as your Saviour.

(VERSES 5-6) That causes David to sleep peacefully and know God will sustain him when he awakes. He will not fear if tens of thousands of his enemies surround him.

(VERSE 7) But David specifically asks the LORD God (whom he calls '**my** *God*') to '*Arise*,' to '*save*' him, and defeat his enemies. This is a request for *physical* victory over his wicked *physical* enemies, by striking them on the cheekbone and breaking their teeth. What is true physically for David then is also true now *spiritually* for anyone who turns from his sins, and asks Jesus to save him and enter his life. Christ saves us by His death on the cross for our sins. He bore our deserved punishment and paid for our many sins there. Now alive again, He sets us free, and causes us to know, trust, serve and rejoice in Him day by day. But we all face spiritual enemies and battles—the world, the flesh and the devil fight against us by overwhelming sins, fears, temptations, bad consciences, unbelief, fear of death, and fear of Hell.

(VERSE 8) '*Salvation belongs to the LORD.*' So trust in the Lord Jesus Christ! Follow Him, with God's help. He will save and deliver you *now* and welcome you in Heaven *forever*. He will guide, encourage, bless and help you and keep you in this life, too, as you pray to Him each day, and get to know His Word, the Bible, also daily. He will also supply good, close fellowship with others who know Him, on Sundays (the Lord's Day) and in the week. *Selah!* Go on, do it!

Psalm 4—Blessing through praying

To the Chief Musician. With stringed instruments. A Psalm of David.
1 Hear me when I call, O God of my righteousness!
You have relieved me in my distress;
Have mercy on me, and hear my prayer.

2 How long, O you sons of men,
Will you turn my glory to shame?
How long will you love worthlessness
And seek falsehood? Selah
3 But know that the LORD has set apart for Himself him who is godly;
The LORD will hear when I call to Him.

4 Be angry, and do not sin.
Meditate within your heart on your bed, and be still. Selah
5 Offer the sacrifices of righteousness,
And put your trust in the LORD.

6 There are many who say,
"Who will show us any good?"
LORD, lift up the light of Your countenance upon us.
7 You have put gladness in my heart,
More than in the season that their grain and wine increased.
8 I will both lie down in peace, and sleep;
For You alone, O LORD, make me dwell in safety.

(VERSE 1) We pray naturally when in danger or distress. A Welsh miner, caught in a terrible pit collapse, told me, 'I saw no atheists down the pit that day. They all prayed!' David knows exactly why he is praying: an answer from his *righteous God*, relief from distress in his oppression by others who want to bring him down in shame, and God's ongoing mercy for his ongoing sins. (He is sinful, just like you and just like me.) If you know Jesus, live for Him. Pray in His name and for His glory. Expect His faithful answers, grace, relief and mercy.

(VERSES 2-3) Ungodly men seek to shame others and bring them down from wanting to live for God's glory. They follow worthless and false things, instead of God Himself. We can slide into that same negative, worthless and false kind of living. But all who know God and follow Him are different. David belongs to God and so he knows God hears when he calls to Him in prayer. If you know Jesus, set aside daily time to pray.

(VERSES 4-5) Like David, all who trust the LORD control their anger and search their hearts (even when thinking things through while in bed) to be sure they are forgiven and cleansed. They offer '*sacrifices of righteousness*' to God. That marks out those trusting the LORD. The best *sacrifice* we can offer now is Jesus as the perfect sacrifice for us when He shed His blood for us, as He bore our sins and was punished on the cross to save us eternally. That is how He bought us back from sin. That is why you should '*put your trust in the LORD.*'

(VERSES 6-7) '*Many*' boastfully doubt or sinfully deny God exists. Others claim God cannot do any good. David prays for the light of God's face to shine on his fellow believers and himself. He recalls how God filled his heart with far more joy than when unbelievers benefit from their lucrative and fruitful harvests, and enjoy their food and drink, no doubt at times in wild parties that flout God's laws and ridicule the Lord who provides their food. God means less to them than the food and drink that He gives to godly and ungodly people alike.

(VERSE 8) Yet, even as David faces enemies of both God and himself, he sleeps in peace and trusts the Lord for the result. God gives him peace and safety. God gives a believer in Christ peace with God, and the peace of God in his heart. If opposed, persecuted and even if martyred for Jesus, anyone trusting in Christ will be kept safe for and in Heaven. Jesus has prepared him, or her, a place there with Him for ever.

Psalm 5—God's protection and favour

To the Chief Musician. With flutes. A Psalm of David.
1 Give ear to my words, O LORD,
Consider my meditation.
2 Give heed to the voice of my cry,
My King and my God,
For to You I will pray.
3 My voice You shall hear in the morning, O LORD;
In the morning I will direct it to You,
And I will look up.

4 For You are not a God who takes pleasure in wickedness,
Nor shall evil dwell with You.
5 The boastful shall not stand in Your sight;
You hate all workers of iniquity.
6 You shall destroy those who speak falsehood;
The LORD abhors the bloodthirsty and deceitful man.

7 But as for me, I will come into Your house in the multitude of Your mercy;
In fear of You I will worship toward Your holy temple.
8 Lead me, O LORD, in Your righteousness because of my enemies;
Make Your way straight before my face.

9 For there is no faithfulness in their mouth;
Their inward part is destruction;
Their throat is an open tomb;
They flatter with their tongue.
10 Pronounce them guilty, O God!
Let them fall by their own counsels;
Cast them out in the multitude of their transgressions,
For they have rebelled against You.

11 But let all those rejoice who put their trust in You;
Let them ever shout for joy, because You defend them;
Let those also who love Your name
Be joyful in You.
12 For You, O LORD, will bless the righteous;
With favor You will surround him as with a shield.

(VERSES 1-3) In the Psalms we often see a great personal need being met by God in answer to the prayer of someone who trusts Him. Here, David is praying to God again. He sets a good practical example of how to pray. He first asks God to '*give ear*', '*consider*', and '*heed*' his cry to Him. He pleads. He cries for help. He addresses God reverently but very personally as '*my King and my God*' because He knows God personally as his Lord. He starts his day's praying '*in the morning*'. He speaks with his '*voice*', so perhaps he prays out loud in an audible voice. He lays out his requests before God and waits expectantly for Him to reply to them. This is no mere dull and dead religious exercise. Do you pray like this? The only thing that stops our prayers reaching God and being answered is unconfessed and unforgiven sin. Jesus died to take our sins and their punishment to the cross where He was punished there for us in our place. When we turn from our sins and ask Jesus to enter and rule our lives as our Lord and Saviour, the sin barrier is broken down and we receive eternal life. As we daily forsake and confess our sins directly to Jesus, He hears our prayers. He answers if we are praying in submission to Him. Do you know Jesus? Do you pray like this each day?

(VERSES 4-6) explain why God answers prayer. He hates all evil and wrongdoing of the wicked and arrogant. He abhors falsehood, bloodthirsty men and deceivers. Such unforgiven wicked men cannot *'stand'* before His holy presence. Can you see why we all need His mercy, His loving forgiveness, and His cleansing from our sins? Can you see why Jesus gave Himself to be punished for our sin in our place? It was so we could be pardoned and know God personally.

(VERSES 7-8) David can worship reverently and humbly only because of the *'multitude'* of God's *'mercy'*. Like us, he needs his LORD God to lead him in His *'righteousness'*, even as his enemies surround him. God will graciously straighten out his sinful paths. What is true for David is true for all sinners everywhere.

(VERSES 9-10) Lying, unfaithful and dishonest mouths of men whose hearts are Hell-bound produce death and deceit. Awaiting these guilty unrepentant rebel sinners are spiritual death, eternal destruction and being banished forever. Such people need to turn and trust in Jesus.

(VERSES 11-12) Contrast this with God's grace to all who take refuge in their defending God and in His mercy. They will sing for joy as they now love His name. He blesses them and counts them as *'righteous'*, not because they have done good but because they trust in Jesus and His righteousness is counted as theirs. God loves, protects and surrounds them with *'favour—as a with a shield.'* If you repent and receive Christ, you are fully included!

Psalm 6—Trust when tried and troubled

To the Chief Musician. With stringed instruments. On an eight-stringed harp. A Psalm of David.

1O LORD, do not rebuke me in Your anger,
Nor chasten me in Your hot displeasure.
2Have mercy on me, O LORD, for I am weak;
O LORD, heal me, for my bones are troubled.
3My soul also is greatly troubled;
But You, O LORD—how long?

4Return, O LORD, deliver me!
Oh, save me for Your mercies' sake!
5For in death there is no remembrance of You;
In the grave who will give You thanks?

6I am weary with my groaning;
All night I make my bed swim;
I drench my couch with my tears.
7My eye wastes away because of grief;
It grows old because of all my enemies.

8Depart from me, all you workers of iniquity;
For the LORD has heard the voice of my weeping.
9The LORD has heard my supplication;
The LORD will receive my prayer.
10Let all my enemies be ashamed and greatly troubled;
Let them turn back and be ashamed suddenly.

❖

(VERSES 1-5) Do you ever feel down and hopeless? Do things seem to be going the 'wrong way' and spinning out of control? The great thing about the Book of Psalms is that we can learn when the writers, such as David, go through such times and tell us about it. This is one of them. David knows God, so he starts with prayer.

Does he feel like praying? Perhaps not! But his kind God answers anyhow. That is true for us now, when access to God by Jesus is for all who trust Christ as their risen Lord and Saviour. See how it all works out here. What are David's heart concerns that cause him to pray and share his troubles with God? He feels he is chastised, under God's *'anger'* and *'hot displeasure'* (which he is not). He feels weak and in agony of body and agony of soul, and so depressed that he might die and is *'greatly troubled'*. It seems never ending to him. No ecstatic feelings here! He prays for God's relief, mercy, healing of both body and soul, deliverance and saving. But even in this 'down time', he recalls God's *'mercies.'* That is the key to his deliverance.

(VERSES 6-7) David pours out his sorrows. Groaning over his pathetic situation only exhausts him still more. Sleepless, his continual tears drench his bed. His eyes grow weak through his grief. Worse still, his haunted mind fears because his enemies are never far away.

(VERSES 8-10) But just as he feels the depth of emotional despair, God begins to answer his prayer. How? He leads David to take a positive hold of the situation in his prayers. Verse 8 is a significant key prayer. Often one prayer, from our heart to God's heart, starts to free up our sad logjam.

David first dismisses the thought of his evil enemies as he now knows that his mighty LORD has heard all his weeping over his troubles. God is involved in the battle! He now realises that. So, he deduces that, as God has also heard him pray for mercy, God really has accepted his prayer!

On this fresh realisation that he is already in relationship with his loving and merciful, prayer-answering God, he can see that the LORD is far bigger and stronger than any and all of his enemies! They will be ashamed, *'greatly troubled'*, turned back, and shamed. When you are feeling down, you, too, can come to trust Him. Jesus died on the cross to bring you to know and trust God. He becomes your mediator in prayer to God, the Father. David triumphs by God's grace. So can you, by knowing Jesus personally. Jesus not only died but also rose again. Through the Holy Spirit, the living Lord enters your life when you trust in Him. You can overcome through Jesus.

Psalm 7—How to trust in God as my Deliverer

A Meditation of David, which he sang to the* Lord *concerning the words of Cush, a Benjamite.
1O Lord my God, in You I put my trust;
Save me from all those who persecute me;
And deliver me,
2Lest they tear me like a lion,
Rending me in pieces, while there is none to deliver.

3O Lord my God, if I have done this:
If there is iniquity in my hands,
4If I have repaid evil to him who was at peace with me,
Or have plundered my enemy without cause,
5Let the enemy pursue me and overtake me;
Yes, let him trample my life to the earth,
And lay my honor in the dust. Selah

6Arise, O Lord, in Your anger;
Lift Yourself up because of the rage of my enemies;
Rise up for me to the judgment You have commanded!
7So the congregation of the peoples shall surround You;
For their sakes, therefore, return on high.
8The Lord shall judge the peoples;
Judge me, O Lord, according to my righteousness,
And according to my integrity within me.

9Oh, let the wickedness of the wicked come to an end,
But establish the just;
For the righteous God tests the hearts and minds.
10My defense is of God,
Who saves the upright in heart.

11God is a just judge,
And God is angry with the wicked every day.
12If he does not turn back,
He will sharpen His sword;
He bends His bow and makes it ready.
13He also prepares for Himself instruments of death;
He makes His arrows into fiery shafts.

14Behold, the wicked brings forth iniquity;
Yes, he conceives trouble and brings forth falsehood.
15He made a pit and dug it out,
And has fallen into the ditch which he made.
16His trouble shall return upon his own head,
And his violent dealing shall come down on his own crown.

17I will praise the Lord according to His righteousness,
And will sing praise to the name of the Lord Most High.

(VERSES 1-5) Twice David says, *'O LORD my God'*. He knows that He can trust in God personally. God saves and delivers him from those stalking him like a lion, to tear and rip him up. Only God can rescue him—no one else can. They obviously falsely accuse him of harming by doing evil to those with whom he had peace, as well and robbing (plundering) others who are against him. David asks God to let his enemies kill him if he is guilty. He knows he is innocent, so he can pray to God like this.

(VERSES 6-10) David's faith is in God. He is confident in God's anger against sin, His justice, His reign over men, and how He judges. He searches our hearts and minds, too. David submits to his *'LORD'* and *'righteous God'* who knows of David's integrity in this matter. He confidently asks God to stop wicked men's violence against him and save and defend him. God sees those whose hearts are right towards Him. He is David's *'defence'* and Saviour. Is He yours?

(VERSES 11-16) David knows he prays to the righteous, divine Judge, who is angry with wrath on sin. He punishes, and will continue to punish, sinners. A man full of evil and falsehood makes trouble for himself. He will be disillusioned about his life and future. He will fall into the pit he digs for another person. The Bible says that what a man sows, he will reap, including violence he seeks to impose on others. God does not miss anything. Sow trouble and reap worse trouble, now in godless living and then eternally in judgment.

(VERSE 17) David thanks the LORD for His perfect righteousness, only possessed by God. His initial prayer asking God to *'save' and 'deliver'* him now turns to *'praise to the name of the LORD Most High'*. This God is his God, his Defender, his Saviour, and his trustworthy Deliverer. Again, is He yours too? Your situation may or may not be like David's. Yet each of us needs to trust in God through Christ to save, deliver and protect us. That is why righteous Jesus—fully God and fully man—came to bear our sins and their judgment when dying in our place on the cross. When we admit our sins, turn from them and trust in the Lord Jesus Christ, the now-living Saviour, we rejoice now and will rejoice eternally.

Psalm 8—Loftiness and lowliness

To the Chief Musician. On the instrument of Gath. A Psalm of David.
1O LORD, our Lord,
How excellent is Your name in all the earth,
Who have set Your glory above the heavens!

2Out of the mouth of babes and nursing infants
You have ordained strength,
Because of Your enemies,
That You may silence the enemy and the avenger.

3When I consider Your heavens, the work of Your fingers,
The moon and the stars, which You have ordained,
4What is man that You are mindful of him,
And the son of man that You visit him?
5For You have made him a little lower than the angels,
And You have crowned him with glory and honor.

6You have made him to have dominion over the works of Your hands;
You have put all things under his feet,
7All sheep and oxen—
Even the beasts of the field,
8The birds of the air,
And the fish of the sea
That pass through the paths of the seas.

9O LORD, our Lord,
How excellent is Your name in all the earth!

❖

(VERSES 1-2) Psalm 8 proclaims the majestic name and glory of our LORD God, as known worldwide. His glory is even above the heavens.

'Heaven' can refer to one of three things. First, it can mean the sky immediately above us, with its clouds and beauty, especially when sunny. Our aeroplanes now fly there. Second, space's vast and infinite domain is also called 'heaven'. This houses the sun, moon, stars, planets, and the whole solar system. Spaceships travel there. Third, Heaven is the eternally blessed place with Christ. No sin, sadness, sickness or sorrow are there. (Read Revelation chapter 21.) All who turn from sin and come to the risen Jesus will be there with Him. You cannot see it now with human eyes. You only get there by personal faith in Jesus crucified. He bore your sins on the cross, was punished for them, and rose again. Innocent children are so impressed as they gaze up at the first two heavens. They praise God naturally. Their knowing by simple unspoiled instinct that God exists silences the empty claims and vain lives of atheists and of God's proud and arrogant enemies who oppose those who love Him.

(VERSES 3-8) David is also struck by God's amazing creation: all He has made in the second heaven are only the work of His '*fingers*'. So, how great is God? That compels David to humbly contrast the incomparable and amazing Almighty God with relatively insignificant mankind.

Consider the vastness of His mere 'finger work' in creating the heavens. This must proclaim loudly how much greater our eternal God is than we are, with our feeble and fallible and passing nature. That is why some rebellious men choose atheism. In fact, man is not even the physically strongest of God's created beings. Obviously, some animals are much stronger. But here we read that man, even though he alone has an ever-living soul, is more than a 'higher' animal with body and spirit. God created man '*a little lower than angels*'. *The Lord Jesus Christ was* willingly made '*lower than the angels*', as God coming to earth as a man to die for and save us (Hebrews 2:7). Yet God put man to rule over His animal kingdom, including birds and fish. And He loves men and women so much that He freely offers us forgiveness and eternal life, if we turn from our sins and trust in Christ, once crucified, now risen and ever living.

(VERSE 9) David sums it all up by repeating verse 1. Note that he calls God '*our LORD*'. A Christian shares his Creator, Redeemer and Lord with all others who trust in Jesus.

Psalm 9—Praise, prayer, justice and judgment

To the Chief Musician. To the tune of "Death of the Son." A Psalm of David.
1 I will praise You, O LORD, with my whole heart;
I will tell of all Your marvelous works.
2 I will be glad and rejoice in You;
I will sing praise to Your name, O Most High.

3 When my enemies turn back,
They shall fall and perish at Your presence.
4 For You have maintained my right and my cause;
You sat on the throne judging in righteousness.
5 You have rebuked the nations,
You have destroyed the wicked;
You have blotted out their name forever and ever.

6 O enemy, destructions are finished forever!
And you have destroyed cities;
Even their memory has perished.
7 But the LORD shall endure forever;
He has prepared His throne for judgment.
8 He shall judge the world in righteousness,
And He shall administer judgment for the peoples in uprightness.

9 The LORD also will be a refuge for the oppressed,
A refuge in times of trouble.
10 And those who know Your name will put their trust in You;
For You, LORD, have not forsaken those who seek You.

11 Sing praises to the LORD, who dwells in Zion!
Declare His deeds among the people.
12 When He avenges blood, He remembers them;
He does not forget the cry of the humble.

13 Have mercy on me, O LORD!
Consider my trouble from those who hate me,
You who lift me up from the gates of death,
14 That I may tell of all Your praise
In the gates of the daughter of Zion.
I will rejoice in Your salvation.

15 The nations have sunk down in the pit which they made;
In the net which they hid, their own foot is caught.
16 The LORD is known by the judgment He executes;
The wicked is snared in the work of his own hands.
Meditation. Selah

17 The wicked shall be turned into hell,
And all the nations that forget God.
18 For the needy shall not always be forgotten;

The expectation of the poor shall not perish forever.

19Arise, O LORD,
Do not let man prevail;
Let the nations be judged in Your sight.
20Put them in fear, O LORD,
That the nations may know themselves to be but men. Selah

This Psalm may seem a little 'heavy' about God as the righteous and just Judge. It also shows how to praise God for who He is, what He has done, and what He will do for those who trust in Him. If you fear at the thought of how He judges and punishes, be very grateful that because Jesus bore our sins, judgment and punishment when He died on the cross, you personally can know His forgiveness, eternal life, and a living relationship with God. That changes the lives of all who receive Christ.

(VERSES 1-2) David gladly praises his '*Most High*' God wholeheartedly, shares God's marvellous wonders with others, and will praise God's name in song. The name '*Jesus*' means 'God saves'. His other name is '*Emmanuel*', meaning 'God with us'. Jesus is fully God and fully man. We should praise Him, too, when we think about what His name means.

(VERSES 3-6) describe unrepentant men and nations opposing God and His people. They are weak compared to God, who judges, rebukes, destroys and blots them out. While God punishes eternally those who refuse to turn from sin and trust in Him for forgiveness, He upholds now and eternally those who do repent and trust Him. (Compare John chapter 3, verses 16 and 36.)

(VERSES 7-8) The LORD reigns for ever in judgment, justice and righteousness. He rules now, too.

(Verses 9-10) God is a refuge for the oppressed and troubled who trust Him. No one seeking Him is ever forsaken by Him. Think on His name.

(VERSES 11-12) Those singing God's praise must proclaim God's deeds to nations. It must include creation, Jesus' incarnation and sin-bearing, rising again, ascending to Heaven, and sending His Holy Spirit. He always listens to cries of the afflicted.

(VERSES 13-14) David's short prayer covers his persecution by those who hate him, his own need for mercy, uplifting by God even near *'the gates of death'*, praising God and rejoicing that God has saved him. A good example for each Christian to follow!

(VERSES 15-17) These verses point to the sad and tragic Godless dying of wicked men and wicked nations, the grave and Hell. Ungodly nations go there and so do the wicked, who are ensnared by what they do. God is always known for His righteous and final justice.

(VERSE 18) God remembers the needy. The afflicted who hope in God are blessed. He will remember the poor. The hope of the afflicted will never perish. God sees and hears them. Christ did not only come for the rich and powerful—though they can trust Him, too, if they will turn from their sins and trust in Jesus—but also for needy and the poor. They will be strong and spiritually rich in Heaven!

(VERSES 19-20) Man cannot prevail and never will prevail against God. Nations must know they are only collections of dying, sinful people. They will be judged by God. God's punishment is one of terror. '*Selah*' means 'Stop and think about that.' How deeply do people and nations need to consider that today—including the people and nation where I live.

Psalm 10–When God seems not to listen

A Song of Confidence in God's Triumph over Evil
1Why do You stand afar off, O LORD?
Why do You hide in times of trouble?
2The wicked in his pride persecutes the poor;
Let them be caught in the plots which they have devised.

3For the wicked boasts of his heart's desire;
He blesses the greedy and renounces the LORD.
4The wicked in his proud countenance does not seek God;
God is in none of his thoughts.

5His ways are always prospering;
Your judgments are far above, out of his sight;
As for all his enemies, he sneers at them.
6He has said in his heart, "I shall not be moved;
I shall never be in adversity."
7His mouth is full of cursing and deceit and oppression;
Under his tongue is trouble and iniquity.

8He sits in the lurking places of the villages;
In the secret places he murders the innocent;
His eyes are secretly fixed on the helpless.
9He lies in wait secretly, as a lion in his den;
He lies in wait to catch the poor;
He catches the poor when he draws him into his net.
10So he crouches, he lies low,
That the helpless may fall by his strength.
11He has said in his heart,
"God has forgotten;
He hides His face;
He will never see."

12Arise, O LORD!
O God, lift up Your hand!
Do not forget the humble.
13Why do the wicked renounce God?
He has said in his heart,
"You will not require an account."

14But You have seen, for You observe trouble and grief,
To repay it by Your hand.
The helpless commits himself to You;
You are the helper of the fatherless.
15Break the arm of the wicked and the evil man;
Seek out his wickedness until You find none.

16The LORD is King forever and ever;
The nations have perished out of His land.
17LORD, You have heard the desire of the humble;

You will prepare their heart;
You will cause Your ear to hear,
18To do justice to the fatherless and the oppressed,
That the man of the earth may oppress no more.

(VERSES 1) The psalmist looks at sinful men instead of looking to God. So he wrongly feels that God is far off when he experiences troubled times. But God can never be far away and Jesus promised that He will never leave or forsake those who put their trust in Him. Because Jesus was punished for your sins on the cross and is alive now, if you forsake your sins and receive Him in your heart, you can know that He is always with you, even in troubles.

(VERSES 2-11) paint a wicked man's life. He is proud; he persecutes and schemes against the weak; he boasts in selfish greed and ignores God and excludes Him from his thoughts. He is haughty and rich; he hates God's laws and judgments; he sneers at enemies; he thinks his future is secure when it is not; he is conceited and out of control with his curses, lies and threats; his evil talk troubles others. He stalks, ambushes, and kills innocent victims. Like a strong lion, he waits, hunts, traps and drags them off them. He tells himself that God has forgotten him and cannot see him.

(VERSES 12-15) give the psalmist's response in prayer to all that has made him doubt if God is 'at home' or listening to him. His prayer is a good, practical lesson for us all. He asks God to arise, lift up His hand, and remember the humble. He asks why the LORD allows a wicked rebel against God to revile Him and fool himself that God will not make him account for his sins. In short, he asks God to judge the wicked. He then affirms to God his confidence that God does see the trouble and grief and will deal with it. Yes, He will hear the one who calls on Him and He will help the fatherless. He will deal with the evil man, too, breaking his power, and judging him. God knows that man's wickedness. All sinners are accountable to God now and eternally.

(VERSES 16-18) reveal the joyful outcome of this episode as the psalmist worships God. When God answers our prayers, we, too, should humbly and thankfully worship and praise Him for who He is and for what He has done for us. The psalmist's worship covers the following: the LORD is the ever-living and everlasting King; He is Victor over the nations and judges them; He hears the cries of the oppressed and fatherless, whom He encourages; He defends the fatherless and oppressed people, so that they no longer are terrified by mere men.

Psalm 11—Taking refuge in the LORD

To the Chief Musician. A Psalm of David.
1In the LORD I put my trust;
How can you say to my soul,
"Flee as a bird to your mountain"?
2For look! The wicked bend their bow,
They make ready their arrow on the string,
That they may shoot secretly at the upright in heart.
3If the foundations are destroyed,
What can the righteous do?

4The LORD is in His holy temple,
The LORD's throne is in heaven;
His eyes behold,
His eyelids test the sons of men.
5The LORD tests the righteous,
But the wicked and the one who loves violence His soul hates.
6Upon the wicked He will rain coals;
Fire and brimstone and a burning wind
Shall be the portion of their cup.

7For the LORD is righteous,
He loves righteousness;
His countenance beholds the upright.

Like so many small Psalms, this one makes a huge impact if we take it to heart. The Holy Spirit brings big blessing from small phrases in the Bible. Think of a few: '*Help, LORD*'; '*Save, LORD*'; '*Look and live*'; '*Lord, remember me*'; '*God, be merciful to me, a sinner*'; '*Believe on the Lord Jesus Christ and you will be saved*'. There are many others. Never underestimate what great good can come from small portions or small phrases of God's Word. It is the infallible and perfect Word of wise and holy God.

(VERSES 1-3) David's starting point is, '*In the LORD put my trust*'. *Another translation, the NIV, helpfully puts this as* '*In the LORD I take refuge*.' To '*trust*' in Christ is to '*take refuge*' in Him. The tombstone of John Berridge, vicar of Everton, near Bedford, reveals that Berridge was born in 1716, ordained in 1744, served as a curate from 1745 to 1755, was vicar of Everton from 1755-93, when he died. There is nothing strange there. But, although religious, he did not realise until 1756 that Jesus died for *him*, to be judged for *him* and for *his* sins, and rose again to enter *his* life to save and forgive *him*. In 1756, he repented of his sin to ask Christ into his life. Earlier, he thought that being religious would save him. His tombstone says he 'Lived proudly on faith and works for salvation till 1754'. But against 1756 that tombstone says: 'Fled to Jesus alone for **refuge**.' He found his refuge in his personal trust in Jesus Christ. Having thus exercised faith in the Saviour, he then had a blessed impact on people. To be saved and forgiven, you must take refuge alone in Jesus. No one is saved by being 'churchy' or religious. Even a church vicar can only be saved if he repents and trusts, or takes '*refuge*', in Jesus alone. David's '*refuge*' is in God, so he refuses to fly away, like a scared bird, when enemies oppose him. David asks, '*When the foundations are being destroyed, what can the righteous do?*' Half of the answer has already been given. Make sure your refuge is in the Lord. Trust in Him alone.

(VERSES 4-6) The rest of the reply to David's question follows: The LORD is holy, He is in place, and He rules. He sees and examines all men. He knows those who trust in Him and so are counted '*righteous*' and live accordingly. He knows and hates wickedness (or sin) and violence. God will judge and punish severely with His burning holy fire, all those committing sin unless they repent, yield to Him, and trust in Him.

(VERSE 7) The second reason why those who turn from sin to God, through Christ, need fear neither wicked opposition, nor God's judgment is, '*The LORD is righteous, He loves righteousness.*' If you know Jesus, God now sees you as clothed in His righteousness, and therefore '*upright*' in His sight. '*His countenance*' (or 'face') looks in mercy and love at those who have repented and trusted Christ. He already regards them as forgiven and '*upright*'. He will do so finally in Heaven for ever. Is *your* refuge in Jesus? Do you trust in Him?

Psalm 12—Bad and good language

To the Chief Musician. On an eight-stringed harp. A Psalm of David.
1Help, LORD, for the godly man ceases!
For the faithful disappear from among the sons of men.
2They speak idly everyone with his neighbor;
With flattering lips and a double heart they speak.

3May the LORD cut off all flattering lips,
And the tongue that speaks proud things,
4Who have said,
"With our tongue we will prevail;
Our lips are our own;
Who is lord over us?"

5"For the oppression of the poor, for the sighing of the needy,
Now I will arise," says the LORD;
"I will set him in the safety for which he yearns."

6The words of the LORD are pure words,
Like silver tried in a furnace of earth,
Purified seven times.
7You shall keep them, O LORD,
You shall preserve them from this generation forever.

8The wicked prowl on every side,
When vileness is exalted among the sons of men.

(VERSE 1) Here is a simple yet significant two-word prayer which you can pray today: '*Help LORD*' David explains why he prays for help: he feels alone as a God-fearing man surrounded by wicked people. *Real* Christians do need close and regular fellowship with each other. They are lonely without it. So, please do meet to hear the Bible in Sunday services, Bible studies and at prayer meetings. Encourage each other personally and informally, too.

(VERSES 2-4) One way someone who trusts and follows Jesus differs from the world around is how he uses his tongue. Bad language is 'out' for someone whose heart Christ has changed. Jesus died for him and now lives in his life through the Holy Spirit. Words are to the heart what amplifiers are to microphones. Wrong talk comes out in many ways. It reveals a heart that needs to be cleansed and changed by faith in Jesus. God will judge every sinner for every evil word—unless and until he or she turns from sin to receive Christ as Lord. This sin includes idle talk, lies, flattery, deception, boasting, pride, conceit, and refusing to let God rule our speech. It includes vile language, filthy words and blasphemy against God, as well as the kinds of sinful and hurtful words already mentioned.

(VERSE 5) God tells David that He sees the oppression and hears the sighing of weak and needy folk facing all this pressure. He then promises to '*arise*' to protect and keep them safe from those speaking evil against them.

(VERSES 6-8) See how God helps such folk. He draws their attention to His Word, the Bible. It contains His actual words which are '*pure*', as you would expect from the God of purity. God's Word is purified as in a refiner's furnace. His inspired words recorded there will be kept and preserved by God '*forever*'. So, please trust and read the Bible daily. Go regularly to hear it taught and preached. God helps all who ask Him and put Him first. You will read there how Jesus shed His blood for us and bore our punishment for our sins in His own sinless body and rose again in that body from the grave. Jesus is the living Word of God of whom the Bible, the written Word of God, speaks.

Although God saves and blesses those who trust and honour Him, wicked men will '*prowl on every side, when vileness is exalted among the sons of men.*' How true that is today in life and in our media. May you honour the Lord and keep close to Him if you are His. For that, you will need a personal and obedient trust in Jesus and in the truth and message of the Bible.

Psalm 13—When tough trials persist

To the Chief Musician. A Psalm of David.
1How long, O LORD? Will You forget me forever?
How long will You hide Your face from me?
2How long shall I take counsel in my soul,
Having sorrow in my heart daily?
How long will my enemy be exalted over me?

3Consider and hear me, O LORD my God;
Enlighten my eyes,
Lest I sleep the sleep of death;
4Lest my enemy say,
"I have prevailed against him";
Lest those who trouble me rejoice when I am moved.

5But I have trusted in Your mercy;
My heart shall rejoice in Your salvation.
6I will sing to the LORD,
Because He has dealt bountifully with me.

(VERSES 1-2) Four times David asks God *'How long?'* The cry *'O LORD'* shows this really does come from his heart. David obviously feels he has been under great pressure for too long. What causes his ongoing stress?

First, rather as in Psalm 10, he feels as if God has forgotten him and hides His face from him. His first two exclamations of *'How long?'* respond to God's seeming remoteness. He should know better than that, and so should anyone who knows Jesus as his Saviour and believes His firm promises. God promises to be always with us and never to leave us.

Second, David asks how long he need wrestle with some troubling thoughts and his sorrowful heart. He surely knows that life is often a battle: fears and sorrows are always near. But it is *'in all these things'* that *'we are more than conquerors through Him who loved us'* (Romans 8:37).

Third, he looks back to problems with his foe. He feels he is losing the battle now. That is to be expected at times today in the battle a Christian has with 'the world, the flesh and the devil'. But God will see us through, if we keep looking to Him, hard as it is at times. We have all been there. We will have victory finally and eternally, if we know Jesus. He has dealt with the only thing able to stop us knowing God—that is our sins. He paid for them in His death when He was punished in our place on the cross for us. The *risen* Lord of glory and victory is always on our side!

(VERSES 3-4) David rightly prays. And we can learn from how he prays. He calls the LORD *'my God'*. He asks his God to look on him and answer him. He asks for God's light to help him see things clearly and to keep him alive. He rightly hates the thought that his enemy should gloat that God could not stop him defeating David. Then all David's foes and God's foes would gloat. His concern is both for his own life for the Lord and for God's glory.

(VERSES 5-6) See what happens in this situation. It starts in dismay and despair. But what then happens when a man prays who knows and follows the LORD and reminds himself of God's *'mercy'*, despite his feelings and weaknesses? As David reviews his trust in God's *'mercy'*, God begins to reassure him. His heart rejoices in God's *'salvation'*—which means God is saving him. *'Salvation'* requires a 'Saviour' who has saved, does save, and will save. Today, when you trust and remember the Lord Jesus as your Saviour, you have very real cause to rejoice and sing to Him for saving you spiritually and for ever. Every born-again child of God through faith in Christ can still say today that *God 'has dealt bountifully with me.'* What is true for you in this life, as a Christian, will be even more *'bountifully'* true for you forever in Heaven!

Psalm 14—Who said, 'There is no God'?

To the Chief Musician. A Psalm of David.
1 The fool has said in his heart,
"There is no God."
They are corrupt,
They have done abominable works,
There is none who does good.

2 The LORD looks down from heaven upon the children of men,
To see if there are any who understand, who seek God.
3 They have all turned aside,
They have together become corrupt;
There is none who does good,
No, not one.

4 Have all the workers of iniquity no knowledge,
Who eat up my people as they eat bread,
And do not call on the LORD?
5 There they are in great fear,
For God is with the generation of the righteous.
6 You shame the counsel of the poor,
But the LORD is his refuge.

7 Oh, that the salvation of Israel would come out of Zion!
When the LORD brings back the captivity of His people,
Let Jacob rejoice and Israel be glad.

(VERSE 1) The man who says, '*There is no God*' is in fact claiming he has seen, considered and assessed all available evidence from all time in history and from all places worldwide, and is personally competent to reach a correct final conclusion, namely, '*There is no God.*' The world calls him an 'atheist': God here calls him a '*fool*'.

A person who says, 'I do not know', is an 'agnostic'. (That word means 'don't know', or 'ignorant'.) To deny dogmatically that God exists makes a person both an 'atheist' and, God says, a '*fool*'. Psalm 14 provides some reasons why he is foolish. Verse 1 opens with: '*The fool has said in his heart, "There is no God."*' This man does not use his head to weigh well all the evidence properly; instead, he carries his prejudice in his heart against God. So, his decision is not based on fact or reason. It comes from his biased feelings. Every thought he now holds about God is prejudiced. However intelligent and educated he may be, his basic intellectual position is therefore dishonest. Why does he act like this? Because, if he believed a holy God was watching him all the time, he knows he would have to repent of his *'corrupt'* and *'abominable'* deeds and ask God for His forgiveness. The first of God's Ten Commandments tells us to put no one and nothing before God. An atheist makes a 'god' of his sinful rejection of God and then worships that 'god'. That is why he cannot do *'good'* in God's eyes until he turns from that particular sin, and all the others, to ask God to pardon and restore him. In Christ, that is what God does for any person—including atheists—who turns to Him, grateful that the Lord Jesus bore the wrath of God the Father against all his sins when Jesus died on Calvary's cross in his place.

(VERSES 2-3) The LORD sees that man cannot, without God's help and the work of His Holy Spirit within, even begin to understand about God, seek God, or keep God's good and holy standards. Each of us has a wayward, corrupt, and sinful heart.

(VERSES 4-6) Explain why sinners remain ignorant of God—unless and until they repent and trust in Jesus. They oppose those who are God's, and proudly refuse to *'call on the LORD'*. One day, dread will overwhelm all sinners who do not repent. Eternal punishment awaits them after death. Compare the peace and security given to *'the generation of the righteous'* believers in their ever-present God. When a *'poor'* believer is opposed by evil men, *'the LORD is his refuge'*. Is He yours?

(VERSE 7) David prays that God's *'salvation of Israel'* would come. Even religious Jews and other religious people need to be saved. David awaits the gladness and rejoicing when God works to restore captive Israel to Himself—even atheists! He restores and blesses anyone who now trusts in Jesus! The big understatement is that sinners restored by God are *'glad'!* Do you know that gladness?

Psalm 15—The heart and life God wants

A Psalm of David.
1LORD, who may abide in Your tabernacle?
Who may dwell in Your holy hill?

2He who walks uprightly,
And works righteousness,
And speaks the truth in his heart;
3He who does not backbite with his tongue,
Nor does evil to his neighbor,
Nor does he take up a reproach against his friend;
4In whose eyes a vile person is despised,
But he honors those who fear the LORD;
He who swears to his own hurt and does not change;
5He who does not put out his money at usury,
Nor does he take a bribe against the innocent.

He who does these things shall never be moved.

Psalm 15 is an excellent and practical way to teach what God looks for in those who know and follow Him. It is as true for born-again folk now, in our New Testament era, as it was for those living in the time of David. Both must aim to please God and bless others. Though often failing, if we know Christ, we repent and keep on aiming high and are helped by His grace.

VERSE 1 starts with God. It deals with the holy walk and talk God looks for from the heart of his follower who wants to live for God. It asks the LORD how anyone can dwell and live with Him. '*Tabernacle*' and '*holy hill*' are ways of describing God's holy dwelling place. Finally, and eternally, these words describe Heaven. You cannot be with God there, nor can you enjoy His presence here by His indwelling Holy Spirit, unless through your personal faith in Christ your heart is clean. A Christian must confess his sins humbly to God through Christ in prayer if he is to enjoy fellowship with God and walk with Him.

VERSES 2-3 show how this should be worked out in daily life. If these verses do not describe your ongoing aim, perhaps your heart still needs His pardon and cleansing. Maybe you have not yet asked Jesus to forgive you and enter your heart to lovingly control it. Or maybe you understand that Jesus Christ has shed His blood and died to be punished for your sins. If you have understood that, have you repented yet and come to Christ? Whether you are a Christian or not, this Psalm details God's standards to seek to always keep with His help. They will bless you and, through you, they will bless many others also.

That is why, in these two verses, God's man speaks the truth from his cleansed heart, walks blamelessly and lives righteously. He seeks neither to slander nor slur nor do evil to anyone. He does not want to. Mean words, lies and acts of deliberately wronging his neighbour must go. A wronged person is his '*fellow man*': he knows that he would not like it if wrong were done to him. So, how can he wrong another, if Jesus has loved him and forgiven all his sins, and become his Lord and Saviour?

VERSES 4-5, the final verses, show positively how a saved man must act. Ongoing failure to do so shouts loud that he needs God to put him right now and help him in future to forsake his sins and trust and follow Jesus Christ. Now see how you should act, helped by God's grace and strength alone: despise vileness in men; honour God-fearing men; keep your word, even when it hurts to do so; generously lend to others without asking for interest; and do not accept bribes or hurt the innocent.

If you trust Jesus and want to be unshaken in your faith, now or eternally, trust Christ and follow God's way shown in this practical little Psalm 15

Psalm 16—Safety and security

A Michtam of David.
1Preserve me, O God, for in You I put my trust.

2O my soul, you have said to the LORD,
"You are my Lord,
My goodness is nothing apart from You."
3As for the saints who are on the earth,
"They are the excellent ones, in whom is all my delight."

4Their sorrows shall be multiplied who hasten after another god;
Their drink offerings of blood I will not offer,
Nor take up their names on my lips.

5O LORD, You are the portion of my inheritance and my cup;
You maintain my lot.
6The lines have fallen to me in pleasant places;
Yes, I have a good inheritance.

7I will bless the LORD who has given me counsel;
My heart also instructs me in the night seasons.
8I have set the LORD always before me;
Because He is at my right hand I shall not be moved.

9Therefore my heart is glad, and my glory rejoices;
My flesh also will rest in hope.
10For You will not leave my soul in Sheol,
Nor will You allow Your Holy One to see corruption.
11You will show me the path of life;
In Your presence is fullness of joy;
At Your right hand are pleasures forevermore.

(VERSES 1-2) David reminds his God of three things: first, for God to preserve him because he puts his trust in God; second, the LORD is his Lord; and third, the only reason for any goodness David possesses is because it comes from God. We, too, can trust in the LORD, surrender to His position as our Lord each day, and realise that as we live closer to Him we see Him changing our moral and spiritual lives by His grace and power.

(VERSE 3) David delights in his fellow '*saints*' (those set aside for God) whom he values as '*excellent*'. If you trust in Christ, fellow Christians become precious to you. The closer you get to Christ, the more you love and esteem others who know and follow Him.

(VERSE 4) He contrasts those whose idolatry makes them pursue other gods. Their sorrows will increase, especially in eternity. Note how David will not take part in any of their idolatrous worship, or even mention their names. All idolatry is sin. The Lord must come first.

(VERSES 5-6) David thanks God for three things: First, he has God Himself as his portion in life and as his inheritance. The Bible says that 'He who has the Son has life; he who does not have the Son of God does not have life' (1 John 5:12). Second, God has dealt well with him and God's influence has worked out well for him; and third, God has given him a *'good inheritance'*. What could be a better inheritance than to have eternal life in Heaven with Jesus?

(VERSES 7-8) It is good and uplifting to thank God often, and David shows he is doing that when he says *'I will bless the LORD.'* Why does David bless and thank God? For God's wonderful counsel (teaching) that keeps David through the night (when problems can seem larger) and the reminder of God's unfailing presence with him at his *'right hand'*. Because of this, David knows he *'shall not be moved'* spiritually. David lives with the fact that God is always near at hand. This is a great privilege and reality for all who trust in the risen Lord Jesus personally.

(VERSES 9-11) Do you recall that David starts by asking to be preserved by God? Now see him rejoicing because God will not only protect and keep him safe and secure in the short term, as he asked. Better still, God will not abandon him to death's decay or to everlasting judgment in Hell. God guarantees him *'the path of life'*, *'fulness of joy'* in His holy presence, and *'pleasures forevermore'* at His right hand in Heaven. In Acts 2:25-32, the Holy Spirit leads Peter, on Pentecost Day, to apply verses 8-11 as a fulfilled prophecy of the resurrected Messiah, the Lord Jesus Christ. Jesus has defeated the grave for us. We have Jesus' promises never to leave or forsake us on earth, and to make us at home in Heaven. Like David, we guilty sinners need God's grace and mercy. But Christ died for our sins. He was punished for our sins in our place and will save us, if we turn from our sins and trust Him as our Saviour and Lord. Are you safe and secure by faith in Him?

Psalm 17—What to ask God to do for me

A Prayer of David.
1Hear a just cause, O LORD,
Attend to my cry;
Give ear to my prayer which is not from deceitful lips.
2Let my vindication come from Your presence;
Let Your eyes look on the things that are upright.

3You have tested my heart;
You have visited me in the night;
You have tried me and have found nothing;
I have purposed that my mouth shall not transgress.
4Concerning the works of men,
By the word of Your lips,
I have kept away from the paths of the destroyer.
5Uphold my steps in Your paths,
That my footsteps may not slip.

6I have called upon You, for You will hear me, O God;
Incline Your ear to me, and hear my speech.
7Show Your marvelous lovingkindness by Your right hand,
O You who save those who trust in You
From those who rise up against them.
8Keep me as the apple of Your eye;
Hide me under the shadow of Your wings,
9From the wicked who oppress me,
From my deadly enemies who surround me.

10They have closed up their fat hearts;
With their mouths they speak proudly.
11They have now surrounded us in our steps;
They have set their eyes, crouching down to the earth,
12As a lion is eager to tear his prey,
And like a young lion lurking in secret places.

13Arise, O LORD,
Confront him, cast him down;
Deliver my life from the wicked with Your sword,
14With Your hand from men, O LORD,
From men of the world who have their portion in this life,
And whose belly You fill with Your hidden treasure.
They are satisfied with children,
And leave the rest of their possession for their babes.

15As for me, I will see Your face in righteousness;
I shall be satisfied when I awake in Your likeness.

(VERSES 1-6) David's cry and prayer to God are personal and urgent. God is asked to *'hear'*, *'attend'*, and *'give ear'*. *'Hear me'* comes first. David has been tested by God and found to be honouring Him. He is determined to speak to please God and to avoid those bent on destroying the good that God seeks. David asks for his footsteps to be in God's paths, and that God will stop him from slipping. He pleads with God to answer his prayers, stating that he has called on God and intends to continue to pray to Him.

(VERSES 7-14) Then, David asks God to show him His *'marvellous lovingkindness'*. By such love, God saves, keeps, and hides from wicked threats and assaults of wicked enemies who surround and threaten him. David next asks God, to *'Keep* ***me****'* as *'the apple of* [God's] *eye'* and *'Hide me under the shadow of* [God's] *wings'*, just as chickens hide under a hen's wings. God *keeps* all who trust in Him now and eternally. Jesus tells those in Jerusalem that He wanted to hide them *'as a hen hides her brood under her wings'*, but they declined His invitation (Luke 13:34). Jesus bore your sins on the cross. His death will hide you from being judged and punished in Hell, if you accept His invitation to repent and trust in Him. Cruel and arrogant foes track David, like a hungry lion, to try to catch and kill him. So, he next pleads for God to deliver him from his evil enemies. The three foes of all who trust and follow Jesus are the world, the flesh and the devil. They oppose Christ and us by promoting sinful thinking and living, wrong desires within us, and by applying satanic power which is, at times, too subtle or too strong for us. But Jesus, our divine Friend, is far stronger and wiser than that evil trio. Always trust and obey Jesus in all problems. David knows God will meet all his earthly needs.

(VERSE 15) David looks forward to waking up in Heaven after death, in his God-given righteousness. He will be satisfied to see God's face and be made like Him. Today, that awaits all sinners who have turned from their sin (this is known as 'repentance') and trusted in Jesus personally! It awaits *you*, too, if *you* repent and trust in Jesus. Well, do you?

Psalm 18—God's unfailing love

To the Chief Musician. A Psalm of David the servant of the* LORD*, who spoke to the* LORD *the words of this song on the day that the* LORD *delivered him from the hand of all his enemies and from the hand of Saul. And he said:

1 I will love You, O LORD, my strength.
2 The LORD is my rock and my fortress and my deliverer;
My God, my strength, in whom I will trust;
My shield and the horn of my salvation, my stronghold.
3 I will call upon the LORD, who is worthy to be praised;
So shall I be saved from my enemies.

4 The pangs of death surrounded me,
And the floods of ungodliness made me afraid.
5 The sorrows of Sheol surrounded me;
The snares of death confronted me.
6 In my distress I called upon the LORD,
And cried out to my God;
He heard my voice from His temple,
And my cry came before Him, even to His ears.

7 Then the earth shook and trembled;
The foundations of the hills also quaked and were shaken,
Because He was angry.
8 Smoke went up from His nostrils,
And devouring fire from His mouth;
Coals were kindled by it.
9 He bowed the heavens also, and came down
With darkness under His feet.
10 And He rode upon a cherub, and flew;
He flew upon the wings of the wind.
11 He made darkness His secret place;
His canopy around Him was dark waters
And thick clouds of the skies.
12 From the brightness before Him,
His thick clouds passed with hailstones and coals of fire.

13 The LORD thundered from heaven,
And the Most High uttered His voice,
Hailstones and coals of fire.
14 He sent out His arrows and scattered the foe,
Lightnings in abundance, and He vanquished them.
15 Then the channels of the sea were seen,
The foundations of the world were uncovered
At Your rebuke, O LORD,
At the blast of the breath of Your nostrils.

16 He sent from above, He took me;
He drew me out of many waters.
17 He delivered me from my strong enemy,

From those who hated me,
For they were too strong for me.
18They confronted me in the day of my calamity,
But the LORD was my support.
19He also brought me out into a broad place;
He delivered me because He delighted in me.

20The LORD rewarded me according to my righteousness;
According to the cleanness of my hands
He has recompensed me.
21For I have kept the ways of the LORD,
And have not wickedly departed from my God.
22For all His judgments were before me,
And I did not put away His statutes from me.
23I was also blameless before Him,
And I kept myself from my iniquity.
24Therefore the LORD has recompensed me according to my righteousness,
According to the cleanness of my hands in His sight.

25With the merciful You will show Yourself merciful;
With a blameless man You will show Yourself blameless;
26With the pure You will show Yourself pure;
And with the devious You will show Yourself shrewd.
27For You will save the humble people,
But will bring down haughty looks.

28For You will light my lamp;
The LORD my God will enlighten my darkness.
29For by You I can run against a troop,
By my God I can leap over a wall.
30As for God, His way is perfect;
The word of the LORD is proven;
He is a shield to all who trust in Him.

31For who is God, except the LORD?
And who is a rock, except our God?
32It is God who arms me with strength,
And makes my way perfect.
33He makes my feet like the feet of deer,
And sets me on my high places.
34He teaches my hands to make war,
So that my arms can bend a bow of bronze.

35You have also given me the shield of Your salvation;
Your right hand has held me up,
Your gentleness has made me great.
36You enlarged my path under me,
So my feet did not slip.

37I have pursued my enemies and overtaken them;
Neither did I turn back again till they were destroyed.
38I have wounded them,

So that they could not rise;
They have fallen under my feet.
39 For You have armed me with strength for the battle;
You have subdued under me those who rose up against me.
40 You have also given me the necks of my enemies,
So that I destroyed those who hated me.
41 They cried out, but there was none to save;
Even to the LORD, but He did not answer them.
42 Then I beat them as fine as the dust before the wind;
I cast them out like dirt in the streets.

43 You have delivered me from the strivings of the people;
You have made me the head of the nations;
A people I have not known shall serve me.
44 As soon as they hear of me they obey me;
The foreigners submit to me.
45 The foreigners fade away,
And come frightened from their hideouts.

46 The LORD lives!
Blessed be my Rock!
Let the God of my salvation be exalted.
47 It is God who avenges me,
And subdues the peoples under me;
48 He delivers me from my enemies.
You also lift me up above those who rise against me;
You have delivered me from the violent man.
49 Therefore I will give thanks to You, O LORD, among the Gentiles,
And sing praises to Your name.

50 Great deliverance He gives to His king,
And shows mercy to His anointed,
To David and his descendants forevermore.

(VERSES 1-6) David gives his Music Director Psalm 18 to sing to mark God's saving him from King Saul and all who seek his life. He praises God, his rock, fortress, deliverer, strength, shield, salvation and stronghold. He recalls crying in his distress to God for help, that God heard and answered him, and that he escaped death.

(VERSES 7-15) David graphically compares God's response to his prayer and fierce onslaught from would-be killers to a wild terrifying storm on land and sea. In poetic style, he describes an earthquake, violent rainstorm, hail, thunder, lightning strikes, mountainous tempestuous waves, and gales. God's same almighty power frightens and scatters his enemies. God is on his side.

(VERSES 16-19) David tells of his rescue by God who reached down, took hold, and drew him out of the troubled waters of all-out enemy action against him. Too weak to save himself, David knew that God saved, supported, and put him in a safe and pleasant place. God rescued him and delighted in him.

(VERSES 20-27) God saves David because he is His praying child, committed to God. What David now says is not to gain merit, but to show what each disciple of the Lord should be like. It describes the character of anyone who turns from selfish living to crown Jesus as his Lord. He should be righteous, clean, obedient, following, keeping God's law, blameless, resisting sin, faithful, pure, and humble. None of us can achieve that by our own efforts. Only by putting our faith in Jesus, who bore our sins and its penalty on the cross, and by asking for His help though the power of the Holy Spirit, can we start to live like that, or even want to.

(VERSES 28-36) David insists that God alone works in and for him, giving him light and courageous strength. God's way is '*perfect*', His word is '*proven*' and He is his shield and Rock. He provides David with strength, security, speed to escape, stability, uplifting, training for battle, and sustaining. '*Your gentleness has made me great,*' says Israel's most famous king. Even his path and walking on it, are God's doing.

(VERSES 37-45) David explains how God has given him victories over his foes and defended him from attacks from some of his '*people*'. All this work by God makes King David now the '*head of the nations*', of whom foreigners hear, fear and tremble.

(VERSES 46-50) David ends as he started—by praising '*the God of his salvation*' and his '*Rock*'. He summarises his thanks for who God is and what He does for him—always a good thing to do. He closes with God's '*great deliverance' and His 'mercy*' to David and to his '*descendants forevermore*'. We can still know that love personally today, if we trust in our crucified and risen Saviour, the Lord Jesus Christ.

Psalm 19—How God speaks to us today

To the Chief Musician. A Psalm of David.
1 The heavens declare the glory of God;
And the firmament shows His handiwork.
2 Day unto day utters speech,
And night unto night reveals knowledge.
3 There is no speech nor language
Where their voice is not heard.
4 Their line has gone out through all the earth,
And their words to the end of the world.

In them He has set a tabernacle for the sun,
5 Which is like a bridegroom coming out of his chamber,
And rejoices like a strong man to run its race.
6 Its rising is from one end of heaven,
And its circuit to the other end;
And there is nothing hidden from its heat.

7 The law of the LORD is perfect, converting the soul;
The testimony of the LORD is sure, making wise the simple;
8 The statutes of the LORD are right, rejoicing the heart;
The commandment of the LORD is pure, enlightening the eyes;
9 The fear of the LORD is clean, enduring forever;
The judgments of the LORD are true and righteous altogether.
10 More to be desired are they than gold,
Yea, than much fine gold;
Sweeter also than honey and the honeycomb.
11 Moreover by them Your servant is warned,
And in keeping them there is great reward.

12 Who can understand his errors?
Cleanse me from secret faults.
13 Keep back Your servant also from presumptuous sins;
Let them not have dominion over me.
Then I shall be blameless,
And I shall be innocent of great transgression.

14 Let the words of my mouth and the meditation of my heart
Be acceptable in Your sight,
O LORD, my strength and my Redeemer.

Psalm 19 shows how God reveals Himself to us in:

- (VERSES 1-6) His *Works (Creation);*
- (VERSES 7-11) His *Words (Revelation);*
- (VERSES 12-13) our sinful *Waywardness (Conviction);*
- (VERSE 14) our God-given *Willingness (Conversion).*

(VERSES 1-6) God's glory is declared by the heavens and skies. They speak to all people in the world, whatever language they use. Each day's dawning and dusk tell us of His constant presence. Daily the sun rises and sets, reminding us of our 24/7 and 52/365 (or 366) God. Have you gazed up and thought, 'A Creator God must have done all that'? Belief in God as Creator is not enough to get you to Heaven. But one song says, 'The great Creator became my Saviour.' That blows my mind. Almighty and all-holy God became Man. He lived a sinless and perfect life, died on the cross to bear our sins and their penalty for us, rose again and ascended to Heaven. He will return in majestic glory. To be with Him in Heaven, you must turn from your sins and ask Jesus to reign in your guilty and humbled heart.

(VERSES 7-11) refer to God's inspired and perfect written Word in which the Psalms form the biggest book. The Old Testament covers from creation to before Jesus was born. The New Testament covers the following: God's becoming as a man in Jesus; His sinless and perfect life; His teaching and miracles; how sinful men rejected Him; His death on the cross for us; His miraculous resurrection; His ascension to Heaven; His coming return to judge those not turning from sin to Him and taking to Heaven all who trust Him. God's Word is perfect, trustworthy, right, enlightening, radiant, pure, everlasting, sure, righteous, very precious and very sweet. It revives the soul and gives wisdom and joy. It warns and rewards each servant of God who keeps it.

(VERSES 12-13) God, through the Holy Spirit, has convicted David of secret faults and wilful sins. David now seeks to be forgiven, free from sin's rule, to have no blame, and to be innocent of secret, presumptuous and great sins.

(VERSE 14) shows how God has changed David's words, thinking, and heart to be willing. His God is now his personal '*strength*' and '*Redeemer*'. Is Jesus that to you, yet?

Psalm 20—Praying before the battle

To the Chief Musician. A Psalm of David.
1May the LORD answer you in the day of trouble;
May the name of the God of Jacob defend you;
2May He send you help from the sanctuary,
And strengthen you out of Zion;
3May He remember all your offerings,
And accept your burnt sacrifice. Selah

4May He grant you according to your heart's desire,
And fulfill all your purpose.
5We will rejoice in your salvation,
And in the name of our God we will set up our banners!
May the LORD fulfill all your petitions.

6Now I know that the LORD saves His anointed;
He will answer him from His holy heaven
With the saving strength of His right hand.

7Some trust in chariots, and some in horses;
But we will remember the name of the LORD our God.
8They have bowed down and fallen;
But we have risen and stand upright.

9Save, LORD!
May the King answer us when we call.

(VERSES 1-5) God gives David, Israel's king and general, the prayer of Psalm 20 for the Temple's music director to sing before an upcoming battle. In Old Testament times, nations often fought each other. Israel needs to conquer the ungodly nations around and about, and exclude their often evil and ungodly influence. Israel, its army and its king must walk closely with the God they serve. It is a comfort to pray before a battle. We have different kinds of battles in our lives to fight: we need to pray, too. David's prayers include the following requests:

- God is asked to answer, even in *'the day of trouble'*;
- God's defending protection;
- God's help and strengthening support;
- God to accept their sacrifices and burnt offerings; and success to achieve their desires and plans as they seek to please God.

David promises to *'rejoice in* [God's] *salvation'* when He gives them victory and to lift up their banners in God's name, to make it clear they are on God's side. Finally, he asks God to grant all these prayers made in His name. We can pray similarly as we battle against the world, the flesh, and the devil and in the trials, temptations and battles we all face.

Look at David's prayers here and elsewhere in the Psalms. Why not adapt some of them for yourself? We do not offer God the same Old Testament sacrifices and burnt offerings. But we have a much better one, in fact, a perfect one, to offer—and we can be confident of God's acceptance. It is the sacrifice of the Lord Jesus Christ that He made in dying for us on the cross when He bore our sins and judgment. God showed He accepted that sacrifice by raising Jesus from the dead to live forevermore! Romans 12:1-2 tell us how to present our bodies as living sacrifices to serve and please the LORD.

(VERSE 6) David knows that God saves him. He answers his godly prayers by His mighty right hand. You can know Jesus as your mighty Saviour, too! If you have not done so yet, receive Him in your heart as your Saviour and Lord. If you already have trusted Jesus, *'As you have received Christ Jesus the Lord, so walk in Him'* (Colossians 2:6).

(VERSES 7-9) Compare vainly trusting in military might to save Israel, with trusting their almighty LORD God. He enables them to *'rise up and stand firm'*. Through faith in the Lord Jesus Christ, the indwelling power of the Holy Spirit, the blessing that comes from daily reading and relying on the Bible, and regular fellowship in a Bible-based church or group, God causes us to *'rise up and stand firm'* too, each day. He is there to save you and answer you when you call on Him. He will help, bless, keep, strengthen, and use you. He loves you.

Psalm 21—Answered prayers and foes

To the Chief Musician. A Psalm of David.
1The king shall have joy in Your strength, O LORD;
And in Your salvation how greatly shall he rejoice!
2You have given him his heart's desire,
And have not withheld the request of his lips. Selah

3For You meet him with the blessings of goodness;
You set a crown of pure gold upon his head.
4He asked life from You, and You gave it to him—
Length of days forever and ever.
5His glory is great in Your salvation;
Honor and majesty You have placed upon him.
6For You have made him most blessed forever;
You have made him exceedingly glad with Your presence.
7For the king trusts in the LORD,
And through the mercy of the Most High he shall not be moved.

8Your hand will find all Your enemies;
Your right hand will find those who hate You.
9You shall make them as a fiery oven in the time of Your anger;
The LORD shall swallow them up in His wrath,
And the fire shall devour them.
10Their offspring You shall destroy from the earth,
And their descendants from among the sons of men.
11For they intended evil against You;
They devised a plot which they are not able to perform.
12Therefore You will make them turn their back;
You will make ready Your arrows on Your string toward their faces.

13Be exalted, O LORD, in Your own strength!
We will sing and praise Your power.

(VERSES 1-7) King David rejoices in God's answers to his praying. Learn to pray more and better, by looking at how David prays. Note that prayer often unleashes for us *'joy in* [His] *strength.'* He starts with '*O LORD*'. After confessing to God our sins (which block our prayers) and asking for God to cleanse us, we are encouraged to focus on God and what He has done for us. David rejoices in God's strength, salvation and God's answers to his other prayers prayed before. He details '*the blessings of goodness*' from God who welcomes his prayers. God's blessings for his earthly king include his life both now and '*for ever and ever*': God gives him eternal life by his trust in the Lord. He knows his victories, kingly glory, splendid majesty, eternal blessings, gladness and joy that God is with him, are *all* gifts to him from God. David '*trusts in the LORD*'. The '*Most*

High' God's never-ending '*mercy*' keeps him firm and sure: '*he will not be moved*' (or '*shaken*'). Focusing on who God is and what He has done for him causes David to praise God humbly. We must pray like that, too, if we know Jesus. In God's great mercy and grace to us, He bore our sins and punishment on the cross so we can know His forgiveness and new life as we receive Him. He will then answer our prayers, too. Make it a godly habit to thank and praise God if you know Jesus as your Saviour.

(VERSES 8-12) reveal the ongoing conflict between David and *God's* enemies, who are also *David's* foes. Learn how to fight our *spiritual* enemies. They are the things and influences in our lives that influence our disobedience, promote wrong, displease God, block our prayers, cause us not to trust and obey the Lord Jesus, and often hurt others. David looks at his foes *through* his Lord. Enemies, problems, temptations, and trials all seem much smaller if you see them *through* the character and strength of your Saviour, who is completely on your side. David states that God will beat his enemies and their supporters. Their evil plots, schemes, and plans cannot block our sovereign God's will. He *will* beat them. When you face hard '*enemies*', look at them with your mighty Lord and Saviour, Jesus Christ, always in your mind. He is *much* stronger! Remember, too, that those who are at enmity with God because they have not repented and put their faith in Christ will be swallowed up in God's wrath upon sin. That is why we should seek to reach them with the gospel that alone can cause a lost sinner to be saved. Remember, too, that Jesus said, '*love your enemies, bless those who curse you, do good to those who hate you, and pray for those who spitefully use you and persecute you*' (Matthew 5:44).

(VERSE 13) David now desires to exalt God by singing and praising his mighty LORD. Prayer often leads to more praise.

Psalm 22—Foretelling key history in advance

1 **My God, My God, why have You forsaken Me?**
Why are You so far from helping Me,
And from the words of My groaning?
2 O My God, I cry in the daytime, but You do not hear;
And in the night season, and am not silent.

3 But You are holy,
Enthroned in the praises of Israel.
4 Our fathers trusted in You;
They trusted, and You delivered them.
5 They cried to You, and were delivered;
They trusted in You, and were not ashamed.

6 But I am a worm, and no man;
A reproach of men, and despised by the people.
7 All those who see Me ridicule Me;
They shoot out the lip, they shake the head, saying,
8 "He trusted in the LORD, let Him rescue Him;
Let Him deliver Him, since He delights in Him!"

9 But You are He who took Me out of the womb;
You made Me trust while on My mother's breasts.
10 I was cast upon You from birth.
From My mother's womb
You have been My God.
11 Be not far from Me,
For trouble is near;
For there is none to help.

12 Many bulls have surrounded Me;
Strong bulls of Bashan have encircled Me.
13 They gape at Me with their mouths,
Like a raging and roaring lion.

14 I am poured out like water,
And all My bones are out of joint;
My heart is like wax;
It has melted within Me.
15 My strength is dried up like a potsherd,
And My tongue clings to My jaws;
You have brought Me to the dust of death.

16 For dogs have surrounded Me;
The congregation of the wicked has enclosed Me.
They pierced My hands and My feet;
17 I can count all My bones.
They look and stare at Me.
18 They divide My garments among them,
And for My clothing they cast lots.

19But You, O LORD, do not be far from Me;
O My Strength, hasten to help Me!
20Deliver Me from the sword,
My precious life from the power of the dog.
21Save Me from the lion's mouth
And from the horns of the wild oxen!

You have answered Me.

22I will declare Your name to My brethren;
In the midst of the assembly I will praise You.
23You who fear the LORD, praise Him!
All you descendants of Jacob, glorify Him,
And fear Him, all you offspring of Israel!
24For He has not despised nor abhorred the affliction of the afflicted;
Nor has He hidden His face from Him;
But when He cried to Him, He heard.

25My praise shall be of You in the great assembly;
I will pay My vows before those who fear Him.
26The poor shall eat and be satisfied;
Those who seek Him will praise the LORD.
Let your heart live forever!

27All the ends of the world
Shall remember and turn to the LORD,
And all the families of the nations
Shall worship before You.
28For the kingdom is the LORD's,
And He rules over the nations.

29All the prosperous of the earth
Shall eat and worship;
All those who go down to the dust
Shall bow before Him,
Even he who cannot keep himself alive.

30A posterity shall serve Him.
It will be recounted of the Lord to the next generation,
31They will come and declare His righteousness to a people who will be born,
That He has done this.

Psalm 22 (written by David) and Isaiah 53 (written by Isaiah) are both key in the Old Testament. They both foretell, in some detail, Jesus' death on the cross, long before crucifixion was ever known in Israel. When were they written? Isaiah 53 about 700-681 BC and Psalm 22 about 1,000 BC—well before Rome crucified criminals in Israel. The Holy Spirit caused history to be recorded in advance.

This teaches us to trust God's Word, the Bible. Its focus is on Jesus. He died for us, rose again, forgives and enters the life of sinners who turn from sin and trust in Him. He gives eternal life to all who put their personal faith in Him. He is only ever a prayer away from anyone who repents and trusts Him.

(VERSES 1–2) This Psalm is set in the immediate context of David's position and feelings of helplessness. He feels that God is far from him. But it is also Messianic, showing aspects of the death of the Lord Jesus Christ hundreds of years before death by crucifixion was known, as if it had already happened. These comments focus on Jesus Christ's death as pictured here. It shows Christ's submission to humble Himself, as God the Son, into a helpless position as Man, to empty Himself, and to be forsaken and judged on the cross by God the Father.

(VERSES 3–5) After proclaiming God's holiness, this is then demonstrated by His faithful dealings with Israel in the past.

(VERSES 6–8) We look beyond David to see the self-humbling of Jesus as a '*worm*', and not as a man. A worm, unlike a snake, never strikes back, and is basically regarded as a lowly creature. See the reproach, lies and spite of those who ridicule Him and mock Him, the Sovereign Lord who became like a worm for us so He could bear our sins on the cross.

(VERSES 9–11) Jesus, the Son of Man, although conceived as a baby by the Holy Spirit through the virgin Mary, knows God as His Father in eternity, from eternity and for eternity. In his vulnerable humanity, the Man, Christ Jesus, seeks divine help as '*there is none to help.*'

(VERSES 12–13) At the cross, hostile men, like menacing animals, encircle and threaten Jesus. They rage and roar at the Lamb of God on the cross. Here His hateful enemies are seen as bulls, lions and (in verse 16) as wild dogs.

(VERSES 14–15) Jesus' body suffers. It is out of joint on the cross. His physical strength is ebbing away. His tongue dries up and sticks to His jaws. Jesus' heart is like melted wax on that cross as He bears our sin and judgment.

(VERSES 16–18) Christ is surrounded by wicked people who behave like wild dogs and cry for His death. His oppressors stare as His hands and feet are pierced. His bones stand out in His suspended and stretched body. His garments are being divided among the soldiers, who cast lots for some of them. What a horrific way to treat any man, especially the sinless Son of God. (Remember Psalm 22 was prophetically written before execution by crucifixion—a Roman, not Jewish form of death penalty—was practised.)

(VERSES 19-21a) Although abandoned on the cross, while bearing our sin and God's wrath on it, Jesus knows that His Father is not far away, and that He, Jesus, will be raised from the dead. He can pray that God the Father hastens to help Him.

(VERSES 21b–24) He knows that His prayer is heard. He will rise from the dead. This was never in doubt: He had often told His disciples that He would rise again from the dead after having been crucified.

(VERSES 25–31) As a result of the crucifixion of the Messiah, blessing will come on all sorts and conditions of people. Seekers will come to Him from all the ends of the world, from all nations, poor and prosperous, from dying and living, and from those yet to come. Only God can accomplish this. They rightly will say, '*He has done this.*'

Psalm 23—The LORD is my Shepherd

A Psalm of David.
1The LORD is my shepherd;
I shall not want.
2He makes me to lie down in green pastures;
He leads me beside the still waters.
3He restores my soul;
He leads me in the paths of righteousness
For His name's sake.

4Yea, though I walk through the valley of the shadow of death,
I will fear no evil;
For You are with me;
Your rod and Your staff, they comfort me.

5You prepare a table before me in the presence of my enemies;
You anoint my head with oil;
My cup runs over.
6Surely goodness and mercy shall follow me
All the days of my life;
And I will dwell in the house of the LORD
Forever.

I heard of a party where guests were asked to amuse each other with a joke, a poem, a song, a trick, some 'magic' or whatever. A professional actor recited Psalm 23. Everyone clapped. A Christian guest had intended to read Psalm 23. After he heard the actor, he became very unsure. But the guests insisted he should read it. So, he did—from his heart. No one clapped after that. A 'holy hush' and some tears followed. He was asked why it was that silence and tears came after he read the psalm, whereas the actor was applauded. He replied: "Well, he knew the *Psalm*, but I know the *Shepherd*." Do *you* know the '*Good Shepherd*', the Lord Jesus Christ, personally? If not, you *can* come to know Him as *your* Good Shepherd.

(VERSES 1-3) Here and throughout this 'Shepherd Psalm', note the words '*my*', '*I*', and '*me*'. Jesus Christ can become *personal to you* if you do not know Him already. He, the Good Shepherd, gave His life for His sheep. He died to take your sins and punishment on the cross. Only if you receive Him into your life as your risen, living Lord will you really grasp that. Forgiveness will then become real to you. Your Good Shepherd will bless you, meet your needs, give you rest and lead you safely. He will lead you to live a righteous life. He restores your sinful and otherwise eternally lost soul. He will guide you to live right. You will come to treasure His name. Jesus means 'God saves'.

(VERSE 4) But there are dark valleys ahead of us all—even the '*valley of the shadow of death*'. But the LORD is there to help you walk '*through*' that darkest '*valley*'. (Many other things in life will lead you *to* that dark valley: only Jesus can lead you '*through*' it.) His presence overcomes your fears. He comforts you. Shepherds in the Middle East carried rods, to beat off wild animals, and staffs, (crooks) to pull wayward sheep out of ditches. Your Good Shepherd will help you in spiritual struggles and against Satan's attacks. He pulls you out of your messes and failures and helps you move forward again. His loving presence, protection, help, care, and guidance are for *you*!

(VERSES 5-6). God gives you security, safety, and assurance spiritually. We are weak and guilty sinners. If your trust is in your Saviour-Shepherd, be sure that '*goodness and mercy*' follow you '*all the days of [your] life*'. Only real Christians have this sure hope. We often need comfort and protection, especially in the '*Valley of the Shadow of death*'. God promises all who trust in Jesus, that they will '*dwell in the house of the LORD* (Heaven) *forever*.' When you receive Christ into your life, you receive eternal life at once and will go to Heaven when you die, instead of eternal judgment which your sins deserve.

Again, do *you* know the Shepherd? You can! If you do not know Him, why not turn from your sin and trust Him now? If you do know Him, be sure to keep close to your loving Shepherd each day and recommend Him to others.

Psalm 24–Creator and Holy King of Glory

A Psalm of David.
1The earth is the LORD's, and all its fullness,
The world and those who dwell therein.
2For He has founded it upon the seas,
And established it upon the waters.

3Who may ascend into the hill of the LORD?
Or who may stand in His holy place?
4He who has clean hands and a pure heart,
Who has not lifted up his soul to an idol,
Nor sworn deceitfully.
5He shall receive blessing from the LORD,
And righteousness from the God of his salvation.
6This is Jacob, the generation of those who seek Him,
Who seek Your face. Selah

7Lift up your heads, O you gates!
And be lifted up, you everlasting doors!
And the King of glory shall come in.
8Who is this King of glory?
The LORD strong and mighty,
The LORD mighty in battle.
9Lift up your heads, O you gates!
Lift up, you everlasting doors!
And the King of glory shall come in.
10Who is this King of glory?
The LORD of hosts,
He is the King of glory. Selah

(VERSES 1-2) The whole Bible teaches (and this is fully endorsed by God the Son, who should know!) that God created the universe in six days and rested to mark one day in seven as special. (This was not because He was tired. He did this to signal that He had finished Creation and to mark the need for created beings to have a weekly rest.)

The universe is His and so is all in it. He founded and established it. That includes our world and its people. This is a good starting point for a 'God Psalm'! To reject God as Creator is to deny His Word, the Bible. Better believe God's Word and God the Son.

Not a single fact can disprove God as Creator. He alone was here at the time! There are, of course, various weak but popular theories and opinions—some well accepted but still wrong—which do not fit the facts and the evidence.

(VERSES 3-6) God is not just the Creator. He is the Holy God, seeking fellowship with men and women now and in eternity in Heaven. But God is holy, clean and pure, and we are not. So, we have a problem. All of us are unholy in thought, word and deed. We cannot approach God and neither can we stand in His presence, any more than darkness can survive light, unless He becomes our *Saviour. We all indeed need 'righteousness from the God of [our] salvation'.* Our sin excludes us from God and Heaven unless we repent from it and trust that Jesus bore our sins in His body on the cross, when punished for us, and rose again to live for ever. He saves all who admit their sins, turn from them, and ask Jesus into their lives. He enters and stays by the Holy Spirit. Then, with God's help, the Christian fights those sins that he once did not care about.

Psalm 24 mentions some sins that may stop a sinner from repenting and receiving eternal life or ruin a Christian's life through failure to forsake sins and surrender to God. Here they are: uncleanness, impurity, idolatry, telling lies (even on oath). We need to be forgiven for and freed from these and many other sins. Only Christ can do that. But He will bless all who trust in Him and, with God's help and strengthening, try to keep clean and pure from sin. God counts those trusting Jesus as righteous before Him. Why? They have a Saviour, Jesus. He not only forgives but also counts all His perfect righteousness as theirs when they put their trust in Him. All must '*seek*' God in personal, real, repentant prayer and faith to come to know Jesus Christ as Lord and Saviour.

(VERSES 7-10) Learn about the coming of the '*King of Glory*', the Lord Jesus Christ. He is '*the LORD strong and mighty.*' He is one of the three Persons in the Triune Godhead of Father, Son and Holy Spirit. God came in flesh to the world that first Christmas. He comes now to individuals through the Holy Spirit when any sinner trusts Him as Saviour. He will come finally, as '*KING OF KINGS AND LORD OF LORDS*' (Revelation 19:16) at His glorious second coming, to judge those who have not turned from sin and trusted Him, and to bless forever all who have.

Which of those two are you?

Psalm 25—Facing trouble with God's help

A Psalm of David.
1To You, O LORD, I lift up my soul.
2O my God, I trust in You;
Let me not be ashamed;
Let not my enemies triumph over me.
3Indeed, let no one who waits on You be ashamed;
Let those be ashamed who deal treacherously without cause.

4Show me Your ways, O LORD;
Teach me Your paths.
5Lead me in Your truth and teach me,
For You are the God of my salvation;
On You I wait all the day.

6Remember, O LORD, Your tender mercies and Your lovingkindnesses,
For they are from of old.
7Do not remember the sins of my youth, nor my transgressions;
According to Your mercy remember me,
For Your goodness' sake, O LORD.

8Good and upright is the LORD;
Therefore He teaches sinners in the way.
9The humble He guides in justice,
And the humble He teaches His way.
10All the paths of the LORD are mercy and truth,
To such as keep His covenant and His testimonies.
11For Your name's sake, O LORD,
Pardon my iniquity, for it is great.

12Who is the man that fears the LORD?
Him shall He teach in the way He chooses.
13He himself shall dwell in prosperity,
And his descendants shall inherit the earth.
14The secret of the LORD is with those who fear Him,
And He will show them His covenant.
15My eyes are ever toward the LORD,
For He shall pluck my feet out of the net.

16Turn Yourself to me, and have mercy on me,
For I am desolate and afflicted.
17The troubles of my heart have enlarged;
Bring me out of my distresses!
18Look on my affliction and my pain,
And forgive all my sins.
19Consider my enemies, for they are many;
And they hate me with cruel hatred.
20Keep my soul, and deliver me;
Let me not be ashamed, for I put my trust in You.
21Let integrity and uprightness preserve me,

For I wait for You.

22Redeem Israel, O God,
Out of all their troubles!

(VERSES 1-3) David faces troubles through treacherous enemies. He prays to his LORD, confirming that he trusts Him. He asks to avoid shame, or enemy triumph over him. He knows God's power and justice are on his side. It is a comfort to trust in God, in trouble, when people are set against us.

(VERSES 4-7) He asks God to show him His ways, teach him and lead him. He knows God is his Saviour: He hopes in and waits on Him all day long. His past sins and rebellion are forgiven. He asks God to remember His *'tender mercies and loving kindnesses'*, but not to remember past sins. The Bible says about our *'sins and their lawless deeds'* that He will remember them *'no more'* (see Hebrews 10:17). God can do that for us because Jesus paid sin's penalty on the cross.

(VERSES 8-11) David looks at how good God is: He is upright, teaches sinners His ways, guides the humble, and is loving and faithful to His covenant keepers. David again feels how big his own sin is and again asks to be pardoned. God did that when he first asked! We can trust His forgiveness, too.

(VERSES 12-15) Marks of a God-fearing man are: God teaches him; he receives God's prosperity (always true spiritually, but not necessarily materially); he inherits a great spiritual inheritance; he has a reverential and loving fear of God; and God helps him understand God's *'covenant'*, and to keep looking to the Lord and so avoid being caught in the net of sinfulness that could trap him. *'Covenant'* describes a legally binding agreement made under seal. The Bible confirms that God will keep His covenant to save, now and eternally, all who turn from sin and trust Him. Jesus also enabled that to be so when He bore our sins' punishment, saving us from Hell. He rose and is alive. He forgives all who come to Him as their living Lord and Saviour to receive His forgiveness and eternal life.

(VERSES 16-22) In a heartfelt last prayer, David looks to his merciful LORD, his only Liberator. God can help in his loneliness, afflictions, trouble, distresses, affliction and pain. God will forgive all David's sins, guard and rescue him from his fierce enemies, keep him from shame, and be his refuge. God gives him integrity and uprightness as David waits upon God. He protects him as he hopes in God. David prays, '*Redeem Israel, O God, out of all their troubles.*' God does *physically* for David what, in Christ, He will do *spiritually* for you.

Psalm 26—Transparent walk—holy life

A Psalm of David.
1Vindicate me, O LORD,
For I have walked in my integrity.
I have also trusted in the LORD;
I shall not slip.
2Examine me, O LORD, and prove me;
Try my mind and my heart.
3For Your lovingkindness is before my eyes,
And I have walked in Your truth.
4I have not sat with idolatrous mortals,
Nor will I go in with hypocrites.
5I have hated the assembly of evildoers,
And will not sit with the wicked.

6I will wash my hands in innocence;
So I will go about Your altar, O LORD,
7That I may proclaim with the voice of thanksgiving,
And tell of all Your wondrous works.
8LORD, I have loved the habitation of Your house,
And the place where Your glory dwells.

9Do not gather my soul with sinners,
Nor my life with bloodthirsty men,
10In whose hands is a sinister scheme,
And whose right hand is full of bribes.

11But as for me, I will walk in my integrity;
Redeem me and be merciful to me.
12My foot stands in an even place;
In the congregations I will bless the LORD.

(VERSES 1-3) David is not boasting about his godly character but is transparently open before God. He asks God to test, try and examine him and his integrity; this shows he is honest before God—who knows all about him. God can check if what he claims is true. Is David blameless, trusting, unwavering and living for God? David focuses on God's lovingkindness and truth and his continual walk in God's truth. Do you also walk before God in such a transparent and Bible-based way that you can tell God about it and ask Him to examine you without fear of being 'found out' for being deceitful?

(VERSES 4-5) Negatives in the Christian life are needed alongside its many positives. There is a 'Divine won't' as well as a 'Divine will'! Because David honours, trusts and walks with God, he rejects what may spoil his relationship with his Lord. So should we! He avoids idolatry and those who practise it, hypocrisy, and evildoing. He does not go to gatherings of evil people. He takes great care not to spend his free time sitting down with wicked men. Obviously, he would meet them to share the good news of forgiveness in order to help them to repent. But he does not voluntarily spend his time with people and in situations which could drag down his life for God. We live in a wicked world, too. We also meet with and, at times, need to work alongside ungodly men. But why emptily 'invest' free time in their pastimes, gatherings and pursuits (Psalm 1:1-2)?

(VERSES 6-8) Because David seeks first God's kingdom and righteousness, he concentrates on spiritual activities that please his LORD, help others, and bless him. He seeks to keep *'clean hands'* morally and spiritually. He proclaims God's praise loudly. He tells of all God's *'wondrous works'*. As a believing Jew, He loves to worship God at the altar of *'[His] house'*, whether earlier at the tabernacle, or later at the temple. They speak of God's Old Testament presence: it reminds him of God's glory. We worship God today both with others at Bible-believing churches and meetings, and also in our own daily devotional times with God when we pray and read our Bibles personally.

Turn from your sins, thank Jesus Christ for dying as your Substitute on the cross when He bore your sins and God's holy wrath on them, as your punishment. Trust fully in Him to forgive and save you. You will then have similar priorities to David. You will make living a clean life your priority and worship and praise God. This you will do both alone and with others and seek to help others to trust Christ to be forgiven and converted. Jesus will never leave you. If that does not paint your relationship with Jesus now, it certainly can in the future.

(VERSES 9-12) So you can see that it is unsurprising that David wants to avoid sinful associations, bloodthirsty men, and wicked schemes of men given to bribery. His blameless life—as already noted—flows from God's saving mercy to this beloved and redeemed sinner. So, David is now on the firm, level ground of assurance. He will praise the LORD in the *'congregations' of believers*. He knows, and so will others, what a wonderful Saviour he has! Those same principles apply to all today who know Jesus personally.

Psalm 27—Why fear, if God is for you?

A Psalm of David.
1The LORD is my light and my salvation;
Whom shall I fear?
The LORD is the strength of my life;
Of whom shall I be afraid?
2When the wicked came against me
To eat up my flesh,
My enemies and foes,
They stumbled and fell.
3Though an army may encamp against me,
My heart shall not fear;
Though war may rise against me,
In this I will be confident.

4One thing I have desired of the LORD,
That will I seek:
That I may dwell in the house of the LORD
All the days of my life,
To behold the beauty of the LORD,
And to inquire in His temple.
5For in the time of trouble
He shall hide me in His pavilion;
In the secret place of His tabernacle
He shall hide me;
He shall set me high upon a rock.

6And now my head shall be lifted up above my enemies all around me;
Therefore I will offer sacrifices of joy in His tabernacle;
I will sing, yes, I will sing praises to the LORD.

7Hear, O LORD, when I cry with my voice!
Have mercy also upon me, and answer me.
8When You said, "Seek My face,"
My heart said to You, "Your face, LORD, I will seek."
9Do not hide Your face from me;
Do not turn Your servant away in anger;
You have been my help;
Do not leave me nor forsake me,
O God of my salvation.
10When my father and my mother forsake me,
Then the LORD will take care of me.

11Teach me Your way, O LORD,
And lead me in a smooth path, because of my enemies.
12Do not deliver me to the will of my adversaries;
For false witnesses have risen against me,
And such as breathe out violence.
13I would have lost heart, unless I had believed
That I would see the goodness of the LORD

In the land of the living.

14 Wait on the LORD;
Be of good courage,
And He shall strengthen your heart;
Wait, I say, on the LORD!

(VERSES 1-3) David declares that *'The LORD is my light and salvation'* and *'The LORD is the strength of my life.'* That is why he can deal openly with *'fear'*, which he does through asking two bold questions and making bold remarks about *'fear'*. That is how he starts this psalm. We all face fear at times, and this psalm has much to teach us.

Having stated who the LORD is and what that means to him, David now knows how to face any fears. Fourteen times he uses *'my'*, *'I'*, or *'me'*. This is not selfishness. God is personal and close to all who trust Him as Lord and Saviour.

Do you see the LORD as your *'light'*, *'salvation'*, and *'strength'* of life? Is God like that to you? You will, only if God's Holy Spirit shows you how bad your sin is, enlightens your mind to grasp God's truth, and shows you Jesus, the *'Light of the world'*, answering your prayer to enter your life as your *'Salvation'* and *'Strength'*. He saves you from sin's penalty in Hell, its power in your life, and its presence in Heaven. When? When you trust in Him, the now-living Lord, and His death, to bear all your sins on the cross and God's judgment against your sins.

The word *'strength'* may also be translated as *'stronghold'*. In David's day, if people were attacked by their enemies, they fled to a fortified *'stronghold'* tower for safe refuge; food stored there saved them. In Christ, God keeps you safe and feeds you spiritually until you move from earth to Heaven. That's why David is not to be afraid! He knows God keeps him, even if an army camps against him! Romans 8:31 asks, *'If God is for us, who can be against us?'* In Christ, we find that God is both our *'strength'* and our *'stronghold'*, now and eternally in Heaven.

(VERSES 4-6) David really wants *'one thing'*. Do you? He wants God's close communion in worship and to sense His beauty. In the tabernacle, temple, or alone, he wants to know God better. We worship and do Bible study together for that same reason. All whom God saves should read the Bible seriously, personally, and with others regularly. Do you do that? It is a blessing! When communing with Christ like that, He hides us from the attacks of the devil, and strengthens us against the approaches of a world that rejects Jesus.

(VERSES 7-12) David now prays for God to hear and mercifully answer him. He seeks God daily. God, whom he calls the *'God of my salvation'*, is his personal Helper-Saviour, who will not reject or forsake him. Some parents do forsake children; but this is not true of God with those trusting Him, who now know Him and now can call Him *'Heavenly Father'* (Matthew 6:26 and 32). When violent, lying foes oppress David, he asks God to save and lead him in God's straight path. God and he are on each other's side!

(VERSES 13-14) David knows God will keep him to see God's goodness in Heaven. He will '*Wait on the LORD; be of good courage, and He [God] shall strengthen [David's] heart.*' When fear assaults us, may we, like David, listen to what God says to us. What is that? '*Wait, I say, on the LORD.*'

Psalm 28—Happy, heard and helped

A Psalm of David.
1To You I will cry, O LORD my Rock:
Do not be silent to me,
Lest, if You are silent to me,
I become like those who go down to the pit.
2Hear the voice of my supplications
When I cry to You,
When I lift up my hands toward Your holy sanctuary.

3Do not take me away with the wicked
And with the workers of iniquity,
Who speak peace to their neighbors,
But evil is in their hearts.
4Give them according to their deeds,
And according to the wickedness of their endeavors;
Give them according to the work of their hands;
Render to them what they deserve.
5Because they do not regard the works of the LORD,
Nor the operation of His hands,
He shall destroy them
And not build them up.

6Blessed be the LORD,
Because He has heard the voice of my supplications!
7The LORD is my strength and my shield;
My heart trusted in Him, and I am helped;
Therefore my heart greatly rejoices,
And with my song I will praise Him.

8The LORD is their strength,
And He is the saving refuge of His anointed.
9Save Your people,
And bless Your inheritance;
Shepherd them also,
And bear them up forever.

(VERSES 1-2) This prayer begins like some other psalms. That can be a *comfort*. It's never good to recite words in a parrotlike way. Whether you follow written liturgy in prayer books or repeat your own usual sequence of words, you can get over-familiar with either or both. Some really do pray set prayers from their heart, but perhaps not always as meaningfully as at first. The *comfort* is to realise that God does expect you to pray and to thank Him for the same subjects, often. That is a good thing to do. Verse 1 says you are *not* like those '*gone down to the pit*' (of death) who remain '*silent*' and so cannot pray. When Christ saves a repentant sinner, his prayer life comes alive. To keep it alive, keep on praying to our helpful, merciful, holy LORD, our Rock. God hears and answers both old and new Christians, whether praying together in a place of worship, or in a prayer meeting, or on your own. Pray in the name of Jesus, God the Son, your Saviour.

(VERSES 3-5) A Christian who values God's holiness must refuse to go with wicked people to behave wickedly. He or she also now recognises that, just as God was right to hold him or her guilty eternally for sinning against God (and others), he or she is right to count guilty all who sin against God. The good news is that God offers mercy, forgiveness and eternal life at once to all repenting from sin and giving their hearts to Jesus, to know and follow Him. He alone suffered our sins' eternal punishment as He died on the cross. If you repent and trust Jesus, the now-living Saviour, you are and will be saved. If you refuse to accept His offer to forgive, you will be a *tragic* loser, for ever destroyed and never built up again.

(VERSES 6-7) David blesses the LORD because *'He has heard the voice of* [his] *supplications.'* David has turned from his sin and trusted the Lord for mercy. If you have not done so yet, you too can turn from your sin, trust in Jesus and be saved. Like David, you can praise God for His mercy, and joy in God as your strength, shield and help. As you trust Him, thank Him and rejoice in singing joyfully to God.

(VERSES 8-9) See how God blesses His people! He strengthens, saves, protects, shepherds, and carries all those who are His children by saving faith. A saved person today can know so much more from the complete Bible than David could have known about our crucified but risen Divine Saviour and Lord, even though God the Holy Spirit spoke to his heart, too. But just as David longs for many more to be saved and blessed by God as he prays *'Save Your people and bless Your inheritance'*, so should everyone who loves Jesus have a desire, and pray, to see God saving and blessing others. David rejoices that God will be their Shepherd and '*bear them up forever*'. What a Saviour to have!

Psalm 29—The voice of the LORD

A Psalm of David.
1 Give unto the LORD, O you mighty ones,
Give unto the LORD glory and strength.
2 Give unto the LORD the glory due to His name;
Worship the LORD in the beauty of holiness.

3 The voice of the LORD is over the waters;
The God of glory thunders;
The LORD is over many waters.
4 The voice of the LORD is powerful;
The voice of the LORD is full of majesty.

5 The voice of the LORD breaks the cedars,
Yes, the LORD splinters the cedars of Lebanon.
6 He makes them also skip like a calf,
Lebanon and Sirion like a young wild ox.
7 The voice of the LORD divides the flames of fire.

8 The voice of the LORD shakes the wilderness;
The LORD shakes the Wilderness of Kadesh.
9 The voice of the LORD makes the deer give birth,
And strips the forests bare;
And in His temple everyone says, "Glory!"

10 The LORD sat enthroned at the Flood,
And the LORD sits as King forever.
11 The LORD will give strength to His people;
The LORD will bless His people with peace.

(VERSES 1-2) God both expects and receives worship from all beings. Here angels and heavenly beings (called '*mighty ones*') are told to '*Give unto the LORD glory and strength due to His name.*' This is emphasised by the use three times of the opening phrase, '*Give unto the LORD.*' This is followed by the command to '*Worship the LORD in the beauty of holiness.*' There is no doubt that the LORD God must be treated with honour, glory, strength and obedience and that He alone should be worshipped. God is worthy of glory and of our strongest service and worship possible. The '*mighty ones*' must '*worship the LORD in the beauty of holiness*'. '*Holiness*' is when any person or thing is 'set apart' for God. His worshippers value His holy, perfect, splendour. To worship God from your heart is to be 'set apart' from sin, and live wholly for Him (Romans 12:1-2).

The fact that the Lord Jesus Christ accepted worship from angels and men underlines that, as God the Son in the Trinity of Father,

Son and Holy Spirit, He is God as well as Man. In fact, the angel announcing Jesus' virgin birth through Mary said, *'Behold, the virgin shall be with child, and bear a Son, and they shall call His name "Immanuel," which is translated, "God with us"'* (Matthew 1:23). That is who Jesus is—*'God with us.'* That is why we should worship Him.

(VERSES 3-9) *'The voice of the LORD'* is repeated six times. To us it means the Bible, the Word of God. In the Bible, God's voice is heard clearly. Jesus used His *'voice of the LORD'* when He told a dead man to come out after four days lying in a tomb (John 11:43). Lazarus did come out—at once! In the beginning of creation 'God said, "*Let there be light' and there was light*"' (Genesis 1:3). The voice of the LORD gives us life and light.

In Psalm 29, *'the voice of the LORD'* means that booming and fearsome echo of God's voice in His storms. No mere man can do that. Listen to mighty waters running free; the shattering sound of violent powerful thunder, as punctuated by the shock of flashing lightning strikes; the crashing roar as huge cedar and oak trees are torn down, broken and twisted in the violent gales; and the trembling desert earthquake booming on.

All God's worshippers in the temple know almighty God is in control, grateful that He is so strong and wonderful. They cry aloud, *'Glory!'* It is good, during a storm, to look at and listen to the thunder and lightning and say quietly, "My strong, loving Father and Saviour are responsible for all that!"

(VERSES 10-11) David moves from creation—the waters, storms, violent winds, and earthquakes—to the Creator. Note this about the LORD: He sits as King over the whole flood; in fact, He *'sits as King forever'; He 'will give strength to His His people'*; and will bless them *'with peace'*.

Your sins made you into God's enemy, and that is why you go the world's way and not God's (James 4:4). But remember that Jesus bore your sins and was punished for them. For you, He has made *'peace through the blood of His cross'* (Colossians 1:12). Turn from sin, trust in Jesus, and He gives you *'peace with God through our Lord Jesus Christ'* (Romans 5:1). He puts His peace within you. You will experience that peace for ever in Heaven because Jesus becomes your *'Prince of Peace'* (Isaiah 9:6).

Psalm 30—The normal life with God

A Psalm. A Song at the dedication of the house of David.
1I will extol You, O LORD, for You have lifted me up,
And have not let my foes rejoice over me.
2O LORD my God, I cried out to You,
And You healed me.
3O LORD, You brought my soul up from the grave;
You have kept me alive, that I should not go down to the pit.

4Sing praise to the LORD, you saints of His,
And give thanks at the remembrance of His holy name.
5For His anger is but for a moment,
His favor is for life;
Weeping may endure for a night,
But joy comes in the morning.

6Now in my prosperity I said,
"I shall never be moved."
7LORD, by Your favor You have made my mountain stand strong;
You hid Your face, and I was troubled.

8I cried out to You, O LORD;
And to the LORD I made supplication:
9"What profit is there in my blood,
When I go down to the pit?
Will the dust praise You?
Will it declare Your truth?
10Hear, O LORD, and have mercy on me;
LORD, be my helper!"

11You have turned for me my mourning into dancing;
You have put off my sackcloth and clothed me with gladness,
12To the end that my glory may sing praise to You and not be silent.
O LORD my God, I will give thanks to You forever.

(VERSES 1-3) This psalm dedicates the Temple. In it, David tells worshippers about daily living with God. In worship and in living, you must be consistent, if the LORD is your Lord. David exalts (meaning *'lifts up'*) God. Why? Because God lifted him up from the depths and rescued him from his enemies and, better still, *'from the grave'*. He prayed for God's help and got it. Keep praying! He answers your prayers, too. The first prayer He must answer is if you know you are sinful, and pray a prayer similar to the prayer a crooked and much-despised tax collector prayed: '*God be merciful to me, a sinner*' (Luke 8:13). Thank Jesus for dying in your place to bear your sins and your punishment for them.

Then you, too, can know victory over death and Hell by trusting the now-risen Jesus.

(VERSES 4-5) *'Saints'* means people who trust the Lord and are set apart for Him and by Him to live for Him under His lordship. They must sing together to praise *'His holy name'*. This is so different from those who so often break the third commandment (Exodus 20:7) by misusing God's name. We learn that, apart from God's eternal wrath remaining on those who do not repent and trust the Lord Jesus, God's anger is short lived for those who know and follow Him. The reason is that He always and at once forgives the sins of those who know Him when they are sincerely sorrowful over their sins, confess them, forsake them, and ask God to pardon and cleanse them. That brings repenting believers the *'joy'* of renewed fellowship with God; but their saving eternal relationship with their Heavenly Father was never in jeopardy.

(VERSES 6-7) It seems that, at one time, King David was foolishly trusting in his own prosperity, strength, or position; that made him feel secure. But circumstances change and real security only comes from realising that its only source is in God by His gracious favour. So, never trust in self or in feelings. Trust in Jesus and keep trusting in the LORD, in His Word, and in the promises you find there. As you pray and read the Bible daily, it will help you do that. So will fellowship with other Christians. When you turn away from your Lord, He seems to hide His face. When you repent and follow Him, you become aware that His smile has returned.

(VERSES 8-10) Note down some specific prayers you prayed which God answered. Here David tells of such a prayer: he feared death was around the corner for him, so he asked God to be merciful to him and help him personally. How did God answer David's prayer for His mercy and help? Read verses 11-12 to see.

(VERSES 11-12) This prayer of thanks and praise is because God answers prayers from the heart for His glory. It encourages you to keep on praying. Remember to thank God for His answered prayers. Thank Him for what He alone did. A praying believer knows his joy is in God, not in what happens. If your heart sings to God—so should your voice! Determine to thank God always and do it!

Psalm 31—At times it can be very hard

1In You, O LORD, I put my trust;
Let me never be ashamed;
Deliver me in Your righteousness.
2Bow down Your ear to me,
Deliver me speedily;
Be my rock of refuge,
A fortress of defense to save me.

3For You are my rock and my fortress;
Therefore, for Your name's sake,
Lead me and guide me.
4Pull me out of the net which they have secretly laid for me,
For You are my strength.
5Into Your hand I commit my spirit;
You have redeemed me, O LORD God of truth.

6I have hated those who regard useless idols;
But I trust in the LORD.
7I will be glad and rejoice in Your mercy,
For You have considered my trouble;
You have known my soul in adversities,
8And have not shut me up into the hand of the enemy;
You have set my feet in a wide place.

9Have mercy on me, O LORD, for I am in trouble;
My eye wastes away with grief,
Yes, my soul and my body!
10For my life is spent with grief,
And my years with sighing;
My strength fails because of my iniquity,
And my bones waste away.
11I am a reproach among all my enemies,
But especially among my neighbors,
And am repulsive to my acquaintances;
Those who see me outside flee from me.
12I am forgotten like a dead man, out of mind;
I am like a broken vessel.
13For I hear the slander of many;
Fear is on every side;
While they take counsel together against me,
They scheme to take away my life.

14But as for me, I trust in You, O LORD;
I say, "You are my God."
15My times are in Your hand;
Deliver me from the hand of my enemies,
And from those who persecute me.
16Make Your face shine upon Your servant;
Save me for Your mercies' sake.

17 Do not let me be ashamed, O LORD, for I have called upon You;
Let the wicked be ashamed;
Let them be silent in the grave.
18 Let the lying lips be put to silence,
Which speak insolent things proudly and contemptuously against the righteous.

19 Oh, how great is Your goodness,
Which You have laid up for those who fear You,
Which You have prepared for those who trust in You
In the presence of the sons of men!
20 You shall hide them in the secret place of Your presence
From the plots of man;
You shall keep them secretly in a pavilion
From the strife of tongues.

21 Blessed be the LORD,
For He has shown me His marvelous kindness in a strong city!
22 For I said in my haste,
"I am cut off from before Your eyes";
Nevertheless You heard the voice of my supplications
When I cried out to You.

23 Oh, love the LORD, all you His saints!
For the LORD preserves the faithful,
And fully repays the proud person.
24 Be of good courage,
And He shall strengthen your heart,
All you who hope in the LORD.

(VERSES 1-5) This multi-prayer of David starts from the truth of the words *'In You, O LORD, I have put my trust.'* The LORD has become his *'rock of refuge'* and his *'fortress of defence'.* Still today, a man who sees his sin and repents to receive mercy and cleansing is forgiven through putting his trust in Jesus as his sole Sin-bearer, Saviour and Sovereign. Jesus becomes his eternal refuge against the world, the flesh and the devil. What blessings has he now in Christ? Liberty from shame, righteous freedom from sin and from judgment. God's ear is always open to him and he has a rock-solid, strong fortress, being built and hidden in Christ. He is led and guided for the sake of Jesus and set free from ensnaring traps. So, he now commits his spirit into the Lord's hands and asks his *'LORD God of truth'* knowing that he has been *'redeemed'* by Him (literally 'bought back' by God) from sin and shame. He belongs to Christ, having been bought by Him.

(VERSES 6-8) Now he hates idolatry but trusts in the LORD. He loves rejoicing and joy in the Lord's *'mercy'* that overcomes *'trouble'* and *'adversities'* and delivers him from *'the hand of the enemy'*. He is in a *'wide place'*, spiritually speaking.

(VERSES 9-13) Yet he still asks for God's *'mercy'* because he is *'in trouble'* still. Grief accompanies his weakness in *'soul'* and in *'body'*. He is weak and sick. He sighs in his failing strength and feels it 'in his bones'. His enemies and neighbours (especially) reproach him. Neighbours treat him with contempt. Mere acquaintances find him repulsive. Those who come across him avoid him, flee from him and forget him. Many slander him as *broken pottery—he has no beauty and cannot do what he was supposed to be doing.* He fears that his conspiring enemies even now scheme to try to take his life. Today, some say that if you walk with God, you will *always* be healthy, wealthy and successful. That is just not true in physical terms.

(VERSES 14-18) But he trusts in God. He calls the LORD *'my God'* and knows his *'times are in* [God's] *hand.'* He asks his God to free him from his foes and persecutors. He asks God to smile upon him and *'save* [him] *for* [God's] *mercies' sake'*. He asks God to deliver him from being *'ashamed'* and repeats detailed prayers for previous blessings from God and against his foes.

(VERSES 19-22) Expecting God's help, he explodes into thankfulness, despite his difficult circumstances. He says to God, *'Oh, how great is Your goodness.'* He thanks God for all the future blessings he knows that God has for those who trust Him now. What an excellent practice! He also thinks back and thanks God for the past blessings God has faithfully given him in answer to his prayers. He rejoices in his prayer-answering God. So can we!

(VERSES 23-24) David now urges all who are set apart for God to love Him. The LORD will preserve His own. David ends with, *'Be of good courage and He shall strengthen your heart.'* To whom does he address this encouragement? To *'All you who hope in the LORD'*. The good news is that this includes *you* if your trust is in the Lord Jesus Christ!

Psalm 32—Forgiven, covered, counted

A Psalm of David. A Contemplation.
1 Blessed is he whose transgression is forgiven,
Whose sin is covered.
2 Blessed is the man to whom the LORD does not impute iniquity,
And in whose spirit there is no deceit.

3 When I kept silent, my bones grew old
Through my groaning all the day long.
4 For day and night Your hand was heavy upon me;
My vitality was turned into the drought of summer. Selah
5 I acknowledged my sin to You,
And my iniquity I have not hidden.
I said, "I will confess my transgressions to the LORD,"
And You forgave the iniquity of my sin. Selah

6 For this cause everyone who is godly shall pray to You
In a time when You may be found;
Surely in a flood of great waters
They shall not come near him.
7 You are my hiding place;
You shall preserve me from trouble;
You shall surround me with songs of deliverance. Selah

8 I will instruct you and teach you in the way you should go;
I will guide you with My eye.
9 Do not be like the horse or like the mule,
Which have no understanding,
Which must be harnessed with bit and bridle,
Else they will not come near you.

10 Many sorrows shall be to the wicked;
But he who trusts in the LORD, mercy shall surround him.
11 Be glad in the LORD and rejoice, you righteous;
And shout for joy, all you upright in heart!

(VERSES 1-2) By God's amazing grace a man whom God saves is '*blessed*' because his '*transgression is forgiven' and* his '*sin is covered*'. God no longer counts that man's sin against him. God changes that forgiven sinner so deeply that '*in his spirit there is no deceit*'. How? Because Jesus bore in His own body on the cross the wrath of God the Father against our sins when He died in our place. Also, the perfect, spotless righteousness and perfection of God the Son, Jesus, is counted by God the Father as covering every repentant sinner's sinful life. God also begins to change that person's sinful heart. All that arises when that sinner humbly confesses his sin, with sorrow, to God, turns from it and asks to be saved by faith in Jesus and through His death for him. All his sins were paid for when counted against Jesus on the cross. So, when a sinner comes to Christ, those sins are no longer counted against him. The blessing of being forgiven, covered, and counted as righteous are for everyone who receives Christ. One of the results is that a deceitful spirit is taken away, too.

(VERSES 3-5) Second Samuel chapters 11 and 12 and Psalm 51 cover David's adultery with Bathsheba, his deceit, murder of Uriah and other soldiers, and his shamefully delayed repentance. We learn now how David suffered badly, even physically. God's heavy hand of conviction was on him. At last, he confessed his sins to God, after the prophet Nathan's bold witness. So, God forgave him and cleansed his sin and guilt.

(VERSES 6-7) When you trust Christ, you start a life of '*godly*' living and praying to God. God then keeps and protects you even in rising waters of danger. He hides you and surrounds you with '*songs of deliverance*'. To walk with God is to turn from sin, trust and obey Jesus through His Word, and follow Him. He blesses you now and will do for ever in Heaven.

(VERSES 8-9) Another result of turning from sin and trusting in the LORD is that as you read His Word, the Bible, each day God instructs, teaches, counsels, guides and watches over you. He wants you to walk with Him and get to know Him better each day. So, do not be mule-headed. Unlike a horse, you should need no controlling '*bit and bridle*' if you walk trusting and obeying the Lord.

(VERSES 10-11) You will escape the '*sorrows of wicked men*' when you trust in the LORD's unfailing and surrounding loving mercy. That is reason to rejoice, be glad and rejoice. By your faith in Jesus, God now counts you, a guilty sinner, as '*righteous*' and '*upright in heart*'. You have good reason to rejoice! And do tell others why.

Psalm 33—'The goodness of the LORD.'

1Rejoice in the LORD, O you righteous!
For praise from the upright is beautiful.
2Praise the LORD with the harp;
Make melody to Him with an instrument of ten strings.
3Sing to Him a new song;
Play skillfully with a shout of joy.

4For the word of the LORD is right,
And all His work is done in truth.
5He loves righteousness and justice;
The earth is full of the goodness of the LORD.

6By the word of the LORD the heavens were made,
And all the host of them by the breath of His mouth.
7He gathers the waters of the sea together as a heap;
He lays up the deep in storehouses.

8Let all the earth fear the LORD;
Let all the inhabitants of the world stand in awe of Him.
9For He spoke, and it was done;
He commanded, and it stood fast.

10The LORD brings the counsel of the nations to nothing;
He makes the plans of the peoples of no effect.
11The counsel of the LORD stands forever,
The plans of His heart to all generations.
12Blessed is the nation whose God is the LORD,
The people He has chosen as His own inheritance.

13The LORD looks from heaven;
He sees all the sons of men.
14From the place of His dwelling He looks
On all the inhabitants of the earth;
15He fashions their hearts individually;
He considers all their works.

16No king is saved by the multitude of an army;
A mighty man is not delivered by great strength.
17A horse is a vain hope for safety;
Neither shall it deliver any by its great strength.

18Behold, the eye of the LORD is on those who fear Him,
On those who hope in His mercy,
19To deliver their soul from death,
And to keep them alive in famine.

20Our soul waits for the LORD;
He is our help and our shield.
21For our heart shall rejoice in Him,

Because we have trusted in His holy name.
22Let Your mercy, O LORD, be upon us,
Just as we hope in You.

(VERSES 1-3) How joyful God wants the praise to be of all He counts as *'righteous' and 'upright'.* Worshipful praise is helped by playing skilfully the harp and stringed instruments, singing a new song, and even accompanying shouts of joy. This is honouring, organised, and enthusiastic praise. Do we worship God like this? We should do.

(VERSES 4-5) The LORD's word *'is right'.* He always works *'in truth.' 'He loves righteousness and justice.'* Little wonder *that 'The earth is full of the goodness of the LORD.'* God's character is stamped all over it.

(VERSES 6-9) Here is a brief summary of how God created the heavens, earth and seas by His Word. Fear and revere Him because the mighty power and authority of His Word made and established all this. As the great Creator, God did all His works of creation simply by His Word!

(VERSES 10-19) God is also sovereign over all nations and all people. He sees and knows everyone and works out His perfect eternal purposes, overruling the plans of nations and peoples. He especially blesses the nation and those people who belong to Him. His choice for them is an eternal inheritance in Heaven: personal faith in the Lord Jesus Christ is the means He uses today to fulfil that plan of His. All who turn from sin and trust that Jesus was punished for them, in dying on the cross while bearing their sin, are forgiven. Each one becomes one of God's people for whom Heaven waits. Have you trusted Him? Are you Heaven-bound for that *'inheritance'*, one day? God looks on and sees the hearts of all men—including you—and He can fashion your heart if you give it to Him. God's power to save, keep and help those who know Him is far above any military or kingly strength or might. He watches over those with godly fear, who hope in Him, rejoicing in His *'mercy'*. He delivers them from death and famine. Eternal life and feeding on the 'Bread of Life' are theirs in Christ.

(VERSES 20-22) Psalm 33 ends with a lovely verse of commitment to the LORD; *'Let Your mercy, O LORD, be upon us, just as we hope in You.'* Will you pray it? Wait and hope in Him as your help and shield. Let your heart rejoice and trust in His holy name and His *'mercy'*. Put all your hope in the Saviour, Jesus Christ.

Psalm 34—God looks after His servants

A Psalm of David when he pretended madness before Abimelech, who drove him away, and he departed.

1 I will bless the LORD at all times;
His praise shall continually be in my mouth.
2 My soul shall make its boast in the LORD;
The humble shall hear of it and be glad.
3 Oh, magnify the LORD with me,
And let us exalt His name together.

4 I sought the LORD, and He heard me,
And delivered me from all my fears.
5 They looked to Him and were radiant,
And their faces were not ashamed.
6 This poor man cried out, and the LORD heard him,
And saved him out of all his troubles.
7 The angel of the LORD encamps all around those who fear Him,
And delivers them.

8 Oh, taste and see that the LORD is good;
Blessed is the man who trusts in Him!
9 Oh, fear the LORD, you His saints!
There is no want to those who fear Him.
10 The young lions lack and suffer hunger;
But those who seek the LORD shall not lack any good thing.

11 Come, you children, listen to me;
I will teach you the fear of the LORD.
12 Who is the man who desires life,
And loves many days, that he may see good?
13 Keep your tongue from evil,
And your lips from speaking deceit.
14 Depart from evil and do good;
Seek peace and pursue it.

15 The eyes of the LORD are on the righteous,
And His ears are open to their cry.
16 The face of the LORD is against those who do evil,
To cut off the remembrance of them from the earth.

17 The righteous cry out, and the LORD hears,
And delivers them out of all their troubles.
18 The LORD is near to those who have a broken heart,
And saves such as have a contrite spirit.

19 Many are the afflictions of the righteous,
But the LORD delivers him out of them all.
20 He guards all his bones;
Not one of them is broken.
21 Evil shall slay the wicked,

And those who hate the righteous shall be condemned.
22The LORD redeems the soul of His servants,
And none of those who trust in Him shall be condemned.

(VERSES 1-3) David, fleeing from King Saul, came before the Philistine ruler of Gath. ('*Abimelech*', in the title of the psalm, means 'ruler'.) The background to this account is 1 Samuel 21 and 22, where we read that this ruler was Achish. He knew very well about David's slaying of Goliath of Gath, the Philistines' military champion, and David's amazing success rate in his battles with Philistine armies. To escape Achish's probable imprisonment or worse, David pretended to be mad. His crafty ruse worked, and he escaped. But he starts Psalm 34, not by saying how clever he was to escape, but by praising God. He urges others to rejoice, glorify God, and exalt His name together with him. Never let work or successful efforts of your own making stop you from praising God. He is in control.

(VERSES 4-7) David may have his escapes from other enemies in mind, or from the Philistines (as from Achish), or from Saul, as he gratefully recalls how he asked God to deliver him, and He did. God saved him from his troubles in answer to his prayer. God can answer your prayers, too. David values godly fear for the LORD, and God's surrounding and delivering him. Answered prayer starts by asking Jesus to forgive and save you. That is why He died in your place on the cross to bear your sins and their penalty. Call on Him to save you. Once you know Him as Saviour, you are in communion with Him to pray to Him. Note that although God is directly involved in saving those who trust Him, He can use His angels, too, to help in our deliverance, even though we might not know this at the time.

(VERSES 8-10) What a wonderful invitation God gives! '*Taste and see that the LORD is good*.' God blesses all who trust in Him. He promises no lack of His supply of needs to any who fear and seek Him. Is that you? God delights to give us good things—judged from His point of view and not always from ours.

(VERSES 11-16) We often see in the Bible that '*the fear of the LORD*' is a reverent yet loving regard for God's awesome holiness. How can you cultivate it and so desire '*life*', love '*many days*' and '*see good*'? The answer given is to refrain from evil speech and deceitful talk. '*Depart from evil and do good; Seek peace and pursue it.*' Do you realise that repentance is not only something that applies when you come to trust Jesus as your Saviour; it is also a principle of godly and blessed living. Always be turning away from wrong and doing good—and God's grace will help you in that. Recognise that God is always watching and listening for your cry if you trust Him. Note that, on the other hand, God is always against evildoers both now and after death.

(VERSES 17-22) See how God looks after those who trust, obey, follow and fear Him. This is so now for those who yield their lives to the Lord Jesus Christ, and aim to please, serve and make Him known to others. When you cry out to Him, He hears and delivers you from all your troubles. He is close to you if your heart is breaking over your sins. He saves you when you feel crushed in spirit. He protects you—even physically. Unlike unbelievers wanting to stay wicked and thus being under God's condemnation, as His servant you are redeemed and will never be condemned. He is your Redeemer in whom you can trust. (Have you noticed that verse 20 also predicted Jesus' crucifixion? See John 19:33-37.)

Psalm 35—Prayer and praise if opposed

A Psalm of David.
1Plead my cause, O LORD, with those who strive with me;
Fight against those who fight against me.
2Take hold of shield and buckler,
And stand up for my help.
3Also draw out the spear,
And stop those who pursue me.
Say to my soul,
"I am your salvation."

4Let those be put to shame and brought to dishonor
Who seek after my life;
Let those be turned back and brought to confusion
Who plot my hurt.
5Let them be like chaff before the wind,
And let the angel of the LORD chase them.
6Let their way be dark and slippery,
And let the angel of the LORD pursue them.
7For without cause they have hidden their net for me in a pit,
Which they have dug without cause for my life.
8Let destruction come upon him unexpectedly,
And let his net that he has hidden catch himself;
Into that very destruction let him fall.

9And my soul shall be joyful in the LORD;
It shall rejoice in His salvation.
10All my bones shall say,
"LORD, who is like You,
Delivering the poor from him who is too strong for him,
Yes, the poor and the needy from him who plunders him?"

11Fierce witnesses rise up;
They ask me things that I do not know.
12They reward me evil for good,
To the sorrow of my soul.
13But as for me, when they were sick,
My clothing was sackcloth;
I humbled myself with fasting;
And my prayer would return to my own heart.
14I paced about as though he were my friend or brother;
I bowed down heavily, as one who mourns for his mother.

15But in my adversity they rejoiced
And gathered together;
Attackers gathered against me,
And I did not know it;
They tore at me and did not cease;
16With ungodly mockers at feasts
They gnashed at me with their teeth.

17 LORD, how long will You look on?
Rescue me from their destructions,
My precious life from the lions.
18 I will give You thanks in the great assembly;
I will praise You among many people.

19 Let them not rejoice over me who are wrongfully my enemies;
Nor let them wink with the eye who hate me without a cause.
20 For they do not speak peace,
But they devise deceitful matters
Against the quiet ones in the land.
21 They also opened their mouth wide against me,
And said, "Aha, aha!
Our eyes have seen it."

22 This You have seen, O LORD;
Do not keep silence.
O LORD, do not be far from me.
23 Stir up Yourself, and awake to my vindication,
To my cause, my God and my LORD.
24 Vindicate me, O LORD my God, according to Your righteousness;
And let them not rejoice over me.
25 Let them not say in their hearts, "Ah, so we would have it!"
Let them not say, "We have swallowed him up."

26 Let them be ashamed and brought to mutual confusion
Who rejoice at my hurt;
Let them be clothed with shame and dishonor
Who exalt themselves against me.

27 Let them shout for joy and be glad,
Who favor my righteous cause;
And let them say continually,
"Let the LORD be magnified,
Who has pleasure in the prosperity of His servant."
28 And my tongue shall speak of Your righteousness
And of Your praise all the day long.

(VERSES 1-10) We often see in the psalms that in David's walk and work for God he has enemies. He enlists God's help against them. What David experiences physically, we face against our spiritual enemies, namely the world, the flesh and the devil. We seek God's help to live for, praise, and work for Him, and make Him known to others. Have you put your trust in Jesus, and in His death on the cross to bear your sins and their penalty? Do you know Him as your risen and living Saviour? If so, pray for His help. He is your '*shield*' (for general defence) and '*buckler*' (for specific 'close quarters' defence). God fights to help you and will *'draw out the spear'* of the enemy for you. He is your *'salvation'*. David targets in prayer all seeking his life, hurt, downfall or capture. He asks God to scatter, chase, confuse, capture and ruin them. He will joy in the LORD and in *'His salvation'*. He praises God for delivering the poor and needy from their stronger plunderers. Far better to be weak and trust in God than to be strong and oppose Him. There can only be one Victor!

(VERSES 11-18) David faces opposition and malice from some lying about what they say about him. He had done them good, yet they repaid him by doing him evil. He was sad and fasted humbly when they were ill. He mourned and wept for them. Yet they rejoiced in his failings and *'adversity'*. They met to gather gleefully when he stumbled. They ganged up on him to attack him with ceaseless slander. They seem like wild animals *'gnashing at'* him with their teeth. He prays desperately for God to rescue him as from lions with their gnashing teeth. But even in this dark time he tells God he will yet thank and praise Him *'in the great assembly'* of believers for answering prayer and rescuing him. Look ahead always to God's faithfulness. And look forward to regular fellowship and worship with others who know and love Christ.

(VERSES 19-28) David anticipates repeated aggressive behaviour against him. He asks God to stop their triumph or gloating over him and over other *'quiet ones in the land'*, but to stay near to defend and vindicate him *'according to* [God's] *righteousness'*. He asks for their shame and confusion and dishonour, and asks for joy for all who support his *'righteous cause'* and continually seek for God to be exalted and magnified. Again, he promises to honour God by his speech and praise. Always look for God to act: praise Him in the darkest times! It often is hard to follow Him, but He keeps, helps and blesses those who honour Him. *'If God is for us, who can be against us?'* (Romans 8:31)

Psalm 36—The basis of the gospel

To the Chief Musician. A Psalm of David the servant of the LORD.
1An oracle within my heart concerning the transgression of the wicked:
There is no fear of God before his eyes.
2For he flatters himself in his own eyes,
When he finds out his iniquity and when he hates.
3The words of his mouth are wickedness and deceit;
He has ceased to be wise and to do good.
4He devises wickedness on his bed;
He sets himself in a way that is not good;
He does not abhor evil.

5Your mercy, O LORD, is in the heavens;
Your faithfulness reaches to the clouds.
6Your righteousness is like the great mountains;
Your judgments are a great deep;
O LORD, You preserve man and beast.

7How precious is Your lovingkindness, O God!
Therefore the children of men put their trust under the shadow of Your wings.
8They are abundantly satisfied with the fullness of Your house,
And You give them drink from the river of Your pleasures.
9For with You is the fountain of life;
In Your light we see light.

10Oh, continue Your lovingkindness to those who know You,
And Your righteousness to the upright in heart.
11Let not the foot of pride come against me,
And let not the hand of the wicked drive me away.
12There the workers of iniquity have fallen;
They have been cast down and are not able to rise.

(VERSES 1-4) David gives his 'bad news' before he can give his 'good news'. That is a good principle in the gospel. Until you realise how bad you are before a holy God, you will not grasp how desperate it is for you to repent from what is wrong in your life and ask Jesus to forgive and cleanse you and become your indwelling Saviour. The Bible says, '*Christ died for the ungodly*' (Romans 5:6). Jesus bore your sins and was punished for them in your place on the cross. He rose again. Only when you turn from sin and receive the living Christ in your life can God, who hates sin but loves you, accept you.

We start this psalm by seeing how God sees you and me: we do not have the fear of God in our minds. We flatter ourselves not to really take in our '*iniquity*' and sinful hatred even when we do become aware of them. We speak words of '*wickedness and deceit*'. We no longer seek to live wisely or a morally good life but even plan wickedness when in bed. We not only go astray by nature; we also set ourselves to follow a wrong course of action. Unsurprisingly, we do '*not abhor evil*'; rather, we choose it. As guilty sinners that describes us all. We all clearly need the Lord Jesus Christ to save us.

(VERSES 5-7a) See how different God is in His character. This describes God the Father, God the Son, and God the Holy Spirit—Three in One and One in Three. God is infinitely merciful, equally faithful, hugely and perfectly righteous, and limitless in His judgements and justice. He preserves all animals and mankind. He is not only infinite but '*precious*' in His '*lovingkindness*'. Can you see how far short you have come because of your sins against God, and how you need Jesus as your perfect sacrifice for your sins in His work of dying on the cross in your place?

(VERSES 7b-9) See what great blessings and benefits God pours out on you if you turn to Him and trust Him. This is reflected in His physical dealings with you, but it also describes perfectly how God blesses you spiritually when you turn from your sins, repent, trust Him, and seek to follow Him and please Him day by day. His blessing is not only in Heaven—He will greatly bless you right now and continually, day by day. Stay close to Him in daily praying, reading and trusting His Word the Bible, and having fellowship regularly with others who are saved by trusting Jesus. He gives refuge and the shadow of His protecting wing to you. He feeds you abundantly spiritually and lets you drink of His delights. He gives you light and insight. A 'bricky' friend of mine, who could not read until He came to Jesus and got a Bible, said in his broad Yorkshire accent, 'It's better *felt* than *telt*.'[1]

(VERSES 10-12) David's prayer is for God to continue to give him His love, make him righteous, and protect him from proud, wicked evildoers, who will finally fall. God will answer that kind of prayer for you too, if you pray it.

1 Telt is an old Scottish or Yorkshire way of saying told, or explained.

Psalm 37—The wicked and the righteous

A Psalm of David.
1Do not fret because of evildoers,
Nor be envious of the workers of iniquity.
2For they shall soon be cut down like the grass,
And wither as the green herb.

3Trust in the LORD, and do good;
Dwell in the land, and feed on His faithfulness.
4Delight yourself also in the LORD,
And He shall give you the desires of your heart.

5Commit your way to the LORD,
Trust also in Him,
And He shall bring it to pass.
6He shall bring forth your righteousness as the light,
And your justice as the noonday.

7Rest in the LORD, and wait patiently for Him;
Do not fret because of him who prospers in his way,
Because of the man who brings wicked schemes to pass.
8Cease from anger, and forsake wrath;
Do not fret—it only causes harm.

9For evildoers shall be cut off;
But those who wait on the LORD,
They shall inherit the earth.
10For yet a little while and the wicked shall be no more;
Indeed, you will look carefully for his place,
But it shall be no more.
11But the meek shall inherit the earth,
And shall delight themselves in the abundance of peace.

12The wicked plots against the just,
And gnashes at him with his teeth.
13The LORD laughs at him,
For He sees that his day is coming.
14The wicked have drawn the sword
And have bent their bow,
To cast down the poor and needy,
To slay those who are of upright conduct.
15Their sword shall enter their own heart,
And their bows shall be broken.

16A little that a righteous man has
Is better than the riches of many wicked.
17For the arms of the wicked shall be broken,
But the LORD upholds the righteous.

18The LORD knows the days of the upright,

And their inheritance shall be forever.
19They shall not be ashamed in the evil time,
And in the days of famine they shall be satisfied.
20But the wicked shall perish;
And the enemies of the LORD,
Like the splendor of the meadows, shall vanish.
Into smoke they shall vanish away.

21The wicked borrows and does not repay,
But the righteous shows mercy and gives.
22For those blessed by Him shall inherit the earth,
But those cursed by Him shall be cut off.

23The steps of a good man are ordered by the LORD,
And He delights in his way.
24Though he fall, he shall not be utterly cast down;
For the LORD upholds him with His hand.

25I have been young, and now am old;
Yet I have not seen the righteous forsaken,
Nor his descendants begging bread.
26He is ever merciful, and lends;
And his descendants are blessed.

27Depart from evil, and do good;
And dwell forevermore.
28For the LORD loves justice,
And does not forsake His saints;
They are preserved forever,
But the descendants of the wicked shall be cut off.
29The righteous shall inherit the land,
And dwell in it forever.

30The mouth of the righteous speaks wisdom,
And his tongue talks of justice.
31The law of his God is in his heart;
None of his steps shall slide.

32The wicked watches the righteous,
And seeks to slay him.
33The LORD will not leave him in his hand,
Nor condemn him when he is judged.

34Wait on the LORD,
And keep His way,
And He shall exalt you to inherit the land;
When the wicked are cut off, you shall see it.
35I have seen the wicked in great power,
And spreading himself like a native green tree.
36Yet he passed away, and behold, he was no more;
Indeed I sought him, but he could not be found.

37Mark the blameless man, and observe the upright;
For the future of that man is peace.
38But the transgressors shall be destroyed together;
The future of the wicked shall be cut off.

39But the salvation of the righteous is from the LORD;
He is their strength in the time of trouble.
40And the LORD shall help them and deliver them;
He shall deliver them from the wicked,
And save them,
Because they trust in Him.

(VERSES 1-7a) If you know the LORD, do not fret or envy because of sinful men. Trust in, delight in, commit to, rest in, and wait for the LORD. He will bless you.

(VERSES 7b-17) Do not harm yourself or others because you fret or are angry. Evil men will be cut off. If you follow and trust God, you will inherit His blessings and peace, despite sinful foes. Their efforts will finally come to nothing. God upholds His own and they find more satisfaction in the little they have than *'the riches of many wicked'*.

(VERSES 18-29) See from these verses what God does if you trust Him. Compare it with the end of the wicked. If you turn from sin to trust in Jesus, who died in your place to take the judgment for your sins, a blessed, enduring, future inheritance (Heaven) is for you. He keeps you from shame and satisfies you. He is near now to bless you. He leads your steps in His way and takes delight in your walk with Him. The wicked perish, and will be cut off for ever without blessings and no more in this world. They cannot be trusted even to repay what they borrow. God guides, loves, upholds and provides for the godly. He blesses their children. They are merciful and generous as a result. The application is, *'Depart from evil, and do good.'* What better *'good'* than to trust Jesus and follow Him? This leads to never being forsaken by God, knowing His protection, and an eternal home in His Heaven. Not so the wicked!

(VERSES 30-38) Again, consider those saved by God's grace. They possess His wisdom and justice, having God's law in their hearts, and walking safely, even through an evil world. God's wisdom, presence, help, keeping, uplifting, peace, and future are signs of His love for those who trust Him, even when they have cruel and committed enemies to face. Compare all that with the wicked. The eternal destruction of those cut off from God, and not restored by repentance and faith, seems so sad. To turn from sin to Christ not only brings us the spiritual blessings that the Father gives to His children, but also rescues is from the mess and judgment that unrepentant sinners experience now and for ever.

(VERSES 39-40) Look at the salvation that God offers those He now regards as righteous. That is even more amazing because by nature all sinners are not '*righteous*', but definitely '*unrighteous*' and wicked. But the Lord Jesus Christ, whose shed blood cleanses all who believe in Him from all their sins, is the One whose perfect righteousness is counted on behalf of guilty sinners as they plead for His mercy, turn from their wicked ways, and receive Christ in their hearts. He now is '*their strength in times of trouble*'. He helps and delivers them. He saves them. Why? '*Because they trust in Him*.' Have you asked Jesus into your life to save you, and are you trusting in Him now?

Psalm 38—When God convicts of sin

A Psalm of David. To bring to remembrance.
1O LORD, do not rebuke me in Your wrath,
Nor chasten me in Your hot displeasure!
2For Your arrows pierce me deeply,
And Your hand presses me down.

3There is no soundness in my flesh
Because of Your anger,
Nor any health in my bones
Because of my sin.
4For my iniquities have gone over my head;
Like a heavy burden they are too heavy for me.
5My wounds are foul and festering
Because of my foolishness.

6I am troubled, I am bowed down greatly;
I go mourning all the day long.
7For my loins are full of inflammation,
And there is no soundness in my flesh.
8I am feeble and severely broken;
I groan because of the turmoil of my heart.

9LORD, all my desire is before You;
And my sighing is not hidden from You.
10My heart pants, my strength fails me;
As for the light of my eyes, it also has gone from me.

11My loved ones and my friends stand aloof from my plague,
And my relatives stand afar off.
12Those also who seek my life lay snares for me;
Those who seek my hurt speak of destruction,
And plan deception all the day long.

13But I, like a deaf man, do not hear;
And I am like a mute who does not open his mouth.
14Thus I am like a man who does not hear,
And in whose mouth is no response.

15For in You, O LORD, I hope;
You will hear, O LORD my God.
16For I said, "Hear me, lest they rejoice over me,
Lest, when my foot slips, they exalt themselves against me."

17For I am ready to fall,
And my sorrow is continually before me.
18For I will declare my iniquity;
I will be in anguish over my sin.
19But my enemies are vigorous, and they are strong;
And those who hate me wrongfully have multiplied.

[20]Those also who render evil for good,
They are my adversaries, because I follow what is good.

[21]Do not forsake me, O LORD;
O my God, be not far from me!
[22]Make haste to help me,
O Lord, my salvation!

(VERSES 1-4) 'Conviction of sin' Is when God's Holy Spirit awakens your conscience to your sins, which are always bad in His eyes. He sees and knows all about them. God punishes sin for ever. The wonder of Christ's gospel is that Jesus has taken that punishment for your sin in your place. He forgives and changes you if you turn from that sin and trust Jesus as your personal Saviour. Psalm 38:1-4 describes how bad David feels as God shows him his sin and guilt. Which sins? We are not told. David feels pain; he is chastened, wounded by arrows of conviction, and pressed down by God's hand. The pain seems even physical. Sometimes sin affects physical well-being. He is heavily burdened by them.

(VERSES 5-8) He knows the pain coming from God's conviction of his conscience is caused by the *'foolishness'* of his sins. He hurts in his flesh, and is *'troubled'*, *'bowed down greatly'*, and mourns throughout the day. His *'bones'*, *'loins'*, *'flesh' and 'heart'* all suffer. These wounds inflicted because of his sins affect his health, well-being and body. He feels wounded, bent, burdened, bruised and worn out. By such conviction of sin, God faithfully shows a guilty sinner how much he needs to come to God to ask for forgiveness, peace, and reconciliation with his offended God.

(VERSES 9-14) God knows all about David's desire to be rid of his sin-sickness troubling his conscience, mind, body and life, and even sight. His plight is worsened because those who loved and befriended him, even relatives, now ignore him. His foes, full of treachery and deceit, seek his harm or death, and speak of it all day long. David wisely behaves like a deaf and mute man—as though he cannot hear or answer them. Sometimes it is wise for us to keep silent.

(VERSES 15-20) God uses conviction of sin and opposition by foes, to drive the guilty and suffering sinner to Him for mercy, grace, salvation and help. David realises this. Do you? If so, turn to Him, now. Follow David's example. He hopes in God, who will answer his prayer to restore him. David prays to God. He asks to overcome both opposition and his own sins by God's grace. He is filled with sorrow for his sins. He confesses them and his guilt to God. He asks for God's help against his foes' hatred of David's aim to do good and please God.

(VERSES 21-22) David ends by asking God not to forsake him but rather to stay close to him, and for His help now. He knows the LORD is His salvation. You can know that by personal faith in Jesus.

Psalm 39—To speak or keep silent?

To the Chief Musician. To Jeduthun. A Psalm of David.
1I said, "I will guard my ways,
Lest I sin with my tongue;
I will restrain my mouth with a muzzle,
While the wicked are before me."
2I was mute with silence,
I held my peace even from good;
And my sorrow was stirred up.
3My heart was hot within me;
While I was musing, the fire burned.
Then I spoke with my tongue:

4"LORD, make me to know my end,
And what is the measure of my days,
That I may know how frail I am.
5Indeed, You have made my days as handbreadths,
And my age is as nothing before You;
Certainly every man at his best state is but vapor. Selah
6Surely every man walks about like a shadow;
Surely they busy themselves in vain;
He heaps up riches,
And does not know who will gather them.

7"And now, Lord, what do I wait for?
My hope is in You.
8Deliver me from all my transgressions;
Do not make me the reproach of the foolish.
9I was mute, I did not open my mouth,
Because it was You who did it.
10Remove Your plague from me;
I am consumed by the blow of Your hand.
11When with rebukes You correct man for iniquity,
You make his beauty melt away like a moth;
Surely every man is vapor. Selah

12"Hear my prayer, O LORD,
And give ear to my cry;
Do not be silent at my tears;
For I am a stranger with You,
A sojourner, as all my fathers were.
13Remove Your gaze from me, that I may regain strength,
Before I go away and am no more."

❖

(VERSE 1) Sometimes we keep a so-called guilty silence. When we should speak, we do not. We may miss a chance to comfort, encourage or even rebuke. Or we fail to say, 'Sorry—I was wrong', or to share the good news of Jesus Christ when someone clearly needs to hear it. David's 'muzzle' here is not wrong: it is to avoid sinful speech before unbelievers.

(VERSES 2-3) But his silence goes too far. He says nothing good either! As he thinks this through, his heart burns within as he is bursting to speak. So, he now speaks.

(VERSES 4-11) What burns within him? It is how short life really is. Considering this carefully helps sinners become Christians. The urgency it produces helps us to trust solely in Jesus' death for our sins on the cross. There, Jesus bore God's wrath on those sins. It also focuses Christians' minds on the urgency to reach others with the gospel so that they can trust in Christ. Compare the brevity of human life with God's eternal nature. See how spending eternity under His blessing (in Heaven) or under His judgment (in Hell) makes this passing life seem relatively trivial. Words to describe your life include: *'handbreadths', 'nothing', 'vapour', 'shadow', 'melt'*, and *'moth'*. It is urgent that you turn from sin and trust the once crucified, now risen Lord Jesus. The Bible says *'Today'* is the day to be saved, *and 'Now'* is the accepted time. To show how much you need Christ, God first shows how hopeless your sinfulness is. He will then answer your prayer: *'Deliver me from all my transgressions'* ('sins'). Your hope is then in Him. God's rebuke and discipline for your sins is so you will turn from them. He then forgives you and blesses you eternally! To gain the whole world and lose your own soul, and so face a lost eternity, is to strike the world's best deal. God lovingly invests long-term blessing in you and in others! Sinners who trust Christ receive eternal life now and enjoy it for ever. Christians want, pray for, and help others to come to trust Jesus as personal Saviour and receive eternal life.

(VERSES 12-13) Like David, we ask God to *'Remove Your gaze from me'* when He judges sin. As we pray that, we look to Jesus, who on the cross bore the sins for all who look for mercy to God. Ask God to hear your prayer and listen to your cry for help. Will you confirm to Him that, with His strength and help, you will follow God in this alien and hostile world? If you will love and follow Jesus, and so live as God's *'stranger'* to this world's ungodly standards, God will bless you greatly.

Psalm 40—When God hears your cry

To the Chief Musician. A Psalm of David.
1I waited patiently for the LORD;
And He inclined to me,
And heard my cry.
2He also brought me up out of a horrible pit,
Out of the miry clay,
And set my feet upon a rock,
And established my steps.
3He has put a new song in my mouth—
Praise to our God;
Many will see it and fear,
And will trust in the LORD.

4Blessed is that man who makes the LORD his trust,
And does not respect the proud, nor such as turn aside to lies.
5Many, O LORD my God, are Your wonderful works
Which You have done;
And Your thoughts toward us
Cannot be recounted to You in order;
If I would declare and speak of them,
They are more than can be numbered.

6Sacrifice and offering You did not desire;
My ears You have opened.
Burnt offering and sin offering You did not require.
7Then I said, "Behold, I come;
In the scroll of the book it is written of me.
8I delight to do Your will, O my God,
And Your law is within my heart."

9I have proclaimed the good news of righteousness
In the great assembly;
Indeed, I do not restrain my lips,
O LORD, You Yourself know.
10I have not hidden Your righteousness within my heart;
I have declared Your faithfulness and Your salvation;
I have not concealed Your lovingkindness and Your truth
From the great assembly.

11Do not withhold Your tender mercies from me, O LORD;
Let Your lovingkindness and Your truth continually preserve me.
12For innumerable evils have surrounded me;
My iniquities have overtaken me, so that I am not able to look up;
They are more than the hairs of my head;
Therefore my heart fails me.

13Be pleased, O LORD, to deliver me;
O LORD, make haste to help me!
14Let them be ashamed and brought to mutual confusion

Who seek to destroy my life;
Let them be driven backward and brought to dishonor
Who wish me evil.
15Let them be confounded because of their shame,
Who say to me, "Aha, aha!"

16Let all those who seek You rejoice and be glad in You;
Let such as love Your salvation say continually,
"The LORD be magnified!"
17But I am poor and needy;
Yet the LORD thinks upon me.
You are my help and my deliverer;
Do not delay, O my God.

(VERSES 1-6) God blesses anyone at any time who cries to Him sincerely for help. It is as true today for a sinner trusting Jesus as personal Saviour as for a Christian in deep need who prays to God to deliver him. How can you pray? Cry urgently to God. Wait patiently for Him to act. He will lift you from sin's slippery filth and set you on a Rock. Jesus is that Rock. He puts a new song in your heart to praise God who has saved and delivered you. Many will see that, fear God and trust Him, too! Like you, they will be '*blessed*'. Proud people and liars cannot save or help you. Only our Triune God, who uses other people who trust Him through His Word, the Bible, can save and help. His wonderful works for us and His loving thoughts towards us are impossible to number. No outdated religious sacrificial ceremony of purification can purify a sinner's heart. But when your heart cries to God, He answers. He also opens your ears to hear Him and His Word.

(VERSES 7-8) This points to the Lord Jesus Christ coming as Messiah (Hebrews 10:5-7). Jesus, the God-Man, came to die on the cross to bear our sins and their penalty, as prophesied. He kept God's law perfectly. He fulfilled His will perfectly. That is why He can save you today. Turn from sin and trust the loving, spotless, eternal Son of God who died and rose again. He still lives. He changes you from within so that you begin to delight to do God's will and have His law written in your heart. Jesus Himself fulfilled verses 7 and 8 perfectly when He came as the Messiah to this world (Psalm 40:8).

(VERSES 9-11) God blesses David, who feels he must make known God's '*righteousness*', '*faithfulness*', '*salvation*', '*lovingkindness*' and '*truth*'. If Jesus is your Lord and Saviour, you should speak out for Him, too. By putting your faith in Jesus alone, His perfect '*righteousness*' is counted as yours. Your own efforts cannot make you righteous. But in His '*faithfulness*', God keeps His promise to forgive and save you when you come to Him through Christ. His '*salvation*' from sin and judgment changes your life. It takes you to Heaven just as Jesus promised in John 14:6! Such is His '*lovingkindness*' and '*truth*'.

(VERSES 12-17) Like David, ask God to act when you are conscious of being surrounded by '*innumerable evils*', and also aware of the many sins of your own. Ask Him to protect you, deliver you and help you, preserve you and deal with any opposition. That is when God's '*tender mercies*', '*lovingkindness*' and '*truth*' are so important to him. David also wants all seeking God to '*rejoice and be glad*' in Him. He asks for saved friends, who love their salvation, to praise and continually magnify God. God is too small in the minds and lives of many; we need to act as clean and efficient magnifying glasses for them. David feels '*poor and needy*', yet he knows and says, '*The LORD thinks upon me.*' He asks his God, his '*help*' and '*deliverer*', to help and deliver him without delay. You can pray like that! Why not even now?

Psalm 41—Help, harm and hope

To the Chief Musician. A Psalm of David.
1Blessed is he who considers the poor;
The LORD will deliver him in time of trouble.
2The LORD will preserve him and keep him alive,
And he will be blessed on the earth;
You will not deliver him to the will of his enemies.
3The LORD will strengthen him on his bed of illness;
You will sustain him on his sickbed.

4I said, "LORD, be merciful to me;
Heal my soul, for I have sinned against You."
5My enemies speak evil of me:
"When will he die, and his name perish?"
6And if he comes to see me, he speaks lies;
His heart gathers iniquity to itself;
When he goes out, he tells it.

7All who hate me whisper together against me;
Against me they devise my hurt.
8"An evil disease," they say, "clings to him.
And now that he lies down, he will rise up no more."
9Even my own familiar friend in whom I trusted,
Who ate my bread,
Has lifted up his heel against me.

10But You, O LORD, be merciful to me, and raise me up,
That I may repay them.
11By this I know that You are well pleased with me,
Because my enemy does not triumph over me.
12As for me, You uphold me in my integrity,
And set me before Your face forever.

13Blessed be the LORD God of Israel
From everlasting to everlasting!
Amen and Amen.

(VERSES 1-3) This promise of God is that there are blessings for him '*who* considers the *poor*'. That word can be extended to mean '*helpless*', or '*powerless*'. It describes someone with little or nothing to offer in return. The motivation today to be so kindly disposed and helpful to someone who cannot pay you back is Christ's love which changed you, if you know Jesus as your Lord and Saviour. You did not deserve His love either, when as a sinner you turned from your sin and asked Christ to save you. It illustrates God's promise in 1 Samuel 2:30 that '*Those who honour me, I will honour.*' See the blessings God gratuitously offers to such a loving person: God delivers him in troubled times, preserves him, keeps him alive, blesses him by overcoming his foes, and strengthens and sustains him when ill. That is as well as the joy of having sins forgiven, peace with God, and a home in Heaven through Jesus' dying for his sins on the cross to take the judgment he deserves and entering his life when he came to Jesus for mercy and forgiveness. It seems so generous of God that He saves us by His loving grace and then rewards our good actions which we have done simply because He has changed us. How kind is our God!

(VERSES 4-9) All this is not theoretical for David. At times you could experience this, too. He feels bad, anyhow, through some sin, the details of which are not given. He confesses that to God. He asks for mercy and healing—probably in spirit and body. His enemies maliciously gloat over him and say he will die. They lie about him. They conspire to slander him far and wide. They whisper falsely about an '*evil disease*' that will kill him. One can imagine what that is. Worse still, his trusted '*familiar friend*', to whom David had given hospitality, turns against him in his need. You can see David's need of the Lord. God is there for you, too, in time of your need.

(VERSES 10-13) It is at times like these that many of us might give up as we feel how weak, poor, helpless and powerless we really are. We could fall into self-pity and start gossiping and arguing. We could become bitter, and even try to 'get even' with our foes. In times like this, follow David's example. Ask God in His mercy to raise you up. The way you will '*repay them*' as a Christian is with God's love and grace that makes you pray for them to come to Christ! Then your arch enemy, the devil, has not won. Remember that Jesus taught you to '*love your enemies, bless those who curse you, do good to those who hate you, and pray for those who spitefully use you and persecute you*' (Matthew 5:44). God will uphold you and bless you in your integrity. He is always with you. You too will be able to praise your unchanging LORD. He is always on your side! Trust Him! He is faithful.

Psalm 42—Hope for the downcast soul

To the Chief Musician. A Contemplation of the sons of Korah.
1As the deer pants for the water brooks,
So pants my soul for You, O God.
2My soul thirsts for God, for the living God.
When shall I come and appear before God?
3My tears have been my food day and night,
While they continually say to me,
"Where is your God?"

4When I remember these things,
I pour out my soul within me.
For I used to go with the multitude;
I went with them to the house of God,
With the voice of joy and praise,
With a multitude that kept a pilgrim feast.

5Why are you cast down, O my soul?
And why are you disquieted within me?
Hope in God, for I shall yet praise Him
For the help of His countenance.

6O my God, my soul is cast down within me;
Therefore I will remember You from the land of the Jordan,
And from the heights of Hermon,
From the Hill Mizar.
7Deep calls unto deep at the noise of Your waterfalls;
All Your waves and billows have gone over me.
8The LORD will command His lovingkindness in the daytime,
And in the night His song shall be with me—
A prayer to the God of my life.

9I will say to God my Rock,
"Why have You forgotten me?
Why do I go mourning because of the oppression of the enemy?"
10As with a breaking of my bones,
My enemies reproach me,
While they say to me all day long,
"Where is your God?"

11Why are you cast down, O my soul?
And why are you disquieted within me?
Hope in God;
For I shall yet praise Him,
The help of my countenance and my God.

(VERSES 1-4) Picture a deer panting hard for water after running fast. The psalmist says his soul thirsts like that for fellowship with his living God. Only our Triune God, Father, Son, and Holy Spirit, is the *'living God'*. All other 'gods' are idols, products of human imagination or ambition, or from a false religion. *'I am the way and the truth and the life. No one comes to the Father except through Me,'* said Jesus (John 14:6). He died on the cross as the only way that our sins and punishment for them could be borne for us. He rose again from death, as the only living Saviour. He lives today! The Bible says, *'But He* [Jesus] *because He continues forever, has an unchangeable priesthood'* and that is why *'He is able to save to the uttermost those who come to God through Him, since He always lives to make intercession for them'* (Hebrews 7:24-25). The psalmist's thirst for God is heightened because he cannot worship God with others and have fellowship with them as in the past. He remembers sharing past joy and thanksgiving.

(VERSES 5-7) The psalmist asks twice in this psalm, *'Why are you cast down, O my soul? And why are you disquieted within me?'* Although he mourns as mockers taunt him *'all day long'* and to arrive at their question, *'Where is your God?'* (see verses 9-10 below), the rest of the psalm shows that he has confidence that God will help him and he shall praise Him, and that he will remember things God has done in the past. He will keep praying, hoping in God, and looking forward to praising God, being helped by Him, and knowing the smile of God's *'countenance'* upon him. When you are tempted not to pray, you should fight back with your knowledge of God's character, past dealings, promises and help. You will win through with that help!

All who trust Christ should worship, pray and thank and worship God together in fellowship each Lord's Day (Sunday) and in the week, too, and daily pray and read the Bible personally. Such a real spiritual thirst is evidence of being saved, shown in a real desire to know God better. It shows a 'born-again' character.

(VERSE 8) He reminds himself of God's love by day and night. Despite feeling low, he sings to God as his prayer to God. Words of hymns can often lead us to pray to God.

(VERSES 9-10) He goes into more details about enemies who taunt him and try to ridicule him all day long. Again, they mock him as they ask, '*Where is your God?*' He knows where his God is: both with him, and ruling from Heaven!

(VERSE 11) Verse 5's question is given the same answer. Put all your hope in God as your personal Saviour and you will praise Him as your God for ever. Only one thing can separate you from God and Heaven—unconfessed sin. Repent, trust and hope in Christ crucified and risen again, and the sin barrier is removed. Eternal life is yours.

Psalm 43—Same again?

[1]Vindicate me, O God,
And plead my cause against an ungodly nation;
Oh, deliver me from the deceitful and unjust man!
[2]For You are the God of my strength;
Why do You cast me off?
Why do I go mourning because of the oppression of the enemy?

[3]Oh, send out Your light and Your truth!
Let them lead me;
Let them bring me to Your holy hill
And to Your tabernacle.
[4]Then I will go to the altar of God,
To God my exceeding joy;
And on the harp I will praise You,
O God, my God.

[5]Why are you cast down, O my soul?
And why are you disquieted within me?
Hope in God;
For I shall yet praise Him,
The help of my countenance and my God.

❖

(VERSE 1) This psalm is believed to be one of about twenty-five psalms written by the 'Sons of Korah'. Most of their psalms are 42-50 and 72-85. Verse 1 does not state who wrote Psalm 43. Originally perhaps it was included as part of Psalm 42. That would explain the repeat of Psalm 42:5 and 42:11 in Psalm 43:5. The Sons of Korah survived when God judged their Levite clan after rebellion against Moses and Aaron. Their descendants served in the Temple in different ways, including as singers and musicians. This reminds us that even rebel families can be restored.

The writer asks God to '*vindicate*' them (clear them from guilt), rescue them and plead his *'cause against an ungodly nation'*. He asks to be delivered from *'deceitful and unjust'* men in that '*ungodly nation'* in which they serve God. Family history teaches them that God is holy.

(VERSE 2) He knows God is his strength. He wrongly thinks that enemy oppression means God has rejected him and now he must *'go mourning'* because of that. But God never said that it would be easy to live for Him in a world hostile to God and His standards. It is not easy today, either.

(VERSES 3-4) Let us see in some detail how this godly psalmist prays specifically when he bears in mind all this opposition, even among the Israelites whom God chose for Himself. He asks for God to shed His '*light*' and His '*truth*' on his path as He leads them. The Bible says that '*God is light*' (1 John 1:5), that Jesus is the '*Light of the World*' (John 9:5), and that God's '*Word is a lamp for my feet and a light to my feet*' (Psalm 119:105). God's work through the Holy Spirit is to enlighten us from the darkness our sins produce, and point us to Jesus, who took our place and punishment for all our wrongdoing in His own body when He suffered and bled on the cross for us. The Bible says that '*if we walk in the light, as* [God] *is in the light, we have fellowship with one another, and the blood of Jesus Christ His Son cleanses us from all sin*' (1 John 1:7). The other thing to guide us, as well as God's '*light*', is His '*truth*'. Jesus is the '*truth*' (John 14:6). The Holy Spirit is '*the Spirit of truth*' (John 15:26). We are to study the Bible carefully, God's Word, as the truth (2 Timothy 2:15). Romans 3:4 says, '*Let God be true but every man a liar.*' We all have lied, but God has never lied. So, to be guided, as the writer seeks, to follow God's holiness, to worship Him, to appreciate His sacrifice (for us by Jesus), to have God as our joy and delight, and to praise Him as my God, I always need God's '*light*' and God's '*truth*'. Pray to God to enlighten you every day as you read through His Word, the Bible.

(VERSE 5) I cannot be dogmatic, but I think personally that the third repetition in two psalms of the two questions the psalmist asks his own soul, namely, '*Why are you cast down, O my soul? And why are you disquieted within me?*' is to enable him to give his final answer with confidence in God. That is based on hope in God, praise for God, and knowing this helps the psalmist to trust the LORD as '*my God*'. Do you trust Him as your God?

Psalm 44—When I do not understand

To the Chief Musician. A Contemplation of the sons of Korah.
1We have heard with our ears, O God,
Our fathers have told us,
The deeds You did in their days,
In days of old:
2You drove out the nations with Your hand,
But them You planted;
You afflicted the peoples, and cast them out.
3For they did not gain possession of the land by their own sword,
Nor did their own arm save them;
But it was Your right hand, Your arm, and the light of Your countenance,
Because You favored them.

4You are my King, O God;
Command victories for Jacob.
5Through You we will push down our enemies;
Through Your name we will trample those who rise up against us.
6For I will not trust in my bow,
Nor shall my sword save me.
7But You have saved us from our enemies,
And have put to shame those who hated us.
8In God we boast all day long,
And praise Your name forever. Selah

9But You have cast us off and put us to shame,
And You do not go out with our armies.
10You make us turn back from the enemy,
And those who hate us have taken spoil for themselves.
11You have given us up like sheep intended for food,
And have scattered us among the nations.
12You sell Your people for next to nothing,
And are not enriched by selling them.

13You make us a reproach to our neighbors,
A scorn and a derision to those all around us.
14You make us a byword among the nations,
A shaking of the head among the peoples.
15My dishonor is continually before me,
And the shame of my face has covered me,
16Because of the voice of him who reproaches and reviles,
Because of the enemy and the avenger.

17All this has come upon us;
But we have not forgotten You,
Nor have we dealt falsely with Your covenant.
18Our heart has not turned back,
Nor have our steps departed from Your way;
19But You have severely broken us in the place of jackals,
And covered us with the shadow of death.

[20]If we had forgotten the name of our God,
Or stretched out our hands to a foreign god,
[21]Would not God search this out?
For He knows the secrets of the heart.
[22]Yet for Your sake we are killed all day long;
We are accounted as sheep for the slaughter.

[23]Awake! Why do You sleep, O LORD?
Arise! Do not cast us off forever.
[24]Why do You hide Your face,
And forget our affliction and our oppression?
[25]For our soul is bowed down to the dust;
Our body clings to the ground.
[26]Arise for our help,
And redeem us for Your mercies' sake.

(VERSES 1-3) God cast out ungodly nations in Canaan's Promised Land to plant Israel there. Korah's sons learned all about that from their fathers. Israel fought, but God alone gave them the victories. He loved them. That continues to cause them to worship Him by writing this psalm and singing it. It is good to sing the truths of the Bible with fellow believers.

(VERSES 4-8) They address God personally as they unite to say, '*You are my King, O God*.' They battle hard against their foes, but trust in God for victory. They boast in God alone and praise Him. Similarly, only personal trust in the Lord gives us victory over sin, death and hell. If we turn from our sin to trust Jesus as our Saviour, He saves us and gives us eternal life. He died at Calvary to bear our sins for which we deserve to be punished. He rose again and lives today. We should also proclaim and praise His name *'all day long'* and *'forever'*.

(VERSES 9-22) So, why do they feel down? They retreated in battle. They were plundered, devoured like sheep and scattered by their enemy. They feel rejected, humbled and left alone by God. Other nations once feared them but now reproach, scorn and ridicule them. Many talk about their downfall. Each man feels the shameful disgrace of being taunted, reproached and reviled by other nations. Their claim is that no specific sins, failures, attitudes, straying or failing to obey have come between them and God. God seems to crush them and put them in darkness. Have they been unfaithful to God? Not that they say they can recall. They feel like sheep for the slaughter, but why? They think that God has done it. Why?

(VERSES 23-26) They ask God to '*Awake*', to rouse Himself from sleep and not to reject them. They ask why He hides from them and forgets their '*affliction and [their] oppression*'. They remind Him of that misery. They ask, '*Arise for our help, and redeem us for Your mercies' sake.*' But God never sleeps. He misses nothing. Do they forget some sin that needs their repentance? God well knows if they need humbling, and to pray to Him from their hearts. How about you?

Psalm 45—Jesus: Saviour, Lord and King

To the Chief Musician. Set to "The Lilies." A Contemplation of the sons of Korah. A Song of Love.

1My heart is overflowing with a good theme;
I recite my composition concerning the King;
My tongue is the pen of a ready writer.

2You are fairer than the sons of men;
Grace is poured upon Your lips;
Therefore God has blessed You forever.
3Gird Your sword upon Your thigh, O Mighty One,
With Your glory and Your majesty.
4And in Your majesty ride prosperously because of truth, humility, and righteousness;
And Your right hand shall teach You awesome things.
5Your arrows are sharp in the heart of the King's enemies;
The peoples fall under You.

6Your throne, O God, is forever and ever;
A scepter of righteousness is the scepter of Your kingdom.
7You love righteousness and hate wickedness;
Therefore God, Your God, has anointed You
With the oil of gladness more than Your companions.
8All Your garments are scented with myrrh and aloes and cassia,
Out of the ivory palaces, by which they have made You glad.
9Kings' daughters are among Your honorable women;
At Your right hand stands the queen in gold from Ophir.

10Listen, O daughter,
Consider and incline your ear;
Forget your own people also, and your father's house;
11So the King will greatly desire your beauty;
Because He is your LORD, worship Him.
12And the daughter of Tyre will come with a gift;
The rich among the people will seek your favor.

13The royal daughter is all glorious within the palace;
Her clothing is woven with gold.
14She shall be brought to the King in robes of many colors;
The virgins, her companions who follow her, shall be brought to You.
15With gladness and rejoicing they shall be brought;
They shall enter the King's palace.

16Instead of Your fathers shall be Your sons,
Whom You shall make princes in all the earth.
17I will make Your name to be remembered in all generations;
Therefore the people shall praise You forever and ever.

(VERSE 1) Psalm 45 deals with the King and his bride at their wedding. But it is also 'Messianic' as it looks forward to the King of kings, the Lord Jesus Christ who is the eternal Son of God. Limited time and space demand only a brief summary, then some New Testament verses are shown to fulfil some prophecies about Jesus in Psalm 45. May our tongues *'write'* about our loving Lord and Saviour to others today!

(VERSES 2-12) The New Testament applies some of these verses to Jesus in Luke 4:22, Hebrews 1:8-9, Hebrews 4:12, Jude 25, and Revelation 1:16, 6:2. They describe Jesus and His bride, the church. If you have repented and trusted Jesus, through His death on the cross for you and your sins, you are part of His spiritual 'bride'. It includes all people from all ages, worldwide, who have turned from sin and given Jesus their trust and love. This King of kings so loved them to shed His blood and pay their sins' penalty on the cross. He entered their lives as their living Saviour and Heavenly bridegroom.

The verses show: His speech is marked by *'gracious words'*; righteousness he loves and wickedness he hates; He is glorious, majestic, in complete charge, with unique power, *'both now and forever'*; He bears a sharp two-edged sword; His throne is forever; He is preeminent; He is joyful; His clothes carry the fragrant herbs used to embalm bodies; He makes His followers glad; kings and the rich must honour Him; He loves and values His spiritual 'bride'. (Let me emphasise this: If you know Jesus as your Saviour, you are part of His bride, too.)

(VERSES 13-15) His bride is 'all *glorious*' and is with the King (Jesus)! Joy and gladness are in *'the King' palace'* (that is, Heaven).

(VERSES 16-17) When fathers die, sons will go on remembering the King. The nations will praise Him for ever. Jesus is Lord!

Now some verses about Jesus: Below are some New Testament truths concerning Psalm 45.

- Luke 4:22 *'All witnessed His amazing and gracious words.'* (See Psalm 45:2.)
- Hebrews 4:12 *'For the word of God is living and powerful, and sharper than any two-edged sword, piercing even to division of soul and spirit and of joints and marrow, and is a discerner of*

the thoughts and intents of the heart.' (See Psalm 45:3.)

- Revelation 1:16 *'Out of His mouth went a sharp double-edged sword, and His countenance was like the sun shining in its strength.'* (See Psalm 45:3.)
- Hebrews 1:8-9 *'But to the Son He says: "Your throne, O God, is forever and ever; A sceptre of righteousness is the sceptre of Your kingdom. You have loved righteousness and hated lawlessness; Therefore God, Your God, has anointed You with the oil of gladness more than Your companions ."'* (SeePsalm 45:6-7.)

Psalm 46—Our Refuge, Strength and Help

To the Chief Musician. A Psalm of the sons of Korah. A Song for Alamoth.
1God is our refuge and strength,
A very present help in trouble.
2Therefore we will not fear,
Even though the earth be removed,
And though the mountains be carried into the midst of the sea;
3Though its waters roar and be troubled,
Though the mountains shake with its swelling. Selah

4There is a river whose streams shall make glad the city of God,
The holy place of the tabernacle of the Most High.
5God is in the midst of her, she shall not be moved;
God shall help her, just at the break of dawn.
6The nations raged, the kingdoms were moved;
He uttered His voice, the earth melted.

7The LORD of hosts is with us;
The God of Jacob is our refuge. Selah

8Come, behold the works of the LORD,
Who has made desolations in the earth.
9He makes wars cease to the end of the earth;
He breaks the bow and cuts the spear in two;
He burns the chariot in the fire.

10Be still, and know that I am God;
I will be exalted among the nations,
I will be exalted in the earth!

11The LORD of hosts is with us;
The God of Jacob is our refuge. Selah

(VERSES 1-3) I can remember, as a boy, having to sing this psalm when I went to the cubs' Church Parade. I was bored. But in later life I have often recited it to myself in need and am so glad I learned it then. These Sons of Korah know a vital secret. They know God as a '*refuge*' to shelter in. In their weakness they have a strong God to give them '*strength*' who is '*ever present' to help*' when trouble comes, as it surely will in life. This '*refuge*', '*strength*', and '*help*' is yours when Jesus Christ becomes your Saviour. The main thing is to know your sins forgiven, peace with God and a home assured in Heaven. All this is yours as you turn your back on your sins and thank God that Jesus died willingly in your place to be punished for you. God forgives you if you receive Christ in your heart to save you. With that eternal security, comes God's '*very present help in*

trouble' and many blessings. Then you can find that His *'perfect love casts out fear'* (1 John 4:18) even in life's biggest catastrophes.

(VERSES 4-6) Heaven is sometimes called the *'New Jerusalem'* (Revelation 3:12, 21:2). Though earthly Jerusalem fell, this one in Heaven will not and can never fall. There is no physical river near the Jerusalem we know, but the perfect river of God's amazing grace brings eternal blessings constantly to Heaven. God is there. All who trust in Jesus will be there. Will you be? God, who melts the earth, will protect His Heaven and all those in it!

(VERSE 7) Here is *the* key! *'The LORD of hosts' is with us.' 'The LORD of hosts'* can be translated *'Almighty God'.* It is no accident that one of Jesus' names is *'Mighty God'* (Isaiah 9:6). He is one of the three Persons in the single Godhead—Father, Son and Holy Spirit. To know Jesus means to know God in your life. But sadly, no Jesus means no God in your life. *'He Himself has said, "I will never leave nor forsake you"'* and that is why *'we may boldly say: "The LORD is my Helper; I will not fear. What can man do to me?'* (Hebrews 13:5-6). After reminding those of us who belong to the Lord that *'The LORD of hosts is with us',* this verse 7 goes on to say that *'The God of Jacob is our refuge.'* Jacob was an 'up and down' man: but God kept and protected him. If you are 'up and down' in your life, God wants to, can and will keep you too, if your trust is in the Lord Jesus Christ. He will be your *'Helper'* too!

(VERSES 8-10) God is all powerful. In judgment He can bring desolation. In mercy He can stop wars and govern nations. He has His timetable when He will do that. Trust in Him, in His power, and in His will. He will finally be *'exalted among the nations'* and *'exalted in the earth.'* He is in control and will keep perfectly to His timetable.

(VERSE 11) The key verse is repeated, to finally remind all who know God through Christ that *'The LORD of hosts is with us; The God of Jacob is our refuge.'* Never forget that, provided that your trust is in the Lord Jesus Christ, God is with you now. He is your fortress, your strength and your help too!

Psalm 47—Crucified, risen, ascended

To the Chief Musician. A Psalm of the sons of Korah.
1Oh, clap your hands, all you peoples!
Shout to God with the voice of triumph!
2For the LORD Most High is awesome;
He is a great King over all the earth.
3He will subdue the peoples under us,
And the nations under our feet.
4He will choose our inheritance for us,
The excellence of Jacob whom He loves. Selah

5God has gone up with a shout,
The LORD with the sound of a trumpet.
6Sing praises to God, sing praises!
Sing praises to our King, sing praises!
7For God is the King of all the earth;
Sing praises with understanding.

8God reigns over the nations;
God sits on His holy throne.
9The princes of the people have gathered together,
The people of the God of Abraham.
For the shields of the earth belong to God;
He is greatly exalted.

(VERSES 1-4) All nations on earth are told to shout with '*the voice of triumph*' and clap their hands to God. He alone is '*awesome*' and to be worshipped: not self, not man, not idols, not religion, but God alone. When the Bible teaches that God is three Persons in One, and One God in three Persons, it is introducing us to this unique God. Why is He '*awesome*'? Because He is the '*great King over all the earth*' who will subdue all people and nations under Him. You can understand, therefore, why the Bible says that Jesus, God the Son, is '*Lord of Lords and King of kings*' (Revelation 17:14; 19:16). He has an agenda, to make His people finally victorious whether they are His earthly people, Israel, or His spiritual and heavenly people, Christians. He chooses for us our inheritance in Heaven because He loves us. By His grace, we shall reign with Him eternally. Every loving father likes to think he has made the right long-term decisions and choices for his children. Why? Because he loves them. Our Heavenly Father—who is perfectly one with the Son and the Spirit—wants the very best for His spiritual children, only even more so. We should stop and think about that most wonderful truth, rather than just take it for granted.

(VERSES 5-7) One of the truly significant miracles achieved by the Lord Jesus Christ was His ascension from earth to Heaven. We often do not hear it referred to when considering the gospel. I think that we tend to assume it at times when we just refer to Jesus' resurrection from the tomb. Jesus died on the cross as the perfect sacrifice for sinners, to bear our sins and be judged for them in our place. He was our perfect penalty-taker and substitute. His resurrection from the dead three days later demonstrates Jesus' power over death. It also shows that God the Father, in raising His Son Jesus from the dead, was fully accepting the substitutionary death on the cross of Jesus in our place. It also confirms that, through the Holy Spirit, the risen Jesus dwells in the heart of each believer. But when He ascended from earth to Heaven, His sinless body, broken on the cross for our sins and raised from the dead with '*the power of an endless life*' (Hebrews 7:16), actually took its place in Heaven. It is that same resurrected and ascended body that Jesus possesses in the Glory. The same Lord Jesus will return in that same glorious body when He comes back once more to earth as '*Lord of Lords and King of kings*'. That is why we are told to praise Him as God! Jesus really is '*King of all the earth*'.

(VERSES 8-9) Our King Jesus is on Heaven's '*holy throne*', over all nations, peoples and those saved by faith, as Abraham was. Jesus is '*greatly exalted*'. (The Hebrew word for '*exalted*' and '*ascended*' is the same.) Is Jesus your Saviour and King? If not, why not bow your heart to Him, in repentance and faith, and worship and follow Him now?

Psalm 48—'Great is the LORD'

A Song. A Psalm of the sons of Korah.
1Great is the LORD, and greatly to be praised
In the city of our God,
In His holy mountain.
2Beautiful in elevation,
The joy of the whole earth,
Is Mount Zion on the sides of the north,
The city of the great King.
3God is in her palaces;
He is known as her refuge.

4For behold, the kings assembled,
They passed by together.
5They saw it, and so they marveled;
They were troubled, they hastened away.
6Fear took hold of them there,
And pain, as of a woman in birth pangs,
7As when You break the ships of Tarshish
With an east wind.

8As we have heard,
So we have seen
In the city of the LORD of hosts,
In the city of our God:
God will establish it forever. Selah

9We have thought, O God, on Your lovingkindness,
In the midst of Your temple.
10According to Your name, O God,
So is Your praise to the ends of the earth;
Your right hand is full of righteousness.
11Let Mount Zion rejoice,
Let the daughters of Judah be glad,
Because of Your judgments.

12Walk about Zion,
And go all around her.
Count her towers;
13Mark well her bulwarks;
Consider her palaces;
That you may tell it to the generation following.
14For this is God,
Our God forever and ever;
He will be our guide
Even to death.

❖

(VERSES 1-3) Long before any other religion stated it, God's Word in the Old Testament said, *'Great is the LORD and greatly to be praised.'* He is great in His character, His eternality, His power, His wisdom, His holiness, His justice, His mercy, His love, and His compassion. Because of how great God is, the Temple on Mount Zion is also holy, because it is where God appears to His people. Because the Temple is on Mount Zion, that is also revered as holy. The word 'holy' means 'set apart'. All real and true holiness and blessing come back to God as their only true Source. That is why, through the gospel of the Lord Jesus Christ, we are blessed with sins forgiven, peace with God, and a home in Heaven. We go right back to the Source when we turn from sin and trust the Lord Jesus Christ as our Lord and Saviour. He was nailed to that cross, bearing our sins and their punishment, so the way is open to us to come to Him and trust in Him. Almighty God's greatness also is known in that He is a '*refuge*' (or '*fortress*') for sinners to hide in. You can shelter there, too, from the judgment of God against your sins. You shelter when you repent of your sins, come to Christ, and rest confidently in Him!

(VERSES 4-8) Various nations attempted to invade Jerusalem but failed. Here we read of one hostile invading army. As their forces advanced on Jerusalem, they were shocked and terrified and fled away in terror, because the God of Jerusalem protected His Jerusalem. They were *'sunk'* as if a mighty sea tempest shattered and swamped a trading fleet of ships, when driven by the east wind. The LORD God Almighty protected His city from those against it and against Him. One day, on God's timetable, physical Jerusalem did fall, but His holy and '*New Jerusalem*' of Revelation chapter 21 is God's eternally secure Heaven coming down to the '*new earth*'. There those redeemed from sin by the shed blood of Jesus will enjoy God forever. Trust Jesus now, and you will be there rejoicing then!

(VERSES 9-13) Consider, if you do know God through faith in Jesus, how to think about God when praising Him. You may be in a building, (like a '*temple*'), or in your own body indwelt by Jesus through the Holy Spirit and therefore called *'the temple of the Holy Spirit'* (1 Corinthians 6:9). Meditate on these subjects: God's unfailing love; the wonder of His name; His worldwide praise; His holiness and righteousness; whether on a holy mountain, or in humble villages, consider His deep judgments; look around and see His greatness; tell future generations about Him. The Christian gospel of sins forgiven, peace with God and a home forever in Heaven is to be shared with others!

(VERSE 14) Just look what a great God you can get to know and get to know better through daily reading the Bible, praying and hearing His Word faithfully taught! He is yours *'for ever and ever'*. He is your Guide throughout life. And Heaven awaits you! When God stops guiding you on earth, it is because you will then be in Heaven with Him and will need no guidance then.

Psalm 49—I cannot take it with me

To the Chief Musician. A Psalm of the sons of Korah.
1Hear this, all peoples;
Give ear, all inhabitants of the world,
2Both low and high,
Rich and poor together.
3My mouth shall speak wisdom,
And the meditation of my heart shall give understanding.
4I will incline my ear to a proverb;
I will disclose my dark saying on the harp.

5Why should I fear in the days of evil,
When the iniquity at my heels surrounds me?
6Those who trust in their wealth
And boast in the multitude of their riches,
7None of them can by any means redeem his brother,
Nor give to God a ransom for him—
8For the redemption of their souls is costly,
And it shall cease forever—
9That he should continue to live eternally,
And not see the Pit.

10For he sees wise men die;
Likewise the fool and the senseless person perish,
And leave their wealth to others.
11Their inner thought is that their houses will last forever,
Their dwelling places to all generations;
They call their lands after their own names.
12Nevertheless man, though in honor, does not remain;
He is like the beasts that perish.

13This is the way of those who are foolish,
And of their posterity who approve their sayings. Selah
14Like sheep they are laid in the grave;
Death shall feed on them;
The upright shall have dominion over them in the morning;
And their beauty shall be consumed in the grave, far from their dwelling.
15But God will redeem my soul from the power of the grave,
For He shall receive me. Selah

16Do not be afraid when one becomes rich,
When the glory of his house is increased;
17For when he dies he shall carry nothing away;
His glory shall not descend after him.
18Though while he lives he blesses himself
(For men will praise you when you do well for yourself),
19He shall go to the generation of his fathers;
They shall never see light.
20A man who is in honor, yet does not understand,
Is like the beasts that perish.

(VERSES 1-4) This psalm is for everyone, everywhere. Each person needs to *'hear this'*—it is too late to listen after death. No matter what your social or financial state, this is for you. Here we see God's wisdom applied that will lead to what is said being understood. The psalmist's ears are open to consider a proverb and he teaches this one in song on his harp. He says it is a *'dark saying'*.

(VERSES 5-9) Here is his *'proverb'* or *'dark saying'*. Presumably some might think it is *'dark'* because it is centred on sin (or *'iniquity'*), the shortness of life, and either having eternal life or facing *'the Pit'* eternally. He asks, *'Why should I 'fear in the days of evil, when the iniquity at my heels surrounds me?'* Make no mistake: evil days are here and will come. Sinful standards and practices are held commonly and snap at our heels and surround us. Many deceive others by pushing their warped beliefs and sinful desires. Most of it is arrogantly anti-God and anti-Bible. Do not let anyone steal the truth of God's Word from you, however 'clever' he or she appears to be. One of the most sinful and selfish errors is the constant emphasis on the deceitful view that what you have is more important than what you are. The tarnished 'god' of today is materialism. It concentrates on how much money you have and what you are 'worth' when you look at all your possessions and incomes. There is no answer to Jesus' question in Mark 8:36: *'What good is it for a man to gain the whole world, yet forfeit his soul?'* Not all the world's wealth can keep you out of eternal Hell. Only Jesus can do that. Neither can anyone rescue you because He is rich. How true it is that *'the redemption of their [lost] souls is costly'*. It cost Jesus His blood and life when He bore your sins and all God's holy punishment against sin, so that you can escape it by turning from sin and asking Jesus to save you and run your life His way.

(VERSES 10-14) Wise and foolish, rich and poor, huge landowners and poor beggars in need, famous and unknown—all these types of people—need to trust Jesus, not to get more wealth, but to get to Heaven. They all will die, like *'the beasts that perish'* or *'like sheep'*, and any beauty they had is transient—but eternity awaits the non-dying souls of all men and women. Wealth is not wrong, if used properly, but it cannot change your Hell to Heaven. Only faith in Christ can do that.

(VERSE 15) The psalmist knows God will *'redeem* [his] *soul from the power of the grave, for He shall receive me'* and take him to be with Him in Glory after death. You can know that certainty too: so be sure to trust in Jesus!

(VERSES 16-20) Make sure you know Jesus Christ personally. Do not envy a man who is rich; he leaves it behind when he dies—then, what if he has not come to Christ? Men admire other rich men. God simply asks—do you know My Son as your Saviour? If so, you will see God's *'light'* and *'understand'* what it is to spend a time of perfect blessing in Heaven.

Psalm 50—What God wants as worship

A Psalm of Asaph.
1The Mighty One, God the LORD,
Has spoken and called the earth
From the rising of the sun to its going down.
2Out of Zion, the perfection of beauty,
God will shine forth.
3Our God shall come, and shall not keep silent;
A fire shall devour before Him,
And it shall be very tempestuous all around Him.

4He shall call to the heavens from above,
And to the earth, that He may judge His people:
5"Gather My saints together to Me,
Those who have made a covenant with Me by sacrifice."
6Let the heavens declare His righteousness,
For God Himself is Judge. Selah

7"Hear, O My people, and I will speak,
O Israel, and I will testify against you;
I am God, your God!
8I will not rebuke you for your sacrifices
Or your burnt offerings,
Which are continually before Me.
9I will not take a bull from your house,
Nor goats out of your folds.
10For every beast of the forest is Mine,
And the cattle on a thousand hills.
11I know all the birds of the mountains,
And the wild beasts of the field are Mine.

12"If I were hungry, I would not tell you;
For the world is Mine, and all its fullness.
13Will I eat the flesh of bulls,
Or drink the blood of goats?
14Offer to God thanksgiving,
And pay your vows to the Most High.
15Call upon Me in the day of trouble;
I will deliver you, and you shall glorify Me."

16But to the wicked God says:
"What right have you to declare My statutes,
Or take My covenant in your mouth,
17Seeing you hate instruction
And cast My words behind you?
18When you saw a thief, you consented with him,
And have been a partaker with adulterers.
19You give your mouth to evil,
And your tongue frames deceit.
20You sit and speak against your brother;

You slander your own mother's son.
[21]These things you have done, and I kept silent;
You thought that I was altogether like you;
But I will rebuke you,
And set them in order before your eyes.

[22]"Now consider this, you who forget God,
Lest I tear you in pieces,
And there be none to deliver:
[23]Whoever offers praise glorifies Me;
And to him who orders his conduct aright
I will show the salvation of God."

(VERSES 1-3) All real worship of God starts with God. Who is He? What has He done? Worship is not a mood, feeling, or a liking for special music. It is not about who worships but about the Lord. He is the '*Mighty One, God the LORD*'. His Word goes out all over the world. God shines out from Zion, His beautiful and holy temple and mountain. He comes like a devouring fire and a raging tempest.

(VERSES 4-6) God summons His people for judgment. They are fully bound to Him by sacrificial covenant and made righteous. Christians come to God through the shed blood of Jesus. He died for us. He paid sins' penalty and punishment on the cross. God's covenant is based on that sacrifice which is to save all who trust in Jesus personally. God's righteousness is even seen if you look up at the heavens and consider. God, our Judge, is righteous in every way.

(VERSES 7-15) God Himself is Israel's God and the God of all who trust in Jesus. He speaks to them now through the Bible. Do read it each day. He shows us our failures, too. The Israelite's issue was not about keeping Old Testament sacrifices; they did keep them. But God did not need them to give Him animals or birds to sacrifice. He owns and knows them all! He never needs them to eat! God seeks hearts giving genuine thanks for His character and acts. He wants His people to keep their vows and promises. When they call on God in troubled times, He will deliver them, and they will glorify Him. That also happens when any sinner turns to Jesus.

(VERSES 16-22) Religious observances can never put sinners right. You can say right words but ignore or reject God's Word. If you steal, are immoral, use bad language, deceive, gossip, or slander people, God sees and hears it all. He will rebuke, accuse, and judge sinners for their sins. After their death, He will judge them eternally and finally.

(VERSE 23) But for anyone who praises God for Jesus' sacrifice, and thereby glorifies God, He prepares the way for such a person to live for Him and to receive His salvation!

Psalm 51—How to say 'Sorry' to God

To the Chief Musician. A Psalm of David when Nathan the prophet went to him, after he had gone in to Bathsheba.
1Have mercy upon me, O God,
According to Your lovingkindness;
According to the multitude of Your tender mercies,
Blot out my transgressions.
2Wash me thoroughly from my iniquity,
And cleanse me from my sin.

3For I acknowledge my transgressions,
And my sin is always before me.
4Against You, You only, have I sinned,
And done this evil in Your sight—
That You may be found just when You speak,
And blameless when You judge.

5Behold, I was brought forth in iniquity,
And in sin my mother conceived me.
6Behold, You desire truth in the inward parts,
And in the hidden part You will make me to know wisdom.

7Purge me with hyssop, and I shall be clean;
Wash me, and I shall be whiter than snow.
8Make me hear joy and gladness,
That the bones You have broken may rejoice.
9Hide Your face from my sins,
And blot out all my iniquities.

10Create in me a clean heart, O God,
And renew a steadfast spirit within me.
11Do not cast me away from Your presence,
And do not take Your Holy Spirit from me.

12Restore to me the joy of Your salvation,
And uphold me by Your generous Spirit.
13Then I will teach transgressors Your ways,
And sinners shall be converted to You.

14Deliver me from the guilt of bloodshed, O God,
The God of my salvation,
And my tongue shall sing aloud of Your righteousness.
15O LORD, open my lips,
And my mouth shall show forth Your praise.
16For You do not desire sacrifice, or else I would give it;
You do not delight in burnt offering.
17The sacrifices of God are a broken spirit,
A broken and a contrite heart—
These, O God, You will not despise.

[18]Do good in Your good pleasure to Zion;
Build the walls of Jerusalem.
[19]Then You shall be pleased with the sacrifices of righteousness,
With burnt offering and whole burnt offering;
Then they shall offer bulls on Your altar.

(VERSES 1-2) Psalm 51 is guilty King David's prayer of confession to God for his sins. What are those sins? Adultery with Bathsheba; attendant dishonesty; murder by proxy of Bathsheba's husband, Uriah, and inevitable killing of soldiers involved; pride; hypocrisy; and unwillingness and slowness to confess his sins. Read 2 Samuel 11:1 to 12:14 for the background. Nathan is God's prophet who confronted David after a long time.

David asks for God's '*mercy*', knowing God's '*lovingkindness*' and '*multitude of [God's] tender mercies*'. He asks for his sins to be blotted out, and for washing and cleansing from his sin. A sincere sorry prayer to God starts like this. Remember why God forgives your sins. Be sure to confess them with shame and then forsake them.

(VERSES 3-4) David no longer hides his sins. He knows them, feels them, admits them and knows they offend God. Although others have suffered because of his sins, his primary offence is against a Holy God who hates all sin. God is right and '*blameless*' to judge him.

(VERSES 5-6) He admits he is a sinner by nature and at heart, since his conception. God wants him to be true and wise in his heart. Already we begin to learn that the gospel can change people from within, though personal faith in Christ.

(VERSES 7-9) He wants real cleansing—'*whiter than snow*'—not just the ceremonial cleansing applied by a shrub called hyssop. He longs for his former joy and gladness. He feels crushed and broken—that is the Holy Spirit at work. He asks God to now look away from his sinfulness and to '*blot out all [my] iniquities*'.

(VERSE 10) David's heartfelt prayer, '*Create in me a clean heart, O God, and renew a steadfast within me*', will not only be answered for him but is also a wonderful prayer for any repenting sinner, however bad he has been, to pray today. Because Jesus died on the cross for guilty and selfish sinners like you and me and carried our sins and took our punishment for them, we learn that through receiving Christ, '*the blood of Jesus Christ His Son cleanses us from all sin'* (1 John 1:7). When we Christians sin, we should also humbly pray to receive a *'clean heart'* and be renewed with a *'steadfast spirit'* from God the Holy Spirit.

(VERSE 11) He asks God to stay with Him, and for His Holy Spirit not to be removed.

(VERSES 12-17) He asks for the joy of God's salvation to be restored to him. God's salvation always produces joy and rejoicing. He also asks for God's *'generous [or 'willing'] spirit'* to *'uphold'* him. Then, when he is restored to his Lord, he will teach sinners God's ways. Some will turn back and be saved. He wants to be saved from the guilt of shedding innocent blood. Then he will praise God for His righteousness. He seeks open lips to praise God with a *'broken and a contrite heart'*. It is not going through the procedures of making animal sacrifices that will save or bless him. God has to have his heart.

(VERSES 18-19) King David can then seek the good of Zion in worshipping God. As he takes part in the sacrifices, his heart must be right with God. If you earnestly confess your sins to God like this, God will cleanse you. That is why Jesus died for you and why He rose again.

Psalm 52—Who owns your lips?

To the Chief Musician. A Contemplation of David when Doeg the Edomite went and told Saul, and said to him, "David has gone to the house of Ahimelech."

1Why do you boast in evil, O mighty man?
The goodness of God endures continually.
2Your tongue devises destruction,
Like a sharp razor, working deceitfully.
3You love evil more than good,
Lying rather than speaking righteousness. Selah
4You love all devouring words,
You deceitful tongue.

5God shall likewise destroy you forever;
He shall take you away, and pluck you out of your dwelling place,
And uproot you from the land of the living. Selah
6The righteous also shall see and fear,
And shall laugh at him, saying,
7"Here is the man who did not make God his strength,
But trusted in the abundance of his riches,
And strengthened himself in his wickedness."

8But I am like a green olive tree in the house of God;
I trust in the mercy of God forever and ever.
9I will praise You forever,
Because You have done it;
And in the presence of Your saints
I will wait on Your name, for it is good.

(VERSES 1-4) Psalm 52 deals with misusing the tongue. But it centres on Doeg the Edomite. He told King Saul, who chased David in order to kill him, that Ahimelech, the priest, innocently helped David when David asked him for help. The outcome? Doeg killed Ahimelech and every priest of Nob, at Saul's cruel and wicked command. (See 1 Samuel 21:1-9 and 22:6-23.) Doeg's sin caused David to compose this psalm. It applies generally to all who say, as Psalm 12:4 puts it, '*With our tongue we will prevail; Our lips are our own; Who is lord over us?*' They need to repent of their sins—including wrong speaking—and trust in Jesus who died in their place on the cross to pay the penalty for their sins. They need to accept God's invitation to forgive them, and to ask God also to control their words. Receiving Jesus brings you a new heart that brings changed language. Our language needs to be changed. Our evil tongues produce boasting, evil planning, deceit, falsehood, unclean thoughts, and harm to others, and it offends our holy God.

(VERSES 5-7) Eternal death and ruin for sin in Hell is the penalty for all sins, including all the offences of your tongue. Jesus paid that penalty for those who repent and trust Him. Those counted '*righteous*', by trusting Jesus, can see the futility of those who do not repent and so are condemned. They resist God, hurt others, and trust in their wealth, not God. They strengthen their wickedness—in short, they go from bad to worse. They will regret that for ever.

(VERSES 8-9) Just contrast their position—now and eternally—with those who '*trust in the mercy of God for ever and ever*'. Right now, those who are forgiven through the shed blood of Jesus and who, at the same time, have the perfect righteousness of the Lord Jesus Christ counted before God as their own, are '*like a green olive tree*'. (Revisit Psalm 1 for a reminder!) They are '*evergreen*'—always experiencing and showing the life of God in their souls through the indwelling Holy Spirit. They flourish spiritually, and love to meet for worship with others whose lives have been changed by faith in Christ. They praise God now and will do for ever in Heaven. They value God's name. (Did you know that '*Jesus*' means '*God saves*', and '*Emmanuel*' means '*God with us*'? See Matthew 1:21,23.) They now look forward to using their tongues in eternal blessing. They will join in praising, with angels and with other saved sinners in Heaven, their wonderful Saviour they have come to love on earth!

So why not tell God you are sorry for all your sins—especially the lies, filth, cruel words, blasphemies, gossip, slander, boasting, hypocrisy and hatred that your lips have uttered? Yield your heart and lips to Jesus.

Psalm 53—God underlines a sad truth

To the Chief Musician. Set to "Mahalath." A Contemplation of David.
1The fool has said in his heart,
"There is no God."
They are corrupt, and have done abominable iniquity;
There is none who does good.

2God looks down from heaven upon the children of men,
To see if there are any who understand, who seek God.
3Every one of them has turned aside;
They have together become corrupt;
There is none who does good,
No, not one.

4Have the workers of iniquity no knowledge,
Who eat up my people as they eat bread,
And do not call upon God?
5There they are in great fear
Where no fear was,
For God has scattered the bones of him who encamps against you;
You have put them to shame,
Because God has despised them.

6Oh, that the salvation of Israel would come out of Zion!
When God brings back the captivity of His people,
Let Jacob rejoice and Israel be glad.

Psalm 53 and Psalm 14 are similar, but not identical. They vary probably because they were written for different audiences. Under the Holy Spirit's influence, a writer can always use similar, or even identical, words at different times. Here, those common words underline the sad, key truth that '*The fool says in his heart, there is no God*.'

The Bible *never* contradicts itself. Any variation is always intended and is never about its truthfulness, but always about its application. Verses 5-6 present the only variations that are more than 'noise level'. They are commented on now. Psalm 53 confirms the main message of Psalm 14.

(Verse 1) The man who says '*There is no God*' implies he has seen, considered and weighed up all the available evidence from all time and all places, and is clever enough to reach an absolute conclusion, namely, '*There is no God*.' The world calls him an 'atheist': God calls him a '*fool*'. A person who says, 'I do not know', is an 'agnostic'. But God says that anyone who dogmatically denies His existence is a fool as well as an atheist.

Some reasons are given why he is foolish. Verse 1 opens with: '*The fool says in his heart, "There is no God."*' The atheist does not use his *head* to weigh all the evidence properly: rather, he carries his prejudice in his '*heart*' against God. Thus, his conclusion is not based on fact or reason. It comes from biased feelings. Every thought he now holds about God is therefore prejudiced. His intellectual position is dishonest. Why? If he believed a holy God watched him all the time, he knows he would have to repent of his '*corrupt*' and '*abominable*' deeds and ask God to forgive him. The first of God's Ten Commandments in Exodus chapter 20 tells us that no one and no thing must be put before God. An atheist makes a 'god' of his sinful rejection of God. He worships that 'god' and so cannot do '*good*' in God's eyes until he turns from that sin, and all the others, to ask humbly for God to pardon and restore him. God does that for any person who turns to the Lord Jesus Christ, thanking Jesus that He bore the wrath of the Father against that person's sins when He died in his place on Calvary's cross.

(VERSES 2-3) God looks down and sees that man cannot, without His help and the work of His Holy Spirit within, begin to '*understand*' about God, seek God, or '*do good*'. None of us can keep His good and holy standards. All of us have wayward, '*corrupt*', and sinful hearts.

(VERSES 4-5) explain why sinners *remain* ignorant of God until they repent and trust in Jesus. They oppose God's people, and proudly refuse to '*call upon God*'. '*Fear*' *will* finally overwhelm all sinners who fail to repent. Eternal punishment awaits them. But '*There they are in great fear where no fear was.*' If only they would trust our Saviour God, they would find that God's '*perfect love casts out fear*'. Psalm 14 says why this is: '*God is with the generation of the righteous.*' Even in Old Testament *physical* battles, God acted to shame those attacking His people. Again, Psalm 14 adds why: '*The LORD is [their] refuge.*' God's grace and mercy make them secure.

(VERSE 6) David prays, '*Oh, that the salvation of Israel would come out of Zion*' *(where God made His presence known in the temple on Mount Zion).* Religious people need to be saved just as much as irreligious people. David awaits gladness and rejoicing when God restores Israel to Himself from their captivity—even their atheists! Today He still restores, blesses and delivers from their captivity because of their sins *anyone* who trusts in Jesus—even today's atheists!

Psalm 54—Saved, delivered, praying

To the Chief Musician. With stringed instruments. A Contemplation of David when the Ziphites went and said to Saul, "Is David not hiding with us?"

1Save me, O God, by Your name,
And vindicate me by Your strength.
2Hear my prayer, O God;
Give ear to the words of my mouth.
3For strangers have risen up against me,
And oppressors have sought after my life;
They have not set God before them. Selah

4Behold, God is my helper;
The Lord is with those who uphold my life.
5He will repay my enemies for their evil.
Cut them off in Your truth.

6I will freely sacrifice to You;
I will praise Your name, O LORD, for it is good.
7For He has delivered me out of all trouble;
And my eye has seen its desire upon my enemies.

(VERSES 1-3) David is persecuted by King Saul and opposed by people from Ziph, the desert which David uses to flee from Saul. The Ziphites are apostate Israelites who help Saul, although they reject Saul's God, and are also against David.

David's opening prayer is good for anyone to pray at anytime, anywhere: '*Save me, O God, by Your name, and vindicate me by Your strength. Hear my prayer, O God.*" This is good in any time of trouble or need. It is also a great response to the gospel of Jesus Christ. Because He took my punishment for my sin when He died as a perfect sacrifice for my sins on the cross, and because He rose again and lives eternally with power, He saves and vindicates me. I was sorry for my sins, so I turned from them. I received Him into my life as my living Lord.

'*Vindicate*' pictures a court trial where the accused is declared 'not guilty' after the facts are examined. The Bible says I am now '*justified by faith*' (Romans 5:1) when I put my trust in the only perfectly righteous One who bore my sins and their punishment, namely the Lord Jesus Christ. I am '*justified*' and '*vindicated*' when I confess and turn from my sins and trust in Jesus. Why? Because my sins are put on to Jesus' account. He paid for them by His shed blood and His perfect righteousness, which God counts as mine by faith in Him even though

I am sinful. If you have not prayed yet for Christ to '*save*' and '*vindicate*' (or '*justify*') you, please do not wait any longer before you do.

It is by God's '*name*' that we are saved. '*Jesus*' means '*God saves.*' He does! Once you know Jesus as your Saviour, you are saved. You also find He answers your other prayers, which you will set aside time to pray each day because you will love Him now. You can pray from the heart, '*Save me, O God, by Your name, and vindicate me by Your might.*' This will lead you to ask the Lord also to pray in future, '*Hear my prayer, O God, give ear to the words of my mouth.*' Can you pray like that? Can you do that now?

(VERSES 4-5) As a saved person, you will always find, especially when opposed, that you can know and say, '*God is my Helper*' in so many ways. He also '*upholds*' those Christians who uphold you in prayer. Prayer is a means of grace and blessing given by God to all who trust in Jesus. As you pray for others, God blesses you, too! David is a physical king, fighting physical battles and wars with physical foes and enemies. The way we 'fight' any who decide to be our physical foes today is on a different and spiritual level. We must pray that God will convict such people of sin, as he did with us, save them, and make them want to follow Him. We should show them Christ's love and grace, even if they hate us and seek to harm us. Jesus said in Luke 6:27, '*I say to you who hear: Love your enemies, do good to those who hate you.*' Through God, we can win this battle, with His help, in His strength, and for His glory.

(VERSES 6-7) See how David now builds on his relationship with his saving Lord. He tells God, '*I will freely sacrifice to You.*' That is the kind of free-will offering, with or without money, that pleases God. That is far more than making Old Testament sacrifices; it means you start by giving the Lord your heart. Missionary pioneer C T Studd said, 'If Jesus Christ be God and died for me, then no sacrifice can be too great for me to make for Him.' Blessings flow from such an attitude. Like David, you will thank the Lord who delivered you '*out of all trouble*'. If you seek your enemies' blessing, that pleases God, blesses others, and blesses you too! It starts with praying that first prayer we looked at in verse 1.

Psalm 55—Trusting God in Trouble

To the Chief Musician. With stringed instruments. A Contemplation of David.

1Give ear to my prayer, O God,
And do not hide Yourself from my supplication.
2Attend to me, and hear me;
I am restless in my complaint, and moan noisily,
3Because of the voice of the enemy,
Because of the oppression of the wicked;
For they bring down trouble upon me,
And in wrath they hate me.

4My heart is severely pained within me,
And the terrors of death have fallen upon me.
5Fearfulness and trembling have come upon me,
And horror has overwhelmed me.
6So I said, "Oh, that I had wings like a dove!
I would fly away and be at rest.
7Indeed, I would wander far off,
And remain in the wilderness. Selah
8I would hasten my escape
From the windy storm and tempest."

9Destroy, O Lord, and divide their tongues,
For I have seen violence and strife in the city.
10Day and night they go around it on its walls;
Iniquity and trouble are also in the midst of it.
11Destruction is in its midst;
Oppression and deceit do not depart from its streets.

12For it is not an enemy who reproaches me;
Then I could bear it.
Nor is it one who hates me who has exalted himself against me;
Then I could hide from him.
13But it was you, a man my equal,
My companion and my acquaintance.
14We took sweet counsel together,
And walked to the house of God in the throng.

15Let death seize them;
Let them go down alive into hell,
For wickedness is in their dwellings and among them.

16As for me, I will call upon God,
And the LORD shall save me.
17Evening and morning and at noon
I will pray, and cry aloud,
And He shall hear my voice.
18He has redeemed my soul in peace from the battle that was against me,
For there were many against me.

19God will hear, and afflict them,
Even He who abides from of old. Selah
Because they do not change,
Therefore they do not fear God.

20He has put forth his hands against those who were at peace with him;
He has broken his covenant.
21The words of his mouth were smoother than butter,
But war was in his heart;
His words were softer than oil,
Yet they were drawn swords.

22Cast your burden on the LORD,
And He shall sustain you;
He shall never permit the righteous to be moved.

23But You, O God, shall bring them down to the pit of destruction;
Bloodthirsty and deceitful men shall not live out half their days;
But I will trust in You.

(VERSES 1-3) We have seen in Psalm 54 that those who trust in the Lord find that He delivers them *'out of all trouble'*. David now pursues that promised help now. As a child speaks directly to a caring parent when he suffers, David asks his Heavenly Father to listen to his prayer and not ignore his plea. He suffers as angry enemies parade their voices, oppression, trouble and wrath against him. He tells his caring Father in this prayer. He sets us good example.

(VERSES 4-8) He trembles in pain, *'terrors of death'*, *'fearfulness, trembling'* and overwhelming '*horror*'. He would like to *'fly away and be at rest'* as a dove flees a violent storm to shelter far away to in a safe desert to escape. He has some real troubles and problems; sometimes Christian have those, too.

(VERSES 9-11) He asks God to confuse and confound his wicked, violent, strife-seeking foes who continuously prowl around the city's walls and streets, making it a place of '*iniqity and trouble*' and '*oppression and deceit*'. They fill the city with a wicked mixture of malice, abuse, fear, violence, strife, destruction, threats, and lies.

(VERSES 12-14) David could handle opposition by a known foe, but sadly a once very close friend is now his foe. They both enjoyed going to worship before with others. They had enjoyed fellowship and friendship in '*sweet counsel together*'. Doubtless they shared thoughts of blessing from God's Word with each other. When a once-believing friend turns against you, it really hurts.

(VERSE 15) We can see why David prays against his enemies. But Christians today must pray for any opposing us to turn to Jesus Christ and receive changed hearts. Romans 5:10 says, *'When we were God's enemies we were reconciled to God through the death of His Son.'* Should we not therefore love and forgive our enemies, too? Jesus bore God's wrath against our sins on the cross to forgive His former *'enemies'* and give them eternal life. God is King and so He can deal with David's Hell-bound foes. So, David confidently prays. But through the gospel, our God tells wicked sinners to repent and trust Jesus. We should pray and work for that. David shares the details of his ex-friend's state with God. That is always a good idea!

(VERSES 16-19) It is right that, in the turmoil and the hurt felt by David, he renews his personal commitment to walk closely with the LORD, whom he knows will save him. He will pray 'morning, noon and night'. He reminds himself that God gives him peace and also that God will deal with his enemies.

(VERSES 20-21) David then shares with God some details of the opposition of his one-time friend now turned enemy. His smooth-sounding words concealed a heart at war with David. Those seemingly soft words were actually like 'drawn swords'. This challenges me too to ask if my heart is at times hypocritical and my words hostile and cruel. If so that needs confessing to God and forsaking, knowing that He will forgive and cleanse where there is repentance.

(VERSES 22-23) Hell (the *'pit of destruction')* awaits rebel unrepentant sinners. But God says to sinners and to Christians, *'Cast your burden on the LORD and He shall sustain you; He shall never permit the righteous to be moved.'* If God washes away your unrighteousness through the shed blood of Jesus, and as the righteous and risen life of Christ He gives to you is yours when you trust the Saviour, your response should surely be like David's: *'But I will trust in You.'* We should do that every day and all day.

Psalm 56—Fear of man? Trust in God!

To the Chief Musician. Set to "The Silent Dove in Distant Lands." A Michtam of David when the Philistines captured him in Gath.

1Be merciful to me, O God, for man would swallow me up;
Fighting all day he oppresses me.
2My enemies would hound me all day,
For there are many who fight against me, O Most High.

3Whenever I am afraid,
I will trust in You.
4In God (I will praise His word),
In God I have put my trust;
I will not fear.
What can flesh do to me?

5All day they twist my words;
All their thoughts are against me for evil.
6They gather together,
They hide, they mark my steps,
When they lie in wait for my life.
7Shall they escape by iniquity?
In anger cast down the peoples, O God!

8You number my wanderings;
Put my tears into Your bottle;
Are they not in Your book?
9When I cry out to You,
Then my enemies will turn back;
This I know, because God is for me.
10In God (I will praise His word),
In the LORD (I will praise His word),
11In God I have put my trust;
I will not be afraid.
What can man do to me?

12Vows made to You are binding upon me, O God;
I will render praises to You,
13For You have delivered my soul from death.
Have You not kept my feet from falling,
That I may walk before God
In the light of the living?

(VERSES 1-2) The cause of David writing Psalm 56 was when the Philistines '*captured him in Gath*'. 1 Samuel 21:10-15 tells of David fleeing from Saul to Gath. They '*captured*' him there. His feigned madness fooled them. The Philistine ruler, King Achish, said he did not want '*madmen*' so they freed David, who then asked God for mercy to escape his proud and many pursuers. They '*hound*'

him '*all day*'. There are '*many who fight against*' him. When you pray for help, be like David and be specific in your requests.

(VERSES 3-4) David feels fear, as we all do. But he is not giving in to it. He determines that '*Whenever I am afraid, I will trust in You.*' Three times—in verse 4 and in verse 10 twice—he volunteers, '*I will praise His word*', as he trusts '*in God*' or '*in the LORD.*' Unsurprisingly, his determination strengthens. He immediately says, '*In God I have put my trust; I will not be afraid.*' He then logically asks, '*What can man do to me?*' The eternal God is on his side. The worst that men can do is to usher him into Heaven sooner than he expected. God cares for those who trust in Him for all eternity. Just think, the eternal God became a man in the Person of the Lord Jesus Christ. He was both fully man and fully God. He went to that cross at Calvary to bear our sins and in our place suffer an eternity of punishment for them, contracted to three hours of suffering in the unexpected midday darkness. At that time, God the Father punished Jesus, God the Son, for our sins. Now, because Jesus rose again from the dead, any sinner who is sorry for his sins and turns from them to trust in Christ need not fear death and Hell. He receives eternal life and awaits a home in Heaven.

(VERSES 5-11) David tells God how his enemies twist his words. They conspire to plot against him. They wait in ambush and note where he goes. They want to kill him. David commits his foes to God, who will deal with them. That is better than taking action himself. He asks God to note his sadness. He knows God can turn his foes back as he asks Him to help. Aware that God is on his side, he confidently prays again as before, trusting and praising God. If that describes you, you also can pray, as David has prayed all those years ago, '*Be merciful to me, O God*' (verse 1), '*I will trust in You*' (verse 3), and '*in God I have put my trust; I will not be afraid. What can man do to me?*' (verse 11).

(VERSES 12-13) David will keep his vows to God and praise Him. His thank offering to God is to praise Him! He is grateful for God's delivering him from death and from falling. Now he can '*walk before God in the light of the living*'. So can you—for ever—if your faith is in Jesus.

Psalm 57—Persecuted but praising.

To the Chief Musician. Set to "Do Not Destroy." A Michtam of David when he fled from Saul into the cave.
1Be merciful to me, O God, be merciful to me!
For my soul trusts in You;
And in the shadow of Your wings I will make my refuge,
Until these calamities have passed by.

2I will cry out to God Most High,
To God who performs all things for me.
3He shall send from heaven and save me;
He reproaches the one who would swallow me up. Selah
God shall send forth His mercy and His truth.

4My soul is among lions;
I lie among the sons of men
Who are set on fire,
Whose teeth are spears and arrows,
And their tongue a sharp sword.
5Be exalted, O God, above the heavens;
Let Your glory be above all the earth.

6They have prepared a net for my steps;
My soul is bowed down;
They have dug a pit before me;
Into the midst of it they themselves have fallen. Selah

7My heart is steadfast, O God, my heart is steadfast;
I will sing and give praise.
8Awake, my glory!
Awake, lute and harp!
I will awaken the dawn.

9I will praise You, O LORD, among the peoples;
I will sing to You among the nations.
10For Your mercy reaches unto the heavens,
And Your truth unto the clouds.

11Be exalted, O God, above the heavens;
Let Your glory be above all the earth.

❖

(VERSE 1) David fled for his life from King Saul, into a cave, probably the cave that is mentioned in 1 Samuel chapter 22 or 24. But his refuge and shelter are under God's wings, like a chick under its mother hen.

(VERSES 2-3) David knows God as his Saviour. He cries out to Him. He trusts His purpose for him. God sends help from Heaven to save him. He halts his enemies. God is full of love and faithfulness. Our hugest need is to be saved from our sins and God's holy, eternal punishment on them. '*God so loved the world that He gave His one and only Son, that everyone who believes in Him may have eternal life*' (John 3:16). Jesus also came from Heaven to earth to save all who trust in Him. Perfectly loving and faithful, He died on the cross bearing your sins and their punishment. Now, if you have not yet done so, you must turn from your sins, cry to God for *His mercy and His truth,* and receive Jesus in your heart as your Lord and Saviour.

(VERSES 4-6) David faces violent men, deadly like lions, and '*ravenous beasts*'. Their teeth and tongues are like spears, arrows and swords. They are cruel, deadly killers. How does David face being killed? By praying for God to be '*exalted*' and for God's glory to be observed worldwide. He wants to live and serve God, but he is ready to die if he has to. Can you say that? He knows they are out to catch him and make him fall. But they are the ones who fall, not David. David is '*bowed down*' at the thought that they are laying a net to trap him. But God is on his side. They will fall into the pit they have dug for David.

(VERSE 7a) Twice David tells God, '*My heart is steadfast*.' It is faithful and settled on God. Christ can make you steadfast.

(VERSES 7b-10) How does David now sing to God with his '*steadfast*' heart? First, with an awakened soul; he knows his Saviour God. Do you? Second, with tuneful musical instruments. Third, he starts early in the morning. Fourth, he sings to and praises God among other nations and peoples. He wants the world to know about his God and Saviour. Do you? Fifth, he praises God's '*mercy*' and '*truth*' and His vast faithfulness which reach into the clouds and the heavens.

(VERSE 11) See how constant and faithful David has become, as God has worked in him. Again, he prays for God to be '*exalted*' and for God's glory to be observed worldwide. Whether in fear of persecution and death or contemplating God's great love and faithfulness, he praises God.

Psalm 58—Bad words: theirs and ours.

To the Chief Musician. Set to "Do Not Destroy." A Michtam of David.
[1]Do you indeed speak righteousness, you silent ones?
Do you judge uprightly, you sons of men?
[2]No, in heart you work wickedness;
You weigh out the violence of your hands in the earth.

[3]The wicked are estranged from the womb;
They go astray as soon as they are born, speaking lies.
[4]Their poison is like the poison of a serpent;
They are like the deaf cobra that stops its ear,
[5]Which will not heed the voice of charmers,
Charming ever so skillfully.

[6]Break their teeth in their mouth, O God!
Break out the fangs of the young lions, O LORD!
[7]Let them flow away as waters which run continually;
When he bends his bow,
Let his arrows be as if cut in pieces.
[8]Let them be like a snail which melts away as it goes,
Like a stillborn child of a woman, that they may not see the sun.

[9]Before your pots can feel the burning thorns,
He shall take them away as with a whirlwind,
As in His living and burning wrath.
[10]The righteous shall rejoice when he sees the vengeance;
He shall wash his feet in the blood of the wicked,
[11]So that men will say,
"Surely there is a reward for the righteous;
Surely He is God who judges in the earth."

(VERSES 1-2) David criticises leaders who pretend to uphold justice but abuse or misuse their powers. Some Bible passages call them '*gods*' (human and self-made) and some call them '*judges*'. They invent unjust practices and treat people violently. These rulers should repent and ask God to forgive and change them. We, too, need to turn from our sins and ask Jesus to forgive and change us. It is not uncommon to find world leaders or our own politicians who fail in ways like this.

(VERSES 3-5) The sinfulness of the corrupt rulers is described. This is true in principle of us all, being 'natural' sinners from birth. We sin so easily. Without Christ, we lie. Our words can be like a cobra's venom, which poisons and harms others. James 3:8 says, *'No man can tame the tongue. It is a restless evil, full of deadly poison.'* Some snakes are untameable by a snake charmer. We sinners cannot tame our own tongues in our own strength. Christ can change our language. Left to ourselves, we could easily lie, take God's name in vain, be abusive, use bad language, gossip, insult and speak unhelpfully. When Jesus died on the cross to bear all our sins and God's punishment for them, remember that He paid the penalty for all our wrong words, too. If you turn from your sins to ask Jesus into your life to become your Lord and Saviour, note that not only must you *'believe in your heart'* on Jesus, but the result will be that *'you confess with your mouth that Jesus is Lord'* (Romans 10:9-10). The first part of your body to show your conversion to Christ is your mouth! What you now will not say, as a Christian, blends well with using your tongue to commend your Lord and Saviour to bless others. When I came to Christ, God's grace and help made my bad language evaporate. I could not achieve that, but God did through His Holy Spirit. I started to want to speak up for Jesus—but (still) nothing like enough. I am still a 'work in progress'.

(VERSES 6-8) David prays for God to nullify these evil men's bad words. We must pray for our words to glorify Jesus and help people. May our unworthy language, also, cease to be like lions' *'fangs'* which injure others, vanish like spilled *'waters'* flowing away, be deprived of their sinful sharpness like *'arrows'* that are blunted, and *'melt away'* like a slug or *'snail'* on a dusty and dry path on a hot day. It would be good if our ungodly language never saw the light of day. We should cut it off before it comes to life.

(VERSES 9-11) David wants to see these wicked men judged by God's *'whirlwind'* removal and destroyed like thorns on a fire by His *'burning wrath'*. He says, *'The righteous shall rejoice'* when he sees the *'vengeance'* of God. The fact that those counted *'righteous'* through faith in Christ will be rewarded by our gracious God, shows that it *'is God who judges in the earth'* perfectly, righteously and finally. We would like to see sinners die to their sinfulness and sins, and come alive to Christ. That is what the gospel does for those who turn to Christ. But there has to be real repentance from sin as well as personal saving faith in the Lord Jesus Christ.

Psalm 59—What God means to David

To the Chief Musician. Set to "Do Not Destroy." A Michtam of David when Saul sent men, and they watched the house in order to kill him.
1Deliver me from my enemies, O my God;
Defend me from those who rise up against me.
2Deliver me from the workers of iniquity,
And save me from bloodthirsty men.

3For look, they lie in wait for my life;
The mighty gather against me,
Not for my transgression nor for my sin, O LORD.
4They run and prepare themselves through no fault of mine.

Awake to help me, and behold!
5You therefore, O LORD God of hosts, the God of Israel,
Awake to punish all the nations;
Do not be merciful to any wicked transgressors. Selah

6At evening they return,
They growl like a dog,
And go all around the city.
7Indeed, they belch with their mouth;
Swords are in their lips;
For they say, "Who hears?"

8But You, O LORD, shall laugh at them;
You shall have all the nations in derision.
9I will wait for You, O You his Strength;
For God is my defense.
10My God of mercy shall come to meet me;
God shall let me see my desire on my enemies.

11Do not slay them, lest my people forget;
Scatter them by Your power,
And bring them down,
O Lord our shield.
12For the sin of their mouth and the words of their lips,
Let them even be taken in their pride,
And for the cursing and lying which they speak.
13Consume them in wrath, consume them,
That they may not be;
And let them know that God rules in Jacob
To the ends of the earth. Selah

14And at evening they return,
They growl like a dog,
And go all around the city.
15They wander up and down for food,
And howl if they are not satisfied.

16But I will sing of Your power;
Yes, I will sing aloud of Your mercy in the morning;
For You have been my defense
And refuge in the day of my trouble.
17To You, O my Strength, I will sing praises;
For God is my defense,
My God of mercy.

(VERSES 1-2) David again asks God to deliver and protect him from his present wicked and bloodthirsty foes, King Saul's men, who watch his house and plot to rise up against him to kill him. David's night escape (1 Samuel 19:11) might be the background for Psalm 59.

(VERSES 3-5) David knows he has done Saul no wrong as he faces the fierce conspiracy to attack him, so appeals to '*the LORD God of hosts, the God of Israel*' who is far stronger than they are. David asks Him to punish opposing nations too and have no mercy on '*wicked transgressors*'. David fights physical battles for physical victories over physical foes. Christians fight on a spiritual level now. We fight by prayer, by trusting God's written Word (the Bible), and by our faith in God's Living Word (Jesus Christ). We must show love and live to please the Lord. Like David, we can ask God individually to '*awake to help me*' and to '*behold*'. We ask God to keep His eye on us, too, to deliver us.

(VERSES 6-8) Psalm 59 echoes about dogs what Psalm 57 says about David's soul being '*among lions*' with sharp teeth, as David's enemies prowl '*about the city at evening*' '*snarling like dogs*'. Their violent words cut like swords. They imply that God cannot hear. God laughs at them and also at enemy nations. He is all-knowing.

(VERSES 9-13) David trusts his loving God as his Strength, fortress, preparer of his way, shield, and sovereign King. If you receive Christ, God will also be those things to you. David now watches for God and follows Him. He asks God to deal with his enemies, by making them wander about and by consuming them finally. He wants all to know that '*God rules over Jacob*'. Now, we want sinful people across the world to be saved by trusting Christ and then following Him.

(VERSES 14-17) As his foes, like growling, '*prowling*', '*howling*' dogs, seek '*food*' in the city, David praises the '*power*' of his saving God, singing '*aloud*' of His '*mercy*', '*defence*', '*strength*', and fortresslike refuge and protection in troubles. To save you for ever from sin and Hell, Jesus paid for your sins, when He was punished in your place on the cross. He now lives for ever. He loves, keeps and protects spiritually all those who trust Him. Hebrews 7:25 says Jesus '*is also able to save to the uttermost those who come to God through Him, since He always lives to make intercession for them.*' Every '*born-again*' sinner has that amazing privilege, comfort and offer made to him by the Lord Jesus Christ. That can include you, too!

Psalm 60—Get up and fight back!

To the Chief Musician. Set to "Lily of the Testimony." A Michtam of David. For teaching. When he fought against Mesopotamia and Syria of Zobah, and Joab returned and killed twelve thousand Edomites in the Valley of Salt.

1 O God, You have cast us off;
You have broken us down;
You have been displeased;
Oh, restore us again!
2 You have made the earth tremble;
You have broken it;
Heal its breaches, for it is shaking.
3 You have shown Your people hard things;
You have made us drink the wine of confusion.

4 You have given a banner to those who fear You,
That it may be displayed because of the truth. Selah
5 That Your beloved may be delivered,
Save with Your right hand, and hear me.

6 God has spoken in His holiness:
"I will rejoice;
I will divide Shechem
And measure out the Valley of Succoth.
7 Gilead is Mine, and Manasseh is Mine;
Ephraim also is the helmet for My head;
Judah is My lawgiver.
8 Moab is My washpot;
Over Edom I will cast My shoe;
Philistia, shout in triumph because of Me."

9 Who will bring me to the strong city?
Who will lead me to Edom?
10 Is it not You, O God, who cast us off?
And You, O God, who did not go out with our armies?
11 Give us help from trouble,
For the help of man is useless.
12 Through God we will do valiantly,
For it is He who shall tread down our enemies.

(VERSES 1-3) Psalm 60 shows how to take defeat, trust God to put things right, and come back to win. Joab and his brother, Abishai, led King David's troops, so David (as king), Joab and Abishai are each rightly said to have killed the 12,000 Edomites. See 2 Samuel 8:13, the title here, and 1 Chronicles 18:12. In 2 Samuel 8:13, a better manuscript text rightly states 'Edomites' rather than 'Syrians'.

While David fought in the north, the Edomites invaded and overcame southern Judah, which caused great distress to David and his men. They think God has, in anger, rejected them by this defeat. They picture it as a great earthquake which shakes the land, tears it apart, and breaks it up. The news of that staggering defeat affects them as if it were alcohol. They feel stupefied about these desperate times here called *'hard things'*. Sometimes Christians face unexpected setbacks, hard to understand or accept. We must always remember that the Lord is there with us (Hebrews 13:5).

(VERSES 4-8) So learn how David and his men respond to defeat, and do the same when you fail. The truly God-fearing men among them take this defeat as a *'banner'* to be unfurled against the enemy. It spurs them to fight back. What a good response to failure! David prays to God, *'Save with Your right hand and hear us and help us.'* He and his troops still regard Shechem, the Valley of Succoth, Gilead, Manasseh, Ephraim and Judah as God's and theirs. Moab, one traditional enemy, is regarded merely as being their washbowl, which a lowly servant would give to them. David will *'cast [his] shoel'* on his continual foe, Edom, as a master would throw his dirty sandals to his servant to be cleaned. He reminds Philistia, an early and frequent foe of David, that Israel will conquer with shouts of victory! They will have to acknowledge that.

Do you remember the triumph cry of Jesus as He died on the cross to bear your sins and their punishment? It was the shout of victory, *'It is finished'* (John 19:30), meaning *'paid in full'* or *'accomplished'*. All your sins were paid for by His perfect sacrifice in your place. If you repent from your sins, the way is open for you to ask the now-resurrected and living Jesus to save you. You will want to acknowledge that in love, if Christ is your Saviour.

(VERSES 9-12) David confidently asks God, despite the recent defeat, for His *'help from trouble'*. Man cannot help. But *'through God [they] will do valiantly* and *'tread down [their] enemies.'* Through Christ you, too, can win in your spiritual conflicts now and in the final victory glory of Heaven, by trusting in your once-crucified now-risen and ever-living Lord and Saviour!

Psalm 61—Feelings, facts, and eternity

To the Chief Musician. On a stringed instrument. A Psalm of David.
1Hear my cry, O God;
Attend to my prayer.
2From the end of the earth I will cry to You,
When my heart is overwhelmed;
Lead me to the rock that is higher than I.

3For You have been a shelter for me,
A strong tower from the enemy.
4I will abide in Your tabernacle forever;
I will trust in the shelter of Your wings. Selah

5For You, O God, have heard my vows;
You have given me the heritage of those who fear Your name.
6You will prolong the king's life,
His years as many generations.
7He shall abide before God forever.
Oh, prepare mercy and truth, which may preserve him!

8So I will sing praise to Your name forever,
That I may daily perform my vows.

(VERSES 1-2) Happily, David does not rely on feelings. They can go up and down for no apparent reason, as well as in response to some calamity or opposition. But he does know that he needs to cry to God. He prays, '*Hear my cry, O God; Attend to my prayer.*' What a privilege that our infinite and almighty God is loving and listening to His people. If you really have turned from your sin and committed your heart to the Lord Jesus Christ to forgive you, bless you, guide you, and help you, then you will know that you have a prayer-hearing God who will answer you. Do pray to Him morning and evening each day. Although David feels distant from God—which is why he feels he prays '*from the end of the earth*'—he still calls out to God. So many of his psalms are examples of how to pray in different circumstances.

Unlike some, who wrongly ease up on praying when they do not feel up to it, he calls on God when his '*heart is overwhelmed*'. He recognises that God is his Rock—solid, settled, reliable—and that He is '*higher than*' David. Many people who feel glum and weak let their heads drop and do not pray as they ought, each day. David looks up to God, his Rock that he knows '*is higher than I*'. Do not look down; look up! Do not trust your feelings—but trust Jesus.

He will never let you down. I remember a time when some folks were making false accusations against me and trying to trap me in various ways. I found that, as well as being aware of those traps, my response was always best to look above to my *'Rock that is higher than I'*. Hebrews 12:1-2 tells us to keep *'looking unto Jesus, the author and finisher of our faith'*. Keep looking upwards to Him.

(VERSES 3-4) A recurring theme in other psalms is repeated here again. God has often been a *'shelter'* (or *'refuge'*) and *'a strong tower from the enemy'* for David. We do like to feel safe, secure, and protected on a long-term basis. That is why the eternal Son of God, Jesus, died for us to take the penalty for our sins in His body on the cross, and then rose again. When you turn your back on your sins, thank Jesus for dying for you, and receive Him into your heart as your living Lord and Saviour, you are placed in Christ as your *'shelter'* or *'refuge'* and your *'strong tower'*. He protects you throughout eternity. Like David, once you experience that, you look forward to dwelling with the Lord Jesus Christ *'forever'* and trusting *'in the shelter of [His] wings'*, just as a newly hatched little chick hides under its mother hen's wings. You will safely *'abide'* there *'forever'* in Him in Heaven. Just think about that! (*'Selah'* is used again.)

(VERSE 5) David has vowed to God to be faithful to his wonderful spiritual heritage, as a man fully committed to God. Similarly, now, each person who truly knows and loves our loving Saviour possesses a godly fear for His name. That name must always be upheld and shared with others. Do not make vows to God unless you mean them: but, assuming they are to do the right things in accordance with the teaching of the Bible, keep your promises to God. Did you ever promise that whenever possible you would read the Bible each day and pray each day, for example? Did you ask God to take your life to bless other people? What God-honouring vows have you made? Do you keep them?

(VERSES 6-8) These verses refer to David's kingdom and to the eternal kingdom of the coming Messiah, the Lord Jesus Christ. By Christ's loving faithfulness, if you trust in Him to save you, you will be there! Until then, keep faithful in daily living for Him. You will need His daily *'mercy and truth'* to preserve you so you can do that.

Will you join David in saying to his Lord, *'So I will sing praise to Your name forever, That I may daily perform my vows'*?

Psalm 62—What God can mean to you

To the Chief Musician. To Jeduthun. A Psalm of David.
1 Truly my soul silently waits for God;
From Him comes my salvation.
2 He only is my rock and my salvation;
He is my defense;
I shall not be greatly moved.

3 How long will you attack a man?
You shall be slain, all of you,
Like a leaning wall and a tottering fence.
4 They only consult to cast him down from his high position;
They delight in lies;
They bless with their mouth,
But they curse inwardly. Selah

5 My soul, wait silently for God alone,
For my expectation is from Him.
6 He only is my rock and my salvation;
He is my defense;
I shall not be moved.
7 In God is my salvation and my glory;
The rock of my strength,
And my refuge, is in God.

8 Trust in Him at all times, you people;
Pour out your heart before Him;
God is a refuge for us. Selah

9 Surely men of low degree are a vapor,
Men of high degree are a lie;
If they are weighed on the scales,
They are altogether lighter than vapor.
10 Do not trust in oppression,
Nor vainly hope in robbery;
If riches increase,
Do not set your heart on them.

11 God has spoken once,
Twice I have heard this:
That power belongs to God.
12 Also to You, O Lord, belongs mercy;
For You render to each one according to his work.

(VERSES 1-8) David makes it clear from the start that his *'soul'* is relying on God alone to receive His *'salvation'*. There is nothing else and no one else that can be my *'rock and my salvation'*. No religion, no good works, no religious leader, no ceremony, no personal history, and no popular teaching or psychology can save you. The divine Lord Jesus Christ, fully God and fully Man, said, *'I am the way, the truth and the life. No one comes to the Father except through Me.'* It is only by seeing my sinfulness and need for cleansing and forgiveness and by turning from my sin to receive Jesus in my life, that I can be saved and so come to know God's unique salvation. Jesus bore my sins and God's wrathful judgment on those sins when He died for me on the cross. He rose again and lives today. The sure evidence that someone turned from his sins and believed in Jesus is that his life is now being changed from the inside out, into someone who is a *'new creation'* (2 Corinthians 5:17). Such a man or woman now follows and obeys God according to His Word, the Bible. Does that describe you? If so, you might be opposed by some people because of how you now live for the God of holiness in a sinful self-centred world. That was often David's experience, as it is now.

This psalm, like many others, centres on David's reaction and response to the intense opposition of evil men who are trying to wipe him out. It starts by his asserting his confidence that God will keep him. David says of God, *'He is my defense; I shall not be greatly moved.'* His foes look to assault him and throw him down. They want him to feel like a *'leaning wall'* that would fall easily under pressure, or like a rickety and unstable *'tottering fence'*. That is how he could feel against this foe, if he were left to himself. His enemies will happily tell lies about him as part of their evil attack. Their words seem to be words of outward blessing, but their hypocritical hearts are cursing him while they speak. Just as David did, they need to be cleansed and to receive new hearts. That is exactly what Jesus Christ gives today to those who turn from wrong in their lives, believe in His atoning death on the cross for them, and trust in Him with all their hearts. Verses 1-8 start and finish with what God is to those who trust in Him. Still today, because Jesus paid the penalty for our sins, if we repent and believe in Him, we find that He takes residence in our hearts by His Holy Spirit. Consider briefly what God does for and is to you when you are saved by such a personal faith in Christ:

- He gives your soul rest now and for ever.
- He defends and stabilises you.

- He saves you from sin's penalty and power now, and from sin's presence in eternity.
- He is the Rock on which you could and should build your life.
- He is your unshakable fortress and refuge.
- He gives you real and certain hope for the future.
- He tells his people to '*trust in Him at all times*' and to '*pour out your heart before Him*',

He can become all that to you too!

(VERSE 9) David reminds us that men are nothing compared to God. Highborn or lowborn, we are all like a passing '*vapour*'. Life is short and eternity is very long, whether separate from Christ in Hell's darkness or present with Him in Heaven's joyful light. Even the well-known '*men of high degree*' in this world's eyes are light-weight compared with God and eternity.

(VERSES 10-12) Hearts which major on increase of material wealth are the losers, especially if that wealth comes from sinful extortion or from robbery. In fact, such sins will bring God's judgment. We should not '*set [our] hearts*' on getting rich. The Lord will '*reward each one according to his work*'. He also possesses '*power*'. God is far too powerful to be deflected from His righteous judgment against sin. He is also loving and merciful and is far too merciful to be deflected from His willingness to give repentant sinners forgiveness and eternal life. Remember the well-known verse in John 3:16: '*God so loved the world that He gave His only begotten Son, that whoever believes in Him should not perish but have everlasting life*' (John 3:16). Christ gives all who believe in Him the never-ending length of '*everlasting life*' and the perfect, God-given quality and length of '*eternal life*' (John 10:28) now!

Psalm 63–You cannot sleep? Try this!

A Psalm of David when he was in the wilderness of Judah.
1O God, You are my God;
Early will I seek You;
My soul thirsts for You;
My flesh longs for You
In a dry and thirsty land
Where there is no water.
2So I have looked for You in the sanctuary,
To see Your power and Your glory.

3Because Your lovingkindness is better than life,
My lips shall praise You.
4Thus I will bless You while I live;
I will lift up my hands in Your name.
5My soul shall be satisfied as with marrow and fatness,
And my mouth shall praise You with joyful lips.

6When I remember You on my bed,
I meditate on You in the night watches.
7Because You have been my help,
Therefore in the shadow of Your wings I will rejoice.
8My soul follows close behind You;
Your right hand upholds me.

9But those who seek my life, to destroy it,
Shall go into the lower parts of the earth.
10They shall fall by the sword;
They shall be a portion for jackals.

11But the king shall rejoice in God;
Everyone who swears by Him shall glory;
But the mouth of those who speak lies shall be stopped.

(VERSES 1-5) The first five verses focus on David's current situation. We know he was '*in the Desert of Judah*' at least twice: once when he was seeking to escape from the pursuing King Saul (1 Samuel 23), and once when, though he was then the king, he fled from his rebel son, Absalom (2 Samuel 15). It seems it was the second occasion that is covered in this psalm, since David refers to himself as '*king*' in verse 11. Whatever his circumstances, David shows his great desire for God and loving respect for Him. He starts with, '*O God, you are my God.*' It is a wonderful thing to belong to the Lord and know that, in one sense, He belongs to you. Doubting Thomas, who believed again in Jesus when he saw Him risen from the dead and had seen the wounds of crucifixion in His hands and side, exclaimed, '*My Lord and my God*' (John 20:28). Can you say the same thing to Jesus? Do you realise that He died to take the punishment for your sins, so have you turned your back on them and received Him into your life? If so, like David, your saved soul will long for fellowship with God, just as a thirsty man's body longs for water in the desert. You will treasure the times when you have sensed being close to God in prayer, like David realised the '*power*' and '*glory*' of God in the '*sanctuary*' in the Tabernacle. You will treasure His changeless '*lovingkindness*' to you—it is more important even than your passing life. You will make thanking and praising God a godly habit as long as you live. Your '*soul*' will feed on the spiritual food of God's Word and sing your praise to Him. That will be marked by '*joyful lips*'.

(VERSES 6-8) David is obviously sleepless. That is always a difficult and tiring affliction to deal with. But he does not waste his time counting sheep! He is a good example to us all. He casts his mind back on what God has done for him. This helps him to '*follow close behind*' his Lord. One of my friends was suffering from insomnia, so he started to pray each time he could not sleep. He said the devil did not like him praying, so he lulled him to sleep. If that did not happen, he kept praying instead. My pal told me, 'So I won whether I slept or stayed awake!' David thinks about God as his helper—and it causes him to sing. He is well aware that God sheltered him '*in the shadow of* [His] *wings*' just like a mother hen shelters her chicks. As he thinks of, prays to, and sings about God, he becomes aware that the powerful '*right hand*' of Almighty God is upholding him. That is a very good result from a sleepless night.

(VERSES 9-11) David's intended killers face Hell's eternal destruction and the sword of judgment. Jackals will eat their bodies out there in Judah's desert. But David '*shall rejoice in God*' and all who revere God's name will praise and glorify God, while it can be said of David's enemies that their '*lies shall be stopped*'.

Comments like this should make everyone ask, 'Will I spend eternity in Heaven and continue rejoicing in God for ever?' or like David's enemies, whose sins had not been repented of and forgiven, will I spend eternity apart from God in Hell, as we saw that verse 9 indicates? It is another way of asking, 'Is Jesus Christ my personal Saviour?'

Psalm 64—From prayer to praise

To the Chief Musician. A Psalm of David.
1Hear my voice, O God, in my meditation;
Preserve my life from fear of the enemy.
2Hide me from the secret plots of the wicked,
From the rebellion of the workers of iniquity,
3Who sharpen their tongue like a sword,
And bend their bows to shoot their arrows—bitter words,
4That they may shoot in secret at the blameless;
Suddenly they shoot at him and do not fear.

5They encourage themselves in an evil matter;
They talk of laying snares secretly;
They say, "Who will see them?"
6They devise iniquities:
"We have perfected a shrewd scheme."
Both the inward thought and the heart of man are deep.

7But God shall shoot at them with an arrow;
Suddenly they shall be wounded.
8So He will make them stumble over their own tongue;
All who see them shall flee away.
9All men shall fear,
And shall declare the work of God;
For they shall wisely consider His doing.

10The righteous shall be glad in the LORD, and trust in Him.
And all the upright in heart shall glory.

(VERSES 1-4) The unseen advantage of David's facing deadly personal opposition is that it causes him to pray often to God from his heart. Difficult circumstances do not determine if we win or lose. Rather, how we deal with them before God is the key. David pleads with God to hear and hide him from *'the secret plots of the wicked'* who conspire and rebel to take his life. Their tongues are like sharpened swords and their *'bitter words'* like *'deadly arrows'*. They also fearlessly look to shoot real arrows at *'blameless'* David in a sudden ambush.

(VERSES 5-6) David's *'evil'* and violent foes *'encourage themselves'*, as an evil team, to hide snares to trap him when no one can see their secret task of *'laying snares'* for him. These wicked, cunning men set their minds and hearts on an unjust and perfect but *'shrewd scheme'* to kill him. Their inward thoughts and hearts are *'deep'* in sinfulness. I know a couple of keen Christian workers who were threatened physically because they were related to men whom the gang hated. It was hard for them. They trusted in God, and He looked after them.

(VERSES 7-9) Brutal and savage aggressors forget that God sees it all and hears it all. The Bible says, '*The eyes of the LORD are in every place, keeping watch on the wicked and the good*' (Proverbs 15:3). He misses nothing—and He needs no video cameras or witnesses. He knows. He will judge all sinners unless they repent and turn to Jesus to save them. He is willing to save the worst of repentant sinners. That is why He bore the sins of such sinners when punished on the cross for them. God's wrath on these wicked men will be far worse than any damage they plan for David. God's '*arrows*' of judgment will strike these men suddenly, if they will not yield to God. Ruin awaits them. They will '*stumble over their own tongue*' probably by incriminating themselves. All who see them fear at the thought of the judgment they face. They will suffer. The Bible says God is full of wrath on sin. He will judge all for their sins unless, in humble repentance, they turn from their sins to Jesus. It is wise to fear God's wrath on sin. One day, sinners will '*declare the work of God*', how God has worked to punish them. They '*shall wisely consider His doing*' as they ponder how God acts as Judge. Best to thank God now that Jesus as Saviour died to save you. Ask for God's pardon. Receive Jesus into your heart.

(VERSE 10) Those who know God's forgiveness in Christ are counted as being '*righteous*' because Jesus' righteousness is counted as theirs. They '*shall be glad in the LORD, and trust in Him.*' All those with hearts made '*upright*' by God's redeeming grace shall glory in the Lord. Are you one of them yet? If not, why not?

Psalm 65—God our Saviour and Creator

To the Chief Musician. A Psalm of David. A Song.
1Praise is awaiting You, O God, in Zion;
And to You the vow shall be performed.
2O You who hear prayer,
To You all flesh will come.
3Iniquities prevail against me;
As for our transgressions,
You will provide atonement for them.

4Blessed is the man You choose,
And cause to approach You,
That he may dwell in Your courts.
We shall be satisfied with the goodness of Your house,
Of Your holy temple.

5By awesome deeds in righteousness You will answer us,
O God of our salvation,
You who are the confidence of all the ends of the earth,
And of the far-off seas;
6Who established the mountains by His strength,
Being clothed with power;
7You who still the noise of the seas,
The noise of their waves,
And the tumult of the peoples.
8They also who dwell in the farthest parts are afraid of Your signs;
You make the outgoings of the morning and evening rejoice.

9You visit the earth and water it,
You greatly enrich it;
The river of God is full of water;
You provide their grain,
For so You have prepared it.
10You water its ridges abundantly,
You settle its furrows;
You make it soft with showers,
You bless its growth.

11You crown the year with Your goodness,
And Your paths drip with abundance.
12They drop on the pastures of the wilderness,
And the little hills rejoice on every side.
13The pastures are clothed with flocks;
The valleys also are covered with grain;
They shout for joy, they also sing.

(VERSES 1-4) Zion is not only the '*city of David*' in Jerusalem. It also pictures the praise of Christians worshipping the Lord today. '*Praise is awaiting You, O God, in Zion.*' Those praising God also keep their vows, or promises, to Him, our loving and saving God who hears our prayers. Christians worldwide are included in '*to You all flesh will come*'. David found that '*iniquities*' prevailed against him. But he knew that God would provide '*atonement*' for their '*transgressions*'. That is still true of all people who confess their sins to God, turn from them in repentance, and trust the Lord Jesus Christ as their sin-bearer, Saviour and Sovereign. We deserved punishment from God in Hell; Jesus bore it in His own body when He died on the cross. He rose again. He lives now. By the Holy Spirit, He enters the lives of all who personally trust in Him. He chose us and brings us together close to Him in prayer, praise and worship. God's blessings fill us when we come to Christ. Even more than those who worshipped in God's '*holy temple*', the born-again Christian '*shall be satisfied with the goodness*' of worshipping with fellow believers in the fellowship of Christ's church.

(VERSES 5-8) The God who answers us changes us from within. We find righteous living for Him to be '*awesome*' since we came to know Christ. We might have thought it was 'irksome' before knowing the '*God of our salvation*'. He is also the almighty God of creation: God created the universe, including this world. We see Him in the stormy and roaring '*far-off seas*'—but our mighty God can calm even them. The huge mountains were formed by His power. The '*tumult of the peoples*' is also under God's control—and already in His timetable of what will happen and when on a global scale.

Wise people '*are afraid of* [God's] *signs*' (also known as '*wonders*'). This kind of fear leads to 'godly reverence' and to people becoming wise. Psalm 111:10 says, '*The fear of the LORD is the beginning of wisdom*.' As each day dawns and each night closes worldwide, God causes His creation to '*rejoice*' across His world. (Just think of the bird choruses, for example.)

(VERSES 9-13) God abundantly supplies our needs. He waters the land. No life could flourish otherwise. Grain decorates the valleys. Many other crops grow, too. God's design is that His creation sustains all life, animal and human. Harvest comes each year in abundance: God is generous. Grass in the meadows feeds the flocks. They, in turn, feed human life. Let us join with the valleys in grateful joy and song to Him!

Our loving, caring God also gives bountiful supplies spiritually to all who are *'born again'* (John 3:3) by faith in Jesus. Thank God for: the Holy Spirit to fill, enable and guide us; the Bible, God's Heavenly bread, to feed us daily as we read it; the gift of praying—come daily to God with your 'sorry-thankyou-please' prayers; Christian fellowship in Bible studies and prayer; worship together on the Lord's day; and service to do for Him in helping others come to know Him and follow Him each day in obedience.

If the *'valleys. . . are covered with grain'* and if *'they shout for joy, they also sing'*, then how much more should those sing for joy who have come personally to know the Lord Jesus Christ, His forgiveness, His eternal life, His Word the Bible, His privilege of prayer, and His Christian family of believers in Him with whom to share worship on the Lord's Day, and fellowship and friendship throughout the week? And our rejoicing will go on unhindered and perfected in Heaven itself.

Psalm 66—How God can change you?

To the Chief Musician. A Song. A Psalm.
1Make a joyful shout to God, all the earth!
2Sing out the honor of His name;
Make His praise glorious.
3Say to God,
"How awesome are Your works!
Through the greatness of Your power
Your enemies shall submit themselves to You.
4All the earth shall worship You
And sing praises to You;
They shall sing praises to Your name." Selah

5Come and see the works of God;
He is awesome in His doing toward the sons of men.
6He turned the sea into dry land;
They went through the river on foot.
There we will rejoice in Him.
7He rules by His power forever;
His eyes observe the nations;
Do not let the rebellious exalt themselves. Selah

8Oh, bless our God, you peoples!
And make the voice of His praise to be heard,
9Who keeps our soul among the living,
And does not allow our feet to be moved.
10For You, O God, have tested us;
You have refined us as silver is refined.
11You brought us into the net;
You laid affliction on our backs.
12You have caused men to ride over our heads;
We went through fire and through water;
But You brought us out to rich fulfillment.

13I will go into Your house with burnt offerings;
I will pay You my vows,
14Which my lips have uttered
And my mouth has spoken when I was in trouble.
15I will offer You burnt sacrifices of fat animals,
With the sweet aroma of rams;
I will offer bulls with goats. Selah

16Come and hear, all you who fear God,
And I will declare what He has done for my soul.
17I cried to Him with my mouth,
And He was extolled with my tongue.
18If I regard iniquity in my heart,
The Lord will not hear.
19But certainly God has heard me;
He has attended to the voice of my prayer.

[20]Blessed be God,
Who has not turned away my prayer,
Nor His mercy from me!

(Verses 1-4) How each person who knows God worships Him will vary in detail from person to person. But below are some reasons for and ways all of us to praise God.

- Joyful shouts from '*all the earth*'.
- Sing to the '*honor of His name*'.
- Appreciate God's '*awesome*' deeds'.
- See the '*greatness of* '[His] *power*'—it makes God's '*enemies*' '*submit*'.
- '*Worship*' and '*sing praises*' to God and to His '*name*'. This is what '*all the earth*' does naturally. We have more reason to do so as those cleansed from our sins and indwelled by the living Saviour!

(Verses 5-7) God is to be praised for the miraculous way He cared for His people, including causing them to cross on dry land through both the Red Sea to escape from Egypt and the River Jordan to enter the Promised Land of Canaan. Also, in mind are His constant watchfulness over '*the nations*' and His desire to prevent rebels to be exalted.

(Verses 8-12) God is also to be praised for preserving the lives of His people and for stopping their feet from slipping. Hard as it was, He tested and refined His people. But He let them taste the refining effects of prison, burdensome slavery and being under hard taskmasters. Despite hard testing, '*through fire and water*', God brought His people to '*a place of abundance*'. Every person who asks to be saved from sin's penalty and power by trusting the Lord Jesus Christ will at times have trials and feel overwhelmed. But the Bible says that God '*who has begun a good work in you will complete it until the day of Christ Jesus*' (Philippians 1:6). If you have come to know Jesus, it is because God showed you your sin, guilt and need of forgiveness and a new life in Christ. Jesus paid the penalty for all your sins when He was nailed to Calvary's cross bearing your sin in your place. When you repented and trusted Jesus, He came into your life by the Holy Spirit. So, He has '*begun a good work*' in you which He will complete. But you do have eternal life already!

(VERSES 13-15) Gratefully, the psalmist gives to God Old Testament sacrifices at this time. This was before the Lord Jesus came to earth as a Man to save us. Today, you are required to give Him your heart, your love and your loyalty.

(VERSES 16-20) If you are His, what change does all this make? You will feel you must tell others of your faith in Christ and *'what He has done for my soul'*. You will cry to Him in prayer and praise; your sin barrier has been broken down! God will now hear your prayers. But beware—God will only hear you from your heart, as one of His followers, if I you are not regarding *'iniquity in* [your] *heart'*. If you harbour sin in your heart, God will not hear you. But you can enjoy that wonderful certainty of knowing that God has heard you, accepts your prayer because you are in Christ and will always treat you with His loving mercy both now and for ever!

Psalm 67—Sowing and reaping

To the Chief Musician. On stringed instruments. A Psalm. A Song.
1 God be merciful to us and bless us,
And cause His face to shine upon us, Selah
2 That Your way may be known on earth,
Your salvation among all nations.

3 Let the peoples praise You, O God;
Let all the peoples praise You.
4 Oh, let the nations be glad and sing for joy!
For You shall judge the people righteously,
And govern the nations on earth. Selah

5 Let the peoples praise You, O God;
Let all the peoples praise You.
6 Then the earth shall yield her increase;
God, our own God, shall bless us.
7 God shall bless us,
And all the ends of the earth shall fear Him.

(VERSES 1-2) Psalm 67 is lovely, simple and short. It is no less God's Word than Psalm 119 (176 verses) or the next Psalm 68 (35 verses). Sometimes it is great to get your teeth into a long psalm. Other times those same key blessings shine through a short psalm. Someone asked an Indian fakir ('a Hindu holy man'—Collins Dictionary) how he could lie on a bed of sharp nails. He said it was easier than lying on a few nails because they stuck in his flesh more than when many nails shared his weight! May the fewer points in this psalm, and other short ones, 'stick in' your mind, heart and life.

The psalmist asks several things in this psalm: he starts by simply asking God to '*be merciful to us and bless us*' and he asks for God to smile on them. God always answers such humble requests for pardon, help and blessing. The psalmist asks his fellow worshipers to stop and think about that—that is what '*Selah*' means. But his reason is selfless and God-honouring: he wants to be so close to God that he can effectively make God's '*way*' known '*on earth*' and God's 'salvation *among all nations*'. D L Moody, the godly, much-used, American evangelist, said, 'You cannot lead someone closer to Christ than you are yourself.' If I want to see others trusting Christ and following Him, I need to live close to Him myself. That means I pray to and live for Him, as well as preach and teach His Word. I should be concerned to see those living near me and others in different countries coming to Christ. Jesus died for all on that cross and will forgive any who turn from sins and trust Him, believing that He shed His blood to bear and pay for their sins. A close walk with Christ means I have a global concern for the gospel to be known widely—to all people however different. God loves them all!

(VERSES 3-5) Look at what the psalmist asks equally for '*all the peoples*' and for the '*nations of the earth*', whatever their race, colour or background. He longs that God is praised, that they become so '*glad*' that they '*sing for joy*', and that they know God is judging them '*righteously*' and governing them '*on earth*'. God wants exactly the same blessings for you, whoever you are and whatever you have done. Turn from your sin, put your trust in Jesus, and it will begin to 'happen'!

(VERSES 6-7) He is convinced that because God is who He is (and remember, He said in 1 Samuel 2:30, '*Those who honor me I will honor*'). God's guaranteed blessings to them will include a high-yield harvest. That naturally refers to grain, but it also applies to life. Galatians 6:7-8 says, '*Whatever a man sow, that he will also reap. . . he who sows to the [Holy] Spirit, will of the Spirit will reap everlasting life*.' Be faithful to the Saviour in whom you believe and '*sow*' the Word of God (the Bible) in your own and in others' lives. He will bless you with a high-yield 'spiritual' harvest. Christians and churches worldwide, who believe in God's Word, the Bible, live it out, and teach it simply, will be blessed, whatever their denomination or name. Across the world many will '*fear Him*' with that godly fear that leads to their coming to Christ, following in His steps, and being a great blessing to many other people.

Psalm 68—The gospel pictured long ago

To the Chief Musician. A Psalm of David. A Song.
1Let God arise,
Let His enemies be scattered;
Let those also who hate Him flee before Him.
2As smoke is driven away,
So drive them away;
As wax melts before the fire,
So let the wicked perish at the presence of God.
3But let the righteous be glad;
Let them rejoice before God;
Yes, let them rejoice exceedingly.

4Sing to God, sing praises to His name;
Extol Him who rides on the clouds,
By His name Yah,
And rejoice before Him.

5A father of the fatherless, a defender of widows,
Is God in His holy habitation.
6God sets the solitary in families;
He brings out those who are bound into prosperity;
But the rebellious dwell in a dry land.

7O God, when You went out before Your people,
When You marched through the wilderness, Selah
8The earth shook;
The heavens also dropped rain at the presence of God;
Sinai itself was moved at the presence of God, the God of Israel.
9You, O God, sent a plentiful rain,
Whereby You confirmed Your inheritance,
When it was weary.
10Your congregation dwelt in it;
You, O God, provided from Your goodness for the poor.

11The Lord gave the word;
Great was the company of those who proclaimed it:
12"Kings of armies flee, they flee,
And she who remains at home divides the spoil.
13Though you lie down among the sheepfolds,
You will be like the wings of a dove covered with silver,
And her feathers with yellow gold."
14When the Almighty scattered kings in it,
It was white as snow in Zalmon.

15A mountain of God is the mountain of Bashan;
A mountain of many peaks is the mountain of Bashan.
16Why do you fume with envy, you mountains of many peaks?
This is the mountain which God desires to dwell in;
Yes, the LORD will dwell in it forever.

17The chariots of God are twenty thousand,
Even thousands of thousands;
The LORD is among them as in Sinai, in the Holy Place.
18You have ascended on high,
You have led captivity captive;
You have received gifts among men,
Even from the rebellious,
That the LORD God might dwell there.

19Blessed be the Lord,
Who daily loads us with benefits,
The God of our salvation! Selah
20Our God is the God of salvation;
And to God the Lord belong escapes from death.

21But God will wound the head of His enemies,
The hairy scalp of the one who still goes on in his trespasses.
22The Lord said, "I will bring back from Bashan,
I will bring them back from the depths of the sea,
23That your foot may crush them in blood,
And the tongues of your dogs may have their portion from your enemies."

24They have seen Your procession, O God,
The procession of my God, my King, into the sanctuary.
25The singers went before, the players on instruments followed after;
Among them were the maidens playing timbrels.
26Bless God in the congregations,
The Lord, from the fountain of Israel.
27There is little Benjamin, their leader,
The princes of Judah and their company,
The princes of Zebulun and the princes of Naphtali.

28Your God has commanded your strength;
Strengthen, O God, what You have done for us.
29Because of Your temple at Jerusalem,
Kings will bring presents to You.
30Rebuke the beasts of the reeds,
The herd of bulls with the calves of the peoples,
Till everyone submits himself with pieces of silver.
Scatter the peoples who delight in war.
31Envoys will come out of Egypt;
Ethiopia will quickly stretch out her hands to God.

32Sing to God, you kingdoms of the earth;
Oh, sing praises to the Lord, Selah
33To Him who rides on the heaven of heavens, which were of old!
Indeed, He sends out His voice, a mighty voice.
34Ascribe strength to God;
His excellence is over Israel,
And His strength is in the clouds.
35O God, You are more awesome than Your holy places.

The God of Israel is He who gives strength and power to His people.

Blessed be God!

(VERSES 1-6) When we see God *'arise'* we may well say, *'Let His enemies be scattered.'* Such is God's power, strength and authority that those who hate Him are as smoke driven away, or wax melted by fire. The wicked will perish at His presence, a perishing that the Bible teaches involves eternal punishment in Hell (John 3:36; Romans 1:18). Those counted *'righteous'* by faith in Christ will be glad personally and *'rejoice before God'* eternally and *'exceedingly'*. It is not hard to see why we must *'sing to God'*, praise His name and *'extol Him who rides on the clouds' by His name YAH* (or *'Yahweh'* or *'Jehovah'* or *'LORD'*). He cares for and defends orphans and widows, builds families for the otherwise *'solitary'* and brings out sad prisoners from *'bounds'* into spiritual *'prosperity'*. (We are all prisoners of sin (John 8:34) and need that liberty of spirit that Christ gives to those who come to know Him and are thereby made *'free indeed'* (John 8:36). Sinful rebels face physical drought, and never-ending spiritual drought also.)

(VERSES 7-10) Earthquakes and rainstorms proclaim Him as He goes out with and refreshes His weary people in the wilderness. The poor receive His bounty. Today, He renews the strength of those who wait on Him (Isaiah 40:31). Mount Sinai itself shakes at the presence of God.

(VERSES 11-14) God scatters kings and armies when He gives *'the word'*, proclaimed by a great company. He enriches people from the spoil taken from His foes. He helps us fight against temptation and sin.

(VERSES 15-18) Rugged enemy mountains do not compare with God's mountain, Sinai, where God reigns as if He was controlling a mighty chariot army. Verse 18 pictures the crucified-and-risen Christ's ascension to Heaven (see Ephesians 4:8).

(VERSES 19-20) The gospel is pictured here. The crucified Christ is both the *'God of our salvation'* and *'the God of salvation'*. Not only has He planned in general the wonderful message of forgiveness for sins, the gift of eternal life, and the escape from eternal Hell to eternal Heaven but each of us who has trusted Him can also say and mean, 'He has borne all my sins and my judgment and delivered me personally from death and Hell.' As well as bearing all the burden of sin and judgment that we deserve, He helps us each day by carrying our burdens of care, too.

(VERSES 21-27) God will crush His foes. He will also defeat our foes, as explained in 1 John 2:16: *'all that is in the world—the lust of the flesh, the lust of the eyes, and the pride of life'*. God's wrath is also on unrepentant sinners, while God's praising people rejoice in Heaven. Some of those praising God are named here. Each saved person's name is written in *'the Lamb's book of life'* (Revelation 21:27).

(VERSES 28-35) David closes this long psalm by praising God for:

- His strength and power. They still help now by the Holy Spirit's living in believers.
- His presence is '*awesome*' in Jerusalem's temple's sanctuary. Any sinner who trusts in Christ becomes the '*Temple of the Holy Spirit*', who lives in him (1 Corinthians 6:19). The Holy Spirit helps David, and you and me, to become more holy and to live changed lives.
- He rebukes warring enemy nations. *'The beasts of the reeds'*—namely the crocodile and hippopotamus—symbolise Egypt. Egypt offers Israel tribute money to beg for peace. So does Ethiopia.
- Worldwide, finally, He will be praised. You will praise Him in Heaven, if—and only if—you know Christ as your Lord and Saviour.
- He rules all nature and the skies He made.
- He strengthens His people, then and now! Our God is indeed '*blessed*' and also a great blesser of those who trust Him!

Psalm 69—Loving your bitter enemies

To the Chief Musician. Set to "The Lilies." A Psalm of David.
1Save me, O God!
For the waters have come up to my neck.
2I sink in deep mire,
Where there is no standing;
I have come into deep waters,
Where the floods overflow me.
3I am weary with my crying;
My throat is dry;
My eyes fail while I wait for my God.

4Those who hate me without a cause
Are more than the hairs of my head;
They are mighty who would destroy me,
Being my enemies wrongfully;
Though I have stolen nothing,
I still must restore it.

5O God, You know my foolishness;
And my sins are not hidden from You.
6Let not those who wait for You, O Lord GOD of hosts, be ashamed because of me;
Let not those who seek You be confounded because of me, O God of Israel.
7Because for Your sake I have borne reproach;
Shame has covered my face.
8I have become a stranger to my brothers,
And an alien to my mother's children;
9Because zeal for Your house has eaten me up,
And the reproaches of those who reproach You have fallen on me.
10When I wept and chastened my soul with fasting,
That became my reproach.
11I also made sackcloth my garment;
I became a byword to them.
12Those who sit in the gate speak against me,
And I am the song of the drunkards.

13But as for me, my prayer is to You,
O LORD, in the acceptable time;
O God, in the multitude of Your mercy,
Hear me in the truth of Your salvation.
14Deliver me out of the mire,
And let me not sink;
Let me be delivered from those who hate me,
And out of the deep waters.
15Let not the floodwater overflow me,
Nor let the deep swallow me up;
And let not the pit shut its mouth on me.

16Hear me, O LORD, for Your lovingkindness is good;

Turn to me according to the multitude of Your tender mercies.
17 And do not hide Your face from Your servant,
For I am in trouble;
Hear me speedily.
18 Draw near to my soul, and redeem it;
Deliver me because of my enemies.

19 You know my reproach, my shame, and my dishonor;
My adversaries are all before You.
20 Reproach has broken my heart,
And I am full of heaviness;
I looked for someone to take pity, but there was none;
And for comforters, but I found none.
21 They also gave me gall for my food,
And for my thirst they gave me vinegar to drink.

22 Let their table become a snare before them,
And their well-being a trap.
23 Let their eyes be darkened, so that they do not see;
And make their loins shake continually.
24 Pour out Your indignation upon them,
And let Your wrathful anger take hold of them.
25 Let their dwelling place be desolate;
Let no one live in their tents.
26 For they persecute the ones You have struck,
And talk of the grief of those You have wounded.
27 Add iniquity to their iniquity,
And let them not come into Your righteousness.
28 Let them be blotted out of the book of the living,
And not be written with the righteous.

29 But I am poor and sorrowful;
Let Your salvation, O God, set me up on high.
30 I will praise the name of God with a song,
And will magnify Him with thanksgiving.
31 This also shall please the LORD better than an ox or bull,
Which has horns and hooves.
32 The humble shall see this and be glad;
And you who seek God, your hearts shall live.
33 For the LORD hears the poor,
And does not despise His prisoners.

34 Let heaven and earth praise Him,
The seas and everything that moves in them.
35 For God will save Zion
And build the cities of Judah,
That they may dwell there and possess it.
36 Also, the descendants of His servants shall inherit it,
And those who love His name shall dwell in it.

❖

(VERSES 1-4) David is being picked on and maligned without cause by countless enemies. He feels he is out of his depth and drowning. Falsely accused of theft, it seems that he feels he must restore what he had never taken anyhow, purely as a good-will token. If you have ever been picked on, you know how he feels. But he very wisely shares it with God. He asks God to save him.

(VERSES 5-6) David has sinned in the past, confessed it, and been forgiven by God. Read and pray through Psalm 51. We, too, have sinned, but we are forgiven if we confess our sins to God, believe Jesus was punished in our place for them, and trust Him. David's concern now is the apparently bad witness to others who seek God but who are deceived into thinking David is a thief. Keen Christians try to be a good example.

(VERSES 7-12) David is wrongly and unjustly scorned, shamed, shunned, insulted and mocked by many, and he is the song of drunkards. Imagine what that all does to the heart of a man who wants to put God first, and follow Him.,

(VERSES 13-29) Troubled David shares his heart with God in real prayer. He seeks God's mercy, deliverance, and salvation. Do you do that when troubled or worried? Why not read slowly though these challenging verses on prayer, and make them your own prayers?

Although David then prays for God to judge his foes, he does commit them to God, rather than retaliate. Born-again sinners do that and ask for their foes to repent, trust in Jesus, and so be blessed and changed by God. Is this thought new to you? Jesus said, '*Love your enemies, bless those who curse you, do good to those who hate you, and pray for those who despitefully use you and persecute you, that you may be sons of your Father in Heaven.*' This way of living is often missing in our lost world. It comes only by God's grace and enabling when Jesus is your Lord and Saviour (Matthew 5:44-45).

(VERSES 30-36) Here is a lesson for us all! David is so confident in God, despite his anguish caused by others, that he concludes by praising and worshipping God and encouraging others to do so! See how encouraging it is to live for Christ when your heart is set to praise Him.

Psalm 70—Small psalm but big issues

To the Chief Musician. A Psalm of David. To bring to remembrance.
1Make haste, O God, to deliver me!
Make haste to help me, O LORD!

2Let them be ashamed and confounded
Who seek my life;
Let them be turned back and confused
Who desire my hurt.
3Let them be turned back because of their shame,
Who say, "Aha, aha!"

4Let all those who seek You rejoice and be glad in You;
And let those who love Your salvation say continually,
"Let God be magnified!"

5But I am poor and needy;
Make haste to me, O God!
You are my help and my deliverer;
O LORD, do not delay.

❖

(VERSE 1) David starts by asking God for four necessary things in just one verse.

FIRST, he asks God to *'Make haste.'* Just as you need an urgent response from the Fire Brigade, if your house is on fire, David sees the urgency of the need for God graciously to answer him.

SECOND, he asks God to *'deliver'* (or *'save'*) him. Yet again he has bitter enemies who would like to see him dead. When a sinner comes to Christ as Saviour, he is saved from sin's penalty for breaking God's laws, sin's dominating power over him now, and sin's punishment in Hell. It is always very urgent to be saved. In 2 Corinthians 6:2 we read, *'Now is the accepted time; behold, now is the day of salvation.'* It will be too late tomorrow for some; life is short and uncertain. Act urgently where salvation is under consideration.

THIRD, he again asks God to *'make haste'*. When Christ enters your life, He does so at the immediate point of faith through His indwelling Holy Spirit. He then wants us each day to be *'being filled with the Spirit'* (that is the tense if the verb in Ephesians 5:18). It is continuous but immediate.

FOURTH, he needs God's presence in his life now so God can *'help'* him right now. If you believe that Jesus died, bearing your sins to atone for those sins on the cross, and rose again to be your living

Saviour, you must reckon on His risen power and you can trust His risen life to enable Him to help you. You will be able to say and know, '*The Lord is my helper; I will not fear. What can man do to me?*" (Hebrews 13:6).

(VERSES 2-3) David's prayer here about his enemies is not vindictive. He simply asks God to shame, confuse, disgrace and turn back all their efforts against him, and bring them to nothing. They mock him as they desire his ruin and even seek his death. Until God humbles them, they will probably never repent and turn to Him anyway.

(VERSE 4) David asks, in comparison, for God to answer the prayers of every person who truly seeks Him. This reminds us of what Jesus taught us to pray in Matthew 7:7-8. '*Ask, and it will be given to you; seek, and you will find; knock, and it will be opened to you. For everyone who asks receives, and he who seeks finds, and to him who knocks it will be opened.*' If you trust Christ and learn to ask, seek and knock, in prayer, God will answer you. Can you see why every person who seeks God—with such a great set of promises to encourage him or her—can '*rejoice and be glad in* [God]'? As each new Christian goes on with Christ, through daily studying the Bible and praying to Him, he will come to '*love* [His] *salvation*' and '*say continually, "Let God be magnified"*'. A true sign of real conversion to the Lord Jesus Christ is that the person who has been saved will want God to be glorified and magnified. God is too small in the thoughts of too many people. We should be like clean and strong magnifying glasses, bringing Him back up to His right size in the minds of men. We must seek to lift Him up to others, both by how we now live, and also by what we now say.

(VERSE 5) But despite God's great love, grace and power, David still sees himself as a poor, needy and weak sinner. But with the Lord as his Saviour, he knows that God will answer him. So, he renews his prayer to God to '*make haste*' to him. He reminds God that, '*You are my Help and my Deliverer.*' But he still asks God not to delay! You can know God in a relationship like that through Christ.

Psalm 71—In youth and in old age

1In You, O LORD, I put my trust;
Let me never be put to shame.
2Deliver me in Your righteousness, and cause me to escape;
Incline Your ear to me, and save me.
3Be my strong refuge,
To which I may resort continually;
You have given the commandment to save me,
For You are my rock and my fortress.

4Deliver me, O my God, out of the hand of the wicked,
Out of the hand of the unrighteous and cruel man.
5For You are my hope, O Lord GOD;
You are my trust from my youth.
6By You I have been upheld from birth;
You are He who took me out of my mother's womb.
My praise shall be continually of You.

7I have become as a wonder to many,
But You are my strong refuge.
8Let my mouth be filled with Your praise
And with Your glory all the day.

9Do not cast me off in the time of old age;
Do not forsake me when my strength fails.
10For my enemies speak against me;
And those who lie in wait for my life take counsel together,
11Saying, "God has forsaken him;
Pursue and take him, for there is none to deliver him."

12O God, do not be far from me;
O my God, make haste to help me!
13Let them be confounded and consumed
Who are adversaries of my life;
Let them be covered with reproach and dishonor
Who seek my hurt.

14But I will hope continually,
And will praise You yet more and more.
15My mouth shall tell of Your righteousness
And Your salvation all the day,
For I do not know their limits.
16I will go in the strength of the LORD God;
I will make mention of Your righteousness, of Yours only.

17O God, You have taught me from my youth;
And to this day I declare Your wondrous works.
18Now also when I am old and grayheaded,
O God, do not forsake me,
Until I declare Your strength to this generation,

Your power to everyone who is to come.

19 Also Your righteousness, O God, is very high,
You who have done great things;
O God, who is like You?
20 You, who have shown me great and severe troubles,
Shall revive me again,
And bring me up again from the depths of the earth.
21 You shall increase my greatness,
And comfort me on every side.

22 Also with the lute I will praise You—
And Your faithfulness, O my God!
To You I will sing with the harp,
O Holy One of Israel.
23 My lips shall greatly rejoice when I sing to You,
And my soul, which You have redeemed.
24 My tongue also shall talk of Your righteousness all the day long;
For they are confounded,
For they are brought to shame
Who seek my hurt.

(VERSES 1-8) This psalm is the psalmist's personal prayer to his LORD from start to end. He reminds God that his trust has been in Him right up to now, from birth and through youth. He still asks his Sovereign LORD to keep him from shame, to deliver him in God's '*righteousness*', and to cause him to '*escape*' as He listens to David's prayer and saves him. He wants the LORD to continue to be his ever-available '*strong refuge*', to save him and deliver him from wicked and cruel men. His hope is in God and has been since birth and throughout his youth. He is determined to always praise God and declare His '*glory all day long*'. He does not merely want to be delivered by God from his foes; he asks God to '*deliver me in your righteousness*'. Note that he seeks more than protection and survival; he wants to live a godly and holy life conforming to God's righteousness. It is a sure mark of conversion to Christ that the person trusting the Lord Jesus Christ as Saviour wants to '*pursue holiness without which no one will see the Lord*' (Hebrews 12:14). Do you know Christ like that? Are you seeking to live a holy life?

(VERSES 9-13) Faced with coming old age and increasing weakness, the psalmist asks God not to '*cast off*' or '*forsake*' him '*in the time if old age*' and when his '*strength fails*'. His enemies conspire to kill him and spread the lie that God has forsaken him. Based on that, they plan to '*pursue and take him*'. They claim '*there is none to deliver him'*, but no one who trusts in God's Word need even ask God not to forsake him or her if their trust is in the Lord Jesus Christ. He who bore your sins and punishment on the cross rose again from the dead and entered your life when you repented of sin and received Him as Saviour is in His relationship with you for ever! God's promise is *'I will never leave you nor forsake you'* (Hebrews 13:5), fulfilling the Old Testament promise (Deuteronomy 31:6) *'Be strong and of good courage, do not fear nor be afraid of them; for the* LORD *your God, He is the One who goes with you. He will not leave you nor forsake you.'* In Matthew 28:20, Jesus assures His disciples, *'I am with you always, even to the end of the age.'* God the Son, the Lord Jesus, cannot and will not break His word. David's requests for God's nearness, speed to help him, and confusion and victory over his enemies will definitely be granted! So will your requests in your spiritual life and battles for Christ.

(VERSES 14-24) David promises his LORD God that he will live in the *'strength'* given him to tell of God's unique *'righteousness'* and *'salvation'*. This has been how he has lived both as a youth and in old age, so he can reach the next generation with God's message of forgiveness. He knows that his Lord who *'has done great things'* will *'revive'*, lift up, and *'comfort* [him] *on every side'*. That is why the *'greatness'* of King David will be *'increased on every side'*.

If you know Christ as your Saviour, pray for the same attitude of gratitude and determination to share, now and in old age, God's word and His gospel of forgiveness with many people. After all,

There is only one thing matters
in this passing world of sin,
That our lives should tell for Jesus:
be of some account for Him.

David is an allrounder—and so should all be who have been *'born again'*. He is not only into living for God and sharing His message with others; he will sing and play for God, rejoice in Him, and talk about His *'righteousness all day long'* in the spirit of true worship.

Psalm 72—The reign of the King's Son

A Psalm of Solomon.
1Give the king Your judgments, O God,
And Your righteousness to the king's Son.
2He will judge Your people with righteousness,
And Your poor with justice.
3The mountains will bring peace to the people,
And the little hills, by righteousness.
4He will bring justice to the poor of the people;
He will save the children of the needy,
And will break in pieces the oppressor.

5They shall fear You
As long as the sun and moon endure,
Throughout all generations.
6He shall come down like rain upon the grass before mowing,
Like showers that water the earth.
7In His days the righteous shall flourish,
And abundance of peace,
Until the moon is no more.

8He shall have dominion also from sea to sea,
And from the River to the ends of the earth.
9Those who dwell in the wilderness will bow before Him,
And His enemies will lick the dust.
10The kings of Tarshish and of the isles
Will bring presents;
The kings of Sheba and Seba
Will offer gifts.
11Yes, all kings shall fall down before Him;
All nations shall serve Him.

12For He will deliver the needy when he cries,
The poor also, and him who has no helper.
13He will spare the poor and needy,
And will save the souls of the needy.
14He will redeem their life from oppression and violence;
And precious shall be their blood in His sight.

15And He shall live;
And the gold of Sheba will be given to Him;
Prayer also will be made for Him continually,
And daily He shall be praised.

16There will be an abundance of grain in the earth,
On the top of the mountains;
Its fruit shall wave like Lebanon;
And those of the city shall flourish like grass of the earth.

17His name shall endure forever;

His name shall continue as long as the sun.
And men shall be blessed in Him;
All nations shall call Him blessed.

18Blessed be the LORD God, the God of Israel,
Who only does wondrous things!
19And blessed be His glorious name forever!
And let the whole earth be filled with His glory.
Amen and Amen.

20The prayers of David the son of Jesse are ended.

(VERSES 1-4) The main application here is to King David and Solomon, *'the king's Son'*. It pictures the rule of the eternal Son of God, Jesus, as Messiah. David's line and Messiah's rule are often linked. Righteous judgment, justice, and defence from attacks for the afflicted, help for the needy, and crushing the oppressor result. A righteous and prosperous world come from Messiah's reign, pictured by Israel's prospering under Solomon.

(VERSES 5-11) When Jesus reigns for ever, He will cause the same blessings, spiritually and physically, as Solomon gives Israel physically. It will be a time of refreshing, righteousness, peace, flourishing, prosperity, and worldwide submission to Him. His enemies will fail, nations will bring Him tribute and serve Him, kings will bow down to Him and bring Him gifts. You may have little to offer Jesus; but you can give Him your heart as His throne room.

(VERSES 12-14) Jesus now delivers any who cry out to Him in prayer. He helps the afflicted and has pity on the weak and needy and saves them from death. He rescues them from violent oppression. Why? Because *'precious shall be their blood in His sight'*. Jesus also helps, takes pity on, and saves those who are needy and weak in their sins. He saves them not only from death, but from Hell itself. He does that today for any sinner who turns from sin, thanks Jesus for having taken his sin and punishment on the cross, and who cries out to Him in submission in prayer. To such people Jesus is *'precious'* (1 Peter 2:7) and so is His shed blood (1 Peter 1:9) and the Christian faith (2 Peter 1:1). Lost sinners who trust in Christ are very precious to Him, too, especially when they finally enter Heaven (Psalm 116:15.)

(VERSES 15-16) Solomon lives a long life. The Lord Jesus lives for ever! He is worthy of our most valuable gifts and prayers. He is to be prayed to *'continually'* and *'praised'* each day. He makes the earth flourish and be fruitful in the city and even on the mountain top.

(VERSES 17-20) Consider these wonderful truths about our triune God: God the Father, God the Son, and God the Holy Spirit, in three Persons but just one God.

- His glorious name endures *'forever'* in Heaven and will *'continue as long as the sun'* on earth.
- He blesses all *'men'* and *'nations'* who call on Him.
- He reigns as *'LORD'*; He is in control.
- He does *'wondrous things'*.
- His *'glory'* will fill the world.

Psalm 73—A real problem solved

A Psalm of Asaph.
1Truly God is good to Israel,
To such as are pure in heart.
2But as for me, my feet had almost stumbled;
My steps had nearly slipped.
3For I was envious of the boastful,
When I saw the prosperity of the wicked.

4For there are no pangs in their death,
But their strength is firm.
5They are not in trouble as other men,
Nor are they plagued like other men.
6Therefore pride serves as their necklace;
Violence covers them like a garment.
7Their eyes bulge with abundance;
They have more than heart could wish.
8They scoff and speak wickedly concerning oppression;
They speak loftily.
9They set their mouth against the heavens,
And their tongue walks through the earth.

10Therefore his people return here,
And waters of a full cup are drained by them.
11And they say, "How does God know?
And is there knowledge in the Most High?"
12Behold, these are the ungodly,
Who are always at ease;
They increase in riches.
13Surely I have cleansed my heart in vain,
And washed my hands in innocence.
14For all day long I have been plagued,
And chastened every morning.

15If I had said, "I will speak thus,"
Behold, I would have been untrue to the generation of Your children.
16When I thought how to understand this,
It was too painful for me—
17Until I went into the sanctuary of God;
Then I understood their end.

18Surely You set them in slippery places;
You cast them down to destruction.
19Oh, how they are brought to desolation, as in a moment!
They are utterly consumed with terrors.
20As a dream when one awakes,
So, Lord, when You awake,
You shall despise their image.

21Thus my heart was grieved,

And I was vexed in my mind.
[22]I was so foolish and ignorant;
I was like a beast before You.
[23]Nevertheless I am continually with You;
You hold me by my right hand.
[24]You will guide me with Your counsel,
And afterward receive me to glory.

[25]Whom have I in heaven but You?
And there is none upon earth that I desire besides You.
[26]My flesh and my heart fail;
But God is the strength of my heart and my portion forever.

[27]For indeed, those who are far from You shall perish;
You have destroyed all those who desert You for harlotry.
[28]But it is good for me to draw near to God;
I have put my trust in the Lord GOD,
That I may declare all Your works.

(VERSE 1) An unshakable principle of God, and thus of the Bible, is that '*God is good, to Israel, to such as are pure in heart.*' Israel is God's special physical people. Also, all those trusting Christ as personal Saviour are His spiritual Israel now. Jews must trust Christ to be saved. If they do, they are then '*the Israel of God*' in both senses (Galatians 6:16). To be '*pure in heart*' you must confess the wickedness of your heart to God, thank Jesus that all your sin was borne and paid for by Him when He was nailed to the cross for you, repent from your sin, and ask Jesus to cleanse your heart and take control of it through His indwelling Holy Spirit. Is that true of you? It can be.

(VERSES 2-16) Asaph's problem here is shared by many today. Briefly, why do the wicked seem to prosper but godly folk suffer? Consider verses 2 to 16 carefully to see what a problem it can be to a real Christian to see so many aspects of the lives who have rejected or neglected putting their faith in Jesus Christ, and yet seem to do well; at the same time there are often keen and selfless Christians who seem to be having a hard and an 'unfair' time. Many unsaved people are prosperous, carefree, healthy, not burdened, proud, violent, sin-hardened, evil-minded, hypocritical in speech, boasting, and openly irreverent about God. Asaph puts his case to God as a suffering godly man. He could not 'get it' until. . .

(VERSES 17-20) Until what? How does Asaph express himself? '*Until I went into the sanctuary of God; Then I understood their end.*' He entered God's sanctuary—the place of prayer, worship and God's Word—and then *he understood their final destiny.* In Heaven, everything that Christians have suffered, however severe, seems light and worth it by comparison. 2 Corinthians 4:17 says, *'For our light affliction, which is but for a moment, is working for us a far more exceeding and eternal weight of glory.'* In Hell, the wicked peoples' most pleasing things they had enjoyed in life, however valuable and pleasing, are nothing compared to Hell's eternal and inescapable punishment on their sins. Consider this from a long-term perspective, very long-term—in fact, for ever!

(VERSES 21-28) Asaph admits that his *'grieved'* heart and *'vexed'* mind were *'foolish and ignorant'.* He was like a *'beast'* before God. But when he thinks about the *'sanctuary'*, the character of God, and the eternality of Heaven and of Hell, he sees sense and truth. God is always with him, guides him now and will take him into Heaven's glory to be with Him. When he weakens and when He dies, *'God is the strength of* [his] *heart and* [his] *portion forever'.* He belongs to God. The Sovereign LORD is his refuge.

He now knows that *'it is good for me to draw near to God.'* He recalls confidently that *'I have put my trust in the LORD God.'* From now on his purpose is to *'declare all* [God's] *works'.* He will keep telling what his Saviour God has done! God has shown him the clear answer to that awkward question that fed his doubts and grievous vexation. Why not share this with others!

Psalm 74—Carry on pleading with God

A Contemplation of Asaph.
1O God, why have You cast us off forever?
Why does Your anger smoke against the sheep of Your pasture?
2Remember Your congregation, which You have purchased of old,
The tribe of Your inheritance, which You have redeemed—
This Mount Zion where You have dwelt.
3Lift up Your feet to the perpetual desolations.
The enemy has damaged everything in the sanctuary.
4Your enemies roar in the midst of Your meeting place;
They set up their banners for signs.
5They seem like men who lift up
Axes among the thick trees.
6And now they break down its carved work, all at once,
With axes and hammers.
7They have set fire to Your sanctuary;
They have defiled the dwelling place of Your name to the ground.
8They said in their hearts,
"Let us destroy them altogether."
They have burned up all the meeting places of God in the land.

9We do not see our signs;
There is no longer any prophet;
Nor is there any among us who knows how long.
10O God, how long will the adversary reproach?
Will the enemy blaspheme Your name forever?
11Why do You withdraw Your hand, even Your right hand?
Take it out of Your bosom and destroy them.
12For God is my King from of old,
Working salvation in the midst of the earth.
13You divided the sea by Your strength;
You broke the heads of the sea serpents in the waters.
14You broke the heads of Leviathan in pieces,
And gave him as food to the people inhabiting the wilderness.
15You broke open the fountain and the flood;
You dried up mighty rivers.
16The day is Yours, the night also is Yours;
You have prepared the light and the sun.
17You have set all the borders of the earth;
You have made summer and winter.

18Remember this, that the enemy has reproached, O LORD,
And that a foolish people has blasphemed Your name.
19Oh, do not deliver the life of Your turtledove to the wild beast!
Do not forget the life of Your poor forever.
20Have respect to the covenant;
For the dark places of the earth are full of the haunts of cruelty.
21Oh, do not let the oppressed return ashamed!
Let the poor and needy praise Your name.

22 Arise, O God, plead Your own cause;
Remember how the foolish man reproaches You daily.
23 Do not forget the voice of Your enemies;
The tumult of those who rise up against You increases continually.

(VERSE 1) Asaph's first two statements might have surprised you: *'O God, why have you cast us off forever? Why does Your anger smoke against the sheep of your pasture?'* Our weakness and lack of trust can tempt us, as with the the psalmist, to think that God is not with us because we suffer unexpected difficulties or setbacks. Think of Joseph, who was sold into slavery by his jealous brothers, and went to Egypt. Years later, after some very serious further setbacks, but then as Egypt's prime minister, and with his frightened brothers grovelling to him there, he said, *'You meant evil against me, but God meant it for good, in order to bring it about as it is this day, to save people alive'* (Genesis 50:20). If you have trusted Jesus to save you, you are always in His hands and purpose. *'And we know that all things work for good to those who love God, to those who are the called according to His purpose'* (Romans 8:28). Trust Him *'whatever'*. Think long term.

(VERSES 2-11) God is asked to remember His own people, and Zion where they met in the temple to worship God. That is now in ruins, like the rest of Jerusalem. A cruel and violent invasion caused it to be axed, smashed, burned, defiled, and crushed. All the *'meeting places of God in the land'* have been burned. Now no inspired prophets speak as God commanded they should. God is mocked, His name reviled. The psalmist asks whether God will always allow this. Why does He not respond to destroy them? This seems to refer to Nebuchadnezzar's cruel invasion in 587 BC.

(VERSES 12-17) The psalmist responds well to his own questions! He concentrates on who God is and what He has done in the past in winning mighty battles, even miraculously. He is *'my King from of old, working salvation in the midst of the earth'*. Today, He still saves those who trust in Jesus and His death on the cross to take the punishment for their sins that separated them from God. Are you included? God is powerful over nature and, for example, still controls the world's water and solar systems, day and night, and throughout all seasons.

(VERSES 18-23) Asaph asks God urgently to:

- Remember that God's enemy has reproached God and blasphemed His name, and does this daily.
- Deliver His people, called here *'Your turtledove'*, from her beastlike enemy.
- Help the oppressed, poor and needy, and help them praise His name.
- Keep His covenant with His people.
- *'Rise up'* to punish His mocking foes who rise up like an increasing tumult.

Despair gives way to prayer. It often does!

Psalm 75—Thanks, praise and eternity

To the Chief Musician. Set to "Do Not Destroy." A Psalm of Asaph. A Song.
1 We give thanks to You, O God, we give thanks!
For Your wondrous works declare that Your name is near.

2 "When I choose the proper time,
I will judge uprightly.
3 The earth and all its inhabitants are dissolved;
I set up its pillars firmly. Selah

4 "I said to the boastful, 'Do not deal boastfully,'
And to the wicked, 'Do not lift up the horn.
5 Do not lift up your horn on high;
Do not speak with a stiff neck.' "

6 For exaltation comes neither from the east
Nor from the west nor from the south.
7 But God is the Judge:
He puts down one,
And exalts another.
8 For in the hand of the LORD there is a cup,
And the wine is red;
It is fully mixed, and He pours it out;
Surely its dregs shall all the wicked of the earth
Drain and drink down.

9 But I will declare forever,
I will sing praises to the God of Jacob.

10 "All the horns of the wicked I will also cut off,
But the horns of the righteous shall be exalted."

(VERSE 1) This worship song starts on the right note, by giving thanks to God. It is a good and godly habit to cultivate thanking God early on in private or public prayer. Here, the reason given for thanking God is *'for Your wondrous works declare that Your name is near'*. When anyone thinks of God's *'wondrous works'*, he uses His name to describe them. Because God has done countless and amazingly *'wondrous works'*, His name is never far away from those who know Him through faith in Christ, and rightly wish to be thankful. That is especially so since Jesus came to earth. Two early names given to our Saviour and Lord are *'JESUS'* and *'Immanuel'*. *'JESUS'* means *'He will save His people from their sins.'* 'Immanuel' means *'God with us'* (Matthew 1:21, 23). Those names remind us of the miraculous *'wondrous works'* of God becoming a man and dwelling with us and what happened on the cross and in the resurrection, when Jesus bore our sins and God's judgment on them that we deserve, and then rose from the dead to live for ever with '*the power of an endless life*' (Hebrews 7:16).

(VERSES 2-8) God's almighty power is demonstrated in many different ways. Here are some areas where His majestic and unique power and authority are seen to apply here.

- The timing of all events is God's.
- He is the supreme, righteous Judge.
- He set up the world and He literally holds it together.
- He warns all wicked and proud people that He hates their sins, boasting, and stiff-necked pride.
- He controls all men's rise and fall.
- All who do not repent of their sin and wickedness will finally drink fully His '*cup*' of wrath against their sin. That is why we all urgently need to receive Christ and make Him known so that we, and others, can be forgiven for our sins, avoid Hell, and gain Heaven.

(VERSE 9) This leads to a personal promise and resolution by Asaph that we would do well to make ours. When he says, '*I will declare forever; I will sing praises to the God of Jacob*', the word '*forever*' has two applications. Of course, it relates to Heaven where the Christian will praise God everlastingly when he will be '*with Christ which is far better*' (Philippians 1:23). But It also implies that '*I will sing praises*' now. The psalms often tell us to do that.

(VERSE 10) God says, '*All the horns of the wicked I will also cut off, but the horns of the righteous shall be exalted.*' Use of the word '*horns*' came from judging an animal's strength by its horns and how it used them in battle. Horns could be locked in combat between two animals. The strongest would win. Horns became a symbol of strength, pride and self-assertion. God says here that finally the proud will be rejected by Him, but those who are counted righteous, through humble faith in the Lord, will be exalted in Heaven.

Psalm 76—Knowing our great God

To the Chief Musician. On stringed instruments. A Psalm of Asaph. A Song.
1 In Judah God is known;
His name is great in Israel.
2 In Salem also is His tabernacle,
And His dwelling place in Zion.
3 There He broke the arrows of the bow,
The shield and sword of battle. Selah

4 You are more glorious and excellent
Than the mountains of prey.
5 The stouthearted were plundered;
They have sunk into their sleep;
And none of the mighty men have found the use of their hands.
6 At Your rebuke, O God of Jacob,
Both the chariot and horse were cast into a dead sleep.

7 You, Yourself, are to be feared;
And who may stand in Your presence
When once You are angry?
8 You caused judgment to be heard from heaven;
The earth feared and was still,
9 When God arose to judgment,
To deliver all the oppressed of the earth. Selah

10 Surely the wrath of man shall praise You;
With the remainder of wrath You shall gird Yourself.

11 Make vows to the LORD your God, and pay them;
Let all who are around Him bring presents to Him who ought to be feared.
12 He shall cut off the spirit of princes;
He is awesome to the kings of the earth.

(VERSES 1-3) Psalm 76 celebrates a famous victory (or possibly victories) that God achieved. We are not told which is in mind. Some commentators think it may refer to the battle against Sennacherib in 701 BC. He tried to besiege Jerusalem. He himself was assassinated later. God '*broke*' the enemy's weapons. Israel and Judah now worship their God who is '*known*' personally. His name is '*great*'. As the attack was against Salem (Jerusalem), the site of Zion's temple, (poetically called '*His tabernacle*', signalling God's dwelling with His people), it was there that God smashed the enemy.

Talking about *knowing God*, Jesus prayed for those who follow Him: '*Now this is eternal life: that they may know You, the only true God, and Jesus Christ, whom You have sent*' (John 17:3). He also said, *'No one comes to the Father except through Me'* (John 14:6). You can *'know'* God now only through personal trust in His eternal Son, Jesus, who bore your sins and their punishment for you on the cross, and now lives to enter the life of any man who repents and asks Christ into his life. When you *'know'* Jesus, you begin to realise how *'great'* our Triune God is.

(VERSE 4) Asaph reminds us of God's unique character. He is *'glorious and excellent'*. His glory, excellence and majestic nature makes mountains look small! Before creating the world, God showed His *'glorious and excellent'* nature and power by saying, *'Let there be light'* (Genesis 1:3) and the text adds, *'and there was light'*. He creates and controls light; He is pure light. God's glorious light is explained in John 1:4-5 as follows: *'In Him was life, and the life was the light of men. And the light shines in the darkness, and the darkness did not comprehend* [or *'overcome'*] *it.'* In John 8:12, Jesus said, *'I am the light of the world.'* Heaven needs no sun because Jesus lights it up with God's glory (Revelation 21:23). Christians are reminded that *'God is light'* and are urged to *'walk in the light'* (1 John 1: 5-7). That is how His glory shines out through every sinner who comes to Christ.

(VERSES 5-10) These verses give details of how God overwhelmed the enemy. He is to be feared. When He is angry, as He is with sin, no one can stand before Him. Only if we are in Christ can we be forgiven and accepted. When God works His judgment, that is an end to the matter. His foes fear and are quiet. Although all Christians would like to see more and more people getting saved by faith in Christ, in some ways the fact that God's wrath is poured out on those who will not turn from their sins to trust in Him wholeheartedly demonstrates God's perfect holiness which is to be praised.

Never forget that because Jesus bore that wrath on the cross for those who would turn their backs on their sins, He is more than willing to show them mercy as guilty sinners. These verses show God as Judge and as Saviour. If we do not know Him as Saviour, we will meet Him, and His wrath on our sin, as Judge. 2 Peter 3:9 says that God *is 'longsuffering toward us, not willing that any should perish but that all should come to repentance'*.

(VERSES 11-12) Our vows today should centre on trusting, following and obeying our Lord and Saviour, by His strength and grace, and to live for Him. We should fulfil them and give Him our all. The '*presents*' He wants us to bring Him in godly fear are our hearts. God says to every '*born-again*' child of His, '*My son, give me your heart*' (Proverbs 23:26). The world's kings and rulers will be judged and fear our '*awesome*' God, one day. We need to grasp that, '*The fear of the* LORD *is the beginning of wisdom*' (Proverbs 9:10).

Psalm 77—When prayer seems empty

To the Chief Musician. To Jeduthun. A Psalm of Asaph.
1I cried out to God with my voice—
To God with my voice;
And He gave ear to me.
2In the day of my trouble I sought the Lord;
My hand was stretched out in the night without ceasing;
My soul refused to be comforted.
3I remembered God, and was troubled;
I complained, and my spirit was overwhelmed. Selah

4You hold my eyelids open;
I am so troubled that I cannot speak.
5I have considered the days of old,
The years of ancient times.
6I call to remembrance my song in the night;
I meditate within my heart,
And my spirit makes diligent search.

7Will the Lord cast off forever?
And will He be favorable no more?
8Has His mercy ceased forever?
Has His promise failed forevermore?
9Has God forgotten to be gracious?
Has He in anger shut up His tender mercies? Selah

10And I said, "This is my anguish;
But I will remember the years of the right hand of the Most High."
11I will remember the works of the LORD;
Surely I will remember Your wonders of old.
12I will also meditate on all Your work,
And talk of Your deeds.
13Your way, O God, is in the sanctuary;
Who is so great a God as our God?
14You are the God who does wonders;
You have declared Your strength among the peoples.
15You have with Your arm redeemed Your people,
The sons of Jacob and Joseph. Selah

16The waters saw You, O God;
The waters saw You, they were afraid;
The depths also trembled.
17The clouds poured out water;
The skies sent out a sound;
Your arrows also flashed about.
18The voice of Your thunder was in the whirlwind;
The lightnings lit up the world;
The earth trembled and shook.
19Your way was in the sea,
Your path in the great waters,

And Your footsteps were not known.
20You led Your people like a flock
By the hand of Moses and Aaron.

(VERSES 1-2) Again, Asaph cries out to God to hear and help him. When you feel you need His help, do the same. The Bible says, *'The Lord is my Helper'* (Hebrews 13:6). He *will* answer. We have noted before that your 'confidence' is that God has said, *'I will never leave you nor forsake you'* (Hebrews 13:5). Asaph uses troubled times to persist in prayer. How wise, although he *feels* no comfort. God answers prayer not because of how you feel, but because He is faithful. Have you considered that those you did not *seem* to 'get through' in prayer, and seeming ineffective to you, actually did reach the Throne of Grace and will be answered even if they have not been answered yet?

(VERSES 3-6) But as Asaph remembers God, he still feels troubled, not peaceful. That may surprise you. As he complains during a sleepless night, when it seems as if God held *'his eyelids open'* he feels worse still. Why? Probably, because as he groans and feels weak and worried, he looks back to better days in nostalgia with an 'if only' attitude. Instead of focusing on God's unchanging faithfulness, he concentrates that 'things ain't what they used to be', as the old song puts it. Circumstances differ now from how they were in 'the former days' of 'long ago' when he sang for joy in the night! He compares his mood then and now. Beware of self-pity! Focus on God!

(VERSES 7-9) As old doubts from the devil return as a result, Asaph asks himself (not God) if he is finally rejected, if God has removed His favour, if God's *'mercy'* has dried up, if God has broken His promise, if God has forgotten to deal graciously, and if God's anger has stopped and replaced His *'tender mercies'*. As he thinks about this, he should work out the same logical answer to each of his doubting questions is 'NO!' That *should* turn him back to God!

(VERSES 10-20) In fact, the evidence that God is still 'in business' is that Asaph now does begin his way back to fellowship with God. He will appeal to how God always handles things, the deeds God has performed, and His mighty power even to work miracles. Determined now to concentrate on God's works and deeds, he soon considers God's holiness, greatness, power, redemption, and details of how He led Israel out of Egypt, through the Red Sea as if it was dry land. When doubts and fears assail you, as they will from time to time, think of God's faithful character and works. If you have trusted Jesus as your Saviour, you are 'redeemed' through Christ's shed blood and risen life. Focus on those miraculous and great works of God for you. He died for you, was punished for your sins, and rose again to live to bless you now and for ever. Your ever-present Lord is a *far* better leader, guide and rescuer than Israel ever had in Moses and Aaron! He is LORD! Keep *'looking unto Jesus, the author and finisher of our faith'* (Hebrews 12:1-2).

Psalm 78—Learning from the past

A Contemplation of Asaph.
1Give ear, O my people, to my law;
Incline your ears to the words of my mouth.
2I will open my mouth in a parable;
I will utter dark sayings of old,
3Which we have heard and known,
And our fathers have told us.
4We will not hide them from their children,
Telling to the generation to come the praises of the LORD,
And His strength and His wonderful works that He has done.

5For He established a testimony in Jacob,
And appointed a law in Israel,
Which He commanded our fathers,
That they should make them known to their children;
6That the generation to come might know them,
The children who would be born,
That they may arise and declare them to their children,
7That they may set their hope in God,
And not forget the works of God,
But keep His commandments;
8And may not be like their fathers,
A stubborn and rebellious generation,
A generation that did not set its heart aright,
And whose spirit was not faithful to God.

9The children of Ephraim, being armed and carrying bows,
Turned back in the day of battle.
10They did not keep the covenant of God;
They refused to walk in His law,
11And forgot His works
And His wonders that He had shown them.

12Marvelous things He did in the sight of their fathers,
In the land of Egypt, in the field of Zoan.
13He divided the sea and caused them to pass through;
And He made the waters stand up like a heap.
14In the daytime also He led them with the cloud,
And all the night with a light of fire.
15He split the rocks in the wilderness,
And gave them drink in abundance like the depths.
16He also brought streams out of the rock,
And caused waters to run down like rivers.

17But they sinned even more against Him
By rebelling against the Most High in the wilderness.
18And they tested God in their heart
By asking for the food of their fancy.
19Yes, they spoke against God:

They said, "Can God prepare a table in the wilderness?
20Behold, He struck the rock,
So that the waters gushed out,
And the streams overflowed.
Can He give bread also?
Can He provide meat for His people?"

21Therefore the LORD heard this and was furious;
So a fire was kindled against Jacob,
And anger also came up against Israel,
22Because they did not believe in God,
And did not trust in His salvation.
23Yet He had commanded the clouds above,
And opened the doors of heaven,
24Had rained down manna on them to eat,
And given them of the bread of heaven.
25Men ate angels' food;
He sent them food to the full.

26He caused an east wind to blow in the heavens;
And by His power He brought in the south wind.
27He also rained meat on them like the dust,
Feathered fowl like the sand of the seas;
28And He let them fall in the midst of their camp,
All around their dwellings.
29So they ate and were well filled,
For He gave them their own desire.
30They were not deprived of their craving;
But while their food was still in their mouths,
31The wrath of God came against them,
And slew the stoutest of them,
And struck down the choice men of Israel.

32In spite of this they still sinned,
And did not believe in His wondrous works.
33Therefore their days He consumed in futility,
And their years in fear.

34When He slew them, then they sought Him;
And they returned and sought earnestly for God.
35Then they remembered that God was their rock,
And the Most High God their Redeemer.
36Nevertheless they flattered Him with their mouth,
And they lied to Him with their tongue;
37For their heart was not steadfast with Him,
Nor were they faithful in His covenant.
38But He, being full of compassion, forgave their iniquity,
And did not destroy them.
Yes, many a time He turned His anger away,
And did not stir up all His wrath;
39For He remembered that they were but flesh,
A breath that passes away and does not come again.

40How often they provoked Him in the wilderness,
And grieved Him in the desert!
41Yes, again and again they tempted God,
And limited the Holy One of Israel.
42They did not remember His power:
The day when He redeemed them from the enemy,
43When He worked His signs in Egypt,
And His wonders in the field of Zoan;
44Turned their rivers into blood,
And their streams, that they could not drink.
45He sent swarms of flies among them, which devoured them,
And frogs, which destroyed them.
46He also gave their crops to the caterpillar,
And their labor to the locust.
47He destroyed their vines with hail,
And their sycamore trees with frost.
48He also gave up their cattle to the hail,
And their flocks to fiery lightning.
49He cast on them the fierceness of His anger,
Wrath, indignation, and trouble,
By sending angels of destruction among them.
50He made a path for His anger;
He did not spare their soul from death,
But gave their life over to the plague,
51And destroyed all the firstborn in Egypt,
The first of their strength in the tents of Ham.
52But He made His own people go forth like sheep,
And guided them in the wilderness like a flock;
53And He led them on safely, so that they did not fear;
But the sea overwhelmed their enemies.
54And He brought them to His holy border,
This mountain which His right hand had acquired.
55He also drove out the nations before them,
Allotted them an inheritance by survey,
And made the tribes of Israel dwell in their tents.

56Yet they tested and provoked the Most High God,
And did not keep His testimonies,
57But turned back and acted unfaithfully like their fathers;
They were turned aside like a deceitful bow.
58For they provoked Him to anger with their high places,
And moved Him to jealousy with their carved images.
59When God heard this, He was furious,
And greatly abhorred Israel,
60So that He forsook the tabernacle of Shiloh,
The tent He had placed among men,
61And delivered His strength into captivity,
And His glory into the enemy's hand.
62He also gave His people over to the sword,
And was furious with His inheritance.
63The fire consumed their young men,
And their maidens were not given in marriage.

64Their priests fell by the sword,
And their widows made no lamentation.

65Then the Lord awoke as from sleep,
Like a mighty man who shouts because of wine.
66And He beat back His enemies;
He put them to a perpetual reproach.

67Moreover He rejected the tent of Joseph,
And did not choose the tribe of Ephraim,
68But chose the tribe of Judah,
Mount Zion which He loved.
69And He built His sanctuary like the heights,
Like the earth which He has established forever.
70He also chose David His servant,
And took him from the sheepfolds;
71From following the ewes that had young He brought him,
To shepherd Jacob His people,
And Israel His inheritance.
72So he shepherded them according to the integrity of his heart,
And guided them by the skillfulness of his hands.

(VERSES 1-8) This long psalm (72 verses), which the Holy Spirit has produced as Asaph engaged in much contemplation, is written to remind Israel of how God dealt with them in the past. It is to teach future generations and their children a very helpful history lesson. Asaph recounts Israel's blessings and backslidings as their forefathers told them. All this is in God's written Word for them to read, heed, and apply. We also should read the Bible daily, ask God to speak to us through it, and apply it. Their children will learn about God's '*wonderful works that He has done*' and see His power, wonders, works, statutes and law. They must ensure that children's children also hear it and obey God. This account specifically starts with Jacob (or 'Israel') the father of the nation and in the line of Abraham, Isaac and Jacob.

Israel's roller-coaster ride shows Israel failing God in a downward trend of forgetting His works, unbelief, stubborn rebellion, disobedience, and unfaithful disloyalty. Now we, who trust in Jesus and in His death as our substitute and sin-bearer who was punished for our sins, must pass on our knowledge of God to children and grandchildren. The risen Lord Jesus loves them as He loves us.

(VERSES 9-12) The bad example of Ephraim's men, in their stubborn rebellion against God, is a clear warning to Israel. Their cowardice, disobedience, and covenant-breaking made them forget

God's miracles and blessings to their forefathers. Like them, we must learn from others' mistakes in the Bible (and from our own) and not repeat them. The psalm traces God's faithfulness to them during their captivity in Egypt.

(VERSES 13-69) THIS IS A SUMMARY. PLEASE READ THE ACTUAL VERSES. In this broad sweep of Israel's history, there are two constants: first, God's faithfulness; and second, Israel's sin. The experience of verses 34-36 seem to recur often in principle: '*When He slew them, then they sought Him; and they returned and sought earnestly for God. Then they remembered that God was their Rock, and the Most High God their Redeemer. Nevertheless they flattered Him with their mouth, and they lied to Him with their tongue.*'

So Israel rebels '*again and again*' against God by tempting Him (Verse 41). This repeated up-and-down pattern is often interrupted by God, who chastises them, often through other nations. They fail to trust and obey God, and rebel. God chastises them. They come to their senses and repent. God forgives, restores, revives and blesses them again. Then the whole roller-coaster ride starts again. The main focus of God's works here is how He causes and engineers Israel's exodus from Egypt (sending plagues and instituting the Passover), the miraculous Red Sea crossing, God's leading them through the desert where He provides food and drink, His replacing Canaan's ungodly nations with Israel and defeating Israel's foes, the return of the Ark of the Covenant, and His replacing the Tabernacle with the Temple. Do you seek God's help to trust and obey Him constantly and daily?

(VERSES 70-72) David is the main writer of the book of Psalms, writing more than anyone else. Asaph tells us simple truths about David. God chose him. He was God's servant. God took him from being a humble shepherd of sheep to shepherd His people, Israel. He became king, not by his own choosing initially. With God's grace and help, he led them in integrity, seeking God's glory. He used his skills to serve and please God, and so caused God's people to be blessed. Christians can learn from David. If you know Christ as your personal Saviour, God has also chosen you to be His servant, to walk in integrity with God, and to bless others. In all of this, remember that the great King David was a sinner, just as you and I are, but God's mercy, forgiveness, grace and help supported him despite his weaknesses. God promises the same to us!

Psalm 79—How to pray when in need

A Psalm of Asaph.
1O God, the nations have come into Your inheritance;
Your holy temple they have defiled;
They have laid Jerusalem in heaps.
2The dead bodies of Your servants
They have given as food for the birds of the heavens,
The flesh of Your saints to the beasts of the earth.
3Their blood they have shed like water all around Jerusalem,
And there was no one to bury them.
4We have become a reproach to our neighbors,
A scorn and derision to those who are around us.

5How long, LORD?
Will You be angry forever?
Will Your jealousy burn like fire?
6Pour out Your wrath on the nations that do not know You,
And on the kingdoms that do not call on Your name.
7For they have devoured Jacob,
And laid waste his dwelling place.

8Oh, do not remember former iniquities against us!
Let Your tender mercies come speedily to meet us,
For we have been brought very low.
9Help us, O God of our salvation,
For the glory of Your name;
And deliver us, and provide atonement for our sins,
For Your name's sake!
10Why should the nations say,
"Where is their God?"
Let there be known among the nations in our sight
The avenging of the blood of Your servants which has been shed.

11Let the groaning of the prisoner come before You;
According to the greatness of Your power
Preserve those who are appointed to die;
12And return to our neighbors sevenfold into their bosom
Their reproach with which they have reproached You, O Lord.

13So we, Your people and sheep of Your pasture,
Will give You thanks forever;
We will show forth Your praise to all generations.

(VERSES 1-4) Asaph again reports on the historic and tragic sacking of Jerusalem as he had done in Psalm 74. The horrific details are engraved on his mind: the Temple defiled; Jerusalem ruined; the birds and beasts eating the corpses left lying around because not enough people were left to bury them; bloodshed that was like running water; and the wicked way that neighbours react to the once-majestic Jerusalem's fate by their reproach, scorn, and derision.

Learn two things about prayer from this:

First, by all means pray to God in detail about what concerns you, because He *is* interested in you and in the details that trouble you, as well as in the main problem.

Second, do not worry about raising in prayer the same thing with God many times. It fits the wide scope of prayer in Matthew 7:7—*'Ask, and it will be given to you; seek, and you will find; knock, and it will be opened to you.'* Asking seems to be a one-time prayer; seeking seems to cover ongoing praying for a particular result; and knocking seems to suggest persistently coming back with the same request. I am sure they all overlap, as well.

(Verses 5-12) Look at the many prayer requests Asaph makes in these verses for his people and for himself:

- His prayer *'How long, O Lord?'* is another way of suggesting to God that it's time for Him to act.
- He asks God to respond in punishing the nations that are anti-God, especially those who devoured His people and ruined His homeland. Today, Christians pray for enemies' conversion, but another good lesson here is to leave revenge to God, and never 'do it yourself'.
- He asks God not still to find them guilty of past sins; this can cover the fact that, once confessed, our sins are completely forgiven and cleansed away through the shed blood of the Lord Jesus Christ; it also covers that current generation of people are not being held guilty because of their fathers' sins that caused God to chastise them in such a hard way.
- He asks for God's *'tender mercies'* to *'come speedily'* to them, because they were *'brought very low'*.
- He asks for God's help, as the God who has saved them: without that help they cannot glorify God.
- He asks God to *'deliver'* (save) and *'provide atonement for* [their] *sins for* [God's] *name's sake'*. If *you* have repented, asked God to deliver (save) *you* and forgive *your* sins, He *has* already done so. Jesus died for you and bore your sins and

punishment on the cross, lives today, and is the Saviour of all who trust in Him. His name means 'God saves'—Jesus does just that! And remember that *'the blood of Jesus Christ His Son cleanses us from all sin'* (1 John 1:7). The tense of the word *'cleanses'* means it *'goes on cleansing'* from sin.

- He asks God to act so the nations will that know He is God. He is the God over all nations.
- He prays for God to hear *'the groanings of the prisoner'*. This would apply to Jewish prisoners held by their enemy. Asaph asks God to save them. But God loves all prisoners. We are all *'prisoners'* of sin—but Jesus can set us free (John 8:34, 36). It applies to physical prisoners, whether in prison because of crime or because of persecution of Christians. Let's pray that God will save, bless and change all prisoners.

(VERSE 13) Asaph promises God that His people ('*sheep of His pasture*') will then thank Him and praise Him for all time. So should we!

Psalm 80—The Saviour and Shepherd

To the Chief Musician. Set to "The Lilies." A Testimony of Asaph. A Psalm.

1 Give ear, O Shepherd of Israel,
You who lead Joseph like a flock;
You who dwell between the cherubim, shine forth!
2 Before Ephraim, Benjamin, and Manasseh,
Stir up Your strength,
And come and save us!

3 Restore us, O God;
Cause Your face to shine,
And we shall be saved!

4 O LORD God of hosts,
How long will You be angry
Against the prayer of Your people?
5 You have fed them with the bread of tears,
And given them tears to drink in great measure.
6 You have made us a strife to our neighbors,
And our enemies laugh among themselves.

7 Restore us, O God of hosts;
Cause Your face to shine,
And we shall be saved!

8 You have brought a vine out of Egypt;
You have cast out the nations, and planted it.
9 You prepared room for it,
And caused it to take deep root,
And it filled the land.
10 The hills were covered with its shadow,
And the mighty cedars with its boughs.
11 She sent out her boughs to the Sea,
And her branches to the River.

12 Why have You broken down her hedges,
So that all who pass by the way pluck her fruit?
13 The boar out of the woods uproots it,
And the wild beast of the field devours it.

14 Return, we beseech You, O God of hosts;
Look down from heaven and see,
And visit this vine
15 And the vineyard which Your right hand has planted,
And the branch that You made strong for Yourself.
16 It is burned with fire, it is cut down;
They perish at the rebuke of Your countenance.
17 Let Your hand be upon the man of Your right hand,
Upon the son of man whom You made strong for Yourself.

18Then we will not turn back from You;
Revive us, and we will call upon Your name.

19Restore us, O LORD God of hosts;
Cause Your face to shine,
And we shall be saved!

(VERSES 1-3) The themes of Psalm 80 are familiar. Asaph reminds the singers who God is—the '*Shepherd of Israel*' who guides feeds and protects His sheep. Jesus said (in John 10:11), '*I am the Good Shepherd. The Good Shepherd lays down his life for the sheep,*' and adds (in John 10:14), '*I know My sheep and My sheep know Me.*' He laid down His life to die on the cross for our sins, suffering God's judgment that would take us eternity to pay without Jesus as our Saviour. God personally knows and cares for every sinner who trusts in Him.

By asking God to 'shine forth' from between the Cherubim, Asaph refers to God's holiness. In the Temple's Holy of Holies were two golden cherubim. Their wings overshadowed the Ark of the Covenant that spoke of God's presence and awesome holiness, where God was worshipped. Asaph asks God to awaken His might to save His people, and to restore them by His smile shining on and saving them. Jesus restores, blesses and saves personally all who come humbly in faith to Him and submit to Him as Lord.

The three Israelite tribes referred to—namely Ephraim, Manasseh and Benjamin—marched together as a unit behind the tabernacle in the wilderness wanderings. Therefore they became very familiar with the ark in all modes of Israelite life. They would know about God's holiness.

(VERSES 4-7) Asaph again asks Almighty God '*How long*' before He ceases to be angry with His backslidden and chastised people and to answer their pleas for blessing. They weep '*in great measure*'. Foes and neighbours mock them. Asaph prays again for spiritual restoration, God's smile and God's salvation to return to them. However bad a sinner is, if he really repents and asks Jesus to save him, Jesus response at once is '*YES*'. He enters his life. There is no need to ask twice.

(VERSES 8-13) When God rescued Israel from Egypt to place them in Canaan, they were like a growing vine covering much land, from the mountains to the sea. God cared for that spreading vine and put walls around it. Now, with walls broken down, passers-by and wild beasts eat the grapes still growing. The vine is cut down and burned. Israel's people are devastated after such cruel and violent enemy destruction. Asaph asks why God has allowed this damage, devastation and devouring of God's vine.

(VERSES 14-19) Asaph asks God to '*return*', inspect and watch over them as a father, and revive Israel. He says that then they will not '*turn back from*' God, and '*will call on* [His] *name*'. He then again prays for their restoration, and God's smile on them to save them. God will raise up the '*son of man*' at His right hand to act, probably referring to David's line. But the Lord Jesus Christ, '*Son of God*' and '*Son of Man*', saves, watches over, revives and restores sinners even now! You will know that full well if you have received Him as your Saviour and follow Him as your Lord.

Psalm 81—Trust and obey

To the Chief Musician. On an instrument of Gath. A Psalm of Asaph.
1Sing aloud to God our strength;
Make a joyful shout to the God of Jacob.
2Raise a song and strike the timbrel,
The pleasant harp with the lute.

3Blow the trumpet at the time of the New Moon,
At the full moon, on our solemn feast day.
4For this is a statute for Israel,
A law of the God of Jacob.
5This He established in Joseph as a testimony,
When He went throughout the land of Egypt,
Where I heard a language I did not understand.

6"I removed his shoulder from the burden;
His hands were freed from the baskets.
7You called in trouble, and I delivered you;
I answered you in the secret place of thunder;
I tested you at the waters of Meribah. Selah

8"Hear, O My people, and I will admonish you!
O Israel, if you will listen to Me!
9There shall be no foreign god among you;
Nor shall you worship any foreign god.
10I am the LORD your God,
Who brought you out of the land of Egypt;
Open your mouth wide, and I will fill it.

11"But My people would not heed My voice,
And Israel would have none of Me.
12So I gave them over to their own stubborn heart,
To walk in their own counsels.

13"Oh, that My people would listen to Me,
That Israel would walk in My ways!
14I would soon subdue their enemies,
And turn My hand against their adversaries.
15The haters of the LORD would pretend submission to Him,
But their fate would endure forever.
16He would have fed them also with the finest of wheat;
And with honey from the rock I would have satisfied you."

(VERSES 1-5) Psalm 81 starts like a hymn, with enthusiastic worship supported by various musical instruments. It is for one of Israel's ordained feasts, very probably the Feast of Tabernacles. Some special celebrations were held when there was a new moon. The Feast of Tabernacles was commanded by God and held on the fifteenth day of Tishri—a New Moon Day in what would be September or October for us today. It commemorated how God had kept and provided for His people in the desert after leaving Egypt and before entering the Promised Land.

(VERSES 6-7) The lifted '*burden*' and the '*baskets*' remind Israel of their slavery in Egypt when they had to carry baskets of bricks to build with. God rescued His distressed people and gave them His laws on Mount Sinai, where they heard thunder. At Meribah (meaning 'strife'), He tested them; they failed and tempted God by asking if He was still with them. When Christ becomes your Saviour, God removes the burden of sin and guilt because Jesus paid for your sins by His death on the cross. You will be tempted and tested, too. If at times you fail to trust the Lord to overcome them, remember 1 John 1:9. '*If we confess our sins*' [directly to God] '*He is faithful and just to forgive us our sins and to cleanse us from all unrighteousness.*'

(VERSES 8-12) God reminded them that He saved them from Egypt and wanted to satisfy all their needs generously. But they neither listened nor submitted to God. So, God left them to their stubborn hearts and their own ways to teach them they really did need Him in charge to change them. Far better to learn that lesson while experiencing the blessing of trusting and obeying your loving God, than while suffering God's chastisement. One hymn says,

Trust and obey, for there's no other way
To be happy in Jesus but to trust and obey.

(VERSES 13-16) These final verses underline the truth of that hymn. Consider the Lord's positive promises to those who do trust and obey Him: they are far better than merely avoiding His chastising hand.

Here we can see that:

- God will subdue Israel's enemies quickly and oppose their foes if His people will listen to and walk in God's ways.
- God will deal with those who hate Him. They will submit before Him and be under His enduring punishment.
- God will feed and satisfy them by the '*finest of wheat*' and by '*honey from the rock*'. This phrase pictures Jesus, our Rock, who gives sweet and satisfying blessing to those who honour and love Him.

Psalm 82—No 'gods', but know God

A Psalm of Asaph.
1God stands in the congregation of the mighty;
He judges among the gods.
2How long will you judge unjustly,
And show partiality to the wicked? Selah
3Defend the poor and fatherless;
Do justice to the afflicted and needy.
4Deliver the poor and needy;
Free them from the hand of the wicked.

5They do not know, nor do they understand;
They walk about in darkness;
All the foundations of the earth are unstable.

6I said, "You are gods,
And all of you are children of the Most High.
7But you shall die like men,
And fall like one of the princes."

8Arise, O God, judge the earth;
For You shall inherit all nations.

(VERSE 1) To understand this psalm best, remember that in verse 1 Asaph introduces God who then speaks from verses 2 to 7. God is pictured as presiding over a big assembly of leaders, possibly the world's leaders. The word '*gods*' is used elsewhere in the Bible to talk of judges and leaders who have a grossly inflated sense of their own importance; in mockery, God now calls them '*gods*'. They try to behave as if they are '*gods*'. Almighty God is *the* only God and the only perfect Judge.

(VERSES 2-5) These '*gods*' are behaving in a very sinful and unfair way. They actually are biased towards the '*wicked*' in their judgments. They defend those who ought to be stopped and punished for the wrong they do. They are prejudiced towards the very ones who should be judged justly, rightly and impartially. How should these judges change, who sin as they judge others? Here are '*gods*' who fail to defend '*the poor and fatherless*' and who fail to '*do justice to the afflicted and needy*'. Needy, unprotected folk should get *extra* care, not less, to '*free them from the hand of the wicked*' and ensure that justice is fairly applied. These '*gods*' behave like this because they also are lost sinners who do not know God's righteousness. For all their proud pomp, they know and understand *nothing* but walk about in spiritual and moral '*darkness*'. They have no right foundation in their lives, and so pass on their warped and unstable standards to a needy, suffering world. How different was Jesus! Consider how He lived, walked, judged and loved! Possessing all power, He never misused it. Instead, He gave Himself up as a righteous, spotless sacrifice for our sins to die on the cross. He was judged in our place there. He rose again in resurrection power and now enters the lives of sinful, needy sinners who turn from their sins and receive Him as their Lord and Saviour. Even today's sinful equivalents of these '*gods*' can be forgiven and have eternal life through personal repentance and trust in Jesus.

(VERSES 6-7) Here is the ultimate test for any man, however great he may claim to be, or others may think he is. Some may see themselves as '*gods*' or be treated as '*gods*' in the world's eyes. Some may even claim to be Christians ('*sons of the Most High*') when they are not. But there is an acid test: death itself. They '*shall die like men*' and '*fall like one of the princes*'. On a death bed a man is a man, and a woman a woman, and nothing more. When the last breath is breathed, each one of has died. The person who died may have been a king, a key politician, a pop star, a sporting hero, or a multi-billionaire. After death comes judgment (Hebrews 9:27) for all—unless Jesus is his or her Saviour.

(VERSE 8) Asaph responds to what God has said by praying, '*Arise, O God, judge the earth; for You shall inherit all nations.*' It is vital to know Jesus as Saviour in your lifetime, rather than meet Him as the all-knowing and righteous Judge of your sins after death. Do you know Him?

Psalm 83—Dealing with God's enemies

A Song. A Psalm of Asaph.
1Do not keep silent, O God!
Do not hold Your peace,
And do not be still, O God!
2For behold, Your enemies make a tumult;
And those who hate You have lifted up their head.
3They have taken crafty counsel against Your people,
And consulted together against Your sheltered ones.
4They have said, "Come, and let us cut them off from being a nation,
That the name of Israel may be remembered no more."

5For they have consulted together with one consent;
They form a confederacy against You:
6The tents of Edom and the Ishmaelites;
Moab and the Hagrites;
7Gebal, Ammon, and Amalek;
Philistia with the inhabitants of Tyre;
8Assyria also has joined with them;
They have helped the children of Lot. Selah

9Deal with them as with Midian,
As with Sisera,
As with Jabin at the Brook Kishon,
10Who perished at En Dor,
Who became as refuse on the earth.
11Make their nobles like Oreb and like Zeeb,
Yes, all their princes like Zebah and Zalmunna,
12Who said, "Let us take for ourselves
The pastures of God for a possession."

13O my God, make them like the whirling dust,
Like the chaff before the wind!
14As the fire burns the woods,
And as the flame sets the mountains on fire,
15So pursue them with Your tempest,
And frighten them with Your storm.
16Fill their faces with shame,
That they may seek Your name, O LORD.
17Let them be confounded and dismayed forever;
Yes, let them be put to shame and perish,
18That they may know that You, whose name alone is the LORD,
Are the Most High over all the earth.

(VERSES 1-4) The annihilation threat to Israel is not new. The Jewish people have suffered many threats and attacks throughout their history, and even relatively recently there was debate about anti-semitism in UK politics. God's ancient physical people are hated and persecuted by some, and so are His spiritual people, Christians. The devil seems to have a masterplan, to oppose God's people though he can never master Almighty God. Here Asaph points out that there are enemy conspiracies and plots to destroy Israel and remove even the remembrance of Israel. He asks God to get involved. Often individual Christians face opposition, too, simply because they do know and follow the Lord Jesus Christ. Here is the best way to handle it: pray to God about it now, just as Asaph did all those years ago.

(VERSES 5-8) As here, where specified, named, historical foes of Israel join to conspire against them, opposition to God's people can come from many sources. It is wise to see and evaluate the threat and it is vital to pray and keep on trusting and following God.

(VERSES 9-12) Asaph comforts himself by thinking back to how God had given His people escape and victory over a variety of powerful, known enemies in their past. For example, the book of Judges shows that Gideon's much-reduced army beat Midian and their chiefs, and that Deborah and Barak defeated Jabin and Sisera—and all those victories would have been impossible without God's help.

(VERSES 13-15) Asaph asks for the defeat of Israel's and God's enemies in ways replicating things seen in nature. Asaph asks God that their power and might will become nothing more than '*whirling dust*' or '*chaff before the wind*'. Instead of being strong enemies to reckon with, they should become insignificant and transient. He asks God to '*pursue*' and '*frighten*' them with His tempestuous storm, to remove them, as a forest fire removes the trees, and to terrify them by His '*tempest*'.

(VERSES 16-18) Asaph wants the shame of their foes to cause onlookers to seek the LORD's '*name*'. God is described by His names. They tell us of His Creatorhood, His Majesty, His Deity, His Perfection, His love, His Sovereignty, His grace and His eternality. That should be our desire, too, that the enemies of the Lord and His gospel will be so conquered by the meaning of the names of God and by the love of God, in sending Jesus to die for them and bear their sins and the penalty for those sins, that they will seek God, and ask Jesus to save them. That is victory! As part of that process Asaph prays for their shame, dismay, and disgrace to drive them to realise that God is the only '*Most High over all the earth*'. It is in seeing our sins, failures and weaknesses that we come humbly as sinners to our perfect Lord for forgiveness, grace and help. If you trust Jesus, you, too, will see yourself as very small, poor and needy but rejoice in God's greatness, and in His mercy and love.

Psalm 84—Longing for God

To the Chief Musician. On an instrument of Gath. A Psalm of the sons of Korah.

1How lovely is Your tabernacle,
O LORD of hosts!
2My soul longs, yes, even faints
For the courts of the LORD;
My heart and my flesh cry out for the living God.

3Even the sparrow has found a home,
And the swallow a nest for herself,
Where she may lay her young—
Even Your altars, O LORD of hosts,
My King and my God.
4Blessed are those who dwell in Your house;
They will still be praising You. Selah

5Blessed is the man whose strength is in You,
Whose heart is set on pilgrimage.
6As they pass through the Valley of Baca,
They make it a spring;
The rain also covers it with pools.
7They go from strength to strength;
Each one appears before God in Zion.

8O LORD God of hosts, hear my prayer;
Give ear, O God of Jacob! Selah
9O God, behold our shield,
And look upon the face of Your anointed.

10For a day in Your courts is better than a thousand.
I would rather be a doorkeeper in the house of my God
Than dwell in the tents of wickedness.
11For the LORD God is a sun and shield;
The LORD will give grace and glory;
No good thing will He withhold
From those who walk uprightly.

12O LORD of hosts,
Blessed is the man who trusts in You!

❖

(VERSES 1-7) The sons of Korah are from the tribe of Levi. They are Kohathites who look after the gates and music in the Temple. Their heart and their work are in the worship of God in the Temple, referred to as a '*tabernacle*' (or '*tent*') here to signify God's presence. A Christian does not base or focus his worship on a building, but on the Lord who has become his Lord and Saviour and is worthy of his praise and worship. But the obvious keen and enthusiastic way that these Temple servants want to worship God is a great example to us today. We should worship God in the fellowship of a Bible-believing church, with others who have turned from their sin to trust the Lord Jesus Christ as their Saviour. The '*LORD of hosts*' is our Almighty Saviour God, worshipped by the Heavenly host of angels. The sons of Korah's desire to worship God is expressed in phrases like '*longs for*', '*faints for*', and '*cry out for the living God*'. God is very much '*living*' in the Trinity of the three Persons of God the Father, God the Son and God the Holy Spirit. The Father planned our salvation from eternity. The Son was crucified to bear our sins and judgment but rose from the dead and lives for ever. The Spirit convicts our hearts of sin, points us to Jesus, and then enters our hearts to give spiritual life.

The writer of the psalm envies a swallow which can nest near the altar. You can only worship God as '*my King and my God*' when you trust and know that Jesus is your personal Saviour. Then you can praise Him during each day, wherever you are. When you do that and rely on God's strength to live a life far different than you could ever live as a non-Christian, you are on a truly blessed and daily '*pilgrimage*' to honour God and see others trust Him. When you travel through life's dry valleys of tears *('Valley of Baca'* means 'Valley of Weeping'), God helps you to drink from His provision of the Holy Spirit in your life. He will help and strengthen you as you keep on trusting and praising Him. Each Lord's Day, plan always to do that with others whenever you can.

(VERSES 8-9) The psalmist asks God to hear his prayer and listen to him. God always hears and listens to us when we pray with a sincere heart in the name of Jesus. He asks God to favour His '*shield*' (the king) who is also God's '*anointed*'. Jesus is our anointed King. Although no earthly monarch can ever compare with King Jesus, we also should pray for '*kings and all who are in authority*'. (1 Timothy 2:2). Every earthly monarch is a dying man or woman; he or she needs to trust in King Jesus as Lord and Saviour just like the rest of us do.

(VERSES 10-12) One day praising the Lord is far better than a thousand days spent with *wicked people* in other ways. '*For the LORD God is a sun and shield; The LORD will give grace and glory.*' The sun brings light and life. A shield protects. God brings you light, life and protection. He adds '*grace and glory*' than no earthly monarch, however good, ever can. God favours those trusting Him. He refuses '*no good thing*' from you if you walk blamelessly with Him each day. That is why we can say to Him: '*Blessed is the man who trusts in* You.' Do you know that blessing personally yourself?

Psalm 85—The way back to God

To the Chief Musician. A Psalm of the sons of Korah.
1LORD, You have been favorable to Your land;
You have brought back the captivity of Jacob.
2You have forgiven the iniquity of Your people;
You have covered all their sin. Selah
3You have taken away all Your wrath;
You have turned from the fierceness of Your anger.

4Restore us, O God of our salvation,
And cause Your anger toward us to cease.
5Will You be angry with us forever?
Will You prolong Your anger to all generations?
6Will You not revive us again,
That Your people may rejoice in You?
7Show us Your mercy, LORD,
And grant us Your salvation.

8I will hear what God the LORD will speak,
For He will speak peace
To His people and to His saints;
But let them not turn back to folly.
9Surely His salvation is near to those who fear Him,
That glory may dwell in our land.

10Mercy and truth have met together;
Righteousness and peace have kissed.
11Truth shall spring out of the earth,
And righteousness shall look down from heaven.
12Yes, the LORD will give what is good;
And our land will yield its increase.
13Righteousness will go before Him,
And shall make His footsteps our pathway.

(VERSES 1-3) There is an interesting parallel throughout this psalm between Israel and the individual Christian. Although thought by some Bible scholars to refer to Judah's return from Babylonian captivity, it could also refer to various stages in the up-and-down history of God's physical people. It reveals a principle seen in both the Old Testament about Israel, and in the New Testament about any sinner who turns to Christ. It starts with God's blessing as He shows favour to restore, forgive and cover sins, and turn from the '*fierceness of* [His] *anger*' and of His '*wrath*'. Israel, including Judah, often knew this in their history as they confessed their wrongs to God, turned from their sins, and trusted Him to forgive them. Similarly, today, a lost sinner—we all are or were lost—who turns from sin and trusts Jesus personally, benefits from God's grace and favour. He is restored to fellowship with the Lord and is forgiven by Him. He is saved through wholehearted personal faith in Jesus, who died for him, bore his sins on the cross, and took God's penalty on those sins in his place. The risen Lord, through the Holy Spirit, enters that person's life, and then begins to change him from within. The same principle of repenting from post-conversion sins and continually putting faith in Christ applies to a Christian's daily life. But at no point has a genuinely *'born-again'* believer ever become 'unsaved' again since trusting Christ. Our current fellowship with our Heavenly Father can be broken—and restored—but our eternal sonship from our Heavenly Father can never be lost or withdrawn.

(VERSES 4-7) God's Old Testament people ask God to restore them, cease His anger and displeasure, revive them, cause them to rejoice in Him, show them His unfailing love and save them. On a spiritual basis, that is how God still blesses any lost sinner who repents and trusts in Jesus Christ. It also foreshadows how a Christian should walk daily with his Lord (1 John 1:7 and 9).

(VERSES 8-9) Israel then, lost sinners now, and those committed to Christ should learn to walk with God as described here. Listen to God's Word. Trust His promises. Refuse and reject sin. If you sin, confess it to God. Ask Him to forgive you and restore your fellowship with Him. Fear Him with a godly, loving fear. Seek His glory in all you are and in all you do. That should describe anyone committed to '*the Lord Jesus, who gave Himself for our sins that He might deliver us from this present evil age, according to the will of our God and Father, to whom be glory forever and ever*' (Galatians 1:4-5).

(VERSES 10-13) The cross where Jesus died is where *'mercy and truth'* met each other, and also where *'righteousness and peace'* met each other. His goodness and righteousness also met our sin and judgment. When we believe that and yield to Jesus, we, too, will begin to harvest His blessing in our lives as He prepares our way to follow Him.

Psalm 86—Our God who answers prayer

A Prayer of David.
1Bow down Your ear, O LORD, hear me;
For I am poor and needy.
2Preserve my life, for I am holy;
You are my God;
Save Your servant who trusts in You!
3Be merciful to me, O Lord,
For I cry to You all day long.
4Rejoice the soul of Your servant,
For to You, O LORD, I lift up my soul.
5For You, Lord, are good, and ready to forgive,
And abundant in mercy to all those who call upon You.

6Give ear, O LORD, to my prayer;
And attend to the voice of my supplications.
7In the day of my trouble I will call upon You,
For You will answer me.

8Among the gods there is none like You, O Lord;
Nor are there any works like Your works.
9All nations whom You have made
Shall come and worship before You, O Lord,
And shall glorify Your name.
10For You are great, and do wondrous things;
You alone are God.

11Teach me Your way, O LORD;
I will walk in Your truth;
Unite my heart to fear Your name.
12I will praise You, O Lord my God, with all my heart,
And I will glorify Your name forevermore.
13For great is Your mercy toward me,
And You have delivered my soul from the depths of Sheol.

14O God, the proud have risen against me,
And a mob of violent men have sought my life,
And have not set You before them.
15But You, O Lord, are a God full of compassion, and gracious,
Longsuffering and abundant in mercy and truth.

16Oh, turn to me, and have mercy on me!
Give Your strength to Your servant,
And save the son of Your maidservant.
17Show me a sign for good,
That those who hate me may see it and be ashamed,
Because You, LORD, have helped me and comforted me.

(VERSES 1-7) It is good, when we view our sins and weaknesses, to remind ourselves of God's character and attitude toward us. David laments that he is '*poor and needy*'. He asks God to hear and answer him, preserve his life, save him, have mercy on him as he cries to God, and make his soul rejoice as he lifts it up to Him. He realises that God is good, forgiving, and to those who call on Him in prayer He is '*abundant in mercy*'. So again he asks God to hear and attend to the '*supplications*' of his prayers. He says that in '*the day of my trouble*' ahead he '*will call upon* [God], *for* [He] *will answer* [him]'. He can look back and remind himself that he did pray to God about all these needs. He has intertwined what he knows about God, both as the basis for his prayers and as an encouragement that God will answer prayers. That is praying as it should be.

What does he say about God?

The LORD is a *personal* God—David says, '*You are my God*' and that is why he prays '*preserve my life*', '*be merciful to me*', and prays *personal* prayers to God for Him to answer David personally. Remember and apply to yourself that God is forgiving, good, abounding in love, merciful and prayer-answering.

(VERSES 8-10) Before continuing with other specific prayers, he worships God in the light of further truths about Him. This mix of who God is and David's needs makes a perfect blend. He prays to his living God who can and will answer him. We should pray like he does.

He extols God's following attributes:

- God is unique—there are no other '*gods*' like Him.
- His deeds are incomparable and '*wondrous*'.
- He merits the nations' worship: after all He made them.
- He is '*great*'. David adds, '*You alone are God.*'

(VERSES 11-13) This leads to two more linked requests: he asks God to teach him His way so he can walk in His truth; and he wants an undivided heart to fear God's name, to praise Him '*with all* [his] *heart*' and '*glorify* [His] *name forevermore*'. He reminds himself again of God's love toward him, and how He has acted to save David before. We pray to the Lord Jesus Christ, and we remember how He has acted to save us. Jesus bled and died on the cross. He was punished there for our sins. He rose again to be the living

Saviour of all who repent and trust in Him. We know that He loves and cares for us. If, like David, we pray selfless prayers that honour God, He will answer positively, bless us, and others through us

(VERSES 14-17) David now prays in more detail—a good way to pray. Detailed prayer means detailed blessing! He wants God to defend and protect him from *'a mob of violent men'* who are out to kill him. He counts on God's compassionate and *'gracious longsuffering'*, and merciful and truthful character. So he asks God, *'Oh, turn to me, and have mercy on me! Give Your strength to Your servant and save'* him. He asks for God to show him *'good'* so that his haters will *'see it and be ashamed'.* Why will they be ashamed? Because they know that it is the *'LORD'* who has *'helped and comforted'* David. They must know they cannot compete with God Almighty! Perhaps they may even repent of their sins and turn to Him for forgiveness and a new start. Some sinners do.

Psalm 87—The blessings of Zion today

A Psalm of the sons of Korah. A Song.
1His foundation is in the holy mountains.
2The LORD loves the gates of Zion
More than all the dwellings of Jacob.
3Glorious things are spoken of you,
O city of God! Selah

4"I will make mention of Rahab and Babylon to those who know Me;
Behold, O Philistia and Tyre, with Ethiopia:
'This one was born there.' "

5And of Zion it will be said,
"This one and that one were born in her;
And the Most High Himself shall establish her."
6The LORD will record,
When He registers the peoples:
"This one was born there." Selah

7Both the singers and the players on instruments say,
"All my springs are in you."

(VERSES 1-2) This worship song to God focuses on '*Zion*', Jerusalem's *poetic* name, mainly used in considering matters of special spiritual value about Jerusalem. The Temple built here, and surrounded by mountains, reminds us of God's special presence with His people. His people meet to praise and worship Him here. Why does God love '*the gates of Zion*' more than '*all the dwellings of the children of Jacob*' or 'Israel'? Gates signify protection—God wishes to protect His people's real worship of Him. Gates also imply access—God offers access to all humble-hearted people who turn from their sin and trust Him as their Lord. That access to Zion has allowed many people, including some Gentiles, to come to know and worship the Lord God Almighty. When you trust the Lord Jesus Christ personally as your Saviour, the Lord protects your spiritual life and your desire to know and worship Him. He also gives you access to worship of Him through Jesus' shed blood. That blood washes all believers in Him from all sin as they own up to it, repent from it and trust that Jesus was punished for them in His body on the cross. They deserved that punishment, but He took it for them. You will also rejoice to find that people from many other nations also trust and worship your Lord Jesus Christ.

(VERSES 3-5) We are told to pause and think *('Selah')* that Zion, this '*city of God*', has '*glorious things. . . spoken*' about it. God is the God of *glory*. Jesus, the eternal Son of God, came from Heaven's *glory* to earth to be born to become our Saviour. Jesus bore our sins and their judgment when He died as our substitute for us on Calvary's cross. Those who turn from their sins to receive the now-living Jesus in their hearts become '*born again*'. They are *en route* to spend eternity in Heaven's *glory*. 1 Timothy 1:11 calls this amazing news '*the glorious gospel of the blessed God*'. '*Rahab*', a traditional, ferocious monster, refers to Egypt, which, with Babylon, was one of Israel's sworn enemies. Israel also has a history of conflict with three other named nations, Philistia, Tyre and Cush (Ethiopia). But their citizens will also come to worship God in Zion! They will regard people born there as privileged. Christians want people from all nations to hear the gospel, come to Christ, and worship our one and only true and living God. Pray for 'new births' to change men and women of all nations, ages, races, and backgrounds as they are '*born again*' in Christ, through the deep work of the Holy Spirit in their lives.

(VERSES 6-7) God keeps a register of those '*born in Zion*'. They will play music and sing in praise. '*All my springs are in You.*' Water from a fountain (or spring) refreshes us, cleanses us, and satisfies our thirst. After they have died, all who trusted in Jesus Christ will live for ever in '*New Jerusalem*' and possess eternally saved souls and resurrected bodies. '*New Jerusalem*' is Heaven come down to a new and perfect Earth. Jesus promises us that His '*living water*' will be there for ever! The names of *all* trusting in Jesus '*are written in the Lamb's book of life*'. (Jesus *is* that '*Lamb*' who became the sacrifice for our sins.) Is *your* name written in His book? (See Revelation 21:2; 3:12; 7:17; 21:27.)

Psalm 88—The ditch of despondency

A Song. A Psalm of the sons of Korah. To the Chief Musician. Set to "Mahalath Leannoth." A Contemplation of Heman the Ezrahite.
1O LORD, God of my salvation,
I have cried out day and night before You.
2Let my prayer come before You;
Incline Your ear to my cry.

3For my soul is full of troubles,
And my life draws near to the grave.
4I am counted with those who go down to the pit;
I am like a man who has no strength,
5Adrift among the dead,
Like the slain who lie in the grave,
Whom You remember no more,
And who are cut off from Your hand.

6You have laid me in the lowest pit,
In darkness, in the depths.
7Your wrath lies heavy upon me,
And You have afflicted me with all Your waves. Selah
8You have put away my acquaintances far from me;
You have made me an abomination to them;
I am shut up, and I cannot get out;
9My eye wastes away because of affliction.

LORD, I have called daily upon You;
I have stretched out my hands to You.
10Will You work wonders for the dead?
Shall the dead arise and praise You? Selah
11Shall Your lovingkindness be declared in the grave?
Or Your faithfulness in the place of destruction?
12Shall Your wonders be known in the dark?
And Your righteousness in the land of forgetfulness?

13But to You I have cried out, O LORD,
And in the morning my prayer comes before You.
14LORD, why do You cast off my soul?
Why do You hide Your face from me?
15I have been afflicted and ready to die from my youth;
I suffer Your terrors;
I am distraught.
16Your fierce wrath has gone over me;
Your terrors have cut me off.
17They came around me all day long like water;
They engulfed me altogether.
18Loved one and friend You have put far from me,
And my acquaintances into darkness.

❖

(VERSES 1-2) This is not a 'happy psalm' of Heman and does not end, like many that go 'through the valley', on to the mountain top of knowing God's faithfulness. But life is like this, and the book of Psalms reflects life; so, we should learn from it. But it starts with a good lesson for us all to heed: despite being despondent and maybe depressed, the psalmist cries out day and night to God. He asks God, his Saviour, to accept and hear his prayer. Someone said that praying and evangelism have in common that there are only two situations where we should pray or evangelise: (1) daily, when we feel like it; and (2) daily, when we do not feel like it! That is living by faith in our Lord and Saviour, Jesus Christ.

(VERSES 3-7) Here is why he is now praying to God: he is troubled and feels near to being spiritually dead (though he is not) and physically as if he was dying (which he is not); he feels he has no strength (which he does have by a weak sinner's trust in his Almighty God and Saviour); he feels God has placed him in darkness (which God may do at times to grow us spiritually or as our loving Father to chastise us); he feels that God has left him *'adrift among the dead'* by which he means that God has forgotten him and cut him off (which He has not done); he feels God's *'wrath lies heavy upon'* him (which is something that can never happen to a '*born again*' child of God, as all God's wrath of judgment was borne by Jesus for him on the cross when He was punished for his sins); and he feels *overwhelmed* by God's circumstantial waves of darkness or chastisement (as it seems to him.) All these things are in the realm of his feelings. It is far better to count on the promise of the Bible than on how you feel. Remember from verse 1 that he is aware that the '*LORD*' is the '*God of* [his] *salvation*'. If you are saved, you are saved for ever (John 10:27-30).

(VERSES 8-18) He now gives his random journal of how this has all affected him. The good thing is that he is sharing all this with his Saviour God who cares for him, just as the Lord Jesus Christ cares for you, even when your feelings do not register this. He twice tells God that daily he spreads his hands out to Him. He calls or cries out to God, including in the morning. He asks God to deal with these problems:

- He is repulsive to his friends, who forsake him.
- He feels confined like a captive.

- He cannot see things as they are.
- He grieves and like a dead man cannot praise God in the dark and he He says God is not at work.
- He feels forgotten by God.
- He feels God has cast him off and hides from him.
- He feels God has afflicted him and kept him close to death, since his youth.
- He feels *'distraught'* because God's wrath and terrors have swamped and destroyed him.
- He blames God for removing his friends and loved ones. In other words, He is lonely.

Other psalmists in similar sad positions reflect on who God really is and are encouraged. He should do that now. Often the lessons from Scripture that we learn in the darkness stand us in good stead for the future. Remember to trust God, trust His Word (the Bible), trust His promises, and trust in Jesus personally. Doubt your doubts and believe your beliefs!

Psalm 89–Remember God and His promised plans

A Contemplation of Ethan the Ezrahite.
1I will sing of the mercies of the LORD forever;
With my mouth will I make known Your faithfulness to all generations.
2For I have said, "Mercy shall be built up forever;
Your faithfulness You shall establish in the very heavens."

3"I have made a covenant with My chosen,
I have sworn to My servant David:
4'Your seed I will establish forever,
And build up your throne to all generations.' " Selah

5And the heavens will praise Your wonders, O LORD;
Your faithfulness also in the assembly of the saints.
6For who in the heavens can be compared to the LORD?
Who among the sons of the mighty can be likened to the LORD?
7God is greatly to be feared in the assembly of the saints,
And to be held in reverence by all those around Him.
8O LORD God of hosts,
Who is mighty like You, O LORD?
Your faithfulness also surrounds You.
9You rule the raging of the sea;
When its waves rise, You still them.
10You have broken Rahab in pieces, as one who is slain;
You have scattered Your enemies with Your mighty arm.

11The heavens are Yours, the earth also is Yours;
The world and all its fullness, You have founded them.
12The north and the south, You have created them;
Tabor and Hermon rejoice in Your name.
13You have a mighty arm;
Strong is Your hand, and high is Your right hand.
14Righteousness and justice are the foundation of Your throne;
Mercy and truth go before Your face.
15Blessed are the people who know the joyful sound!
They walk, O LORD, in the light of Your countenance.
16In Your name they rejoice all day long,
And in Your righteousness they are exalted.
17For You are the glory of their strength,
And in Your favor our horn is exalted.
18For our shield belongs to the LORD,
And our king to the Holy One of Israel.

19Then You spoke in a vision to Your holy one,
And said: "I have given help to one who is mighty;
I have exalted one chosen from the people.
20I have found My servant David;
With My holy oil I have anointed him,
21With whom My hand shall be established;
Also My arm shall strengthen him.

22 The enemy shall not outwit him,
Nor the son of wickedness afflict him.
23 I will beat down his foes before his face,
And plague those who hate him.

24 "But My faithfulness and My mercy shall be with him,
And in My name his horn shall be exalted.
25 Also I will set his hand over the sea,
And his right hand over the rivers.
26 He shall cry to Me, 'You are my Father,
My God, and the rock of my salvation.'
27 Also I will make him My firstborn,
The highest of the kings of the earth.
28 My mercy I will keep for him forever,
And My covenant shall stand firm with him.
29 His seed also I will make to endure forever,
And his throne as the days of heaven.

30 "If his sons forsake My law
And do not walk in My judgments,
31 If they break My statutes
And do not keep My commandments,
32 Then I will punish their transgression with the rod,
And their iniquity with stripes.
33 Nevertheless My lovingkindness I will not utterly take from him,
Nor allow My faithfulness to fail.
34 My covenant I will not break,
Nor alter the word that has gone out of My lips.
35 Once I have sworn by My holiness;
I will not lie to David:
36 His seed shall endure forever,
And his throne as the sun before Me;
37 It shall be established forever like the moon,
Even like the faithful witness in the sky." Selah

38 But You have cast off and abhorred,
You have been furious with Your anointed.
39 You have renounced the covenant of Your servant;
You have profaned his crown by casting it to the ground.
40 You have broken down all his hedges;
You have brought his strongholds to ruin.
41 All who pass by the way plunder him;
He is a reproach to his neighbors.
42 You have exalted the right hand of his adversaries;
You have made all his enemies rejoice.
43 You have also turned back the edge of his sword,
And have not sustained him in the battle.
44 You have made his glory cease,
And cast his throne down to the ground.
45 The days of his youth You have shortened;
You have covered him with shame. Selah

46How long, LORD?
Will You hide Yourself forever?
Will Your wrath burn like fire?
47Remember how short my time is;
For what futility have You created all the children of men?
48What man can live and not see death?
Can he deliver his life from the power of the grave? Selah

49LORD, where are Your former lovingkindnesses,
Which You swore to David in Your truth?
50Remember, Lord, the reproach of Your servants—
How I bear in my bosom the reproach of all the many peoples,
51With which Your enemies have reproached, O LORD,
With which they have reproached the footsteps of Your anointed.

52Blessed be the LORD forevermore!
Amen and Amen.

This summary of Psalm 89 (52 verses) tells how God keeps His covenant with David *(verses 1-4),* how He is worthy of praise *(verses 5-18),* and how God's covenant with David brings blessing *(verses 19-37).* Then, after a good and biblical start, Ethan dips into his dark feelings—depressive feelings which forget God's faithfulness and promises. He complains that God seems to have broken His covenant promises and let down David and Israel. He even doubts if God is faithful (verses 38-51*).* But despite his complaints and questions, Ethan ends by praising '*the LORD forever*'. Always praise God, even if your faith wobbles because you wrongly relied on your feelings *(*verse 52).

(VERSES 1-2) *Ethan* begins by pledging, *'I will sing of the mercies of the LORD forever.'* God is not only known for His mercy as a general quality of God. He has many '*mercies*' to cover our many sins. Yet it is that general quality of having '*mercy*' that twins with His amazing quality of '*faithfulness*' that the psalmist will make known and now states is established *'in the very heavens'.* It is lasting and obvious.

(VERSES 3-4) By a covenant, God has sworn to His chosen servant, David, that He will establish his seed for ever and that he will have an eternal throne. This is a promise of the Messiah to come, the Lord Jesus Christ.

(VERSES 5-18) See what Ethan has had revealed to him by God the Holy Spirit of some of God's attributes:

- He is praiseworthy.
- He is to be awesome and greatly to be feared.
- He is divinely unique.
- He is to be feared and revered by His separated people.
- He is mighty.
- He is faithful.
- He rules over nature.
- He defeats His people's enemies, including nations that are against Him.
- As Creator, He founded the heavens and the earth.
- He is powerful.
- He is exalted.
- He is righteous and *'just'.*
- He is merciful and truthful.
- His presence gives light that helps people to walk *'in the light'* and rejoice.
- He is glorious and strong.
- He defends His people as their *'shield'* and possesses their king.
- He is holy: *'the Holy One of Israel'.*

(VERSES 19-37) God has made His covenant with David and with His people. He abounds in faithfulness, mercy, love, lovingkindness and truth. God will not change. He will uphold David and his posterity, from whom will come the Messiah, the Lord Jesus Christ. Note that in communing with His people, the following facts about God:

- He finds, anoints, sustains and strengthens His servants against their enemies.
- He hears those who call on Him.
- He will punish their sin.
- He never betrays anyone's trust in Him.
- He will establish them *'forever like the moon'.*

(VERSES 38-45) The knowledge of God's character does not stop

Ethan wondering again why things have not worked out the way he wants. Life is like that, sometimes, and we must accept God's overriding goodness and faithfulness, even when our preferences are not realised or we become disappointed for a while. (See Romans 8:28.) As we saw in the previous psalm, it is important to trust God's character, promises, Word and Saviour.

(VERSES 46-51) Ethan's weakness to believe God in remembrance of harder times returns yet again. This drives him to ask God to remember that his time is limited and that His servants are being reproached. The seeming futility of human life surfaces, but that is to forget God, His character, His promises, His Word, His Saviour and His past faithful details.

(VERSE 52) However the psalm ends with a reverent and more appropriate note: *'Blessed be the LORD forevermore!'* Maybe Ethan is learning after all! This third book of the Psalms ends by underlining this with the phrase *'Amen and Amen'*.

Psalm 90—Eternity and brevity

A Prayer of Moses the man of God.
1LORD, You have been our dwelling place in all generations.
2Before the mountains were brought forth,
Or ever You had formed the earth and the world,
Even from everlasting to everlasting, You are God.

3You turn man to destruction,
And say, "Return, O children of men."
4For a thousand years in Your sight
Are like yesterday when it is past,
And like a watch in the night.
5You carry them away like a flood;
They are like a sleep.
In the morning they are like grass which grows up:
6In the morning it flourishes and grows up;
In the evening it is cut down and withers.

7For we have been consumed by Your anger,
And by Your wrath we are terrified.
8You have set our iniquities before You,
Our secret sins in the light of Your countenance.
9For all our days have passed away in Your wrath;
We finish our years like a sigh.
10The days of our lives are seventy years;
And if by reason of strength they are eighty years,
Yet their boast is only labor and sorrow;
For it is soon cut off, and we fly away.
11Who knows the power of Your anger?
For as the fear of You, so is Your wrath.
12So teach us to number our days,
That we may gain a heart of wisdom.

13Return, O LORD!
How long?
And have compassion on Your servants.
14Oh, satisfy us early with Your mercy,
That we may rejoice and be glad all our days!
15Make us glad according to the days in which You have afflicted us,
The years in which we have seen evil.
16Let Your work appear to Your servants,
And Your glory to their children.
17And let the beauty of the LORD our God be upon us,
And establish the work of our hands for us;
Yes, establish the work of our hands.

(VERSES 1-11) The much-used Bible phrase '*man of God*' often describes His prophets, including Moses (Deuteronomy 33:1). God revealed His messages to prophets *either* to '*foretell*' God's future plans, *or* to *'forth-tell'* by proclaiming and applying His messages to the prophet's hearers. *'Man of God' now* describes someone who has turned from his sins, trusted that on the cross Jesus died in his place to be judged and punished for those sins, and then fully committed his life to Jesus as his Lord and Saviour. Such people grow into men and women of God by daily walking ever closer with God.

Moses contrasts God's everlasting nature, before and after creation, with the short and passing life of man. A thousand years are like a passing day to our eternal Lord. Our bodies die. They are like grass that withers in a day, or like a four-hour *'watch in the night'*, which has gone by dawn. Seventy years seems a fair lifespan, if you consider the whole of humanity, but it does vary up or down in many different places. If we do get a further ten years to reach eighty years, those extra years often bring *'labor and sorrow'* and pass quickly. Birdlike, our soul one day flies off into eternity. But which eternity? There are only two options. Saved or lost? Blessed or punished? In Heaven or in Hell? Our all-seeing God knows us and is angry with us for our open *'iniquities'* and for our *'secret sins'*. His eternal *'wrath'* awaits us *unless we repent and trust in Jesus.*

(VERSES 12-17) It is vitally urgent to apply these sombre, eternal truths, whether you are a *'born-again'* Christian, or not. Whether or not you know Christ personally as your Lord and Saviour, *whoever you are*, ask God to *'Teach* [you] *to number* [your] *days, that* [you] *may gain a heart of wisdom'*. The Bible says we all need all the wisdom that God will freely give if we ask Him for it (James 1:5). Only then can we make wise choices. Half-hearted Christians lose their satisfaction and joy in Christ. To *'be glad all* [your] *days'*, ask for God to reveal His *'work'* to you and His *'glory'* to your children. When we grow daily in our understanding ourselves of God's amazing works, such as creation, redemption, regeneration, and glorification, we become more joyful and established as Christians. We then are in a better position to present God's glory to our children, be they physical or spiritual children, Are you a half-hearted Christian? Submit afresh to Christ (Romans 12:1-2). Pray and study your Bible humbly every day. But if you have *not yet* turned from your sins to ask Christ to save you and take charge of your heart, ask God *now* to open your eyes to His great love, endless mercy and amazing grace. If you *really* mean it, He *will* lead you to put your trust in Jesus. You will never be sorry!

Psalm 91—The 'air raid psalm'

1He who dwells in the secret place of the Most High
Shall abide under the shadow of the Almighty.
2I will say of the LORD, "He is my refuge and my fortress;
My God, in Him I will trust."

3Surely He shall deliver you from the snare of the fowler
And from the perilous pestilence.
4He shall cover you with His feathers,
And under His wings you shall take refuge;
His truth shall be your shield and buckler.
5You shall not be afraid of the terror by night,
Nor of the arrow that flies by day,
6Nor of the pestilence that walks in darkness,
Nor of the destruction that lays waste at noonday.

7A thousand may fall at your side,
And ten thousand at your right hand;
But it shall not come near you.
8Only with your eyes shall you look,
And see the reward of the wicked.

9Because you have made the LORD, who is my refuge,
Even the Most High, your dwelling place,
10No evil shall befall you,
Nor shall any plague come near your dwelling;
11For He shall give His angels charge over you,
To keep you in all your ways.
12In their hands they shall bear you up,
Lest you dash your foot against a stone.
13You shall tread upon the lion and the cobra,
The young lion and the serpent you shall trample underfoot.

14"Because he has set his love upon Me, therefore I will deliver him;
I will set him on high, because he has known My name.
15He shall call upon Me, and I will answer him;
I will be with him in trouble;
I will deliver him and honor him.
16With long life I will satisfy him,
And show him My salvation."

❖

(VERSES 1-8) Psalm 91 was called the 'air raid psalm' in World War II when bombs were falling thick and fast on battered London. People found great comfort in it. Psalms are like that: you may read one in a completely different context from the one in which it was written or for which it was primarily intended, but God still uses that psalm now to bless those who read it and trust Him many years later. Its basic message is that God protects and blesses you if you put your trust in

Him. That trust is richly illustrated as dwelling '*in the secret place of the Most High*', resting '*under the shadow of the Almighty*', making the LORD God your '*refuge*' to hide in and your '*fortress*' which no enemy can take by storm, being sheltered like a chick under its mother hen's wings, and having God's faithfulness protect you like an elevated shield. Any physical protection is temporary and limited in this world, but God's saving power is eternal and absolute. If your personal trust really is in God the Son, the Lord Jesus Christ, God's saving power will keep you for ever. Nothing can stop that, including any '*snare*' set to catch you, '*perilous pestilences*' and plagues, any '*terror*' of the night, whatever '*arrows*' are fired at you, and major calamities and destruction claiming many others around you. If you turn from sin and trust Jesus' death on the cross in your place, where He bore your sins and judgment, God will save you not only from all those terrifying things spiritually, but also from the deserved eternal judgment against your sins in Hell. God is in control of your life also, when Christ is your Lord: your earthly life will last until He knows when to call you home to Heaven. But unrepentant people will sadly receive '*the punishment of the wicked*'.

(VERSES 9-13) Spiritually speaking, if you seek to '*dwell*' (spend time) with the LORD as your '*refuge*', God will keep you, protect you, and help you overcome every evil means that Satan would try to use to ruin your spiritual walk with God. Those things may, like the great lion, be too strong for you to combat or, like a cobra, be too quick and sly to outwit and beat. But God will keep you from spiritual harm and your life will avoid disaster through faith in Christ. This does not mean you have no problems or battles, physically and spiritually. But, in knowing Christ, you know God graciously will protect, keep, help and bless you—and see you through finally.

(VERSES 14-16) If you know God, and thus benefit from His blessings of salvation, now and eternally in Heaven, you will:

- Love Him, '*because He first loved* [you]' (1 John 4:19);
- Know, identify with and honour His 'name';
- '*Call upon*' Him in your prayers and be answered;
- Have a satisfying '*long life*'. That is good: but to experience *eternal* '*salvation*' is even longer and better!

Psalm 92—Flourishing and fruitful

A Psalm. A Song for the Sabbath day.
1 It is good to give thanks to the LORD,
And to sing praises to Your name, O Most High;
2 To declare Your lovingkindness in the morning,
And Your faithfulness every night,
3 On an instrument of ten strings,
On the lute,
And on the harp,
With harmonious sound.
4 For You, LORD, have made me glad through Your work;
I will triumph in the works of Your hands.

5 O LORD, how great are Your works!
Your thoughts are very deep.
6 A senseless man does not know,
Nor does a fool understand this.
7 When the wicked spring up like grass,
And when all the workers of iniquity flourish,
It is that they may be destroyed forever.

8 But You, LORD, are on high forevermore.
9 For behold, Your enemies, O LORD,
For behold, Your enemies shall perish;
All the workers of iniquity shall be scattered.

10 But my horn You have exalted like a wild ox;
I have been anointed with fresh oil.
11 My eye also has seen my desire on my enemies;
My ears hear my desire on the wicked
Who rise up against me.

12 The righteous shall flourish like a palm tree,
He shall grow like a cedar in Lebanon.
13 Those who are planted in the house of the LORD
Shall flourish in the courts of our God.
14 They shall still bear fruit in old age;
They shall be fresh and flourishing,
15 To declare that the LORD is upright;
He is my rock, and there is no unrighteousness in Him.

(VERSES 1-5) Psalm 92 is written with Sabbath day worship in mind. Each week, this is the day when non-essential work gives way to thinking about the Lord, praising Him, talking with Christians about Him in fellowship, and sharing the gospel with those who do not know Christ. God's moral law, the Ten Commandments, teaches that one day in seven is to be kept for the Lord as a Sabbath, or 'cessation' from normal work and life. The apostles, under

God's guidance, kept that timeless one-in-seven principle, but changed the day to mark Jesus' resurrection from the dead which happened on the first day of the week, our Sunday. This first-day Sabbath is now called 'the Lord's day'. The command to keep it still applies, and so do God's great blessings promised to all who try to do that (Isaiah 58:13-14).

Verses 1-5 describe how we should keep the Lord's day by honouring God, even more than usual, instead of the work and other activities and pleasures of the week. They are:

- Praising the Lord, with music, all day;
- Remembering the '*Most High*' God;
- Morning proclamation of His '*lovingkindness*';
- Evening recalling of His '*faithfulness*';
- Rejoicing in His works and thoughts. We do that when we read His Word, the Bible, and especially recall His work of creation, and especially as we worship the Lord Jesus Christ though His death on the Cross in our place to pay the penalty for our sins, His rising from the dead, His giving us His Holy Spirit, His ascending to Heaven, and His entering our hearts as our Saviour and Lord.
- The Lord's Day is the day that most churches remember the broken body and the shed blood of Jesus, and we are told that as we celebrate that we '*proclaim the Lord's death till He comes*' (1 Corinthians 11:26).

(VERSES 6-9) If you know Jesus as your Saviour, do you sometimes wonder why there are those who don't seem to be able to 'get it' about how great it is to know Christ? These verses confirm they lack any *sense* of knowing God outside of faith in Christ. They are '*senseless forever*'. They just '*do not know*'. They find it hard to grasp that their lives are like grass that flourishes and then is '*destroyed forever*'. Christians and non-Christians all will die, but then, what a difference! Those who know the Lord will be with Him for ever in Heaven. Those who have not repented and trusted Christ will be scattered and will perish in '*everlasting destruction*'. Pray for them. Show them Christ's love. Share God's good news with them. Through that, the Holy Spirit brings light to darkened souls, as He did for all who received Christ as Saviour.

(VERSES 10-15) Compare the blessings received by those of us who have repented of our sins and given our lives to the Lord Jesus Christ. Our many spiritual blessings from God include:

- Spiritual strength (like a wild ox!);
- Anointed by the Holy Spirit (like oil);
- Victory over our spiritual enemies: the world, the flesh and the devil;
- Flourishing spiritual life ('*palm tree*');
- Growth in grace (like a cedar tree);
- Being '*planted*' in God's presence;
- Flourishing praise (in God's courts);
- Bearing '*fruit*'—even '*in old age*';
- Staying spiritually fresh and flourishing;
- Proclaiming Jesus as our Rock and our righteous Lord.

Psalm 93–The character of God

1The Lord reigns, He is clothed with majesty;
The Lord is clothed,
He has girded Himself with strength.
Surely the world is established, so that it cannot be moved.
2Your throne is established from of old;
You are from everlasting.

3The floods have lifted up, O Lord,
The floods have lifted up their voice;
The floods lift up their waves.
4The Lord on high is mightier
Than the noise of many waters,
Than the mighty waves of the sea.

5Your testimonies are very sure;
Holiness adorns Your house,
O Lord, forever.

(Verse 1-2) This short psalm has much to teach us. We start with some basic, but very important, truths about God. Think about what we learn about God.

First, *'The Lord reigns.'* He is Sovereign. He is King. Whether thinking about His Creation or Salvation, God is in control.

Next, He is *majestic* as King. He is the only ruler who can always, without reservation, be properly called *'Your Majesty.'*

He is *strong*: in fact, He is Almighty! Not only that, but *'He has girded Himself with strength.'* It was always His strength.

He is both the *Creator and the Sustainer of the world,* as well as the rest of His universal creation. Colossians 1:16-17 says that *'by Him all things were created that are in heaven and that are on earth, visible and invisible, whether thrones or dominions or powers. All things were created through Him and for Him. And He is before all things and in Him all things consist'* (meaning they *'hold together'*.)

Then, He is *eternal* and so without start or finish. Eternity comes under His sovereign and majestic control. That is why, with our time-limited minds we find it hard to grasp that what God does in eternity is for eternity, although on earth it may have a historical date when it becomes a reality down here. Jesus died as the Lamb of God, who was sacrificed bearing and being punished for our sins. If you turn from sin and trust in Jesus, He saves you from the eternal punishment of Hell and gives you His eternal blessings of Heaven. He gives you eternal life *now*. Jesus is '*the Lamb slain from the foundation of the world*', even though He died for us at a point in time about 2,000 years ago, on the cross at Calvary in Jerusalem (Revelation 13:8). Also, although it is true for all of us that at a point in time trusted Jesus as our Saviour to give us eternal life, we read that God '*chose* us *in Him before the foundation of the world, that we should be holy and without blame before Him in love*' (Ephesians 1:4).

(VERSES 3-4) He is '*almighty*' over nature. The sea can be very agitated, angry and terrifying—have you been in a storm at sea, facing mighty waves like mobile mountains and valleys? Our mighty '*LORD on high*' is even '*mightier*' than the sea's '*noise of many waters, than the mighty waves of the sea*'. He is Lord over it.

(VERSE 5a) In all this mind-boggling power and majesty, God's word ('*testimonies*' as in Psalm 119) '*are very sure*'. When the Bible says something is '*sure*' it means it is '*sure*'. When it says it is '*very sure*' it means it is '*very sure*'. His perfect Word reflects His perfect character and describes it perfectly, too!

(VERSE 5b) We read that '*holiness adorns Your house, O LORD, forever*'. God is pure and holy. He hates sin and so He *must* punish sin and *never* allow it in Heaven to ruin Heaven as it ruins earth. The Holy Spirit shows me my sin. He leads me to trust Jesus, and then enters my heart. God wants me to be and live as a holy person. Are you seeking to be holy? Do you live in a '*holy*' way? 'Holy' literally means 'set apart from and set apart for'. The person who trusts, knows, loves, and follows the Lord Jesus Christ has been set apart from sin and the desires of this world to please himself. He has been set apart to honour Jesus in every aspect of his daily living. We will, one day, be at home with Christ, in His '*house*' which is adorned by holiness. Let us practise our holiness now!

Psalm 94—Comforted when anxious

1O LORD God, to whom vengeance belongs—
O God, to whom vengeance belongs, shine forth!
2Rise up, O Judge of the earth;
Render punishment to the proud.
3LORD, how long will the wicked,
How long will the wicked triumph?

4They utter speech, and speak insolent things;
All the workers of iniquity boast in themselves.
5They break in pieces Your people, O LORD,
And afflict Your heritage.
6They slay the widow and the stranger,
And murder the fatherless.
7Yet they say, "The LORD does not see,
Nor does the God of Jacob understand."

8Understand, you senseless among the people;
And you fools, when will you be wise?
9He who planted the ear, shall He not hear?
He who formed the eye, shall He not see?
10He who instructs the nations, shall He not correct,
He who teaches man knowledge?
11The LORD knows the thoughts of man,
That they are futile.

12Blessed is the man whom You instruct, O LORD,
And teach out of Your law,
13That You may give him rest from the days of adversity,
Until the pit is dug for the wicked.
14For the LORD will not cast off His people,
Nor will He forsake His inheritance.
15But judgment will return to righteousness,
And all the upright in heart will follow it.

16Who will rise up for me against the evildoers?
Who will stand up for me against the workers of iniquity?
17Unless the LORD had been my help,
My soul would soon have settled in silence.
18If I say, "My foot slips,"
Your mercy, O LORD, will hold me up.
19In the multitude of my anxieties within me,
Your comforts delight my soul.

20Shall the throne of iniquity, which devises evil by law,
Have fellowship with You?
21They gather together against the life of the righteous,
And condemn innocent blood.
22But the LORD has been my defense,
And my God the rock of my refuge.

[23]He has brought on them their own iniquity,
And shall cut them off in their own wickedness;
The LORD our God shall cut them off.

(VERSES 1-3) God is holy. He hates sin. He is the Judge. God the Son will judge all sinners after death who have not trusted Him as Saviour before death. Heaven or Hell? That is the issue at stake. He judges fairly but severely. Only God is to be trusted about taking vengeance: never 'do it yourself'. The psalmist asks God '*how long*' before He pays back proud and wicked people, who now '*triumph*'.

(VERSES 4-7) Like those '*wicked*' sinners, we too have sinful hearts and are proud and arrogant at times. They '*boast*', '*break in pieces*' and '*afflict*' God's people, kill '*widows*', foreigners and '*fatherless*' children. They insult God by saying He neither sees nor understands. You hopefully do not go to their extremes of sin, but never forget that we all have sinned against God and need His forgiveness, just as they do. Worldwide today, some still persecute Christians as these wicked people persecuted God's people years ago. Pray for them regularly.

(VERSES 8-11) God sees them as '*senseless*' and as '*fools*'—as are all people who deny He exists. He made our ears and eyes: of course, He sees and hears! He '*instructs*' and '*teaches*' so of course He can correct and teach knowledge. God knows everything, including their sinful and futile thoughts. He will punish them.

(VERSES 12-19) Discipline for the believer differs from punishment for the wicked. It is a blessing to be so taught from God's Word. All who trust the Lord find rest and relief in knowing Him even in '*days of adversity*'. People with personal faith in Christ are never rejected, unlike the wicked in their eternal '*pit*'. God never casts off or forsakes those who come to Him. When you turn from sins and ask Jesus to forgive and save you, your sins are counted as His, even though He is and always has been sinlessly perfect. Jesus paid the penalty for those sins in His death for you. He treats all His righteousness as yours. God treats and accepts you as '*upright in heart*' simply by your faith in Christ. You then begin to '*follow*' Him in His righteous teachings. He stops your downward slide into sin. He supports you. When you are anxious, He comforts you. He gives you joy. Verse 19 is worth thinking about closely: '*In the multitude of my anxieties within me, Your comforts delight my soul.*'

(VERSES 20-23) In all the struggles and misery that cruel and corrupt opposition cause, the LORD becomes your '*fortress*' and your '*rock*' in whom you take refuge. You need Him especially as you will experience the opposition of '*the throne of iniquity, which devises evil by law*'. They will gather together against those seeking God's righteousness, with a view to kill the innocent.

Just as He will defend, keep and bless you, God the Judge will punish them, unless they repent and trust Jesus. Pray for them to do that! Like God, we would rather that sinners turn from sin and come to know our life-changing God of salvation.

Psalm 95–Wonder, worship, wandering and warning

1Oh come, let us sing to the LORD!
Let us shout joyfully to the Rock of our salvation.
2Let us come before His presence with thanksgiving;
Let us shout joyfully to Him with psalms.
3For the LORD is the great God,
And the great King above all gods.
4In His hand are the deep places of the earth;
The heights of the hills are His also.
5The sea is His, for He made it;
And His hands formed the dry land.

6Oh come, let us worship and bow down;
Let us kneel before the LORD our Maker.
7For He is our God,
And we are the people of His pasture,
And the sheep of His hand.

Today, if you will hear His voice:
8"Do not harden your hearts, as in the rebellion,
As in the day of trial in the wilderness,
9When your fathers tested Me;
They tried Me, though they saw My work.
10For forty years I was grieved with that generation,
And said, 'It is a people who go astray in their hearts,
And they do not know My ways.'
11So I swore in My wrath,
'They shall not enter My rest.' "

(VERSES 1-5) This psalm deals with wonder, worship and warning. Intended for Old Testament Jews, it applies in principle still to all *'born-again'* sinners. It starts with wonderful truths about God, easily taken for granted and not marvelled at as we ought. These truths should make us *'sing to the LORD'* and *'shout joyfully to the Rock of our salvation'*. Why? Our God is good, gracious and *'the great God'* as well as *'the great King'*. He is not evil or against us. We should approach Him *'with thanksgiving'* and *'with psalms'*. The heights and depths of nature are His. He made both the *'sea'* and *'the dry land'*. We cannot *'worship and bow down'* without lifting Him up in praise. We cannot do that from the heart until and without becoming, as verse 7 puts it, *'the people of His pasture and the sheep of His hand'* by trusting the Good Shepherd who gave His life for His sheep. Then we can know and praise with joy our Triune Saviour God. The Lord Jesus Christ (God the Son) is One in the Godhead with God the Father and God the Holy Spirit: Three in One and One in Three. We only come to know God as Saviour, when we believe that Jesus died on the cross in our place, bearing our sin and the penalty that sin deserves. We confess our sins to Him, with shame. We thank Him for dying for us and rising from death. We humbly ask Him to enter our lives to forgive and save us and become our Lord and Master. We then know personally our '*Rock of salvation*' on whom we build the rest of our lives. We then realise He really is 'the *great God and the great King above all gods*'. And our amazing Creator and Saviour God loves *you*!

(VERSES 6-7a) It is obvious that our hearts, should '*worship and bow down*' as we '*kneel before the LORD our Maker*'. Better still He becomes our personal Shepherd when we trust in Christ. We become His '*sheep*' under His loving care (Psalm 23).

(VERSES 7b-11) With every blessing comes a loving warning from God to the children of Israel. Their up-and-down faith and lack of obedience robbed them of much blessing and made them wander in the wilderness for forty years, until a whole generation died out and a fresh trust and obedience in the Promised Land was offered to their successors, under Joshua's leadership. They had failed to honour God '*in the day of trial in the wilderness*'. So, they went astray and made a potentially short journey in the wilderness into a hard forty-year slog. Moreover, they missed the blessings awaiting them in Canaan. The rebellion at '*Meribah*' ('rebellion' or 'quarrelling') followed their grumbling about lack of water. '*Massah*' ('testing' of God) was where they came when their leaders failed to believe that God would supply them with water. Meribah and Massah show how they failed to trust God. If you trust Jesus as your Saviour now, you can never lose your Heavenly home or salvation; but failure to trust and obey God can rob you of blessings *en route*. Beware! Keep close to Him in reading your Bible and praying each day, and cultivating worship and Christian fellowship during the week and on the Lord's day, Sunday.

Psalm 96—Good news for all the nations

1Oh, sing to the LORD a new song!
Sing to the LORD, all the earth.
2Sing to the LORD, bless His name;
Proclaim the good news of His salvation from day to day.
3Declare His glory among the nations,
His wonders among all peoples.

4For the LORD is great and greatly to be praised;
He is to be feared above all gods.
5For all the gods of the peoples are idols,
But the LORD made the heavens.
6Honor and majesty are before Him;
Strength and beauty are in His sanctuary.

7Give to the LORD, O families of the peoples,
Give to the LORD glory and strength.
8Give to the LORD the glory due His name;
Bring an offering, and come into His courts.
9Oh, worship the LORD in the beauty of holiness!
Tremble before Him, all the earth.

10Say among the nations, "The LORD reigns;
The world also is firmly established,
It shall not be moved;
He shall judge the peoples righteously."

11Let the heavens rejoice, and let the earth be glad;
Let the sea roar, and all its fullness;
12Let the field be joyful, and all that is in it.
Then all the trees of the woods will rejoice
13before the LORD.
For He is coming, for He is coming to judge the earth.
He shall judge the world with righteousness,
And the peoples with His truth.

(VERSES 1-3) These verses must foresee the wonder of the glorious gospel of our Lord Jesus Christ! There is a '*new song*' to sing, and it is for '*all the earth*'. The LORD is to be praised for it, and it is right to '*proclaim the good news of His salvation from day to day*' and '*declare His glory among the nations, His wonders among all people*'. The good news that God offers is for everyone, everywhere. One song puts it like this:

> *'Every person in every nation, in each succeeding generation*
> *has the right to hear the news that Christ can save.'*

All people in the whole wide world, however nice or religious they may be, have sinned against God in thought, word and deed. Every person is not only a lost sinner but a dying lost sinner. Is there any good news that can bring forgiveness to sinners, and eternal life to those who must go through the '*valley of the shadow of death*' (Psalm 23:4)? Yes, there is! The eternal Son of God became a sinless and perfect man, died to bear the sins and judgment of sinners, and rose again to an endless life. He is the One who, through the Holy Spirit, enters and changes the lives of all who turn from their sins and ask Jesus to enter their lives as Lord and Saviour. When you know Jesus, this news is so good that you feel you must praise God for it and share it with lost sinners who need to be saved by the only living Saviour, the Lord Jesus Christ. In short, verses 1 to 3 make sense to you.

(VERSES 4-9) Someone who is saved by Christ realises that '*the LORD is great*' and '*greatly to be praised*'. He is the real, living Creator whose '*honour and majesty*' and '*strength and beauty*' show up all religious idols—thought to be gods by some in their ignorance—as nothing. They do not have life, strength or glory, as does our eternal God of salvation. We should '*Give to the LORD the glory due His name*'. And, yes, we do have '*an offering*' to bring to God making us acceptable to Him. It is Jesus' perfect and sinless sacrifice as the '*Lamb of God*' on the cross to take the punishment for our sins. With our faith in Christ and in His sacrifice for us, we then can worship God '*in spirit and in truth*' (John 4:24).

(VERSES 10-13) *All nations* need to know:

- '*The LORD reigns*': He is in charge. That gladdens all those who know Him.
- He judges '*the peoples righteously*'.
- All His creation welcomes Him: the heavens, earth, sea, fields, trees and forests, for example.
- He will come '*to judge the earth*'.
- Righteousness and truth mark His final judgments.

Jesus told His disciples to '*Go into all the world and preach the gospel to every creature*' (Mark 16:15). He wants every person in the world to have the opportunity to repent of their sins and trust Him as Saviour and Lord. That is why real Christians should be sharing daily His good news with others all over the world.

Psalm 97—A great result of conversion

1The LORD reigns;
Let the earth rejoice;
Let the multitude of isles be glad!

2Clouds and darkness surround Him;
Righteousness and justice are the foundation of His throne.
3A fire goes before Him,
And burns up His enemies round about.
4His lightnings light the world;
The earth sees and trembles.
5The mountains melt like wax at the presence of the Lord,
At the presence of the LORD of the whole earth.
6The heavens declare His righteousness,
And all the peoples see His glory.

7Let all be put to shame who serve carved images,
Who boast of idols.
Worship Him, all you gods.
8Zion hears and is glad,
And the daughters of Judah rejoice
Because of Your judgments, O LORD.
9For You, LORD, are most high above all the earth;
You are exalted far above all gods.

10You who love the LORD, hate evil!
He preserves the souls of His saints;
He delivers them out of the hand of the wicked.
11Light is sown for the righteous,
And gladness for the upright in heart.
12Rejoice in the LORD, you righteous,
And give thanks at the remembrance of His holy name.

(VERSE 1) When a good, kind, loving, honest and powerful king is in charge, his subjects rejoice. The LORD, our promise-keeping, covenant-keeping, caring, loving, righteous, just, truthful and Almighty Ruler, *is* in charge. The whole world should rejoice—even all the '*multitude of isles*' scattered all over the globe in its vast seas and oceans.

(VERSE 2) He is so holy and glorious that darkness veils Him from the sight of mere human beings. But we are in darkness for another reason—our sin. We need to trust in Jesus, who is the '*light of the world*' (John 8:12). He shines so brightly that He replaces the need of the sun and moon to shine in Heaven itself (Revelation 21:23). His rule is based on the light of His perfect righteousness and justice.

(VERSES 3-9) Fire implies both holiness and judgment on sin. Jesus is the holy Judge. God's awesome presence—unless veiled in flesh as it was because Jesus was fully God and fully man at the same time—is likened to a flashing electric storm, and an earthquake that makes '*mountains melt like wax at the presence of the LORD*'. The heavens proclaim to all who 'read' them that God is their righteous and glorious Creator. How different from those who worship empty idols, which cannot hear, see or speak. All men and women ought to worship the true God. Those who do, then in Zion and Judah and now worldwide, rejoice that their personal God, the LORD, is '*Most High above all the earth*' and '*exalted far above all gods*'. Make sure that you regard no one and nothing in this world as more important to you than your holy Triune God, God the Father, God the Son and God the Holy Spirit. Your idol could be an obvious religious idol or anything or anyone or any preoccupation or ambition you allow to become an idol in your life. Idolatry is a sin; resist it!

(VERSES 10-11) When a sinner has been saved, God counts him as being 'righteous' for two reasons. First, his sins are *washed away* because he has trusted in Jesus, whose blood was shed for him on the cross when He bore that man's sins and was punished for them. Second, though that person is by nature an unrighteous sinner, all Jesus' perfect righteousness is *counted as his* through his trust in Jesus. My spiritual mentor, Professor Verna wright, taught me a verse, as a young Christian, that summarises these two truths about righteousness:

'Upon a life I did not live,Upon a death I did not die:
Another's life, another's death, I stake my whole eternity.'

Here are some evidences that a sinner has been converted. He now hates evil. His saved soul is preserved by God, who keeps him faithful and delivers him from wicked people. He now knows Christ's and the Bible's light on his thinking, and He is glad and joyful. Conversion to Christ is a wonderful experience, and awaiting Heaven to come is still better!

(VERSE 12) If *you* know that Jesus has cleansed you from sin, and God counts *you* as righteous, rejoice and praise the Lord as you remember His name, the Lord Jesus Christ!

Psalm 98—Jesus: Judge or Saviour?

A Psalm.
1 Oh, sing to the LORD a new song!
For He has done marvelous things;
His right hand and His holy arm have gained Him the victory.
2 The LORD has made known His salvation;
His righteousness He has revealed in the sight of the nations.
3 He has remembered His mercy and His faithfulness to the house of Israel;
All the ends of the earth have seen the salvation of our God.

4 Shout joyfully to the LORD, all the earth;
Break forth in song, rejoice, and sing praises.
5 Sing to the LORD with the harp,
With the harp and the sound of a psalm,
6 With trumpets and the sound of a horn;
Shout joyfully before the LORD, the King.

7 Let the sea roar, and all its fullness,
The world and those who dwell in it;
8 Let the rivers clap their hands;
Let the hills be joyful together
9 before the LORD,
For He is coming to judge the earth.
With righteousness He shall judge the world,
And the peoples with equity.

(VERSES 1-3) In some ways Psalm 98 seems like an echo from Psalm 96. Usually when I repeat myself it is because I forgot what I said in the first place! But the Bible often repeats truths and promises. They are good, so God reminds us of them again! As in Psalm 96, we are urged: *'Oh, sing to the LORD a new song!'* Christianity loves to put truths to music so we can join in; singing helps us remember those truths. I realised that Jesus is God when I sang and thought over the truths of the Christmas carols! Now I know it is a clear, constant theme of the Bible. *The Bible Panorama* comments on Psalm 98: 'The new song to be sung to the LORD is because of His marvellous deeds, victory, salvation, righteousness, revelation, mercy and faithfulness.' Just add the word '*grace*' (Ephesians 2:8-9) and '*love*' (1 John 4:9-10) to make it almost an exhaustive list of words that are bedrock in the message of the gospel. Think about Jesus' cruel death on the cross to bear our sins and their penalty. When we turn from the wrong in our lives to receive Christ as our Lord, Saviour and Friend, we begin to realise that the list of words quoted above, and found in this Psalm, perfectly describe what Christ did to save us. How sad that many people will not see their urgent need to repent and to receive the Lord Jesus into their hearts as their personal Lord and Saviour.

(VERSES 4-6) What joy the worship of God can produce across the world. Shouts of joy, jubilant song, music including from the harp, trumpet-playing, a ram's horns' blasts, and even joyful shouts underline the infectious joy which can become yours when the Lord Jesus is your Lord and King. Is He your Saviour, Lord and King?

(VERSES 7-9) Nature itself is put forth again as worshipping and rejoicing in God, its Designer and Creator (Genesis 1 and 2). Nature's 'choir members' include the sea and its occupants, the world and all living in it, the rivers and the hills. This reminds us how man naturally wonders at nature. He thinks instinctively, 'Whoever did that must be great.' Look at the stars in the night sky, and marvel. Mankind and nature involuntarily proclaim the Lord's wonders before their Creator.

But the joy of such worship cannot hide a sober and frightening fact. Jesus will come to earth to judge its peoples righteously and fairly. '*And as it is appointed for men to die once, and after this the judgment, so Christ was offered once to bear the sins of many*' (Hebrews 9:27-28). *Either* face *Judge* Jesus *after death* and be judged for all your sins, *or* trust *Saviour* Jesus *before death*. He was judged on the cross in your place for you. Eternal Hell awaits all unrepentant people to be judged by Jesus. Eternal Heaven awaits all who trust Him as Saviour. Will you be judged or saved? Do *you* need to trust Him *now*?

To those who trust the Lord Jesus Christ and receive eternal life, the praise of God, already sparked off by creation, hits the highest notes of sins forgiven, peace with God, eternal life now, and a home in Heaven for ever! '*Oh, sing to the LORD a new song!*' from the Psalms, ascends into deeper, wider and louder praise in Heaven when the worshippers of Jesus there, as Revelation 5:9-10 tells us, sing '*a new song, saying:*

> *"You are worthy to take the scroll,*
> *And to open its seals:*
> *For You were slain,*
> *And have redeemed us to God by Your blood*
> *Out of every tribe and tongue and people and nation,*
> *And have made us kings and priests to our God;*
> *And we shall reign on the earth."'*

Psalm 99—God's amazing character

1The LORD reigns;
Let the peoples tremble!
He dwells between the cherubim;
Let the earth be moved!
2The LORD is great in Zion,
And He is high above all the peoples.
3Let them praise Your great and awesome name—
He is holy.

4The King's strength also loves justice;
You have established equity;
You have executed justice and righteousness in Jacob.
5Exalt the LORD our God,
And worship at His footstool—
He is holy.

6Moses and Aaron were among His priests,
And Samuel was among those who called upon His name;
They called upon the LORD, and He answered them.
7He spoke to them in the cloudy pillar;
They kept His testimonies and the ordinance He gave them.

8You answered them, O LORD our God;
You were to them God-Who-Forgives,
Though You took vengeance on their deeds.
9Exalt the LORD our God,
And worship at His holy hill;
For the LORD our God is holy.

(VERSES 1-4) God's amazing character has many aspects. He is eternal, all-knowing, everywhere, self-revealing, almighty, righteous, just, merciful, loving, gracious, forgiving, judging, long-suffering, and creating. But Psalm 99 also emphasises He is '*awesome*' and '*holy*'. '*The LORD reigns*.' That fact should cause all '*peoples*' (which can also be translated '*nations*') to '*tremble*'. Powerful people groups can become arrogant and over-confident. When most powerful they can easily forget that once so-called 'impregnable' nations held that 'top spot' but fell from it. Proverbs 14:34 says, '*Righteousness exalts a nation, but sin is a reproach to any people*.' Almighty God who reigns and judges is '*awesome*'. He has unlimited power, strength and knowledge. He is '*holy*', hates all sin and *will* punish it. The Bible teaches that the '*LORD*' who is '*great in Zion*' is not only '*high above all the peoples*' but is rightly the Judge of all nations and people everywhere. All will be judged for sins against Him, unless they confess their sin, turn from it, and cast themselves on God's mercy by asking the Lord Jesus Christ to forgive them and lead them in His wisdom, holiness, and love. Only then can they, or we, '*praise* [His] *great and awesome name*' and live holy lives, knowing that '*He is holy*'.

If you turn to Jesus, God sends His Holy Spirit to live in you and His holy Word, the Bible, to guide and help you to live a holy life for God. You *will* be blessed. From then on '*your body is a temple of the Holy Spirit, who is in you, whom you have from God, and you are not your own.*' The same passage goes on to apply this important truth of Christianity by reminding us that '*you were bought at a price; therefore glorify God in your body and in your spirit, which are God's*' (1 Corinthians 6:19-20).

(VERSE 5) Verses 5 and 9 are similar. '*Exalt*' and '*worship*' '*the LORD our God*' because '*He is holy*'. God asks His people to praise Him *both 'at His footstool' and 'at His holy hill'*. Mount Zion's temple *was* His '*footstool*' for His people. All thrones of Israel's kings had footstools on which their subjects knelt before them. Now the Lord Jesus, our King of kings, chooses believers' hearts as His footstools. Worship *only* Him there—no one else and nothing else!

(VERSES 6-8) Throughout Israel's history, His people have '*called upon the LORD, and He answered them*'. Leaders who prayed include Moses, Aaron, and Samuel. God gave His Law through Moses. All three were priests. All but Aaron were prophets. The Israelites also prayed, as Moses led them in the desert from Egypt's slavery to Canaan's Promised Land. God led them by a pillar of fire at night, and a pillar of cloud by day. He forgave them but also dealt with their sins. In our Christian journey through life, God forgives us *for eternity*, but insists that daily we confess and turn from sins committed *en route*. We never lose our salvation but we can lose fellowship with God through any unconfessed sin. He expects us to keep '*His testimonies and the ordinance He gave*' us. In other words, keep to His Word, the Bible, to trust, follow and obey it.

(VERSE 9) Remember always to '*exalt' and worship*' your awesome and holy Saviour God. Follow Him each day in holiness.

Psalm 100—The thankful heart

A Psalm of Thanksgiving.
1Make a joyful shout to the LORD, all you lands!
2Serve the LORD with gladness;
Come before His presence with singing.
3Know that the LORD, He is God;
It is He who has made us, and not we ourselves;
We are His people and the sheep of His pasture.

4Enter into His gates with thanksgiving,
And into His courts with praise.
Be thankful to Him, and bless His name.
5For the LORD is good;
His mercy is everlasting,
And His truth endures to all generations.

❖

(VERSE 1) Someone has called this short Psalm 'an *exuberant* psalm'. It certainly starts with the loudest form of praise possible for a human being (a '*shout*'), in the happiest of all human emotions ('*joyful*'), from the widest possible range of worshippers ('*all you lands*'), to the most important and influential Person in the whole universe ('*the LORD*'). This is a small psalm which seeks to make a huge impact! It is *God's* Word, so we should heed the commands of this psalm just as much as we need to heed those in the 176 verses of marathon Psalm 119.

Note *why* this command for enthusiastic worship for all is made: it is as a '*Psalm of Thanksgiving*'. The Bible says so much so often about why those who know God should give Him thanks *in* all situations in our lives (even if not *for* all situations). If you have come to know that you have eternal life now, and Heaven to come, through trusting the Lord Jesus Christ as your Saviour, Friend, and loving Master, you will *want* to thank Him often and always.

Just think of His love for you in dying on that cruel cross, bearing your sins, taking your punishment for them, and being separated from God the Father for the only time in eternity. He did that so you could be forgiven and know Him personally both now and for ever. Even if you have not yet turned from your sins and trusted Jesus, surely you can see the most important thing in life is to be ready for its end, and to know God as your Father throughout eternity. To come to know Jesus really is a cause to give thanks. There are many other daily blessings, large and small, to thank God for as well.

(VERSE 2) All that explains why you should *'Serve the LORD with gladness'* and *'come before His presence with singing.'* Even if your vocal cords are out of tune, your *heart* can be in tune with God through your relationship with the Lord Jesus Christ. Your *heart* will *'sing'*!

(VERSE 3) *'LORD'*, in small capitals, refers to our covenant-keeping God. His Hebrew name, spelled without vowels, 'YHWH', was thought to be far too holy to say out loud. It later became 'Jehovah' to say easily. God, the great Creator, made us as body, soul and spirit. When Jesus becomes our Saviour and Shepherd, we become His people, and spiritually one of *'the sheep of His pasture'*. He then protects, feeds, cares for, guides and blesses us. (Read Psalm 23 to see just *how* blessed we are individually to be able to say and know that *'The LORD is my Shepherd.')*

(VERSE 4) The way to worship God is to praise Him for who He is and for what He has done for you. If you know Christ as your Saviour, do thank Him and remember His name. Your Saviour is the Lord Jesus Christ. So, He is the Sovereign God, who saves, and the anointed Messiah and the eternal Son of God. His other name, *'Immanuel'* simply *means 'God with us'* (Matthew 1:23). Jesus is fully God and fully Man. He is the only sinless and perfect Man who ever lived and died—and, in His case, rose again and ascended to Heaven!

(VERSE 5) The Lord's love and faithfulness will never end in your life or in all eternity, if you are trusting Him as your personal Lord and Saviour.

Psalm 101—Negatives and positives?

A Psalm of David.
1I will sing of mercy and justice;
To You, O LORD, I will sing praises.

2I will behave wisely in a perfect way.
Oh, when will You come to me?
I will walk within my house with a perfect heart.

3I will set nothing wicked before my eyes;
I hate the work of those who fall away;
It shall not cling to me.
4A perverse heart shall depart from me;
I will not know wickedness.

5Whoever secretly slanders his neighbor,
Him I will destroy;
The one who has a haughty look and a proud heart,
Him I will not endure.

6My eyes shall be on the faithful of the land,
That they may dwell with me;
He who walks in a perfect way,
He shall serve me.
7He who works deceit shall not dwell within my house;
He who tells lies shall not continue in my presence.
8Early I will destroy all the wicked of the land,
That I may cut off all the evildoers from the city of the LORD.

(VERSE 1) In this psalm, David, known in 2 Samuel 23:1 as the *'The anointed of the God of Jacob, and the sweet palmist of Israel'*, announces his personal intention to sing *'to You, O LORD'*. The reason is to *'sing of mercy and justice'* and to *'sing praises'*.

So the truths about God that move David to praise Him now are God's *'mercy and justice'*. *Justice without mercy* would sentence all to Hell to be punished for ever for the mountain of sins committed against God in our lifetimes, whether long or short. Hebrews 9:27 states clearly that *'it is appointed for men to die once, but after this the judgment'*. The only possible verdict must be 'Guilty'—just as charged. Romans 1:18 adds that God's wrath is *'revealed from heaven against all the ungodliness and unrighteousness of men who suppress the truth in unrighteousness'*. But *mercy without justice* would ignore God's holiness, that hates and judges sin, and would welcome the contaminant of sin into Heaven, like welcoming the Covid 19 virus into a hospital. But Jesus *'Himself bore our sins in His own body on the tree* [the cross]', that we, having died to sins, might *'live for righteousness'*. In our hearts we are thereby spiritually *'healed'* from our sins. By the Holy Spirit now in us, we start to grow as Christians. Does that describe you and your own experience of Jesus?

(VERSES 2-5) Such a real step of repenting from your sins and submitting to the Lord Jesus Christ makes you desire to live for the Lord a wise and blameless life. You know you always need the privilege of having God with you. He alone can come afresh to you each day and enable you to *'walk'* with a *'perfect heart'*. That affects all areas of your life, so you can please God, and as a result, know His daily blessings. Decide not to look at anything *'wicked'*, including filth, pornography and ungodly television, as well as what you read. Hate the sinful deeds of men with no faith. Do not allow yourself to get too close to them but do meet with and show forth Christ to them. Also stay as far away in your very closest relationships as you can from those who are of a *'perverse heart'* (meaning so sinful as to be foolish) and any form of *'wickedness'*. Do not allow unfair slandering of others in secret. Simply refuse to listen and say so, and why. Resist sinful pride (first, in your own heart) and do not encourage it in others, either.

(VERSES 6-8) From all the above and from verses 7 and 8, you can see that to be negative about sinful things is to be positive in seeking to please God. Reject lying to endorse truth. Do not swear or blaspheme to encourage good and godly speech. Say no to theft (of small or big things) and you promote honesty. King David plans to oppose deceit and lies. He also aims to apply those standards in how he rules others. But he seeks close fellowship and friendship with those who are the Lord's and try to live blamelessly and faithfully to the Lord, called here, *'the faithful of the land'*. Let us seek to do the same!

Psalm 102—'Down' but certainly not 'out'

A Prayer of the afflicted, when he is overwhelmed and pours out his complaint before the LORD.
1Hear my prayer, O LORD,
And let my cry come to You.
2Do not hide Your face from me in the day of my trouble;
Incline Your ear to me;
In the day that I call, answer me speedily.

3For my days are consumed like smoke,
And my bones are burned like a hearth.
4My heart is stricken and withered like grass,
So that I forget to eat my bread.
5Because of the sound of my groaning
My bones cling to my skin.
6I am like a pelican of the wilderness;
I am like an owl of the desert.
7I lie awake,
And am like a sparrow alone on the housetop.

8My enemies reproach me all day long;
Those who deride me swear an oath against me.
9For I have eaten ashes like bread,
And mingled my drink with weeping,
10Because of Your indignation and Your wrath;
For You have lifted me up and cast me away.
11My days are like a shadow that lengthens,
And I wither away like grass.

12But You, O LORD, shall endure forever,
And the remembrance of Your name to all generations.
13You will arise and have mercy on Zion;
For the time to favor her,
Yes, the set time, has come.
14For Your servants take pleasure in her stones,
And show favor to her dust.
15So the nations shall fear the name of the LORD,
And all the kings of the earth Your glory.
16For the LORD shall build up Zion;
He shall appear in His glory.
17He shall regard the prayer of the destitute,
And shall not despise their prayer.

18This will be written for the generation to come,
That a people yet to be created may praise the LORD.
19For He looked down from the height of His sanctuary;
From heaven the LORD viewed the earth,
20To hear the groaning of the prisoner,
To release those appointed to death,
21To declare the name of the LORD in Zion,

And His praise in Jerusalem,
22When the peoples are gathered together,
And the kingdoms, to serve the LORD.

23He weakened my strength in the way;
He shortened my days.
24I said, "O my God,
Do not take me away in the midst of my days;
Your years are throughout all generations.
25Of old You laid the foundation of the earth,
And the heavens are the work of Your hands.
26They will perish, but You will endure;
Yes, they will all grow old like a garment;
Like a cloak You will change them,
And they will be changed.
27But You are the same,
And Your years will have no end.
28The children of Your servants will continue,
And their descendants will be established before You."

(VERSES 1-2) The author of Psalm 102 is not given. The sad, afflicted writer feels faint. He shares his heart with God and asks God to hear and answer him quickly in his distress. God does hear and answer.

(VERSES 3-11) This man sees nothing but surrounding trouble and problems. His life is passing. His bones ache. His heart seems like withered grass. His appetite has gone. He is just '*skin and bones*'. He feels alone, like a desert pelican or owl, or a lone sparrow on a roof. His enemies taunt and curse him. His tears flow into his drink. He (wrongly) feels rejected by a wrathful God. As he prays to God, he will see that is not so.

(VERSES 12-17) His mindset changes. Why? He now focuses on God, His character and attributes. God is the King, eternal, full of mercy, in control of time, to be feared, over the nations, glorious, prayer-answering, is kind to the destitute and needy, and listens to their pleas for help.

(VERSES 18-22) This needy man now looks ahead. He knows God is in charge. From Heaven God sees the earth, even hears prisoners' groans and sets free those who are condemned. We all groan as slaves of sin, condemned eternally for our sins. But Jesus died and was punished for our sins to free us from judgment. Alive now, He answers all condemned sinners' prayers for forgiveness. He will be praised forever.

(VERSES 23-28) This man realises how short life is, but how everlasting is the God who created the heavens and the earth. All who know Him will live in His presence after death. These last verses are applied in Hebrews chapter 1 to the changeless and timeless Lord Jesus Christ. They show that He is none other than God Himself. Put your trust safely in Him!

Psalm 103—How is your soul?

A Psalm of David.
1Bless the LORD, O my soul;
And all that is within me, bless His holy name!
2Bless the LORD, O my soul,
And forget not all His benefits:
3Who forgives all your iniquities,
Who heals all your diseases,
4Who redeems your life from destruction,
Who crowns you with lovingkindness and tender mercies,
5Who satisfies your mouth with good things,
So that your youth is renewed like the eagle's.

6The LORD executes righteousness
And justice for all who are oppressed.
7He made known His ways to Moses,
His acts to the children of Israel.
8The LORD is merciful and gracious,
Slow to anger, and abounding in mercy.
9He will not always strive with us,
Nor will He keep His anger forever.
10He has not dealt with us according to our sins,
Nor punished us according to our iniquities.

11For as the heavens are high above the earth,
So great is His mercy toward those who fear Him;
12As far as the east is from the west,
So far has He removed our transgressions from us.
13As a father pities his children,
So the LORD pities those who fear Him.
14For He knows our frame;
He remembers that we are dust.

15As for man, his days are like grass;
As a flower of the field, so he flourishes.
16For the wind passes over it, and it is gone,
And its place remembers it no more.
17But the mercy of the LORD is from everlasting to everlasting
On those who fear Him,
And His righteousness to children's children,
18To such as keep His covenant,
And to those who remember His commandments to do them.

19The LORD has established His throne in heaven,
And His kingdom rules over all.

20Bless the LORD, you His angels,
Who excel in strength, who do His word,
Heeding the voice of His word.
21Bless the LORD, all you His hosts,

You ministers of His, who do His pleasure.
22 Bless the LORD, all His works,
In all places of His dominion.

Bless the LORD, O my soul!

(VERSES 1-5) David is praising his Lord again. The Bible teaches human beings are body, soul and spirit. Hebrews 4:12 says '*For the word is living and powerful, and sharper than any two-edged sword, piercing even to the division of soul and spirit, and of joints and marrow.*' '*Joints and marrow*' obviously refer to our physical *body*. 'Soul' is that eternal part of you which *either* is saved, if you trust Christ as your Saviour and so will go to Heaven, *or* lost if you do not repent and trust Jesus and will go to Hell. David calls his soul his '*inmost being*'. '*Spirit*' is 'the *you* that is in you'. *You* are more than a body. *You* still exist if you lose your arms and legs! Animals have spirits but not eternal souls. It can be hard to distinguish between soul and spirit. Some use the two words interchangeably. Do remember all the '*benefits*' God gives your soul if you are saved: He forgives its '*iniquities*' (sins), heals its '*diseases*', redeems it from '*destruction*', crowns it with '*lovingkindness and tender mercies*', satisfies it with '*good things*', and renews it. What a great benefit package of grace! (Compare Psalm 103:2 with Psalm 116:8-12.)

(VERSES 6-18) David turns from considering man's soul to considering God's character. He is righteous, just, self-revealing, kind to the oppressed, '*merciful*', '*gracious*', '*slow to anger*', '*abounding in mercy*', not always striving with us or angry, not treating us as severely as He could, being as merciful as the heavens are high, utterly forgiving as far as east is from west, pitying, knowing everything about us, and just as His mercy is '*from everlasting to everlasting*', so is He. Man's soul will live on eternally—lost or saved—but his body is passing and, just as grass and flowers, he will wither and die. But saved men and women, while alive, know His love and they influence future generations for Him, keep His covenant, and obey His commandments. That demonstrates the reality of their saving faith in Christ, by repentance and trust in Him, who carried their sins and penalty for them on the cross, and then rose again.

(VERSES 19-22) The LORD's kingdom '*rules over all*' from Heaven. David praises His glorious and almighty Saviour-God and urges God's '*angels who excel in strength*' and '*who do His word*' also to

'*Bless the* L*ORD*.' All the hosts of Heaven and all God's servants, who seek to do His will, are encouraged to join this 'praise choir'. So are God's created works everywhere! David remembers His own privilege and duty when he ends the psalm with, '*Bless the* L*ORD*, *O my soul.*' Will *you* join in too?

Psalm 104—God's clothing, creation and claim

1Bless the LORD, O my soul!

O LORD my God, You are very great:
You are clothed with honor and majesty,
2Who cover Yourself with light as with a garment,
Who stretch out the heavens like a curtain.

3He lays the beams of His upper chambers in the waters,
Who makes the clouds His chariot,
Who walks on the wings of the wind,
4Who makes His angels spirits,
His ministers a flame of fire.

5You who laid the foundations of the earth,
So that it should not be moved forever,
6You covered it with the deep as with a garment;
The waters stood above the mountains.
7At Your rebuke they fled;
At the voice of Your thunder they hastened away.
8They went up over the mountains;
They went down into the valleys,
To the place which You founded for them.
9You have set a boundary that they may not pass over,
That they may not return to cover the earth.

10He sends the springs into the valleys;
They flow among the hills.
11They give drink to every beast of the field;
The wild donkeys quench their thirst.
12By them the birds of the heavens have their home;
They sing among the branches.
13He waters the hills from His upper chambers;
The earth is satisfied with the fruit of Your works.

14He causes the grass to grow for the cattle,
And vegetation for the service of man,
That he may bring forth food from the earth,
15And wine that makes glad the heart of man,
Oil to make his face shine,
And bread which strengthens man's heart.
16The trees of the LORD are full of sap,
The cedars of Lebanon which He planted,
17Where the birds make their nests;
The stork has her home in the fir trees.
18The high hills are for the wild goats;
The cliffs are a refuge for the rock badgers.

19He appointed the moon for seasons;
The sun knows its going down.

20You make darkness, and it is night,
In which all the beasts of the forest creep about.
21The young lions roar after their prey,
And seek their food from God.
22When the sun rises, they gather together
And lie down in their dens.
23Man goes out to his work
And to his labor until the evening.

24O LORD, how manifold are Your works!
In wisdom You have made them all.
The earth is full of Your possessions—
25This great and wide sea,
In which are innumerable teeming things,
Living things both small and great.
26There the ships sail about;
There is that Leviathan
Which You have made to play there.

27These all wait for You,
That You may give them their food in due season.
28What You give them they gather in;
You open Your hand, they are filled with good.
29You hide Your face, they are troubled;
You take away their breath, they die and return to their dust.
30You send forth Your Spirit, they are created;
And You renew the face of the earth.

31May the glory of the LORD endure forever;
May the LORD rejoice in His works.
32He looks on the earth, and it trembles;
He touches the hills, and they smoke.

33I will sing to the LORD as long as I live;
I will sing praise to my God while I have my being.
34May my meditation be sweet to Him;
I will be glad in the LORD.
35May sinners be consumed from the earth,
And the wicked be no more.

Bless the LORD, O my soul!
Praise the LORD!

(VERSE 1-2a) In this psalm we praise God as Creator. As in Genesis 1 and 2, and throughout the Bible, we learn that God designed and created all things. Trust and obey Him because He is God the great Creator. 1 Corinthians 6:19,20 asks if you do not know that *'you are not your own'* and then adds that *'you were bought at a price'*. God has an even greater claim on you, if you have turned from your sins and received Jesus Christ as your Saviour. He *bought* you with His own precious blood on the cross in dying in your place as a sinless sacrifice, bearing the judgment for your sins. He *bought* you. God's Holy Spirit lives in the born-again sinner's life, so God also *possesses* you. In any case, God is worthy of everyone's praise as Creator. He can be known *personally*. The psalm starts, *'Bless the* LORD, *O my soul'* and *'O* LORD *my God, You are very great.'* We have a *'very great'* and *personal* God! He is clothed in *'honour'* and *'majesty'*. Part of His clothing is *'light'*. In this dark world, *'God is light'* (1 John 1:5) and Jesus said, *'I am the light of the world. He who follows Me shall not walk in darkness, but have the light of life'* (John 8:12).

(VERSES 2b-30) See God's hand of creation, design and preservation. This shouts to us of God's amazing and varied creation: heavens; sky; clouds and world's water system; winds; earth as a foundation; lakes, rivers, streams and springs; mountains and valleys; planned preservation of animals and birds by providing food and water, and places for them to live; *'fruit of* [His] *works'* (meaning all food that grows seasonally); grass for animals; plants and food for mankind; oil; trees; moon marking out the seasons and sun marking out each day; darkness and light each day; sea and all its fish and inhabitants (including *'Leviathan'*—probably an extinct dinosaur); life cycles for every creature—and this is also true, of course, for man (who alone has an ever-living soul).

(VERSES 31-35) In the light of God's glory, eternality, and fearsome power, the psalmist knows the claim that the Creator has on him as a created being. Throughout his life, he will honour God by song, praise and meditation which pleases his holy God, and by rejoicing in His Lord. Even creation shows God is too holy for uncleansed sinners to live with. But, when we repent and trust in the Lord Jesus Christ, *'the blood of Jesus,* [God's] *Son, cleanses us from all sin'* (1 John 1:7). So we know Him now personally and will joyfully dwell with God in Heaven. Join in now with the psalmist: *'Bless the* LORD, *O my soul! Praise the* LORD.*'*

Psalm 105–The sweep of history (Part 1)

1Oh, give thanks to the LORD!
Call upon His name;
Make known His deeds among the peoples!
2Sing to Him, sing psalms to Him;
Talk of all His wondrous works!
3Glory in His holy name;
Let the hearts of those rejoice who seek the LORD!
4Seek the LORD and His strength;
Seek His face evermore!
5Remember His marvelous works which He has done,
His wonders, and the judgments of His mouth,
6O seed of Abraham His servant,
You children of Jacob, His chosen ones!

7He is the LORD our God;
His judgments are in all the earth.
8He remembers His covenant forever,
The word which He commanded, for a thousand generations,
9The covenant which He made with Abraham,
And His oath to Isaac,
10And confirmed it to Jacob for a statute,
To Israel as an everlasting covenant,
11Saying, "To you I will give the land of Canaan
As the allotment of your inheritance,"
12When they were few in number,
Indeed very few, and strangers in it.

13When they went from one nation to another,
From one kingdom to another people,
14He permitted no one to do them wrong;
Yes, He rebuked kings for their sakes,
15Saying, "Do not touch My anointed ones,
And do My prophets no harm."

16Moreover He called for a famine in the land;
He destroyed all the provision of bread.
17He sent a man before them—
Joseph—who was sold as a slave.
18They hurt his feet with fetters,
He was laid in irons.
19Until the time that his word came to pass,
The word of the LORD tested him.
20The king sent and released him,
The ruler of the people let him go free.
21He made him LORD of his house,
And ruler of all his possessions,
22To bind his princes at his pleasure,
And teach his elders wisdom.

23 Israel also came into Egypt,
And Jacob dwelt in the land of Ham.
24 He increased His people greatly,
And made them stronger than their enemies.
25 He turned their heart to hate His people,
To deal craftily with His servants.

26 He sent Moses His servant,
And Aaron whom He had chosen.
27 They performed His signs among them,
And wonders in the land of Ham.
28 He sent darkness, and made it dark;
And they did not rebel against His word.
29 He turned their waters into blood,
And killed their fish.
30 Their land abounded with frogs,
Even in the chambers of their kings.
31 He spoke, and there came swarms of flies,
And lice in all their territory.
32 He gave them hail for rain,
And flaming fire in their land.
33 He struck their vines also, and their fig trees,
And splintered the trees of their territory.
34 He spoke, and locusts came,
Young locusts without number,
35 And ate up all the vegetation in their land,
And devoured the fruit of their ground.
36 He also destroyed all the firstborn in their land,
The first of all their strength.

37 He also brought them out with silver and gold,
And there was none feeble among His tribes.
38 Egypt was glad when they departed,
For the fear of them had fallen upon them.
39 He spread a cloud for a covering,
And fire to give light in the night.
40 The people asked, and He brought quail,
And satisfied them with the bread of heaven.
41 He opened the rock, and water gushed out;
It ran in the dry places like a river.

42 For He remembered His holy promise,
And Abraham His servant.
43 He brought out His people with joy,
His chosen ones with gladness.
44 He gave them the lands of the Gentiles,
And they inherited the labor of the nations,
45 That they might observe His statutes
And keep His laws.

Praise the LORD!

Psalms 105 and 106 are Parts 1 and 2 of the wide sweep of Israel's history. Neither of these long psalms (45 and 48 verses respectively) are now covered in detail, but in outline, in these commentaries on the psalms. We do, however, take a more detailed look at verses 16-24 (below). Please do read slowly all of these two psalms. The outlines are largely based on the author's book, *The Bible Panorama*.

(VERSES 1–3) *Salute Him*: God is to be saluted in thanksgiving, calling on Him, proclaiming His deeds, singing to Him, and talking of His works. His holy name is to be gloried in. This will enable the hearts of those who seek Him to rejoice.

(VERSE 4) *Seek Him*: His people must always seek the LORD, His strength and His face.

(VERSES 5–45) *See Him*: His works throughout history for His people are to be remembered. It is here that we see God in His faithfulness, power and grace; these characteristics have been manifested abundantly in the past. The sweep of Israel's history, including the exodus from Egypt and entering the promised land, is rehearsed in the rest of this psalm. What God promised to Abraham, He confirmed to Isaac and Jacob, made possible through Joseph, and progressed towards through Moses and Aaron.

(Psalm 106 will resume this sweep of history and then take us further.) God is faithful and sovereign.

A more detailed look at verses 16-24 on 'Joseph', a son of Jacob

Do you ever wonder why God allows some distressing and troubling experiences in your life, as though He owes you an easy life? We accept others' hardships far more easily! Some say that, if God is first in your life, nothing can go wrong. But the Bible does not teach that. Look at Jesus: He lived a perfect life, free from sin. Yet He was rejected, nailed to a cross, and punished there in our place by God the Father for *our* sins. The Bible says that *'all who desire to live godly in Christ Jesus will suffer persecution'* (2 Timothy 3:12). Why not take time to read Joseph's true story in Genesis: chapters 37, 39, 40, 41, 42, 43, 44, 45, 46, 47, 48, 49, 50. Joseph was sold into slavery by his jealous brothers, then treated well and did well, then was wrongly imprisoned after a false charge against him, then rose to become Egypt's powerful prime minister who was second only to Pharoah, then saved his father Jacob (or Israel) and his family, as well as various nations, from starvation. He said his brothers meant to harm him, but God meant it for his good and to bless others. More important is how this pictures Jesus, who despite living a perfect life was also rejected by His own people, suffered for us when He died on the cross to be judged for our sins, rose again to a new life, and is the King of kings and Lord of lords. He still saves us and people from all nations today, too—not from physical famine but from being judged for our sins, if we turn from sin and trust Him.

Psalm 106—The sweep of history (Part 2)

1Praise the LORD!

Oh, give thanks to the LORD, for He is good!
For His mercy endures forever.

2Who can utter the mighty acts of the LORD?
Who can declare all His praise?
3Blessed are those who keep justice,
And he who does righteousness at all times!

4Remember me, O LORD, with the favor You have toward Your people.
Oh, visit me with Your salvation,
5That I may see the benefit of Your chosen ones,
That I may rejoice in the gladness of Your nation,
That I may glory with Your inheritance.

6We have sinned with our fathers,
We have committed iniquity,
We have done wickedly.
7Our fathers in Egypt did not understand Your wonders;
They did not remember the multitude of Your mercies,
But rebelled by the sea—the Red Sea.

8Nevertheless He saved them for His name's sake,
That He might make His mighty power known.
9He rebuked the Red Sea also, and it dried up;
So He led them through the depths,
As through the wilderness.
10He saved them from the hand of him who hated them,
And redeemed them from the hand of the enemy.
11The waters covered their enemies;
There was not one of them left.
12Then they believed His words;
They sang His praise.

13They soon forgot His works;
They did not wait for His counsel,
14But lusted exceedingly in the wilderness,
And tested God in the desert.
15And He gave them their request,
But sent leanness into their soul.

16When they envied Moses in the camp,
And Aaron the saint of the LORD,
17The earth opened up and swallowed Dathan,
And covered the faction of Abiram.
18A fire was kindled in their company;
The flame burned up the wicked.

19They made a calf in Horeb,
And worshiped the molded image.
20Thus they changed their glory
Into the image of an ox that eats grass.
21They forgot God their Savior,
Who had done great things in Egypt,
22Wondrous works in the land of Ham,
Awesome things by the Red Sea.
23Therefore He said that He would destroy them,
Had not Moses His chosen one stood before Him in the breach,
To turn away His wrath, lest He destroy them.

24Then they despised the pleasant land;
They did not believe His word,
25But complained in their tents,
And did not heed the voice of the LORD.
26Therefore He raised His hand in an oath against them,
To overthrow them in the wilderness,
27To overthrow their descendants among the nations,
And to scatter them in the lands.

28They joined themselves also to Baal of Peor,
And ate sacrifices made to the dead.
29Thus they provoked Him to anger with their deeds,
And the plague broke out among them.
30Then Phinehas stood up and intervened,
And the plague was stopped.
31And that was accounted to him for righteousness
To all generations forevermore.

32They angered Him also at the waters of strife,
So that it went ill with Moses on account of them;
33Because they rebelled against His Spirit,
So that he spoke rashly with his lips.

34They did not destroy the peoples,
Concerning whom the LORD had commanded them,
35But they mingled with the Gentiles
And learned their works;
36They served their idols,
Which became a snare to them.
37They even sacrificed their sons
And their daughters to demons,
38And shed innocent blood,
The blood of their sons and daughters,
Whom they sacrificed to the idols of Canaan;
And the land was polluted with blood.
39Thus they were defiled by their own works,
And played the harlot by their own deeds.

40Therefore the wrath of the LORD was kindled against His people,
So that He abhorred His own inheritance.

[41]And He gave them into the hand of the Gentiles,
And those who hated them ruled over them.
[42]Their enemies also oppressed them,
And they were brought into subjection under their hand.
[43]Many times He delivered them;
But they rebelled in their counsel,
And were brought low for their iniquity.

[44]Nevertheless He regarded their affliction,
When He heard their cry;
[45]And for their sake He remembered His covenant,
And relented according to the multitude of His mercies.
[46]He also made them to be pitied
By all those who carried them away captive.

[47]Save us, O LORD our God,
And gather us from among the Gentiles,
To give thanks to Your holy name,
To triumph in Your praise.

[48]Blessed be the LORD God of Israel
From everlasting to everlasting!
And let all the people say, "Amen!"

Praise the LORD!

(VERSES 1–5) **Remembrance** Having first praised the LORD and given thanks to Him for His goodness, enduring *'mercy'*, *'mighty acts'*, unique praiseworthiness and for His particular dealings, the psalmist asks God to remember him and to give him His salvation with all its attendant benefits, and cause him to *'rejoice'* in the nation's *'gladness'* and *'glory'* with His *'inheritance'*.

(VERSES 6-46) **Review** Nevertheless, the psalmist identifies himself in confession with the sins of the people of Israel. He sees himself as no different in heart from them. He then reviews the seesaw of Israel's repentance and rebelliousness against the ever-ready mercy and grace of God when God's people turn back to Him. He charts Israel through from Egypt via the Red Sea and wilderness wanderings to Moses and Aaron, by name. He then summarises the period from Joshua to Jeremiah, without naming them. Always in focus are God's goodness and mercy, and His people's fickleness.

(VERSES 47-48) **Request** This reminder of human sinfulness and God's merciful grace causes him to ask God to save His people. Again, he ends on the same note of praise that opened the psalm.

A more detailed focus at verses 34-40 on why God told Israel to destroy their foes in Canaan.

The nations in Canaan's 'Promised Land' were evil. God knew that Israel would be contaminated by their evil and become like them if they survived. So, He commanded His people to destroy those evil nations. They worshipped idols. Idolatry involved both sexual perversion and horrific child sacrifice. Those living in those nations killed their own sons and daughters as sacrifices offered to idols. Sadly, when Israel did rebel, these same abominable things did actually happen. That is why God was so hard on Israel in judgment to make them come back to Him in repentance. God is a holy God who hates sins, and sin's effects on others.

Psalm 107–Why should we thank the LORD?

1Oh, give thanks to the LORD, for He is good!
For His mercy endures forever.
2Let the redeemed of the LORD say so,
Whom He has redeemed from the hand of the enemy,
3And gathered out of the lands,
From the east and from the west,
From the north and from the south.

4They wandered in the wilderness in a desolate way;
They found no city to dwell in.
5Hungry and thirsty,
Their soul fainted in them.
6Then they cried out to the LORD in their trouble,
And He delivered them out of their distresses.
7And He led them forth by the right way,
That they might go to a city for a dwelling place.
8Oh, that men would give thanks to the LORD for His goodness,
And for His wonderful works to the children of men!
9For He satisfies the longing soul,
And fills the hungry soul with goodness.

10Those who sat in darkness and in the shadow of death,
Bound in affliction and irons—
11Because they rebelled against the words of God,
And despised the counsel of the Most High,
12Therefore He brought down their heart with labor;
They fell down, and there was none to help.
13Then they cried out to the LORD in their trouble,
And He saved them out of their distresses.
14He brought them out of darkness and the shadow of death,
And broke their chains in pieces.
15Oh, that men would give thanks to the LORD for His goodness,
And for His wonderful works to the children of men!
16For He has broken the gates of bronze,
And cut the bars of iron in two.

17Fools, because of their transgression,
And because of their iniquities, were afflicted.
18Their soul abhorred all manner of food,
And they drew near to the gates of death.
19Then they cried out to the LORD in their trouble,
And He saved them out of their distresses.
20He sent His word and healed them,
And delivered them from their destructions.
21Oh, that men would give thanks to the LORD for His goodness,
And for His wonderful works to the children of men!
22Let them sacrifice the sacrifices of thanksgiving,
And declare His works with rejoicing.

23Those who go down to the sea in ships,
Who do business on great waters,
24They see the works of the LORD,
And His wonders in the deep.
25For He commands and raises the stormy wind,
Which lifts up the waves of the sea.
26They mount up to the heavens,
They go down again to the depths;
Their soul melts because of trouble.
27They reel to and fro, and stagger like a drunken man,
And are at their wits' end.
28Then they cry out to the LORD in their trouble,
And He brings them out of their distresses.
29He calms the storm,
So that its waves are still.
30Then they are glad because they are quiet;
So He guides them to their desired haven.
31Oh, that men would give thanks to the LORD for His goodness,
And for His wonderful works to the children of men!
32Let them exalt Him also in the assembly of the people,
And praise Him in the company of the elders.

33He turns rivers into a wilderness,
And the watersprings into dry ground;
34A fruitful land into barrenness,
For the wickedness of those who dwell in it.
35He turns a wilderness into pools of water,
And dry land into watersprings.
36There He makes the hungry dwell,
That they may establish a city for a dwelling place,
37And sow fields and plant vineyards,
That they may yield a fruitful harvest.
38He also blesses them, and they multiply greatly;
And He does not let their cattle decrease.

39When they are diminished and brought low
Through oppression, affliction, and sorrow,
40He pours contempt on princes,
And causes them to wander in the wilderness where there is no way;
41Yet He sets the poor on high, far from affliction,
And makes their families like a flock.
42The righteous see it and rejoice,
And all iniquity stops its mouth.

43Whoever is wise will observe these things,
And they will understand the lovingkindness of the LORD.

(VERSES 1-3) The Book of Psalms is divided into five sections. Psalms 105 and 106, which close off the fourth section, both start with *'Give thanks to the LORD'* and then tell you why to thank Him as they summarise Israel's up-and-down history. Psalm 107, which starts the fifth and last section of Psalms, also starts with *'Give thanks to the LORD'* and then also summarises why. It continues, *'for He is good; His mercy endures forever'*. That itself is a summary of this psalm, where God's dealings with His people is traced not so much in periods of history, but geographically concerning those God *'redeemed from the hand of the enemy, and gathered out of the lands, from the east and from the west, from the north and from the south'*. It has been pointed out by John MacArthur that Israelites over the ages have been delivered from Babylon to the east, from the Philistines to the west, from Syria and Assyria to the north, and from Egypt to the south. Just as God has blessed those who belong to Him from each quarter of the globe, so the Lord Jesus Christ now commands Christians in these words: *'Go therefore and make disciples of all the nations, baptizing them in the name of the Father and of the Son and of the Holy Spirit, teaching them to observe all things that I have commanded you, and lo I am with you always, even to the end of the age'* (Matthew 28:19-20).

Bearing in mind that general thanks are due to the LORD for His mercy, redemption, and gathering in of His captive people from far and wide from enemy hands, we now will see specifically why He should be thanked from all points of the compass. Each of the four sections will end with a repeat of *'Oh that men would give thanks to the LORD for His goodness, and for His wonderful works to the children of men.'* Not only evangelism and teaching but also thanksgiving to our truly good God is to be a worldwide task to do to His glory. See verses 7-8, 15-16, 21-22, and 31-32, which conclude each of the four sections before the psalm gives us a final general summary from verses 33-43. We now will see what specific things God should be thanked for from each of the four designated areas.

(VERSES 4-8) God has delivered Israel from wilderness wanderings, dealing with their hunger and thirst and their other *'troubles'* and *'distresses'*. God led them *'by the right way, that they might go to a city for a dwelling place'*. He feeds us spiritually through daily reading of the Bible and prayer, keeps us in His peace in and during many troubles and distresses of life, and guides us as we keep close to the Lord Jesus Christ who is our guide.

(VERSES 9-16) God has also delivered Israel from the *'darkness' of the 'shadow of death'* and liberated them from their *'chains'* and from the *'gates of bronze'* and *'bars of iron'* that held them captive. Jesus gives us eternal life and frees us from sin if we trust Him and follow Him as our Lord and Saviour.

(VERSES 17-22) Even those whose own sinfulness and foolishness led them into grave problems, troubles, distresses and being near to death, have found out that the LORD saved them when they cried out to Him. He healed them and saved them from destruction. They are encouraged to *'sacrifice the sacrifices of thanksgiving'* and *'declare His works with rejoicing'.* We should thank God for saving us from death and Hell's destruction, and to engage in giving thanks, rejoicing and telling others of the amazing work of salvation that God has done in us through His Holy Spirit, as well as the work of Jesus in His sacrifice for us on the cross, where He carried our sins and was punished in our place for them, and then His work of rising again from the dead, nevermore to die!

(VERSES 23-32) God has often saved His people from both physical and spiritual storms that stagger us and would prevent us getting to the safe haven we seek; but He has saved us and got us to our safe destinations time after time. We should remember to thank Him for all that in fellowship with other Christians and in the presence of the '*elders'* of our churches.

(VERSES 33-43) God sometimes judges people by reversing their blessings to make them realise their dependence upon Him, and repent to return to Him. But He graciously does just the reverse in His grace to provide all the things we need, bot physically and spiritually, and helps us to grow and be blessed. He loves to bless the poor and to shepherd the families. The psalmist deduces that observant, wise people will understand God's lovingkindness. We need to reflect on that, trust Him, obey Him, and always be grateful for His gracious hand upon us.

Psalm 108—Is my heart 'steadfast'?

A Song. A Psalm of David.
1O God, my heart is steadfast;
I will sing and give praise, even with my glory.
2Awake, lute and harp!
I will awaken the dawn.
3I will praise You, O LORD, among the peoples,
And I will sing praises to You among the nations.
4For Your mercy is great above the heavens,
And Your truth reaches to the clouds.

5Be exalted, O God, above the heavens,
And Your glory above all the earth;
6That Your beloved may be delivered,
Save with Your right hand, and hear me.

7God has spoken in His holiness:
"I will rejoice;
I will divide Shechem
And measure out the Valley of Succoth.
8Gilead is Mine; Manasseh is Mine;
Ephraim also is the helmet for My head;
Judah is My lawgiver.
9Moab is My washpot;
Over Edom I will cast My shoe;
Over Philistia I will triumph."

10Who will bring me into the strong city?
Who will lead me to Edom?
11Is it not You, O God, who cast us off?
And You, O God, who did not go out with our armies?
12Give us help from trouble,
For the help of man is useless.
13Through God we will do valiantly,
For it is He who shall tread down our enemies.

(VERSES 1-3) This psalm of David combines the same thoughts we have seen in Psalms 57 and 60. It is a good thing at times to repeat the same praises to God as long as your heart is in it. A '*steadfast*' heart is not a 'stuck fast' heart! One dictionary says 'steadfast' means 'unwavering or determined in purpose, loyalty etc'. This psalm shows how a steadfast-hearted person thinks, behaves, believes and values God's truth. Ask yourself as you read this psalm, 'Am I really steadfast-hearted for God?' If so, I too will sing with my soul spiritually, as well as with voice and instruments '*among the peoples*' who love the LORD. I should praise God from first morning light. I will also *'sing praises to* [the LORD] *among the nations'*, just as surely as I will seek to share the gospel with all people. I will not be ashamed of Him.

(VERSES 4-5) What causes David to praise with his steadfast heart? It is God's *'great' 'mercy'* and *'truth'*, which are literally immeasurable in their height. It causes him to seek God to be exalted, even *'above the heavens'*, and show His *'glory above all the earth'*.

(VERSE 6) David's steadfast heart comes from asking God to save and help with His all-powerful *'right hand'* those who wish to worship God. He knows God delivers *'His beloved'* and saves sinners *'with* [His] *right hand.'* God also listens to our prayers; that is why David says God will *'hear me'*. We start to be steadfast when we ask the Lord Jesus Christ to save us from our sins and from Hell, and to help us to turn from those sins and receive Christ in our hearts. He will deliver us from the power of the devil and the downward drag of the world. Jesus took our place, our sins, and our punishment for them, when He died on the cross and was judged there for us by God the Father. He rose again to give us fellowship with our living Saviour, through the Holy Spirit.

(VERSES 7-10) As in Psalm 60:6-8, God's people, along with David, regard Shechem, the Valley of Succoth, Gilead, Manasseh, Ephraim and Judah as God's and theirs. Moab, one traditional enemy, is seen only as their washbowl, which a lowly servant is employed to give to them. David will *'toss* [his] *sandal'* on his continual foe, Edom, as a master will throw his dirty sandals to his servant to clean. He warns Philistia, an early and frequent foe of David, that Israel will conquer them with victory shouts. In short, if we know and praise our crucified, risen Lord and Saviour, we join with *all* His saved people. He is also all-powerful over all who do not love or serve Him. He is *the* eternal Sovereign, Creator, Redeemer, and Judge.

(VERSES 11-13) But David feels rejected by God, as he points to times of defeat by foes, probably caused by God's people sinning against Him. So, David openly prays to God about it—a good example for us if, and when, we lose ground through sin. He asks God to help them. Only God can help—not man. He knows that keeping close to God will ensure their victory. We know that too. If we trust in Him, He defeats our enemies and gives us success where we never could win otherwise.

Psalm 109—When the guilty accuse the innocent

To the Chief Musician. A Psalm of David.
1Do not keep silent,
O God of my praise!
2For the mouth of the wicked and the mouth of the deceitful
Have opened against me;
They have spoken against me with a lying tongue.
3They have also surrounded me with words of hatred,
And fought against me without a cause.
4In return for my love they are my accusers,
But I give myself to prayer.
5Thus they have rewarded me evil for good,
And hatred for my love.

6Set a wicked man over him,
And let an accuser stand at his right hand.
7When he is judged, let him be found guilty,
And let his prayer become sin.
8Let his days be few,
And let another take his office.
9Let his children be fatherless,
And his wife a widow.
10Let his children continually be vagabonds, and beg;
Let them seek their bread also from their desolate places.
11Let the creditor seize all that he has,
And let strangers plunder his labor.
12Let there be none to extend mercy to him,
Nor let there be any to favor his fatherless children.
13Let his posterity be cut off,
And in the generation following let their name be blotted out.

14Let the iniquity of his fathers be remembered before the LORD,
And let not the sin of his mother be blotted out.
15Let them be continually before the LORD,
That He may cut off the memory of them from the earth;
16Because he did not remember to show mercy,
But persecuted the poor and needy man,
That he might even slay the broken in heart.
17As he loved cursing, so let it come to him;
As he did not delight in blessing, so let it be far from him.
18As he clothed himself with cursing as with his garment,
So let it enter his body like water,
And like oil into his bones.
19Let it be to him like the garment which covers him,
And for a belt with which he girds himself continually.
20Let this be the LORD's reward to my accusers,
And to those who speak evil against my person.

21But You, O God the LORD,
Deal with me for Your name's sake;

Because Your mercy is good, deliver me.
22For I am poor and needy,
And my heart is wounded within me.
23I am gone like a shadow when it lengthens;
I am shaken off like a locust.
24My knees are weak through fasting,
And my flesh is feeble from lack of fatness.
25I also have become a reproach to them;
When they look at me, they shake their heads.

26Help me, O LORD my God!
Oh, save me according to Your mercy,
27That they may know that this is Your hand—
That You, LORD, have done it!
28Let them curse, but You bless;
When they arise, let them be ashamed,
But let Your servant rejoice.
29Let my accusers be clothed with shame,
And let them cover themselves with their own disgrace as with a mantle.

30I will greatly praise the LORD with my mouth;
Yes, I will praise Him among the multitude.
31For He shall stand at the right hand of the poor,
To save him from those who condemn him.

❖

(VERSES 1-5) There is no such thing as perfect justice this side of Heaven, even when a country's legal system is basically fair and well administered. Any honest lawyer will confirm that. Here we have David, always a sinner (as we all are), but here being maliciously attacked with false accusations on points where he is innocent. He shows how a man of prayer and praise should respond. The God to whom he prays often, and praises constantly, is the One to whom David takes his problems. He simply but openly gives God the details about those who wickedly, deceitfully, dishonestly, and hatefully have turned against him. Worse still, he thought they were his friends and treated them with godly love. Have you been there? Have you ever been treated like that? Have you ever treated others sinfully like this?

(VERSES 6-20) The Old Testament law says how such people are to be severely punished. David now reminds God of what He said should be applied as punishment for these sins. God hates all sin and will punish it. Even now, *'The wages of sin is death, but the gift of God is eternal life in Christ Jesus our Lord'* (Romans 6:23). Unless we repent and trust in Jesus, we face as our spiritual *'death'*, which is eternal punishment for our sins against God and against others.

But we know that Jesus took our punishment in our place when He died on the cross for us. When we repent and trust Him, we are at once forgiven and receive eternal life, now and in Heaven. When you sin against others, first own up to God and ask Him to forgive and save you and change your future conduct; then tell the person you hurt that you are sorry and ask for his or her pardon too. But notice that even if sin is either judged because of rebellion against God and evil done to others or pardoned through faith in Christ, there are often very harmful consequences to others. Of course, a converted sinner stops behaving in a wicked way, and also will know God's peace that overcomes all fear and regret.

(VERSES 21-29) David then asks God, *'Deal with me for* [God's] *name's sake; Because* [His] *mercy is good, deliver me.'* He then details how *'poor and needy'* he is and has become. His heart is *'wounded within'* him. He feels 'weak-kneed' and *'feeble'*. He is 'feeble' and the target of his foes' ridicule and insults. But the way up is down! As he lowers himself before God, he knows God will help him and lift him up. He trusts his Sovereign LORD God. He knows that God will deal with and shame his sinful foes.

(VERSES 30-31) As we often see with David, when he starts with God and shares a real problem with Him, he ends up by praising God, both individually and *'among the multitude'*. God is faithful and will *'stand at the right hand of the poor'*. By *'the poor'*, more than the financially needy folks are included. It includes *'the poor and needy man'* who is being *'persecuted'* (see verse 16). God is on our side when we feel we have nothing much to offer Him. So keep trusting and praising Him!

Psalm 110—Short psalm—long blessings!

A Psalm of David.
1The LORD said to my Lord,
"Sit at My right hand,
Till I make Your enemies Your footstool."
2The LORD shall send the rod of Your strength out of Zion.
Rule in the midst of Your enemies!

3Your people shall be volunteers
In the day of Your power;
In the beauties of holiness, from the womb of the morning,
You have the dew of Your youth.
4The LORD has sworn
And will not relent,
"You are a priest forever
According to the order of Melchizedek."

5The Lord is at Your right hand;
He shall execute kings in the day of His wrath.
6He shall judge among the nations,
He shall fill the places with dead bodies,
He shall execute the heads of many countries.
7He shall drink of the brook by the wayside;
Therefore He shall lift up the head.

(VERSES 1-3) For a better grasp of these verses, read Matthew 22:41-46, Mark 12:35-37, and Luke 20:41-44. These show how Jesus puts these truths to Pharisees who try to trap Him and deny His Deity.

He takes the initiative from the Pharisees and asks them whose son is the Christ (or 'Messiah'). They reply, *'the Son of David'*. Correct! The Messiah's line comes from David. An ancestor can be called 'father' and a descendant 'son', so Jesus is the *'Son of David'*. But there is more! The Pharisees reject Jesus as God. So, Jesus shows that Christ is *both* David's Lord *and also* his descendant. The *'LORD'* God, God the Father, says David calls Him *'Lord'*. Jesus shows that, as Messiah, He is *both* David's descendant *and* David's divine eternal Lord. Jesus is *both* God *and* sinless man.

We read, too, that the Lord Jesus Christ rules and will have the final victory on earth and in Heaven. That follows His earlier victories on the cross, at the tomb, and in His ascension. As God the Son, He shares all His victories with God the Father and God the Holy Spirit. Jesus' willing followers reflect God's *holy majesty* and will also triumph finally as they follow Jesus (Revelation 19:11-21).

(VERSE 4) Another deep truth follows from both Old and New Testaments. Note that when God gives His word, He keeps it! *'The* LORD *has sworn and will not relent.'* Rely completely on His Word, the Bible. Study it each day. God's faithfulness includes that, if you repent of your sins, believe Jesus died and was punished by God the Father for you on the cross, and receive Him into your heart as your Lord and Saviour, you *are* saved. You receive eternal life. God cleanses you from all sin, and lives in your heart by the Holy Spirit.

God also keeps His Word about the work of Jesus. Jesus is a *'priest for ever according to the order of Melchizedek'*. Priests descended from Aaron. They all died or retired. Their regular and many sacrifices never could take away sins. Sinners were forgiven until the next sacrifice. Unique Melchizedek appeared and took tithes from Abraham.

He is at least a type of Christ: some think he is an actual Old Testament appearance of Jesus. As *'king of righteousness'* and *'king of peace'*, he had no (human) father or mother, and neither start nor end. *'Made like the Son of God,* [He] *remains a priest continually'* (Hebrews chapters 5, 6 and 7, especially 7:1-3). He pictures Jesus, who sacrificed His life to pay the penalty for our sins *'once for all'* (Hebrews 7:27). He now continues as Priest eternally. (See Hebrews 7:25.) At Calvary (the *final* altar), the Lord Jesus Christ (the *final* Priest) made the *final* Sacrifice for sins (*Himself*). His sacrifice is both perfect and complete as well as being eternally effective.

(VERSES 5-7) *'The* LORD *is at your right hand'* to save you if He has become your Saviour. He will also judge all sinners and nations, including kings. Think of brook Kidron flowing in Gethsemane, where Jesus prayed before going to the cross for us. He drank from it and prayed: *'My Father, if it is possible, may this cup be taken from Me. Yet not as I will, but as You will'* (Matthew 26:39). After His lonely but selfless prayer at Gethsemane, His head was lifted up to face Calvary's judgment for us and for our sins. How brave, loving and sacrificial. Trust, love and follow Him. He drank that bitter cup of suffering and judgment for you and for me.

Psalm 111—Worship, works and wisdom

1Praise the LORD!

I will praise the LORD with my whole heart,
In the assembly of the upright and in the congregation.

2The works of the LORD are great,
Studied by all who have pleasure in them.
3His work is honorable and glorious,
And His righteousness endures forever.
4He has made His wonderful works to be remembered;
The LORD is gracious and full of compassion.
5He has given food to those who fear Him;
He will ever be mindful of His covenant.
6He has declared to His people the power of His works,
In giving them the heritage of the nations.

7The works of His hands are verity and justice;
All His precepts are sure.
8They stand fast forever and ever,
And are done in truth and uprightness.
9He has sent redemption to His people;
He has commanded His covenant forever:
Holy and awesome is His name.

10The fear of the LORD is the beginning of wisdom;
A good understanding have all those who do His commandments.
His praise endures forever.

(VERSE 1) This simple verse teaches two very important lessons to everyone who has been *'born again'* by trusting in Jesus as Lord and Saviour. Remember that according to Jesus and the Bible, the *only* people who can legitimately say they are 'Christians' are those who have been *'born again'* (John 3:3-7).

First, a Christian should always praise the Lord, even in hard circumstances. And that should be done wholeheartedly. Our lives and words should help others, both believers and unbelievers, to have the highest view of our Saviour God. That is why each should be able to say honestly that *'I will praise the LORD with my whole heart.'*

Second, we should not only do that when on our own: we should worship God wholeheartedly before Christian leaders ('in *the assembly of the upright*'), and also along with our fellow believers in services and meetings (*'and in the congregation'*), as well as in daily life.

(VERSES 2-9) There are so many reasons to praise God. See if you can add any to this list taken from these verses:

- God does great works, such as Creation, Redemption, Resurrection, Conversion.
- God's deeds show His honour and glory.
- God is righteous for ever.
- God makes His wonders memorable.
- God is gracious and compassionate.
- God feeds those who fear Him.
- God keeps and honours His word and promises: *'He will ever be mindful of His covenant.'*
- God is powerful: He use His power to help and bless His people — Israel then physically, and Christians now spiritually.
- God's works are always centred on truth and justice.
- God's precepts (teachings) are *'sure'*. They showGod is eternally faithful and upright.
- God provides redemption for us. Redemption means to 'buy back'; Jesus bought us back from sin, selfishness, judgment and Hell by taking the penalty and punishment for our sins on the cross and rising again. We become God's people if we turn from our sins and trust in Jesus.
- God's covenant—His eternally binding commitment to us—through Christ, really is for ever! Heaven is for keeps, also!
- God is holy. He hates all sin—including ours—and we must seek to be holy.
- God is awesome: to the Christian, He is Saviour, Friend, Father, and Comforter. But on sinners who will not repent from sin and trust in Him, His awesome holiness and justice will be poured out eternally in judgment in Hell. That is why He '*now commands all people everywhere to repent*' (Acts 17:30). Have you repented?

(VERSE 10) One of the Bible's best-known verses is '*The fear of the LORD is the beginning of wisdom.*' Holy reverence and awe for God, and right fear of being judged for our sins should lead us to repent and ask Him to forgive us and become our Lord and Master. We then begin to know His wisdom as we ask for it (James 1:5) and daily learn His Word, the Bible, which is packed with His wisdom and truth. It is vital to follow that wise teaching by obeying what He commands in the Bible. This produces *'good understanding'* and praise to God for ever!

Psalm 112—Consequences of blessing

1Praise the LORD!

Blessed is the man who fears the LORD,
Who delights greatly in His commandments.

2His descendants will be mighty on earth;
The generation of the upright will be blessed.
3Wealth and riches will be in his house,
And his righteousness endures forever.
4Unto the upright there arises light in the darkness;
He is gracious, and full of compassion, and righteous.
5A good man deals graciously and lends;
He will guide his affairs with discretion.
6Surely he will never be shaken;
The righteous will be in everlasting remembrance.
7He will not be afraid of evil tidings;
His heart is steadfast, trusting in the LORD.
8His heart is established;
He will not be afraid,
Until he sees his desire upon his enemies.

9He has dispersed abroad,
He has given to the poor;
His righteousness endures forever;
His horn will be exalted with honor.
10The wicked will see it and be grieved;
He will gnash his teeth and melt away;
The desire of the wicked shall perish.

(VERSE 1) Every true spiritual blessing in life starts with God. That is why the best hymns we can sing today focus on God and not mainly on how we feel—though the two are not always incompatible. So, Psalm 112 again bids us first to '*Praise the LORD*'. Then we are told that God's blessing comes to '*the man who fears the LORD*'. We have noted before that such *fear* of Him, on the part of those who know Him as their Lord and Saviour, though faith in Jesus Christ, is a reverential and loving fear, not a terror-stricken panic. If you know the Lord Jesus, through His death on the cross when He bore your sins and was punished for them in your place, this psalm says that a big change in your life is that now you will '*delight greatly*' to obey His commands. Jesus said, '*If you love Me, keep My commandments*' (John 14:15).

(VERSES 2-9) What blessed consequences follow for those made '*upright*' by their obedient trust in the Lord! Here they are:

- Their children are blessed: that can be *both physical* children, *and* those to whom you are a *spiritual* parent.
- God provides His prosperity—*always* spiritually in Christ, and *at times* physically, too.
- Enduring righteousness: first we are counted as righteous through faith in Jesus, and then He changes us and makes us begin to live righteously in practice, to please Him.
- Light in darkness: Jesus, the '*Light of the world*' (John 8:12), is always with us in the darkest situations and problems. His Word brings light, too. As this light is for those who are '*gracious and full of compassion, and righteous*', God changes those who are not naturally so to become like that. Ask Him to do that for you. He will if you trust Jesus as Saviour, put Him first in your life as your Lord, and obey Him as the Bible teaches you should.
- God's presence makes those who obey Him deal graciously and generously lend to others.
- A certainty that God gives and guides believers in Him with discretion.
- A steadfast trust in God, security, a firmness in faith, and lack of fear even when the news is bad.
- Final triumph as they follow Christ. This is *always eternally* true! Even those who are martyred for their faith in Christ end up in Heaven with Jesus. Here, on earth, we triumph, if Christ is exalted and we keep close to Him—and He blesses us for that.
- A generosity to others, especially the poor.
- A practical growth in righteousness, and a way to live powerfully and honourably for God.

(VERSE 10) There is a sad but clear contrast between the man described above who trusts in the Lord, and so obeys Him, and the unrepentant '*wicked*' man who goes his own way. Not only will he achieve *nothing* lasting, but, worse still, he will be eternally separateed from God in Hell. His state of vexation and gnashing his teeth will continue for ever. But if, even now, he repents of his sins and trusts in Jesus, he will be forgiven, blessed and changed by God.

Psalm 113—Why 'Praise the LORD'?

1Praise the LORD!

Praise, O servants of the LORD,
Praise the name of the LORD!
2Blessed be the name of the LORD
From this time forth and forevermore!
3From the rising of the sun to its going down
The LORD's name is to be praised.

4The LORD is high above all nations,
His glory above the heavens.
5Who is like the LORD our God,
Who dwells on high,
6Who humbles Himself to behold
The things that are in the heavens and in the earth?

7He raises the poor out of the dust,
And lifts the needy out of the ash heap,
8That He may seat him with princes—
With the princes of His people.
9He grants the barren woman a home,
Like a joyful mother of children.

Praise the LORD!

(VERSES 1-3) We can learn so much about praising the Lord from this psalm's first three verses. Before I came to know Christ, I rarely praised God unless I, or my loved ones, benefited from something unusually good. I was very selfish. Then, after seeing how my sister's life changed after she received Christ, I began to think through the gospel and ended up by realising that I was a guilty sinner who deserved God's punishment, that Jesus was both God and sinless man, and had borne my sins and their penalty for me when He died on the cross. I believed that because Jesus rose again, He could live in my life by the Holy Spirit if I turned from my sins and asked God to forgive me and enter my life as my Lord. When that happened it *did* cause me to *'praise the LORD'*, who had become my Saviour. As I read the Bible each day, I began to see how great and loving God really is. I began to praise Him *for who He is,* as well as for what *He had done, is doing,* and *will do* for me and for *many others* worldwide.

Now learn four things about praising the LORD; you can do it!

- If I serve the LORD, that increases my desire to praise Him—He is a loving and kind Lord.

- Praise His Name. There are many names used for God in the Bible. The two I love most are '*Jesus*' which means 'God saves', and '*Emmanuel*' which means 'God with us'. We praise Him because He saves us and is with us!
- The LORD should be praised at all times, '*from this time forth and forevermore*' and whether the sun or the moon are visible.
- His name is to be praised *geographically* wherever the sun shines—in other words, *everywhere!*

If you know the Lord Jesus, these four occasions to praise Him are for you too! Someone said that there are only two occasions when a Christian should praise the Lord: first, when he feels like it; and second, when he doesn't feel like it!

(VERSES 4-6) Think of '*all nations*' with their billions of people, huge natural resources, armaments, and finances: '*The LORD is high above*' all of them and over what they have and can do. But He is even more exalted than that! His glory is also '*above the heavens*', whether atmospheric heavens that planes fly across, starry heavens which are infinite and beyond our ability to fully explore, or Heaven which awaits all who repent and trust in our Creator-Redeemer God, the Lord Jesus Christ. Not only is our Triune God (Father, Son and Holy Spirit) '*the LORD our God who dwells on high*'. He actually '*humbles Himself* [meaning 'He stoops'] *to behold the things that are in the heavens and in the earth*'. God is so exalted and majestic yet interested in you and me.

(VERSES 7-9) God's principle of blessing is to raise those who are cast down, like a '*barren woman*' who becomes a '*joyful mother of children*' and gives them a home to live in. The '*poor*' and '*needy*' are lifted from the '*dust*' and '*ash heap*' respectively to Heaven's glory. Jesus taught that '*everyone who exalts himself will be humbled, and he who humbles himself will be exalted*' (Luke 18:14). Only those will be in Heaven who have humbled themselves over their wrongdoings and guilt, repented of their sins and trusted in Jesus.

No wonder we end the psalm *with 'Praise the LORD'!* If you know Jesus, '*Praise the LORD*'. If you do not know Him, trust Him now! You will then have eternal reasons to '*Praise the LORD*'.

Psalm 114—The Exodus remembered

1When Israel went out of Egypt,
The house of Jacob from a people of strange language,
2Judah became His sanctuary,
And Israel His dominion.

3The sea saw it and fled;
Jordan turned back.
4The mountains skipped like rams,
The little hills like lambs.
5What ails you, O sea, that you fled?
O Jordan, that you turned back?
6O mountains, that you skipped like rams?
O little hills, like lambs?

7Tremble, O earth, at the presence of the LORD,
At the presence of the God of Jacob,
8Who turned the rock into a pool of water,
The flint into a fountain of waters.

(VERSES 1-2) Psalm 114 refers to Israel's leaving Egypt, known as the 'Exodus', which you can read about in the book of Exodus chapters 12-14. God's plan was first to take Israel out of Egypt, and then to take the influence of Egypt (especially its idolatry and ungodliness) out of Israel. So, the southern tribe of Judah, including Jerusalem, was to be God's dedicated *'sanctuary'*. The ten northern tribes of Israel were also to be under God's control *('His dominion')*. After their cruel slavery in Egypt, God brought out His people on that first Passover to know and follow Him.

This also is a valuable picture and principle for those of us who have been set free from the penalty and power of sin through the death and resurrection of the Lord Jesus Christ. He was judged and punished on the cross for our sins, and then rose from the dead to conquer death as well as sin. As we are forgiven and freed from the slavery, caused not by Egypt but by our sins, we, too, are bidden by God to live holy lives. *'Holy'* means being 'set apart' for God. We *are* already counted as holy; by His grace and help we must now *live* in a holy way. We do not belong to ourselves; Jesus has bought us to be His. The Bible says, in 1 Corinthians 6:19: *'Do you not know that your body is the temple of the Holy Spirit who is in you, whom you have from God, and you are not your own? For you were bought at a price; therefore glorify God in your body and in your spirit, which are God's.'*

(VERSES 3-6) Nature itself responds to the greatness of God's power and authority. He parted the Red Sea to let Israel out of Egypt. Forty years later, He parted the Jordan to allow them to enter Canaan's Promised Land. The God who takes the Christian out of sin's dominion also leads him into a place of blessing for all who follow Jesus, who daily read and obey the Bible and who keep a prayerful walk with the Lord and especially on the Lord's day seek fellowship with others saved by faith in Christ. The earthquake described may be that on Mount Sinai when, in awesome circumstances, God revealed His law, the Ten Commandments. If the Creator God wants to get attention by earthquakes, He can make mountains skip *'like rams'* and He can make hills *'like lambs'*, which run and jump.

(VERSES 7-8) When God shows His majestic and powerful presence in our small part of His created world (earth is a very tiny part of His universe), the least the earth can do is to quake! We, too, need to recognise His dazzling holiness and His hatred for and judgment on sin. Yet He is also *'the God of Jacob'*. Jacob was the father of the twelve tribes of Israel, but also a man who often failed; his name means 'supplanter' or 'twister'. God still deals with sinners who trust but fail Him—just like Jacob, like me and like you. At Meribah (or Massah), God twice brought water from the flinty rock. Jesus is our Rock: He quenches our thirst for reality and for God, now and eternally, and for all who repent and trust Him. Have you repented? Do you trust in Christ?

Psalm 115—God or gods?

1Not unto us, O LORD, not unto us,
But to Your name give glory,
Because of Your mercy,
Because of Your truth.
2Why should the Gentiles say,
"So where is their God?"

3But our God is in heaven;
He does whatever He pleases.
4Their idols are silver and gold,
The work of men's hands.
5They have mouths, but they do not speak;
Eyes they have, but they do not see;
6They have ears, but they do not hear;
Noses they have, but they do not smell;
7They have hands, but they do not handle;
Feet they have, but they do not walk;
Nor do they mutter through their throat.
8Those who make them are like them;
So is everyone who trusts in them.

9O Israel, trust in the LORD;
He is their help and their shield.
10O house of Aaron, trust in the LORD;
He is their help and their shield.
11You who fear the LORD, trust in the LORD;
He is their help and their shield.

12The LORD has been mindful of us;
He will bless us;
He will bless the house of Israel;
He will bless the house of Aaron.
13He will bless those who fear the LORD,
Both small and great.

14May the LORD give you increase more and more,
You and your children.
15May you be blessed by the LORD,
Who made heaven and earth.

16The heaven, even the heavens, are the LORD's;
But the earth He has given to the children of men.
17The dead do not praise the LORD,
Nor any who go down into silence.
18But we will bless the LORD
From this time forth and forevermore.

Praise the LORD!

❖

(VERSE 1) A characteristic of sinful men is that so often we want to be acknowledged, praised and glorified. Someone has said that self-made man loves to worships his creator—*himself!* A coincidence of the English language is that the middle letter in the word 'sin' is 'I'— *I* live for what *I* want, *I* do want *I* like, and *I* do not care too much about others. When I was a young man, I remember a popular saying, 'Blow you Jack—I'm all right.' The symptoms of this worldwide spiritual disease are still very evident today.

But what a difference there is when someone trusts, knows, loves and follows the Lord—though the temptation to be selfish is always near. Psalm 115 starts by saying, *'Not unto us, LORD, not unto us but to Your name give glory.'* We should live to glorify our Lord. When you think of God's great love for us in giving His only Son, Jesus, to come to earth to live a sinless life, to die in the place of the guilty to bear the penalty for our sins, and then to rise again to be the living Saviour of all who will turn from sin and trust Him, you can see why we should seek to glorify Him. Note that His *'mercy'* and His *'faithfulness'* to us are what causes us to want to glorify Him.

(VERSES 2-8) God hates idolatry, whether physical, visible idols on display, or the idols that have taken God's place in our hearts, lives, thoughts and ambitions. The idols to which people bow down are a tragic waste of time. They are mute, blind, deaf, senseless, useless, lame, and lifeless. The worshippers' sinful worship of idols is as ineffective as their idols are—even if they belong to a so-called 'Christian' church. The second and longest of the Ten Commandments, referred to often in the Bible, says that idols should not even be made, and that it is wrong to bow down to them or worship them (Exodus 20:4-6).

(VERSES 9-11) By contrast, trust in the Lord God. He helps, shields, and blesses His physical children (the Jews), their priests, and *those 'who fear the LORD—trust in the LORD.'* All non-Jews are included, too, no matter who they are or where they live. *'God so loved the world, that He gave His only begotten Son, that whoever believes in Him should not perish but have everlasting life'* (John 3:16). Why *'perish'* eternally when *'eternal life'* is offered by trusting the Saviour who died for you?

(VERSES 12-15) The blessings God gives to all those just mentioned are offered to their children, too. In His Word, God, our powerful Creator and loving Redeemer, has made that promise. He *cannot* lie. The *children* we can see blessed by God's grace, as we share the gospel with them and try to help them trust Christ and understand the Bible, are not just our physical offspring where we are their mothers and fathers. There are 'spiritual children' to see blessed, too. They are the ones who have become *'children of God'* spiritually by faith by receiving the Jesus Christ in their hearts (John 1:12; John 3:3 and 7).

(VERSES 16-17) Like the psalmist, we should be grateful that the LORD, who owns the heavens, has generously given this earth to man. Those who die not believing in Christ will *never* praise God. They will face His eternal judgment in Hell. Those who know the Lord will praise Him *'from this time forth and forevermore'* in Heaven.

Little wonder, that we end with the golden words, *'Praise the LORD!'*

Psalm 116—God is merciful

1I love the LORD, because He has heard
My voice and my supplications.
2Because He has inclined His ear to me,
Therefore I will call upon Him as long as I live.

3The pains of death surrounded me,
And the pangs of Sheol laid hold of me;
I found trouble and sorrow.
4Then I called upon the name of the LORD:
"O LORD, I implore You, deliver my soul!"

5Gracious is the LORD, and righteous;
Yes, our God is merciful.
6The LORD preserves the simple;
I was brought low, and He saved me.
7Return to your rest, O my soul,
For the LORD has dealt bountifully with you.

8For You have delivered my soul from death,
My eyes from tears,
And my feet from falling.
9I will walk before the LORD
In the land of the living.
10I believed, therefore I spoke,
"I am greatly afflicted."
11I said in my haste,
"All men are liars."

12What shall I render to the LORD
For all His benefits toward me?
13I will take up the cup of salvation,
And call upon the name of the LORD.
14I will pay my vows to the LORD
Now in the presence of all His people.

15Precious in the sight of the LORD
Is the death of His saints.

16O LORD, truly I am Your servant;
I am Your servant, the son of Your maidservant;
You have loosed my bonds.
17I will offer to You the sacrifice of thanksgiving,
And will call upon the name of the LORD.

18I will pay my vows to the LORD
Now in the presence of all His people,
19In the courts of the LORD's house,
In the midst of you, O Jerusalem.

Praise the LORD!

(VERSES 1-2) The LORD has heard the psalmist's *'voice and supplications.'* He always does! That is what the gospel is all about. As I saw how sinful I was and my need to be forgiven, I cast myself on God's mercy and cried out to Him. I turned from sin to receive Christ as my Lord and Saviour. He died on the cross for me, bearing my sins and their judgment. He rose again and now lives in my heart. Two results follow: *'I love the LORD'* and *'I will call upon Him as long as I live.'*Those are marks of conversion for anyone who trusts in Jesus. The rest of this psalm tells what to expect if we trust in Jesus to save us.

(VERSES 3-7) God saves us from fear of death. He is with us in trouble and sorrow. He continues to save and protect us when we are in great need. He is compassionate, gracious, righteous and *'bountifully'* generous. He gives us rest in our souls, even in hard times. He always answers a prayer that effectively says, *'O LORD, I implore You, deliver my soul.'*

(VERSES 8-11) The psalmist stops and focuses on what the LORD has done for him. The three aspects he mentions are a wonderful preview of the gospel of the Lord Jesus Christ. He saves our soul from the spiritual and eternal death of Hell when we trust in Him and saves us for Heaven. He gives us joy in place of sadness and tears. And He gives us a new walk with Him day by day as our Lord, Saviour and Friend. Previously, he had been occupied with his affliction caused by the dishonesty and sinfulness of liars with whom he was in contact. For us today, we can proclaim to them the One who is *'the Way, the Truth and the Life'!*

(VERSES 12-14) The *'cup of salvation'* speaks of the satisfaction of being saved. We now call on God in prayer and honour and keep our promises to Him along with others who know Him, *'in the presence of all His people'.* That is His church. It exists locally where people meet together who know Christ, and it exists universally and consists of all people from all times and in all places, including Heaven, who are saved by faith in Christ.

(VERSES 15-17) Every saved person is what the Bible calls a 'saint', which means being set apart to live for Christ each day. Our death is precious to God because we will then share Heaven with Him and others. If you are a true '*servant*' of the Lord, He sets you free! That makes you give the sacrifice of thanksgiving to Him and causes you to often '*call on the name of the LORD*'.

(VERSES 18-19) The psalmist obviously greatly values meeting together with others who know God, in Zion's temple in Jerusalem. It is there that he will praise the Lord and renew his vows to serve, honour, follow and worship God. That is also why Christians meet together, especially on Sunday (the Christian's Sabbath known as 'the Lord's Day'), to praise our triune God, whom we know in our lives as Father, Son and Holy Spirit. This is all because Jesus is the Saviour of all who cast themselves on His mercy.

'*Praise the LORD!*' is a command as well as a joyful recommendation! He alone is worthy of praise and worship, as the first three of the Ten Commandments make very clear (Exodus 20:1-6).

Psalm 117—Short psalm—long blessing

1 Praise the LORD, all you Gentiles!
Laud Him, all you peoples!
2 For His merciful kindness is great toward us,
And the truth of the LORD endures forever.

Praise the LORD!

Psalm 117 is the shortest psalm in the book of Psalms, consisting of only two verses. It is also the Bible's shortest chapter. Here is the middle chapter of all the chapters in the Bible! You are half way through God's Word. Although it is short, the benefits and blessings it describes and encourages are truly endless. In fact, they last through all eternity for all trusting in Jesus Christ!

Because it is so short, we examine it phrase by phrase. Why not pray over each simple phrase as you read it or hear it read?

(VERSE 1) *'Praise the LORD,'*

It is always the right thing to do to praise God. This short psalm starts and finishes with *'Praise the LORD'*. From the start of our Christian lives—since Jesus became our Saviour in answer to our personal faith placed in Him—until our dying day, may our aim always be to praise God, and live in such a way that helps others to praise Him, too. In Heaven, for the first time, we will praise Him perfectly, because sin and self and worldly influences will not be there and *'we shall see Him as He is'* (1 John 3:2).

'all you Gentiles;' It is no surprise that the Bible says that *'God so loved the world that He gave His only begotten Son, that whoever believes in Him should not perish but have everlasting life'* (John 3:16), or that Jesus told His disciples to *'go into all the world and preach the gospel to every creature'* (Mark 16:15).

There is a challenging song which starts:

Every person in every nation,
In each succeeding generation,
Has the right to hear the news
that Christ can save.

God wants people from all nations to trust in the Lord Jesus Christ and praise Him.

'Laud [Extol] *Him. . .'*

Do you see yourself as a sinner who needs to repent and turn from your sins? Do you believe that the penalty for your sins has been paid for by Jesus when He was punished on the cross in your place? If so, have you trusted in Jesus yet as your living Saviour and Lord? If you do, seek to *'extol'* the Lord by what you now say and do. *'Extol'* means to elevate or raise. Many people ignore God, but when they note that you lift up His name in the way you worship or witness, and live life to please God, they see what a wonderful, life-changing, Lord and Saviour Jesus is.

'. . . all you peoples.'

Every people group in the world, as well as every nation, is filled with individuals who Christ died to save and who need to come to know Him. This mirrors the meaning of *'all you Gentiles'*.

(VERSE 2) *'For His merciful kindness is great toward us. . .'*

The Bible teaches that *'God is love'* (1 John 4:16). God's love is shown in everyday situations worldwide. But the Bible says that *'God demonstrates his own love for us, in that while we were still sinners, Christ died for us'* (Romans 5:8). It talks about *'the Son of God, who loved me and gave Himself for me'* (Galatians 2:20). It confirms that *'greater love has no one than this, than to lay down one's life for his friends'* (John 15:13). Whichever way you look at it, *'His merciful kindness is great toward us.'*

'. . .and the truth of the LORD endures forever.'

God is faithful. 1 Corinthians 1:9 says, *'God is faithful, by whom you were called into the fellowship of His Son, Jesus Christ our Lord.'* His unfailing faithfulness is shown by the way He always keeps His promises, such as, *'If we confess our sins, He is faithful and just to forgive us our sins and to cleanse us from all unrighteousness'* (1 John 1:9). Remember to confess your sins directly to God and ask for His cleansing. He will purify you from them. He is faithful, and He has promised!

'Praise the LORD!'

We finish as we began! Learn to praise God at *all* times.

Psalm 118—The enduring love of God

1Oh, give thanks to the LORD, for He is good!
For His mercy endures forever.

2Let Israel now say,
"His mercy endures forever."
3Let the house of Aaron now say,
"His mercy endures forever."
4Let those who fear the LORD now say,
"His mercy endures forever."

5I called on the LORD in distress;
The LORD answered me and set me in a broad place.
6The LORD is on my side;
I will not fear.
What can man do to me?
7The LORD is for me among those who help me;
Therefore I shall see my desire on those who hate me.
8It is better to trust in the LORD
Than to put confidence in man.
9It is better to trust in the LORD
Than to put confidence in princes.

10All nations surrounded me,
But in the name of the LORD I will destroy them.
11They surrounded me,
Yes, they surrounded me;
But in the name of the LORD I will destroy them.
12They surrounded me like bees;
They were quenched like a fire of thorns;
For in the name of the LORD I will destroy them.
13You pushed me violently, that I might fall,
But the LORD helped me.
14The LORD is my strength and song,
And He has become my salvation.

15The voice of rejoicing and salvation
Is in the tents of the righteous;
The right hand of the LORD does valiantly.
16The right hand of the LORD is exalted;
The right hand of the LORD does valiantly.
17I shall not die, but live,
And declare the works of the LORD.
18The LORD has chastened me severely,
But He has not given me over to death.

19Open to me the gates of righteousness;
I will go through them,
And I will praise the LORD.
20This is the gate of the LORD,

Through which the righteous shall enter.

21I will praise You,
For You have answered me,
And have become my salvation.

22The stone which the builders rejected
Has become the chief cornerstone.
23This was the LORD's doing;
It is marvelous in our eyes.
24This is the day the LORD has made;
We will rejoice and be glad in it.

25Save now, I pray, O LORD;
O LORD, I pray, send now prosperity.
26Blessed is he who comes in the name of the LORD!
We have blessed you from the house of the LORD.
27God is the LORD,
And He has given us light;
Bind the sacrifice with cords to the horns of the altar.
28You are my God, and I will praise You;
You are my God, I will exalt You.

29Oh, give thanks to the LORD, for He is good!
For His mercy endures forever.

(VERSES 1-4) God's goodness and enduring *'mercy'* make us thank Him and reverentially fear Him. Who is thanking Him for His enduring love? *'Israel'*, God's people; the priests in *'the house of Aaron'*; and people who *'fear the LORD'* anywhere. That includes us today if we have trusted in Jesus as our Saviour. He took our sins and God's punishment on them when He died on the cross for us and rose again.

(VERSES 5-9) Times of distress do come to those who love and follow the Lord. But He answers our prayers and liberates us from it. He is on our side—there is no need to fear those who wish to harm us. God is our Helper (Psalm 54:4). Through Him we can have the victory over whatever assaults us. Trusting in man, even in princes, is useless. Trusting and taking refuge in the Lord is far better! So next time you feel overwhelmed, ask God to help you. If you know Jesus as your Saviour, He will!

(VERSES 10-14) God's physical people, Israel, fight physical battles against physical enemies who hate both God and them. Like a swarm of bees, they surround and outnumber them. God helps His servant and his forces to beat their enemy. Even when it seemed as if his foes will win, he *says, 'The LORD helped me.'* He rejoices that the *'LORD is* [his] *strength and* [his] *song and He has become* [his] *salvation'.* In our spiritual battles, we fight three forces: against a world system of thinking and living that has no time for the Bible and for Jesus; against our indwelling sin which strives to overcome us with temptations as if we do not love or belong to Christ; and against the devil and his unseen and ungodly spiritual forces. We are not strong enough ourselves, but we are in Christ (Philippians 4:13).

(VERSES 15-18) Joyful victory shouts acknowledge that God enables us to win. The Lord's valiant and exalted *'right hand'* achieves that. But at times, our Father God will chasten us to keep us from sin. That will be always justifiable and reasonable. But we never face spiritual death; we have eternal life in Christ!

(VERSES 19-26) When God saves me (meaning He has *'become my salvation'*) I will *'praise the LORD'* and seek to live righteously. God is righteous and wants His forgiven and cleansed children to be righteous. Verses 19-26 are also 'Messianic'—about Jesus. He is *'the stone which the builders rejected'* but who became the *'Chief Cornerstone'* on that first Lord's Day when He rose up from the grave, having paid for our sins. You, too, can pray, *'Save now, I pray, O LORD.'* He will certainly bless you as you do.

(VERSES 27-29) God is the LORD who *'has given us light'.* An animal sacrifice had to be bound *'with cords to the horns of the altar'.* Jesus needed only His love to keep Him as our sacrifice for our sins. He could have left the cross at any time, but He stayed there to pay for our sins completely. Now He asks us to voluntarily live for Him as a living sacrifice (Romans 12:1-2). Twice we read, *'You are my God.'* If Christ is your Saviour, He is your God, too. So, we continue to thank Him for His enduring '*mercy*'. How we need it! How we need Him.

Psalm 119—The wonder of God's Word

ALEPH
1Blessed are the undefiled in the way,
Who walk in the law of the LORD!
2Blessed are those who keep His testimonies,
Who seek Him with the whole heart!
3They also do no iniquity;
They walk in His ways.
4You have commanded us
To keep Your precepts diligently.
5Oh, that my ways were directed
To keep Your statutes!
6Then I would not be ashamed,
When I look into all Your commandments.
7I will praise You with uprightness of heart,
When I learn Your righteous judgments.
8I will keep Your statutes;
Oh, do not forsake me utterly!

BETH
9How can a young man cleanse his way?
By taking heed according to Your word.
10With my whole heart I have sought You;
Oh, let me not wander from Your commandments!
11Your word I have hidden in my heart,
That I might not sin against You.
12Blessed are You, O LORD!
Teach me Your statutes.
13With my lips I have declared
All the judgments of Your mouth.
14I have rejoiced in the way of Your testimonies,
As much as in all riches.
15I will meditate on Your precepts,
And contemplate Your ways.
16I will delight myself in Your statutes;
I will not forget Your word.

GIMEL
17Deal bountifully with Your servant,
That I may live and keep Your word.
18Open my eyes, that I may see
Wondrous things from Your law.
19I am a stranger in the earth;
Do not hide Your commandments from me.
20My soul breaks with longing
For Your judgments at all times.
21You rebuke the proud—the cursed,
Who stray from Your commandments.
22Remove from me reproach and contempt,
For I have kept Your testimonies.

23Princes also sit and speak against me,
But Your servant meditates on Your statutes.
24Your testimonies also are my delight
And my counselors.

DALETH
25My soul clings to the dust;
Revive me according to Your word.
26I have declared my ways, and You answered me;
Teach me Your statutes.
27Make me understand the way of Your precepts;
So shall I meditate on Your wonderful works.
28My soul melts from heaviness;
Strengthen me according to Your word.
29Remove from me the way of lying,
And grant me Your law graciously.
30I have chosen the way of truth;
Your judgments I have laid before me.
31I cling to Your testimonies;
O LORD, do not put me to shame!
32I will run the course of Your commandments,
For You shall enlarge my heart.

HE
33Teach me, O LORD, the way of Your statutes,
And I shall keep it to the end.
34Give me understanding, and I shall keep Your law;
Indeed, I shall observe it with my whole heart.
35Make me walk in the path of Your commandments,
For I delight in it.
36Incline my heart to Your testimonies,
And not to covetousness.
37Turn away my eyes from looking at worthless things,
And revive me in Your way.
38Establish Your word to Your servant,
Who is devoted to fearing You.
39Turn away my reproach which I dread,
For Your judgments are good.
40Behold, I long for Your precepts;
Revive me in Your righteousness.

WAW
41Let Your mercies come also to me, O LORD—
Your salvation according to Your word.
42So shall I have an answer for him who reproaches me,
For I trust in Your word.
43And take not the word of truth utterly out of my mouth,
For I have hoped in Your ordinances.
44So shall I keep Your law continually,
Forever and ever.
45And I will walk at liberty,
For I seek Your precepts.

46 I will speak of Your testimonies also before kings,
And will not be ashamed.
47 And I will delight myself in Your commandments,
Which I love.
48 My hands also I will lift up to Your commandments,
Which I love,
And I will meditate on Your statutes.

ZAYIN
49 Remember the word to Your servant,
Upon which You have caused me to hope.
50 This is my comfort in my affliction,
For Your word has given me life.
51 The proud have me in great derision,
Yet I do not turn aside from Your law.
52 I remembered Your judgments of old, O LORD,
And have comforted myself.
53 Indignation has taken hold of me
Because of the wicked, who forsake Your law.
54 Your statutes have been my songs
In the house of my pilgrimage.
55 I remember Your name in the night, O LORD,
And I keep Your law.
56 This has become mine,
Because I kept Your precepts.

HETH
57 You are my portion, O LORD;
I have said that I would keep Your words.
58 I entreated Your favor with my whole heart;
Be merciful to me according to Your word.
59 I thought about my ways,
And turned my feet to Your testimonies.
60 I made haste, and did not delay
To keep Your commandments.
61 The cords of the wicked have bound me,
But I have not forgotten Your law.
62 At midnight I will rise to give thanks to You,
Because of Your righteous judgments.
63 I am a companion of all who fear You,
And of those who keep Your precepts.
64 The earth, O LORD, is full of Your mercy;
Teach me Your statutes.

TETH
65 You have dealt well with Your servant,
O LORD, according to Your word.
66 Teach me good judgment and knowledge,
For I believe Your commandments.
67 Before I was afflicted I went astray,
But now I keep Your word.
68 You are good, and do good;

Teach me Your statutes.
69The proud have forged a lie against me,
But I will keep Your precepts with my whole heart.
70Their heart is as fat as grease,
But I delight in Your law.
71It is good for me that I have been afflicted,
That I may learn Your statutes.
72The law of Your mouth is better to me
Than thousands of coins of gold and silver.

YOD
73Your hands have made me and fashioned me;
Give me understanding, that I may learn Your commandments.
74Those who fear You will be glad when they see me,
Because I have hoped in Your word.
75I know, O LORD, that Your judgments are right,
And that in faithfulness You have afflicted me.
76Let, I pray, Your merciful kindness be for my comfort,
According to Your word to Your servant.
77Let Your tender mercies come to me, that I may live;
For Your law is my delight.
78Let the proud be ashamed,
For they treated me wrongfully with falsehood;
But I will meditate on Your precepts.
79Let those who fear You turn to me,
Those who know Your testimonies.
80Let my heart be blameless regarding Your statutes,
That I may not be ashamed.

KAPH
81My soul faints for Your salvation,
But I hope in Your word.
82My eyes fail from searching Your word,
Saying, "When will You comfort me?"
83For I have become like a wineskin in smoke,
Yet I do not forget Your statutes.
84How many are the days of Your servant?
When will You execute judgment on those who persecute me?
85The proud have dug pits for me,
Which is not according to Your law.
86All Your commandments are faithful;
They persecute me wrongfully;
Help me!
87They almost made an end of me on earth,
But I did not forsake Your precepts.
88Revive me according to Your lovingkindness,
So that I may keep the testimony of Your mouth.

LAMED
89Forever, O LORD,
Your word is settled in heaven.
90Your faithfulness endures to all generations;

You established the earth, and it abides.
91They continue this day according to Your ordinances,
For all are Your servants.
92Unless Your law had been my delight,
I would then have perished in my affliction.
93I will never forget Your precepts,
For by them You have given me life.
94I am Yours, save me;
For I have sought Your precepts.
95The wicked wait for me to destroy me,
But I will consider Your testimonies.
96I have seen the consummation of all perfection,
But Your commandment is exceedingly broad.

MEM
97Oh, how I love Your law!
It is my meditation all the day.
98You, through Your commandments, make me wiser than my enemies;
For they are ever with me.
99I have more understanding than all my teachers,
For Your testimonies are my meditation.
100I understand more than the ancients,
Because I keep Your precepts.
101I have restrained my feet from every evil way,
That I may keep Your word.
102I have not departed from Your judgments,
For You Yourself have taught me.
103How sweet are Your words to my taste,
Sweeter than honey to my mouth!
104Through Your precepts I get understanding;
Therefore I hate every false way.

NUN
105Your word is a lamp to my feet
And a light to my path.
106I have sworn and confirmed
That I will keep Your righteous judgments.
107I am afflicted very much;
Revive me, O Lord, according to Your word.
108Accept, I pray, the freewill offerings of my mouth, O Lord,
And teach me Your judgments.
109My life is continually in my hand,
Yet I do not forget Your law.
110The wicked have laid a snare for me,
Yet I have not strayed from Your precepts.
111Your testimonies I have taken as a heritage forever,
For they are the rejoicing of my heart.
112I have inclined my heart to perform Your statutes
Forever, to the very end.

SAMEK
113I hate the double-minded,

But I love Your law.
114You are my hiding place and my shield;
I hope in Your word.
115Depart from me, you evildoers,
For I will keep the commandments of my God!
116Uphold me according to Your word, that I may live;
And do not let me be ashamed of my hope.
117Hold me up, and I shall be safe,
And I shall observe Your statutes continually.
118You reject all those who stray from Your statutes,
For their deceit is falsehood.
119You put away all the wicked of the earth like dross;
Therefore I love Your testimonies.
120My flesh trembles for fear of You,
And I am afraid of Your judgments.

AYIN
121I have done justice and righteousness;
Do not leave me to my oppressors.
122Be surety for Your servant for good;
Do not let the proud oppress me.
123My eyes fail from seeking Your salvation
And Your righteous word.
124Deal with Your servant according to Your mercy,
And teach me Your statutes.
125I am Your servant;
Give me understanding,
That I may know Your testimonies.
126It is time for You to act, O LORD,
For they have regarded Your law as void.
127Therefore I love Your commandments
More than gold, yes, than fine gold!
128Therefore all Your precepts concerning all things
I consider to be right;
I hate every false way.

PE
129Your testimonies are wonderful;
Therefore my soul keeps them.
130The entrance of Your words gives light;
It gives understanding to the simple.
131I opened my mouth and panted,
For I longed for Your commandments.
132Look upon me and be merciful to me,
As Your custom is toward those who love Your name.
133Direct my steps by Your word,
And let no iniquity have dominion over me.
134Redeem me from the oppression of man,
That I may keep Your precepts.
135Make Your face shine upon Your servant,
And teach me Your statutes.
136Rivers of water run down from my eyes,

Because men do not keep Your law.

TSADDE
137 Righteous are You, O LORD,
And upright are Your judgments.
138 Your testimonies, which You have commanded,
Are righteous and very faithful.
139 My zeal has consumed me,
Because my enemies have forgotten Your words.
140 Your word is very pure;
Therefore Your servant loves it.
141 I am small and despised,
Yet I do not forget Your precepts.
142 Your righteousness is an everlasting righteousness,
And Your law is truth.
143 Trouble and anguish have overtaken me,
Yet Your commandments are my delights.
144 The righteousness of Your testimonies is everlasting;
Give me understanding, and I shall live.

QOPH
145 I cry out with my whole heart;
Hear me, O LORD!
I will keep Your statutes.
146 I cry out to You;
Save me, and I will keep Your testimonies.
147 I rise before the dawning of the morning,
And cry for help;
I hope in Your word.
148 My eyes are awake through the night watches,
That I may meditate on Your word.
149 Hear my voice according to Your lovingkindness;
O LORD, revive me according to Your justice.
150 They draw near who follow after wickedness;
They are far from Your law.
151 You are near, O LORD,
And all Your commandments are truth.
152 Concerning Your testimonies,
I have known of old that You have founded them forever.

RESH
153 Consider my affliction and deliver me,
For I do not forget Your law.
154 Plead my cause and redeem me;
Revive me according to Your word.
155 Salvation is far from the wicked,
For they do not seek Your statutes.
156 Great are Your tender mercies, O LORD;
Revive me according to Your judgments.
157 Many are my persecutors and my enemies,
Yet I do not turn from Your testimonies.
158 I see the treacherous, and am disgusted,

Because they do not keep Your word.
159Consider how I love Your precepts;
Revive me, O LORD, according to Your lovingkindness.
160The entirety of Your word is truth,
And every one of Your righteous judgments endures forever.

SHIN
161Princes persecute me without a cause,
But my heart stands in awe of Your word.
162I rejoice at Your word
As one who finds great treasure.
163I hate and abhor lying,
But I love Your law.
164Seven times a day I praise You,
Because of Your righteous judgments.
165Great peace have those who love Your law,
And nothing causes them to stumble.
166LORD, I hope for Your salvation,
And I do Your commandments.
167My soul keeps Your testimonies,
And I love them exceedingly.
168I keep Your precepts and Your testimonies,
For all my ways are before You.

TAU
169Let my cry come before You, O LORD;
Give me understanding according to Your word.
170Let my supplication come before You;
Deliver me according to Your word.
171My lips shall utter praise,
For You teach me Your statutes.
172My tongue shall speak of Your word,
For all Your commandments are righteousness.
173Let Your hand become my help,
For I have chosen Your precepts.
174I long for Your salvation, O LORD,
And Your law is my delight.
175Let my soul live, and it shall praise You;
And let Your judgments help me.
176I have gone astray like a lost sheep;
Seek Your servant,
For I do not forget Your commandments.

Psalm 119 is the Bible's longest chapter. To try to summarise this 'Everest' of the psalms is like trying to itemise the contents of a huge treasure chest on a postcard! I simply share some key thoughts from each of its 22 sections of 8 verses.

Each section starts with letters from the Hebrew alphabet. The major themes are the wonder and the effect of God's written word, also known as: laws, testimonies, precepts, statutes, commandments, and judgments .

Reading *about* Psalm 119 is fine, but the best thing to do is to read it, or hear it read. Try reading *all of it* slowly yourself. It is like a bunch of important keys. Perhaps the main 'key' and the first in the quoted '*Nun*' section is verse 105: '*Your word is a lamp to my feet and a light to my path.*' God guides you personally step by step and also in long term, as you read, learn, trust and obey His precious Word. Is darkness in you or around you? The light of His Word reveals Jesus, the Light of the world, who bore your sins and judgment and rose again.

Verses 1–8: Aleph: UNDEFILED AND UNASHAMED

See the blessings and results of keeping God's law.

Verses 9–16: Beth: SEEKING AND SINNING

If you wholeheartedly seek for God through His Word, it keeps you from sin.

Verses 17–24: Gimel: DESIRE AND DELIGHT

If you thirst for God's enlightening Word, He will delight and counsel you.

Verses 25–32: Daleth: SORROW AND STRENGTH

God's Word brings you personal help, revival, teaching and strength, in your 'down times'.

Verses 33–40: He: TEACHING AND TURNING

Avoid coveting, selfish gain and looking at worthless things by obeying and longing for God's reviving Word.

Verses 41–48: Waw: TRUST AND TESTIMONY

Use God's Word to answer sceptics and to witness, even to kings! Meditate on His Word.

Verses 49–56: Zayin: COMFORT AND COMMITMENT

As you keep and obey God's law, God comforts you if you suffer and are opposed.

Verses 57–64: Heth: COMMANDS AND COMPANIONS

Despite opposition, keeping God's Word emphasises mercy for you and oneness with other uncompromising believers.

Verses 65–72: Teth: ASTRAY AND AFFLICTED

Affliction can deepen your belief in, obedience to, and delighting in God's Word. It can help you not to stray from Him.

Verses 73–80: Yod: LEARNING AND LOVE

The comfort of God's merciful kindness is yours if you seek to understand and learn God's commands and meditate on His precepts.

Verses 81–88: Kaph: PERSECUTION AND PRECEPTS

If times of intense persecution tempt you to despair, hope in and reviving help from God will come to you through His Word.

Verses 89–96: Lamed: EVERLASTING AND ENDURING

Everything about God is everlasting and enduring, including His faithfulness and His Word, which keeps those who delight in God and in His law.

Verses 97–104: Mem: WISDOM AND WALK

Living for God's law gives supernatural wisdom, amazing understanding, a holy walk with Him and brings you honeylike sweetness to your soul.

Verses 105–112: Nun: LAMP AND LIGHT

By the light of God's Word, you are guided in both the short and long term. Your joy and determination to keep on come as you commit yourself to the Bible.

Verses 113–120: Samek: SEPARATION AND SAFETY

As you reject ungodly standards and lovingly keep God's holy statutes, you will be upheld and sustained spiritually by God.

Verses 121–128: Ayin: DECREES AND DISCERNMENT

In testing and tiring times ask God to teach you His decrees and ask God for His discernment. His commands will seem as pure gold to you.

Verses 129–136: Pe: LONGING AND LAW

A real thirst and longing for God's wonderfully enlightening testimonies, words, commands, mercy and blessing are in sharp contrast to the sorrow over those who disobey His law.

Verses 137–144: Tsadde: RIGHTEOUS AND RIGHT

God is everlastingly righteous and upright. His judgments, testimonies, word, precepts, commandments, statutes and law reflect this.

Verses 145–152: Qoph: CALLING AND CLOSE

Calling out to God (mentioned twice) and a third request to '*Hear my voice*' underline that your personal prayer is fed and helped if you obey, keep, hope in, and meditate on God's Word. You keep close to the Lord like this.

Verses 153–160: Resh: REVIVAL AND REVELATION

Spiritual personal revival comes through God's revealed Word, His judgements, and His lovingkindness.

Verses 161–168: Shin: AWE AND ABHOR

A heartfelt awe and rejoicing in God's word will make you hate and abhor any kind of falseness, and cause you to praise God continually, obey His Word, enjoy great personal peace, and know that comforting sense of God's omniscience.

Verses 169–176: Tau: SUPPLICATION AND SEEKING

Ask to understand God's Word. Ask Him to deliver you and seek you as a shepherd seeks a straying sheep.

Have you asked Jesus to become *your 'Good Shepherd'*? He gave His life for lost sheep like us to bear our sins and their punishment on the cross. Have you turned from your sin and asked Him, the Living Word, into your life? Is your prayer, *'I long for your salvation, O LORD'*? If so, *He will answer it.*

Psalm 120—Plea, punishment and peace

A Song of Ascents.
1In my distress I cried to the LORD,
And He heard me.
2Deliver my soul, O LORD, from lying lips
And from a deceitful tongue.

3What shall be given to you,
Or what shall be done to you,
You false tongue?
4Sharp arrows of the warrior,
With coals of the broom tree!

5Woe is me, that I dwell in Meshech,
That I dwell among the tents of Kedar!
6My soul has dwelt too long
With one who hates peace.
7I am for peace;
But when I speak, they are for war.

(VERSES 1-2) This is the first psalm of fifteen, from Psalm 120 to Psalm 134, to be called *'A song of ascents'*. The Jewish pilgrims sang these songs each year as they ascended Mount Zion in Jerusalem to the temple. The songs marked three Feasts of the Old Testament: those of Unleavened Bread, Pentecost (also called Weeks or Harvest), and Ingathering (also called Booths or Tabernacles). They prepared the pilgrims to worship God in the temple. They carry spiritual messages for all whose heart is open to God. We do not know who this psalmist is, but he seems to be Jewish and has lived outside Israel amongst enemies of Judaism. (We see this in verse 5.) He is distressed because of the opposition of people who tell lies and are deceitful. That still can happen today, wherever we may live. In that distress, he calls on God in prayer. That is always the best and the right thing to do. He shares his distress with God. Even though God knows about our griefs, sorrows, and worries, He always asks us to lay them before Him. First Peter 5:7 urges us to be *'casting all your care upon Him, for He cares for you'*. If you have put your trust in the Lord Jesus Christ as your living Saviour, you can readily grasp that He carries your worries and cares, too. He who has already borne all your sins and the punishment for them that you deserve can easily carry your concerns as well—and He will. Jesus said, *'Come to me, all you who labor and are heavy laden, and I will give you rest'* (Matthew 11:28). The psalmist asks for deliverance from those lies and from that deceit. We can pray that in two good ways. One way is to ask God to deliver us from others who lie and act deceitfully. The other way is to ask God to keep us from doing that ourselves, and to speak, think and act as Jesus would like us to.

(VERSES 3-4) The psalmist is also very much aware that God will judge and punish those who distort the truth and live a lie. God's judgment always hits its target as a sharp arrow. His arrow never misses. God will punish all unrepentant sinners. *Any* sinner who has turned to Jesus to forgive him is saved. On the cross, Jesus bore eternal punishment for sinners to save those who repent and trust Him. The *'coals of the broom tree'* indicate the fire which burns the wood of a broom tree and so produces red-hot glowing charcoal. In the Bible, fire often speaks of judgment. Hell is eternal. It is pictured as a fire that never goes out. Some say that is 'only a picture'. But pictures are usually less real than the reality pictured. If fire is only a *picture* of Hell, the greater reality of everlasting and conscious punishment on sins is far worse. That is why Christ was punished for us and bore our Hell in His own body (1 Peter 2:24).

(VERSES 5-7) Meshech is in Asia Minor (modern-day Turkey) and Kedar is in Arabia. The psalmist has obviously lived in both places. He has experienced great opposition, probably to him personally as a foreigner worshipping the Almighty God revealed in the Bible. Today, that happens worldwide and in our own country. The psalmist wants peace. They want war. Christians often still meet that situation. Some suffer greatly because of it. Jesus is the *'Prince of Peace'* (Isaiah 9:6). He makes peace for sinners through the blood of His cross (Colossians 1:20). May we know His peace and blessing as we seek to make peace in a troubled world (Matthew 5:9). When we know the Prince of Peace and follow Him, we are better placed to help to bring peace to others.

Psalm 121—God's constant care

A Song of Ascents.
1 I will lift up my eyes to the hills—
From whence comes my help?
2 My help comes from the LORD,
Who made heaven and earth.

3 He will not allow your foot to be moved;
He who keeps you will not slumber.
4 Behold, He who keeps Israel
Shall neither slumber nor sleep.

5 The LORD is your keeper;
The LORD is your shade at your right hand.
6 The sun shall not strike you by day,
Nor the moon by night.

7 The LORD shall preserve you from all evil;
He shall preserve your soul.
8 The LORD shall preserve your going out and your coming in
From this time forth, and even forevermore.

(VERSES 1-2) This psalm is the second *'song of ascent'* in a cluster of fifteen psalms. It seems to offer a solution to Psalm 120's problem of oppression by lies, deceit and aggressive intent coming from those who oppose God's children. Those who know God look for God's peace in all dealings, while others seek war. The answer given in the first two verses is for God's children, when opposed by those war-loving foes, to *'lift up'* their eyes. Their gaze, however, is to be far higher than the inspiring mountains which they can see, or the heavens stretching over those mountains. They must look to the ultimate Source of all help and blessing, namely the LORD Himself. He made the mountains—and the heavens too. There is no higher Person to look to for help than the great Creator Himself. That is why He is described as *'the LORD who made heaven and earth'*. Just think about the words of one hymn, 'The great Creator became my Saviour, and all God's fulness dwells in Him.' The Almighty God took on flesh, lived a sinless and faultless life, and went to the cross to bear our sins and take the just judgment for those sins in His own body. He was smitten by God in our place so we could be forgiven, freed and receive eternal life.

(VERSES 3-6) Half of Psalm 121 is taken by detailing how God really has continuous and unfailing care for His own physical people,

Israel. God treats them as His own children, though the word 'children' is not used. We become His spiritual children now when we receive Him in our hearts as our Lord and Saviour. John 1:11-13 tells us that Jesus *'came to His own, and His own did not receive him. But as many as received Him, to them He gave the right to become children of God, to those who believe in His name: who were born, not of blood, nor of the will of the flesh, nor of the will of man, but of God.'* Although many reject or ignore that Jesus is the Lord, and will not turn to Him, all those who do receive Him in their hearts become *'children of God'* spiritually. These *'born-again'* sinners received Him by belief in Him as their Saviour. They are not born as spiritual children of God. They do not do that because they follow a man-made plan to become a child of God. Neither can anyone else make them one, not even their own fathers. It is God's work as they believe fully in Christ and trust in Him. When you belong to God like that, He watches over you ceaselessly. He will not let you slip if you walk with Him. He never goes to sleep as He watches over you. He shades and protects you by day and by night. This really is 24/7 care from your loving Father in Heaven. You have *become* His blood-bought child!

(VERSES 7-8) The summary of God's care for those who know Him—and that includes you, if you repent and trust in Christ as we have just discussed—is that, although assailed at times, you will be kept from suffering evil and doing evil if you walk with Him. He watches over your life—and that includes the fact that you can never lose the eternal life you have in the Lord Jesus Christ. Wherever you go, whatever you do, however you do it, and whomever you may meet or be with, in all your comings and goings, God is watching over you. That is true in earth and always true in Heaven, too!

Psalm 122—Unimaginable glory!

A Song of Ascents. Of David.
1I was glad when they said to me,
"Let us go into the house of the LORD."
2Our feet have been standing
Within your gates, O Jerusalem!

3Jerusalem is built
As a city that is compact together,
4Where the tribes go up,
The tribes of the LORD,
To the Testimony of Israel,
To give thanks to the name of the LORD.
5For thrones are set there for judgment,
The thrones of the house of David.

6Pray for the peace of Jerusalem:
"May they prosper who love you.
7Peace be within your walls,
Prosperity within your palaces."
8For the sake of my brethren and companions,
I will now say, "Peace be within you."
9Because of the house of the LORD our God
I will seek your good.

(VERSES 1-2) This short psalm is set against the background of worship. It is the third of a *'song of ascents'* and is sung by the Israelites as the pilgrims ascend Mount Zion, Jerusalem, on their way to worship God in the temple there. Although each person who knows God is to praise and worship Him individually and personally, worship also includes worshipping God together with others. So, the psalmist, David, says to his Jewish brothers, *'Let us go into the house of the LORD.'* He does not just say 'I am going to worship': he wants others to join together to do it. He wants to worship God as an individual and also in fellowship with others who know the Lord.

It is just the same today for those who know the Lord Jesus Christ as their Saviour. They have come to Christ one by one to receive God's forgiveness and eternal life. As individuals have realised that Jesus died on the cross for them, to bear their sins and take God's wrath and punishment for them, and as they have asked the risen Lord Jesus to enter their hearts by the Holy Spirit, they have been individually *'born again'* (John 3:3, 7). Just as babies are born one by one, so are people *'born again'* one by one by faith in the Lord

Jesus Christ. However, the Bible tells us to meet with others to worship God, for fellowship, and to praise Him (Hebrews 10:25). Each of us also needs to read our Bibles each day and pray daily on our own with the Lord. The temple at Jerusalem was regarded as the place where God was present. The Bible says the Lord is present in the heart of each person who trusts in Jesus, and, also when two or three (or more) believers meet together in His name (Matthew 18:20). That is what a church is. It is not a building but a group of people who know, worship, serve and follow Jesus together. When those of us who have received Jesus as Saviour get to Heaven, that time for ever with the Lord will be perfect!

(VERSES 3-5) As the pilgrims travel to Jerusalem, they sing these *'songs of ascent'*. They must have great delight at the prospect that, like the tribes of Israel, they go *'to give thanks to the name of the LORD'.* We aim to thank and praise Him, too. Do you recall again that the two names *'Jesus'* and *'Immanuel'*, which are given to our Saviour in Matthew 1:21 and 1:23, mean 'God saves' (or 'Saviour') and 'God with us'? Those of us trusting Christ are so grateful that Jesus has saved us from sin, death, and Hell, and that He is with us 24/7 as our ever-present God. That is why God regards each of our bodies as a temple of the Holy Spirit. We must make Him Lord of our bodies, in practice, and seek to honour, worship and serve Him as we daily present our bodies fully to Him (1 Corinthians 6:19-20, Romans 12:1-2).

(VERSES 6-9) It is because Jerusalem is so linked with the temple and worship of God that David asks people to pray for peace in Jerusalem. He wants it to be *peaceful* and *secure* for the people of God to worship. He asks this *'for the sake of* [his] *brethren and companions'.* He also seeks Jerusalem's *'peace'* and *'prosperity'* for the sake of *'the house of the LORD our God'.* Today's application for us is to pray that people will come to prosper spiritually and have *'peace'* with God through faith in the Lord Jesus Christ, and so worship the LORD with the inner *'peace'* Christ gives. Every converted sinner has eternal *security* in Christ because he will be with Jesus for ever in Heaven. As we pray for peace in physical Jerusalem today, look, too, at the wonderful long-term scenario where Heaven *prospers* unimaginably as the *New Jerusalem* pictured in Revelation 21. The *'tabernacle of God is with men'* there and so *'He will dwell with them.'* The *'men'* it refers to are those of us, men and women, who have received Christ and so are accepted by our forgiving God of love. Revelation 21:27 says that every single sin will be kept out, and *'only those who are written in the Lamb's book of life'* will be there. So, how can anyone get into Heaven, as we are all sinners? The answer is that for all of us who repent and trust in Christ, *'the blood of Jesus Christ His Son cleanses us from all sin'* (1 John 1:7). Heaven, as the *New Jerusalem,* is described in Revelation 21 in dazzling detail. Read it all to see what blessing awaits true Christians there, by God's grace. But here is a sample from verse 4 to think about: *'And God will wipe every tear from their eyes; there will be no more death, nor sorrow, nor crying. There shall be no more pain, for the former things have passed away. . . .* Verse 23 adds that this New Jerusalem (Heaven) *'had no need of the sun or of the moon to shine in it, for the glory of God illuminated it. The Lamb* [Jesus] *is its light.'* What a privilege to be there for ever with Jesus and all the saved from all time, plus all the angels, to praise our Saviour without anything holding us back!

Psalm 123—The LORD who is Lord

A Song of Ascents.
1Unto You I lift up my eyes,
O You who dwell in the heavens.
2Behold, as the eyes of servants look to the hand of their masters,
As the eyes of a maid to the hand of her mistress,
So our eyes look to the LORD our God,
Until He has mercy on us.

3Have mercy on us, O LORD, have mercy on us!
For we are exceedingly filled with contempt.
4Our soul is exceedingly filled
With the scorn of those who are at ease,
With the contempt of the proud.

(VERSE 1) This fourth *'song of ascents'* is written by David and focuses on worshipping the *'LORD our God'.* All prayers and praise should be directed to Him, whether in a building or not. The temple enables God's people to worship God together. We *cannot* do that unless and until we have come to *know* Him as *our* LORD and *our* God. That means two things. *First,* we have turned from our sins in repentance and understood that the Lord Jesus Christ, God the Son, died in our place on the cross to bear in His body our sins and God's punishment for them. *Second,* we have yielded our hearts and lives to our risen and ever-living Lord and Saviour. This first happened when we came in prayer to Him to ask Him to forgive us and enter into our lives. So, we now know the LORD God as *'our'* Lord and Saviour. We now should yield to Jesus every day. (Romans 12:1-2 tells us how to do that.)

(VERSE 2) *'LORD'* (spelled L-O-R-D in block letters) means 'Jahweh' or 'Jehovah'. This is not a *description* of God, but a *personal* name for Him. It presents our God as the only one true living God, and as a Person. 'Lord' (not in blocks) describes a person who is in overall charge. The Lord Jesus Christ is both 'LORD' ('Jehovah') and 'Lord' (the One in overall charge). He is our personal God who is in charge of all things. That is why He is called *'Lord of lords and King of kings'* in Revelation 17:14. If we know Jesus as our 'Lord' we can, in prayer, lift our eyes to Him as our 'LORD God' who has saved and does save us from sin, death and Hell, and will welcome us into Heaven after death, where He is worshipped for ever! Jesus, our *'Lord of lords and King of kings'*, has His throne *both* in Heaven *and* in the hearts of every *'born-again'* Christian. Is He *your* Lord?

A slave in Israel was under the master's or mistress's ownership and control. Slaves did not debate what to do; they simply kept their eyes on their owners who gave them 'the nod', or looked meaningfully at them to tell them to come to their owner, or signalled with their hand. The slaves served them and did what they were told. We are told to look to God in prayer like that for a different reason—to receive His loving *'mercy'*. When we look to God in our need for forgiveness and help, He answers us in His grace, and gives us the *'mercy'* we so much need. He never says, "No!" if our heart is right as we look to Him.

(VERSE 3b-4) But God's *'mercy'* not only causes our sins to be forgiven and shows that God accepts us through Christ. God also gives us many smaller *'mercies'*. Lamentations 3:22-23 states, *'Through the LORD's great mercies we are not consumed, because His compassions fail not. They are new every morning; great is Your faithfulness.'* God loves you and wants to help you in mercy to deal with your life and its problems. Here, God's people suffer much contempt, scorn and ridicule from proud and arrogant unbelievers. Christians worldwide still face that, and much worse, today. What is the answer?

Keep close to the Lord, pray for your opposers, and ask for God to help you love them for Christ's sake. Jesus said, in Matthew 5:43-45, *'You have heard that it was said, "You shall love your neighbor and hate your enemy." But I say to you, love your enemies, bless those who curse you, do good to those who hate you, and pray for those who spitefully use you and persecute you, that you may be sons of your Father in heaven.'* God blesses all who do that. But we need a changed heart and the Holy Spirit's indwelling power to live like that. That can only happen after we have received the Lord Jesus Christ as our Lord and Saviour.

Psalm 124—The LORD is 'on our side'

A Song of Ascents. Of David.
1"If it had not been the LORD who was on our side,"
Let Israel now say—
2"If it had not been the LORD who was on our side,
When men rose up against us,
3Then they would have swallowed us alive,
When their wrath was kindled against us;
4Then the waters would have overwhelmed us,
The stream would have gone over our soul;
5Then the swollen waters
Would have gone over our soul."

6Blessed be the LORD,
Who has not given us as prey to their teeth.
7Our soul has escaped as a bird from the snare of the fowlers;
The snare is broken, and we have escaped.
8Our help is in the name of the LORD,
Who made heaven and earth.

(VERSES 1-5) This fifth *'song of ascents'* is written by the most prolific writer of psalms, David. He starts with *'If'* and then repeats it for emphasis. This is not the *'if'* of doubt, but the *'if'* as in *'what if?'* He is so convinced and assured of the LORD's protecting presence with him that he expresses it to show just the reverse of doubt. Here is a small psalm which dispenses great assurance to all believers. So, what is David saying? Speaking for the body of the Lord's people, whom he leads, He knows that *'the LORD'* has always *been 'on our side'* and still is. That is true for each individual believer and is also true for the community he represents, namely the Israelite people. It is equally true now for every individual who has put his trust in the crucified and risen Lord Jesus Christ, as well as for every assembly and gathering of sinners who have been *'born-again'*. It applies too to the universal Church of God, which consists of every person throughout the whole world and throughout all time who has been saved by personal faith in the Lord Jesus Christ. The LORD really is *'on our side'*. Romans 8:31 asks a question and answers it with another one: *'What, then, shall we say to these things? If God is for us, who can be against us?'* In the next verse it adds, *'He who did not spare His own Son, but delivered Him up for us all, how shall He not with Him, also freely give us all things?'* From that we take confidence that, *first*, God is always with and for us, if our trust is in Jesus, and *second*, because God gave His *very*

best in sending His Son to die for us to take the penalty for our sins, when He died on the cross, there is no end to the good, blessed, and God-honouring things He will give us to live our Christian lives. That promise is for you personally, too!

David now concentrates on the feared *tsunami* of angry and violent enemy opposition which would have swamped and swallowed up His people without God on their side. For the Christian, this applies to the strength of our main opposition from the world, the flesh, the devil, and strong temptations so hard to withstand. Without God the Father as our Father, God the Son as our Saviour, and God the Holy Spirit to strengthen, counsel and help us, we would fail miserably and give up. But our Triune God *is always 'on our side'.*

(VERSES 6-7) Imagine facing a snarling, man-eating lion! A friend comes and rescues you. Or think of a bird caught in a snare. A bird-lover breaks the snare and the bird flies away. When God delivers Christians from our spiritual foes, we should praise and thank Him, live for Him, and share His message of forgiveness with many. The Bible has many promises to encourage and help us in such situations. Here is one: '*No temptation has overtaken you except such as is common to man; but God is faithful, who will not allow you to be tempted beyond what you are able, but with the temptation will also make the way of escape, so that you may be able to bear it.*' (1 Corinthians 10:13). That is for you, too!

(VERSE 8) '*Our help is in the name of the LORD, who made heaven and earth.*' Psalm 54:4 confirms this by saying, '*Behold, God is my helper; the Lord is the one who upholds my life.*' All of His power as our Creator/Saviour is ours!

Psalm 125—Mountainous blessings!

A Song of Ascents.
[1]Those who trust in the LORD
Are like Mount Zion,
Which cannot be moved, but abides forever.
[2]As the mountains surround Jerusalem,
So the LORD surrounds His people
From this time forth and forever.

[3]For the scepter of wickedness shall not rest
On the land allotted to the righteous,
Lest the righteous reach out their hands to iniquity.

[4]Do good, O LORD, to those who are good,
And to those who are upright in their hearts.

[5]As for such as turn aside to their crooked ways,
The LORD shall lead them away
With the workers of iniquity.

Peace be upon Israel!

(VERSES 1-2) As the Jewish pilgrims go to Mount Zion to worship God in the temple there, they will see the mountains around Jerusalem and ascend Mount Zion itself. Now the psalmist uses that mountainous background to illustrate this sixth '*song of ascent*'.

Mount Zion is solid, stable and enduring. Spiritually, so is everyone whose personal faith is in the LORD. If you put your trust in the Lord Jesus Christ as your Saviour and Lord, you will know God and build a solid relationship with Him that cannot be shaken or destroyed. You receive eternal life the instant that you receive Christ in your life. Like a river of blessing, that eternal life will flow into God's fathomless ocean of salvation in Heaven for ever. To deepen and build up that relationship on earth, read your Bible and pray to God each day, and have regular fellowship with other Christians, and enjoy good teaching and preaching from the Bible, each week. Be encouraged that God's presence, grace, help, strength and love surround you like the mountains around Jerusalem. That will never change, either! And this is all by the amazing grace and love of God. Jesus died for you on the cross. He bore your sins and was punished in your place, so you need never face eternal judgment in Hell. He literally went through Hell for you on the cross so you can be in Heaven with Him. What a Saviour! It is vital to trust in Him.

(VERSE 3) A *'sceptre'* is an ornamental rod carried by the person with authority and power. It is used here as a picture of that authority and power. God will not allow the *'sceptre'* of wickedness to *'rest on the land allotted to the righteous'*. He will act to ensure that ongoing evil will not *'rest'* over His people. This is gloriously true in Heaven: no sin or impurity is there (Revelation 21:27). Every true Christian will see the same truth increasing in his life because Romans 6:14 says, *'Sin shall not have dominion over you, for you are not under law but under grace.'* If God allowed Israel to remain under wicked authority, His people would become wicked. If a Christian permitted sin to be his master, instead of Christ, he would go sadly astray. And Heaven with *any* sin there would not and could not continue to be Heaven. God hates any sin of any kind from anyone, anywhere.

(VERSE 4) *'Upright'* refers to people who are made righteous in God's sight by trusting in the Lord. God continues to *'do good'* to them every day. He is at work in the hearts of every sinner who repents and receives Christ as his living Saviour. Philippians 1:6 says, *'He who has begun a good work in you will complete it until the day of Jesus Christ.'* Our salvation will not evaporate or fail.

(VERSE 5a) Here is a warning to anyone who fails to repent of his sins and will not trust and follow Christ but chooses the *'crooked ways'* of sin and selfishness. God will *'lead* [him] *away with the workers of iniquity'*. Hell awaits him. Heaven welcomes those who turn from sin, trust in Christ, and so read, believe, and follow the Bible's teachings.

(VERSE 5b) Pray for *'peace upon Israel'*. Have *'peace with God'* (Romans 5:1) and the *'peace of God'* by knowing and walking closely with the Lord Jesus Christ and so know the that *'the God of peace will be with you'* (Philippians 4:7,9).

Psalm 126—Sow in tears—reap in joy

A Song of Ascents.
1When the LORD brought back the captivity of Zion,
We were like those who dream.
2Then our mouth was filled with laughter,
And our tongue with singing.
Then they said among the nations,
"The LORD has done great things for them."
3The LORD has done great things for us,
And we are glad.

4Bring back our captivity, O LORD,
As the streams in the South.

5Those who sow in tears
Shall reap in joy.
6He who continually goes forth weeping,
Bearing seed for sowing,
Shall doubtless come again with rejoicing,
Bringing his sheaves with him.

(VERSES 1-3) Psalm 126, the seventh *'song of ascents'*, marks some unspecified joyful event in Israel's national history. It seems highly likely that it was written about one of the three returns from the Babylonian captivity, whether under Zerubbabel, under Ezra, or under Nehemiah. Zion, and its temple and worship, are now in the minds of the worshippers. The psalm is probably true of each partial return and also of the three returns as a whole. God's people were so used to captivity that the prospect of returning seemed like a dream to them. Laughter and joy are theirs now! Other nations recognise what God has done for them. So do they. They are quick to give the glory to God: *'The LORD has done great things for us, and we are glad.'* The same sentiments are often expressed when someone trusts in Jesus Christ and finds his life is changing. Also, Christians who have backslidden and then come back to the Lord often express those same sentiments and thank God for restoring them. In each case, onlookers who know the people concerned often comment on the change the Lord has made in them. Some of the unconverted onlookers also come to realise that Jesus bore their sins and judgment and receive Him in their hearts as Lord and Saviour. Others who are believers are often challenged to come afresh to the Lord to surrender to Him again. It is a joyful and *'great'* thing to sing about, and to tell others about, when you are made right with God!

(VERSE 4) In summer, the southern area near Beersheba, called the Negev, is very dry and parched. But when spring comes, the streams are swollen and flowing, thus changing the arid area into one where things grow, and people are not thirsty. It could be that this return is not the final of the three returns and so, by asking God to *'Bring back our captivity, O LORD, like streams in the South'* the psalmist may be urging God to complete Israel's return. Doubtless, he also asks God's blessing on the return in question. We rejoice to receive a 'spiritual spring' of conversion, restoration, or renewal from God. He waters us spiritually each day through His Holy Spirit and through His Word, as we pray and study the Bible individually. In church life, those 'streams' of blessing flow through prayer meetings, Bible studies, worship, hearing God's Word on the Lord's Day, and sharing the gospel with others.

(VERSES 5-6) Sowing in *tears* probably primarily refers to repentance in captivity by disobedient Israel. True repentance towards God always brings forgiveness and restoration, and joy as a result. But there is also a striking gospel application, often made by Bible teachers and preachers. Those who truly come to know Christ long to see others also trusting Jesus for forgiveness, eternal life and a home in Heaven for ever. With compassion for lost people, they sow the *'seed'* of the gospel of the crucified and risen Lord Jesus *'in tears'*. There will be a harvest (*'sheaves'*) of people who turn from sin, receive Christ, and are won for God. And that brings *'joy'* to all! Do you have compassion for lost people that? Do you seek to sow gospel seed to others each day?

Psalm 127—Live with meaning for God.

A Song of Ascents. Of Solomon.
1 Unless the LORD builds the house,
They labor in vain who build it;
Unless the LORD guards the city,
The watchman stays awake in vain.
2 It is vain for you to rise up early,
To sit up late,
To eat the bread of sorrows;
For so He gives His beloved sleep.

3 Behold, children are a heritage from the LORD,
The fruit of the womb is a reward.
4 Like arrows in the hand of a warrior,
So are the children of one's youth.
5 Happy is the man who has his quiver full of them;
They shall not be ashamed,
But shall speak with their enemies in the gate.

(VERSES 1-2) Solomon, King David's son, who authors this psalm, the eighth *'song of ascents'*, also wrote in the book of Ecclesiastes 1:2 these words: *'"Vanity of vanities" says the Preacher, "Vanity of vanities, all is vanity."'* The NIV translates this as *'Meaningless'* and *'Utterly meaningless.'* Ecclesiastes is God's record of how a man without God looks at life. Life seems empty to so many without Christ as their Saviour. Solomon now writes in this psalm about doing three things *'in vain'* and therefore they become *meaningless*. The lesson here is unless God is with us and helps us in what we do, then, as Christians, we will get nowhere and accomplish nothing that pleases Him. That is why we should daily pray for the day ahead and look back at the end of it with thanks to God for how He has helped us during the day.

The three things relate to builders building, watchmen watching, and living without proper sleep. These are all very practical matters. *Building, watching, waking and sleeping:* we need God in all of these things. One of the first things to do after believing in the living Christ, and in His substitutionary death for you on the cross where He was punished in your place and for your sins, is to open up the whole of your life to Him, to ask Him to be in charge of every part of it. The more you share with Him, trust and obey Him, the more He blesses you.

You may never build a house or act as the lookout (watchman) for a city. And maybe you are now happy with your waking and sleeping patterns. But if you trust in Christ, you need your life to be *built* on the solid Rock of Jesus Christ and biblical teaching. In Matthew 26:41 and Mark 14:38, Jesus says, *'Watch and pray lest you enter into temptation. The spirit indeed is willing, but the flesh is weak.'* We need God's help to '*watch*' against temptations to sin, so He can strengthen us to live for Him. We need His help to be disciplined about *time asleep and awake* to serve and glorify Him.

Many young adults rise too late and go to bed too late. Some people are slaves to their jobs to make a lot of money: they get up too early and work too late. At times we all need to do that for good reasons, but not as a pattern for living. We need wisdom and discipline and we need to ensure that each day starts and finishes with the Bible and prayer if we know Jesus. God promises wisdom to all who ask Him for it (James 1:5). We do need to be in touch with Him to ask for wisdom. Live *meaningfully* for God and for others; please Him and bless them.

(VERSES 3-5) *Physical* children are a blessing to many families, especially if parents are good role models, and the children are raised well. This is a prime parental duty, especially for those who follow Christ. But keen Christians *also* pray to have *spiritual* children and help people of all ages to turn to Christ, and so be '*born-again*'. They must act in a caring, loving and spiritual parental role, so 'baby converts', however old in years, grow well as children of God. You could be eighty years old, yet if you just came to receive Christ as your Saviour, you would be a spiritual babe.

Whether spiritual or physical, or both, our children are like arrows. They are sent to places we cannot reach easily. They can represent and even defend their parents, as the *'gate'* reference suggests, seeing that business and legal matters were often transacted at the city gates. If we are faithful as God's children, it helps them to be faithful as well. It is good when the physical family becomes a spiritual one too, and serves our mutual Heavenly Father.

Psalm 128—Present and future blessings

A *Song of Ascents*.
1Blessed is every one who fears the LORD,
Who walks in His ways.

2When you eat the labor of your hands,
You shall be happy, and it shall be well with you.
3Your wife shall be like a fruitful vine
In the very heart of your house,
Your children like olive plants
All around your table.
4Behold, thus shall the man be blessed
Who fears the LORD.

5The LORD bless you out of Zion,
And may you see the good of Jerusalem
All the days of your life.
6Yes, may you see your children's children.

Peace be upon Israel!

(VERSE 1) This ninth '*song of ascents*' starts with an important Bible principle which extends beyond Jewish pilgrims going to worship God in the temple on Mount Zion in Jerusalem. It applies to all who repent of sin and trust in the Lord Jesus Christ as Saviour. It is that everyone who '*fears*' (reverentially) the only all-powerful and personal '*LORD*' God is '*blessed*'. '*Blessed*' refers to true happiness that is the envy of everyone. We are '*blessed*' when we put our faith and confidence in Jesus, who died on the cross to carry our sins and God the Father's judgment of wrath on them, and conquered death by rising again. He blesses us now with eternal life if we trust in Him. This blessedness is for ever. One result of that trust, as part of Christian conversion, is we acquire and deepen that reverential and loving '*fear*' of God. That leads us to '*walk in His* [God's] *ways*'. We cannot seriously claim to know the Lord Jesus, or to fear God, unless we start to walk in a way that pleases the Lord. Do you know the Lord Jesus? Do you fear God? Do you walk in His ways?

(VERSES 2-4) One of the results of fearing God and trusting Christ is that you honour him in your work, both daily work and Christian work for Him. That means you can put food on the table. God also blesses you and prospers you *spiritually*, and sometimes physically, too. In an imperfect world, and as imperfect people, at times we all may face times of difficulties, illness, hardships, opposition and deprivation. Unlike Heaven, there is nothing perfect in this world except Jesus and God's Word. But if I walk with God, I walk *through* these times. Psalm 23:4 says, *'Yea, though I walk through the valley of the shadow of death, I will fear no evil, for You are with me.'* (Note the words *'walk'* and *'through.'*) Romans 8:37 says that *'in all these things we are more than conquerors through Him who loved us.'* (Note the phrase *'in all these things'.*) Remember that when we get to Heaven, all will be *perfectly* fulfilled for ever! But we are blessed on earth too. *'The man* [who is] *blessed who fears the LORD'* is a man who lives a godly life at home, supports his wife well, and helps her to bring up their children in a godly background where they hear the gospel and are taught to trust the Bible. His wife will be spiritually fruitful, like a vine, with or without children, but if she has children, she will see them grow in the protection and guidance of a family which honours God. God's family plan is simple: it is one man with one woman in marriage for life. And godly people look to have *spiritual* children too—those *'born-again'* by faith in Christ and obeying Him.

(VERSES 5-6) Psalmist and pilgrims alike long that the *'LORD bless* [them] *out of Zion. . . all the days of* [their] *life'* and see both *'Jerusalem'* and *'Zion'* prosper. God's blessing will flow through children to grandchildren and be crowned by God's *'Peace'* on Israel. *'Peace'* is far more than no war or conflict. Philippians 4:7 says that *'the peace of God, which surpasses all understanding, will guard your hearts and your minds through Christ Jesus'.* Christians experience that peace now, *and* eternally, and pray for it for future generations.

To summarise: check whether you trust in Jesus, fear God reverentially, walk with Christ daily, seek blessing for future generations, and rejoice in God's peace.

Psalm 129—Opposed but still going

A Song of Ascents.
1"Many a time they have afflicted me from my youth,"
Let Israel now say—
2"Many a time they have afflicted me from my youth;
Yet they have not prevailed against me.
3The plowers plowed on my back;
They made their furrows long."
4The LORD is righteous;
He has cut in pieces the cords of the wicked.

5Let all those who hate Zion
Be put to shame and turned back.
6Let them be as the grass on the housetops,
Which withers before it grows up,
7With which the reaper does not fill his hand,
Nor he who binds sheaves, his arms.
8Neither let those who pass by them say,
"The blessing of the LORD be upon you;
We bless you in the name of the LORD!"

(VERSES 1-3) This tenth *'song of ascents'* underlines how Israel suffered much at the hands of other nations. This included their slavery in Egypt during four hundred years there, and seventy years of captivity in Babylon. At other times, they were attacked and oppressed by other nations. The long furrows on their ploughed back may point to the flogging some received, as Jesus did before He was crucified. Israel demonstrates how God acts and applies His principles in changed situations. Israel nationally also pictures spiritually an individual Christian. A Christian is a child of God who also has trials and temptations. He loses some and wins others, depending on how close he lives to Christ and the truths of the Bible. But just as Israel can say, *'they have not prevailed against me'*, because God is on their side, so each Christian can say that Christ enables him to stand in temptation and persecution. Paul said, *'I can do all things through Christ who strengthens me'* (Philippians 4:13). All this is possible only by God's grace and strength. We can never succeed spiritually unless we keep 'short accounts' with God over our sins. That means we confess and forsake our sins as soon as we are aware of them. We also must cultivate our relationship with Christ daily through personal Bible study, prayer, fellowship regularly with other Christians, and each Sunday keeping the Lord's Day to worship Him and hear His Word preached.

(VERSE 4) When Israel was bound, enslaved and in captivity, God got them out! They did not stay in Egypt as slaves. In their exodus from Egypt, God's almighty hand delivered them with great power. They did return from Babylonian captivity, even if in three waves. They did resist, overcome, or recover from others' attacks. So today, God's promises to Christians include Romans 6:14, *'For sin shall not have dominion over you, for you are not under law, but under grace'*, and 1 Corinthians 10:13, *'No temptation has overtaken you except such as is common to man; but God is faithful, who will not allow you to be tempted beyond what you are able, but with the temptation will also make the way of escape, that you may be able to bear it.'* God will *either* keep you out of temptation *or* give you the strength to overcome it.

(VERSES 5-8) The psalmist's prayer for God is that He will deal physically with the physical enemies who hate Zion and God's worshippers there, and it has three parts to it: *first,* may they *'be put to shame and turned back'*; *second,* may they be unproductive and unsuccessful (grass growing on a roof cannot be compared with crops growing in a field, and there can be no reaping or harvest there); and *third,* as judgment may they know what it feels like to have no blessing from God and no one to wish it upon them. At harvest, there was a regular greeting of blessing between people, as you can see between Boaz and his workers in Ruth 2:4. No harvest means no harvest blessing. But we should pray to seek God's mercy and grace on those who oppose us, so that they will be converted to Christ. It could well be that they have first to taste some negatives, like the three in the prayer we looked at, before they will call on the Lord to save them. Meanwhile, pray for them.

Psalm 130—Praying from the depths

A Song of Ascents.
1Out of the depths I have cried to You, O LORD;
2Lord, hear my voice!
Let Your ears be attentive
To the voice of my supplications.

3If You, LORD, should mark iniquities,
O Lord, who could stand?
4But there is forgiveness with You,
That You may be feared.

5I wait for the LORD, my soul waits,
And in His word I do hope.
6My soul waits for the Lord
More than those who watch for the morning—
Yes, more than those who watch for the morning.

7O Israel, hope in the LORD;
For with the LORD there is mercy,
And with Him is abundant redemption.
8And He shall redeem Israel
From all his iniquities.

(VERSES 1-2) This eleventh *'song of ascents'* does not mention Jerusalem, Zion, the temple, or any of Israel's foes. It concentrates on two very different persons. One is the LORD and the other is the psalmist. It ends by addressing Israel because the result of serious (even if short) 'one-on-ones' with God always spills over to the blessing of others. The psalmist is so honest with his Lord; that always guarantees blessing.

He cries to God *'out of the depths'.* He *seems* to speak audibly as he prays—that is not a 'must do' but sometimes it helps to focus our prayers when we are alone with God. He submissively asks God to *'hear* [his] *voice,'* and to listen attentively. We need never to ask the LORD to do that, but He is always pleased to hear and see that the person praying is in earnest. What are the *'depths'* from which the psalmist prays? We will see in verses 3 and 4, but the key here is that he is crying out for *God to 'be attentive to the voice of* [his] *supplications'.* He is in earnest and is praying often.

Probably the most commended prayer in the New Testament is that of the despised tax collector in Luke 18:13. *'Standing afar off,* [he] *would not so much raise his eyes to heaven, but beat his breast, saying, "God, be merciful to me, a sinner."'* He knew he needed God's forgiveness for his sins. Jesus said God heard his humble prayer but rejected the proud pretence at praying by the religious hypocritical Pharisee.

(VERSES 3-4) Verse 3 asks the *question 'If You LORD, should mark iniquities, O Lord, who could stand?'* Verse 4 goes on to say *'But there is forgiveness with You, that You may be feared.'* Only a sinner needs to pray for God's forgiveness. We are all sinners and need to come and pray for God's merciful forgiveness. The psalmist clearly feels the burden of his sins. God the Holy Spirit is at work in him to convict him of guilt. One hymn says, *'Quicken my conscience till it feels the loathsomeness of sin.'* We need to feel our sins and confess and turn from them.

There is *bad news* and *good news* for us. The *bad news* is that I am so sinful that I cannot *stand* before a holy God, who keeps *a record of sins.* That is why God can judge fairly. I am lost and condemned eternally because of my sins. But the *good news* is that God is gracious and forgiving. He forgives all who confess their sins to Him, repent of them, and come to God to be forgiven and restored. How can He do that? Because Jesus has borne our sins and taken God's wrathful punishment for them on the cross. His perfect righteousness is counted as ours when we trust in Jesus to forgive us. *'If we confess our sins, He is faithful and just to forgive us our sins and to cleanse us from all unrighteousness'* (1 John 1:9). When we are forgiven through faith in Christ, we begin to fear God with love and reverence. Psalm 111:10 and Proverbs 9:10 both say, *'The fear of the LORD is the beginning of wisdom.'*

(VERSES 5-6) A man on watch during the night, like a city watchman or a shepherd, watches until light breaks. The soul of the psalmist waits on God for mercy, like that. He knows it will come. But meanwhile he confidently puts his hope in God's Word. What a privilege it is for us to know that, although God is supremely loving and sin-hating, He always responds in mercy and forgiveness to us when we own up to our sins, turn from them, and ask Him to forgive us.

(VERSES 7-8) The psalmist urges Israel to hope in God, too. God's mercy never fails. He fully redeems from *'all their sins'* all who trust in Him and will do so for Israel. Just like someone kind and loving might have bidden to buy a slave in the slave market to then give him his freedom and treat him like a son, so our Redeemer, the Lord Jesus Christ, paid for our freedom by shedding His blood on the cross and taking the judgment for sins that we deserve. But the living Saviour set us free and also sets us free inside by His indwelling Holy Spirit. We become *'born-again'* and a child in the family of God. Do you trust in Jesus as your Redeemer?

Psalm 131—Humble, calm and secure!

A Song of Ascents. Of David.
1LORD, my heart is not haughty,
Nor my eyes lofty.
Neither do I concern myself with great matters,
Nor with things too profound for me.

2Surely I have calmed and quieted my soul,
Like a weaned child with his mother;
Like a weaned child is my soul within me.

3O Israel, hope in the LORD
From this time forth and forever.

(VERSE 1) This twelfth of fifteen successive *'songs of assents'* follows well from Psalm 130. Why? Psalm 130 focuses on the psalmist's relationship with God, and especially his sense of sinful unworthiness before his holy LORD. He knows he needs God's mercy and forgiveness. That is why he now claims to God that *his 'heart is not haughty nor* [his] *eyes lofty'*. To make that claim with no sense of his sinfulness or need for mercy would be extremely proud and show haughtiness which he insists he does not possess! But he says these things because he knows he has nothing to be proud of, or to boast about. Here is a very different attitude. Only God's grace can enable us to see that *'all our righteousnesses like as filthy rags'* (Isaiah 64:6) and make the logical argument in Romans 7:14-20 that includes those verses 18-19: *'I know that in me (that is in my flesh) nothing good dwells; for to will is present with me, but how to perform what is good I do not find. For the good that I will to do, I do not do; but the evil I will not to do, that I practise.'* None of us can repent of sins and trust in the Lord Jesus Christ as Saviour without seeing our need shamefully to admit that *'whoever commits sin is a slave of sin'* (John 8:34).

Speaking personally, only as I come humbly like that to Christ, who bore my sins and was punished for them in my place on the cross, can I then freely and gratefully admit that some *'great matters'* are *'too wonderful for me'* to grasp. Being forgiven for all my sins and receiving eternal life in Christ are certainly two of the greatest *'matters'* which always *'are too profound for me'*.

(VERSE 2) But the sinner who admits his sin and trusts fully in the Lord Jesus Christ, and in His death and resurrection, finds that his soul within him is *'calmed and quieted'*. God's peace entered his heart when the risen and living Prince of peace, Jesus, entered it through the Holy Spirit. His soul is like a weaned child, who has full confidence in his mother. She once fed him herself but has gradually enabled him to eat solid food and now he feels content. He is at peace. He trusted his mother, and still does. He is happy to be under her care and loving control. A person who becomes *'born-again'* feels like this about the Saviour he has received and trusts.

(VERSE 3) This third and final verse points out to Israel then, and to every saved sinner now, that there are two aspects of being saved by God. (We call that 'salvation'.) We are told to *'hope in the LORD from this time forth and forever'*. Do you have your *'hope in the LORD'* right *now*? If so, you will find that Jesus saves you *now* from sin's dominating power in your life. You can also be legitimately and joyfully sure that you *will be* saved *'forever'* in Heaven, in the presence of your Lord and Saviour, Jesus Christ. *'Hope'* in Christ in the Bible does not mean *wishful thinking about an uncertain future*. It implies a sure and certain knowledge of something that is sure to happen but is not yet fully realised and experienced in Christ. You can know that you *have* eternal life right *now*! 1 John 5:11-12 says, *'God has given us eternal life, and this life is in His Son. He who has the Son has life.'* That includes you, if your trust is in the Lord Jesus Christ as your Lord and Saviour.

Psalm 132—Kings and priests forever with Jesus

A Song of Ascents.
1LORD, remember David
And all his afflictions;
2How he swore to the LORD,
And vowed to the Mighty One of Jacob:
3"Surely I will not go into the chamber of my house,
Or go up to the comfort of my bed;
4I will not give sleep to my eyes
Or slumber to my eyelids,
5Until I find a place for the LORD,
A dwelling place for the Mighty One of Jacob."

6Behold, we heard of it in Ephrathah;
We found it in the fields of the woods.
7Let us go into His tabernacle;
Let us worship at His footstool.
8Arise, O LORD, to Your resting place,
You and the ark of Your strength.
9Let Your priests be clothed with righteousness,
And let Your saints shout for joy.

10For Your servant David's sake,
Do not turn away the face of Your Anointed.

11The LORD has sworn in truth to David;
He will not turn from it:
"I will set upon your throne the fruit of your body.
12If your sons will keep My covenant
And My testimony which I shall teach them,
Their sons also shall sit upon your throne forevermore."

13For the LORD has chosen Zion;
He has desired it for His dwelling place:
14"This is My resting place forever;
Here I will dwell, for I have desired it.
15I will abundantly bless her provision;
I will satisfy her poor with bread.
16I will also clothe her priests with salvation,
And her saints shall shout aloud for joy.
17There I will make the horn of David grow;
I will prepare a lamp for My Anointed.
18His enemies I will clothe with shame,
But upon Himself His crown shall flourish."

❖

(VERSES 1-5) The background to this psalm is rich in content and context from the Bible. It is the thirteenth *'song of ascents'* dealing with the desire to worship God, both in Zion's temple then, and in our lives now. It does not say if David wrote it, but it deals with matters which involve King David and point us to the Lord Jesus Christ, the Messiah King. What is included in the *'afflictions'* that David suffered? He had many; some came as a result of his own sin. Others were because he did follow the Lord and was strongly opposed by men. He had a great desire to see Israel worship, serve and follow God, and that inspired him to bring back to Jerusalem the Ark of the Covenant, central to the Old Testament worship of God, both in the tabernacle and later in the temple. Solomon, supported by David, built the temple on Mount Zion, where the Ark was housed and worship took place. David had vowed to God to work tirelessly night and day so Israel would worship the LORD, with the Ark in its place there. Although God is *everywhere,* Zion's temple focused the worshippers' attention on God's presence and the need to worship Him. The tabernacle and the temple are each described as *'the LORD's dwelling place for the Mighty One of Jacob'.* (Jacob was later named Israel by God.)

(VERSES 6-9) The Ark points to God's presence. It is now in its proper place. Once it was moved to Jerusalem from Kiriath Jearim, (or Jaar). Finally, it went to Zion's temple, built by Solomon. The psalmist wants the priests to be righteous, and the worshippers to be joyful in song. (See 2 Chronicles 6:41-42, 2 Samuel 6:1, Exodus 25:30, 1 Chronicles 13-16, and 1 Samuel 25:6 give the context.)

(VERSES 10-12) God promised and swore that David's descendants would rule after him (2 Samuel 23:5). He was anointed as king, but His greatest descendant, the Lord Jesus Christ (His *'Anointed'* or 'Messiah') will *'sit upon* [David's] *throne for evermore'.* Jesus is the *'KING OF KINGS AND LORD OF LORDS' (Revelation 19:16, 1 Timothy 6:15).* No failure to obey God, by many covenant-breaking kings, could stop Jesus, the sinless and perfect King, from reigning for ever.

(VERSES 13-18) Jerusalem's Mount Zion is God's physical resting place on earth for worship by the children of Israel. God sits in Heaven and His footstool on earth is pictured here. Perfect praise will be His for ever in the *'new Jerusalem',* which pictures Heaven (Revelation 21:1-5). The poor are satisfied; the priests are clothed *'with salvation',* and the saved people, *'the saints',* joyfully *'shout aloud for joy'.* We come from the poverty of our sin, to receive invaluable spiritual riches in Christ. Each *'born-again'* sinner has been made into a king and a priest by personal faith in Jesus (Revelation 1:5-6). His sin is washed away by Jesus' death for him on the cross where He bore the punishment of God's judgment for the sinner's sin on Himself. Jesus is my sacrifice, my King, and my great High Priest. He is *'the Son of God, who loved me and gave himself for me'* (Galatians 2:20). I have eternal life solely through personal faith in Him.

David's *strength* (signified by his *'horn'*), *'lamp'*, victory over *'his enemies'* being put to shame, and flourishing *reign* are all mentioned. The Lord Jesus Christ's *strength* is for anyone who turns from sin and trusts Him. He is our *Light* in a dark world. His *victory* on the cross and His rising from death give us *victory* through Him eternally. We shall enjoy the Lord Jesus Christ's perfect *reign* of love for ever with Him in Heaven.

Do you know Jesus and all these generous benefits He freely gives to those who trust in Him? If you repent and receive Him, you will!

Psalm 133—Unity and God's blessing

A Song of Ascents. Of David.
1Behold, how good and how pleasant it is
For brethren to dwell together in unity!

2It is like the precious oil upon the head,
Running down on the beard,
The beard of Aaron,
Running down on the edge of his garments.
3It is like the dew of Hermon,
Descending upon the mountains of Zion;
For there the LORD commanded the blessing—
Life forevermore.

(VERSE 1) David concentrates on true unity between those who know the LORD. He calls them *'brethren'* (or *'brothers')*. Here, in this fourteenth *'song of ascents'*, are principles of blessing which are timeless. Those who turn from their sins and trust in Christ, and in His death on the cross as their substitute to suffer the penalty their sins deserve, become *'born-again'* and *'children of God'* (John 3:7, John 1:12). God the Father is their Father, God the Son their Saviour, and God the Holy Spirit their indwelling Helper. They become spiritual *brothers* (and sisters) in Christ. At once they find a common bond with all other *brothers* in Christ. This oneness is hard to explain to a non-Christian but is real to the one who trusts the Lord Jesus Christ as Lord and Saviour. That unity really is *'good' and 'pleasant'*. Old or young, he discovers a close and new relationship with previously unknown people who may differ greatly from him. This oneness transcends age, sex, race, colour, nationality, politics, jobs, money, gifts, interests, or which sports teams you might support! Galatians 3:28 says of those of us who have received Jesus in our hearts, that we are *'are all one in Christ Jesus'*. It is a oneness that the devil hates and will seek to attack. Sadly, our sinful hearts help him at times. We need to be humble in our relationships with other Christians, and always put Jesus first. We are always to be *'endeavoring to keep the unity of the Spirit in the bond of peace'* (Ephesians 4:3). Sometimes that means that we need to apologise from our hearts when we wrong a brother or sister in Christ. First, we ask the Lord to forgive us for that sin. A mark of conversion to Jesus is a willingness to admit our sin, confess it to God, and then forsake it. Never allow yourself to spoil what God has given us, namely that *'good and pleasant'* unity. Let us rather *'dwell together in unity.'* It will please Jesus, help your fellow Christians, and be a blessing to you too!

(VERSE 2) This unity is illustrated by the anointing of Aaron, the Chief Priest of Israel (Exodus 29:7, 30:30). The anointing oil was richly blended (Exodus 30:22-33) and poured over Aaron. The oil and its perfume spread down from his head, over his face, beard and body, clothed in his priestly robes. True *'good' and 'pleasant'* unity in Christ is like that between sinners who have come to know Jesus, no matter which Bible-believing church they attend. It starts at conversion when Christ enters their lives through the Holy Spirit. Oil in the Bible often pictures the Holy Spirit. Like Aaron's oil, God's Spirit affects our *heads* as He makes our thinking more Bible-based and God-honouring. He can even change our *faces*: many Christians often *look* more joyful than before they were converted! The same Spirit leads us to use our *bodies* and minds to serve and follow the Lord (Romans 12:1-2). There is a *'fragrance'* of new spiritual life around many committed Christians. Second Corinthians 2:15 says that *'we are to God the fragrance of Christ among those who are being saved and those who are perishing'.*

(VERSE 3) Mount Hermon, in the north of Israel, feeds the Jordan river when its snow melts. A high precipitation rate means that its very heavy dew refreshes its vegetation. Close fellowship in Christ refreshes those who trust Christ. It also helps others, who thirst for reality, to come to Jesus. He said, in Revelation 21:6, *'I will give of the fountain of water of life freely to him who thirsts.'* Lost sinners are more likely to be won through those who know God's blessing in unity together. They will see the difference that Jesus makes among those who seek to join together for fellowship, worship and service.

Psalm 134—Prayer, praise and blessing

A Song of Ascents.
1 Behold, bless the LORD,
All you servants of the LORD,
Who by night stand in the house of the LORD!
2 Lift up your hands in the sanctuary,
And bless the LORD.

3 The LORD who made heaven and earth
Bless you from Zion!

(VERSE 1) Psalm 134 is the fifteenth and last *'song of ascents'* sung by the Israelite pilgrims *en route* to Mount Zion's temple. They have arrived! This three-verse psalm marks that event. The pilgrims now address *'all you servants of the LORD, who by night stand in the house of the LORD'*. Who are these *'servants of the LORD'*? They are the priests and the Levites. The priests are the descendants of Aaron, the first priest. They operate for a limited time unless they die before that time is completed. They conduct worship and offer the various sacrifices, all of which are now fulfilled in the Lord Jesus Christ, and in His work on the cross when He bore our sins and paid our penalty. We now are cleansed, forgiven, and we enjoy fellowship with God as a result. Jesus became our Great High Priest for ever. The Bible teaches He is the final priest. He lives today to continue as our Priest. We need no other priest to represent us before God, and no more sacrifice to be offered. Jesus, the last priest, gave Himself, the last sacrifice, on the cross, the last altar. Though some churches still call ministers 'priests', Jesus is the *only* way to come to God for pardon, eternal life, and fellowship (John 14:6, Acts 4:12). *'He is also able to save to the uttermost those who come to God through Him, since He always lives to make intercession for them. For such a High Priest was fitting for us, who is holy, harmless, undefiled, separate from from sinners, and has become higher than the heavens.'* (You can read about this in Hebrews 4:14 to 5:10, and 6:13 to 7:28.) The Levites maintained the temple and its contents, prepared offerings, and helped the priests. When the tabernacle was used before the temple was built, they carried the tabernacle and its contents from one place to another. It seems that the first and second verses record the pilgrims' appreciation of the temple *servants* who enable them to worship there. They are especially grateful that these men work through the night. Our caring Great High Priest, The Lord Jesus Christ, watches over us and listens to us every second of time. The third verse records the priests' final blessing on the pilgrims who travelled to worship God together at Zion. The *born-again* sinner worships God because our High Priest was also our final and complete sacrifice for our sins, when He bore God's wrath against sin on the cross for us, as He gave Himself for us. He blesses us greatly.

(VERSE 2) Lifting up of hands in prayer and praise was a physical feature of some Old Testament prayer and worship. It was also used as a picture of prayer. It is similarly used in 1 Timothy 2:8 where Paul says he wants *'that men everywhere, lifting up holy hands to lift up holy hands in prayer, without wrath and doubting'*. The physical attitude of the body is secondary, but we must regularly pray to God and praise Him together. Daily each of us should do that, read the Bible and pray its teachings into the way we live our lives.

(VERSE 3) Again we are reminded that the One to whom we pray, in the name of Jesus, is the Almighty Creator who inhabits a far greater place than Zion, namely Heaven itself. Jesus has forgiven and cleansed us from the only thing that could stop our communing in prayer with God, namely our sin. We now have open access to God in prayer 24/7. Use it well and often. We must pray, both with fellow believers when we can, and daily in personal prayer. Let us cultivate the habit of praying during the day to God, as well, as we live our daily lives. The Bible says we should *'pray without ceasing'*. (1 Thessalonians 5:17). God does and will answer our prayer and continue to bless us by His amazing grace.

Psalm 135–Praising God: why and who?

1Praise the LORD!

Praise the name of the LORD;
Praise Him, O you servants of the LORD!
2You who stand in the house of the LORD,
In the courts of the house of our God,
3Praise the LORD, for the LORD is good;
Sing praises to His name, for it is pleasant.
4For the LORD has chosen Jacob for Himself,
Israel for His special treasure.

5For I know that the LORD is great,
And our LORD is above all gods.
6Whatever the LORD pleases He does,
In heaven and in earth,
In the seas and in all deep places.
7He causes the vapors to ascend from the ends of the earth;
He makes lightning for the rain;
He brings the wind out of His treasuries.

8He destroyed the firstborn of Egypt,
Both of man and beast.
9He sent signs and wonders into the midst of you, O Egypt,
Upon Pharaoh and all his servants.
10He defeated many nations
And slew mighty kings—
11Sihon king of the Amorites,
Og king of Bashan,
And all the kingdoms of Canaan—
12And gave their land as a heritage,
A heritage to Israel His people.

13Your name, O LORD, endures forever,
Your fame, O LORD, throughout all generations.
14For the LORD will judge His people,
And He will have compassion on His servants.

15The idols of the nations are silver and gold,
The work of men's hands.
16They have mouths, but they do not speak;
Eyes they have, but they do not see;
17They have ears, but they do not hear;
Nor is there any breath in their mouths.
18Those who make them are like them;
So is everyone who trusts in them.

19Bless the LORD, O house of Israel!
Bless the LORD, O house of Aaron!
20Bless the LORD, O house of Levi!

You who fear the LORD, bless the LORD!
21 Blessed be the LORD out of Zion,
Who dwells in Jerusalem!

Praise the LORD!

(VERSES 1-2) The word '*praise*' occurs five times in four verses. This psalm is full of reasons to '*praise the LORD*'. It starts by urging the '*servants of the LORD*', the priests and Levites mentioned in Psalm 134, to do so. We will end this psalm by seeing who else should praise Him.

(VERSES 3-5) The initial reasons given for praising God are given here. Praise is not just emotional, though our emotions should be involved fully, but there are good, solid reasons why He deserves praise and why we should give it. Here are some reasons given to praise the LORD:

- He is '*good*', not malevolent.
- It is '*pleasant*' to '*sing praises to His name*.' It pleases both Him and us.
- He chose Israel as His. He chose Christians too! (See Ephesians 1:3-8.)
- He is '*great*' and 'is *above all gods*'.

(VERSES 6-14) Why claim that the LORD is '*great*' and '*above all gods*'?

- He does whatever pleases Him. We are very glad that our God's goodness ensures He is pleased by good things.
- He is in charge of the heavens, the earth, the seas—even the deepest.
- He is over all weather.
- His '*signs and wonders*' caused Israel to leave slavery in Egypt.
- He gave Israel the lands of the strong nations in the Promised Land.
- From no possession, He gave His people the Promised Land to inherit.
- His name is eternal, and His fame is known through all generations.

- He will *'judge His people'* which means He will justify them with *'compassion'*. Bear in mind that the Lord Jesus Christ did that for sinners when He died on the cross, bearing their sins and God's wrathful punishment on them. His greatest miracle of rising from the dead meant those who repent and receive Him as Lord and Saviour are justified by their faith alone in Him alone.

(VERSES 15-18) Now compare the greatness of the living LORD with mute, sightless, deaf and lifeless idols which other nations vainly and ignorantly worship. Little wonder that God forbids idolatry in the Ten Commandments in Exodus 20:4

(VERSES 19-21) So who should *'praise the LORD'*? The Israelites, the priests, Levites, and *'you who fear the LORD'*, including *you* if you know Jesus as your personal Saviour.

Psalm 136—God's love lasts how long?

1 Oh, give thanks to the LORD, for He is good!
For His mercy endures forever.
2 Oh, give thanks to the God of gods!
For His mercy endures forever.
3 Oh, give thanks to the LORD of lords!
For His mercy endures forever:

4 To Him who alone does great wonders,
For His mercy endures forever;
5 To Him who by wisdom made the heavens,
For His mercy endures forever;
6 To Him who laid out the earth above the waters,
For His mercy endures forever;
7 To Him who made great lights,
For His mercy endures forever—
8 The sun to rule by day,
For His mercy endures forever;
9 The moon and stars to rule by night,
For His mercy endures forever.

10 To Him who struck Egypt in their firstborn,
For His mercy endures forever;
11 And brought out Israel from among them,
For His mercy endures forever;
12 With a strong hand, and with an outstretched arm,
For His mercy endures forever;
13 To Him who divided the Red Sea in two,
For His mercy endures forever;
14 And made Israel pass through the midst of it,
For His mercy endures forever;
15 But overthrew Pharaoh and his army in the Red Sea,
For His mercy endures forever;
16 To Him who led His people through the wilderness,
For His mercy endures forever;
17 To Him who struck down great kings,
For His mercy endures forever;
18 And slew famous kings,
For His mercy endures forever—
19 Sihon king of the Amorites,
For His mercy endures forever;
20 And Og king of Bashan,
For His mercy endures forever—
21 And gave their land as a heritage,
For His mercy endures forever;
22 A heritage to Israel His servant,
For His mercy endures forever.

23 Who remembered us in our lowly state,
For His mercy endures forever;

[24]And rescued us from our enemies,
For His mercy endures forever;
[25]Who gives food to all flesh,
For His mercy endures forever.

[26]Oh, give thanks to the God of heaven!
For His mercy endures forever.

This seems to be a responsive song, where one person reads the first line and another (or others) read the refrain: *'For His mercy endures forever.'* In a sense, the story is constantly interrupted by the 'audience' interjecting their response to the truths being sung.

(VERSES 1-4) There are twenty-six verses in this psalm. Each one carries the same last five words: *'His mercy endures forever.'* The same phrase comes another fourteen times in the Bible, all in the Old Testament, making forty times in all. Do not believe anyone saying the Old Testament is full of judgment and the New Testament is full of love. They are both full of God's love and judgment, reflecting His balanced nature. Various Bible versions translate the NKJV word *for 'mercy'* (AV, NKJV) as *'love'* (NIV), *'steadfast love'* (ESV), and *'lovingkindness'* (NASB). No single English word is deep or wide enough to convey the full nature and depth of God's mercy. It is a *merciful, kind, steadfast and everlasting love* that God has for sinners. That alone explains why *'God so loved the world that He gave His one and only Son'*—to die on the cross as our substitute to be punished for our sins—*'that whoever believes in Him shall not perish but have everlasting life'* (John 3:16). We read who God is: *'good'*, sovereign over all other *'gods'* and *'lords'*, and the Almighty who *'alone does great wonders'*.

(VERSES 5-9) The first mention of His *'great wonders'* is that He is Creator. He created the *'heavens'*, the *'earth'*, the *'sun'* and the *'moon and stars'*. No one else can ever do, repeat or destroy that!

(VERSES 10-15) He is the Deliverer, as He proves to His people Israel when He takes them out of the might of Egypt. He overcomes the Egyptians. He mightily liberates Israel, divides the Red Sea, and destroys Pharaoh and his enemy forces. He is our Saviour and mighty Deliverer today, too.

(VERSE 16) He leads Israel *through* the *'wilderness'*, keeping, and feeding them. He does that for us in our spiritual wildernesses, too.

(VERSES 17-22) He powerfully acts to keep His promises, defeats *'great kings' and 'famous kings'*. Thus He gives His people Canaan's Promised land. He keeps His promises to us, still, and always will. Trust in our faithful God now!

(VERSE 23) He remembers our lowliness as guilty and weak sinners, and still gives us His loving mercy.

(VERSES 24-26) He rescues and feeds His lowly, sinful, and undeserving people. It was true for Israel then. It is true now for every sinner who repents and trusts in the Lord Jesus Christ as his Lord and Saviour because *'His mercy endures forever.'* That is something for which every blood-bought sinner could and should always *'give thanks to the God of heaven!'*

Psalm 137—Hanging up the harps

[1]By the rivers of Babylon,
There we sat down, yea, we wept
When we remembered Zion.
[2]We hung our harps
Upon the willows in the midst of it.
[3]For there those who carried us away captive asked of us a song,
And those who plundered us requested mirth,
Saying, "Sing us one of the songs of Zion!"

[4]How shall we sing the LORD's song
In a foreign land?
[5]If I forget you, O Jerusalem,
Let my right hand forget its skill!
[6]If I do not remember you,
Let my tongue cling to the roof of my mouth—
If I do not exalt Jerusalem
Above my chief joy.

[7]Remember, O LORD, against the sons of Edom
The day of Jerusalem,
Who said, "Raze it, raze it,
To its very foundation!"

[8]O daughter of Babylon, who are to be destroyed,
Happy the one who repays you as you have served us!
[9]Happy the one who takes and dashes
Your little ones against the rock!

(VERSES 1-4) God's people are captives in Babylon. They long to worship God, as before, in the temple on Mount Zion, Jerusalem. Jerusalem lies wrecked and desolate, except for a few 'nobodies' who are left behind by the Babylonians.

As they remember all this in the river plains of Babylon, beside the Tigris and Euphrates rivers, they weep. Ridiculed and tormented there in captivity, they hang their harps on the tall poplar trees, out of the sight and touch of their tormentors. They had hoped to continue praising God with their harps in Babylon, but to do so would lead to ridicule of and mocking of God by those who jeer at the downcast captives. They jokingly urge them to *'Sing us one of the songs of Zion'*. They will not do that on demand, in that hostile and *'foreign land'*, just to quench the cruel Babylonian sense of humour or enjoyment at their expense. They say, *'How shall we?'* and will not do it. If we widen that principle today, many who love Christ feel unable to sing some popular worldly songs which offend biblical holiness. We should sing praise to God wholeheartedly, of course, when we can. As the hymn writer puts it, 'Take my lips and let them sing ever, only for my King.'

(VERSES 5-6) Sometimes we do not realise just how much we value something until it has gone. In Babylon, God's people feel like that. They long for the worship of God, typified and helped by His temple on Zion. If you are a real Christian, does this challenge you? By 'real Christian' I mean that you believe Jesus has borne you sins and their punishment on the cross, and you have turned from your sin and self to ask Him into your life as your Lord and Saviour? Is that true of you? If so, each Lord's Day (Sunday) you should plan to go to a church or fellowship which believes and teaches the Bible and, each week, to its Bible study and prayer meeting. If you let any of that slip, you will know you have missed something vital that honours God. It is the same to miss your daily walk with God through reading the Bible and praying each day. As someone put it cleverly, '*Seven days without reading the Bible and praying makes one weak.*' (Note the play on words—'weak' not '*week*'!) Missing that time of spiritual blessing by forgetting Jerusalem is so real to the captive psalmist that he feels he would rather be without his right hand and its skills, and without his tongue and his ability to speak. That is how vital being in ongoing communion with God and other believers is to him. He says this is '*Above my chief joy.*' How about you?

(VERSES 7-9) He now expresses his righteous anger for how the Babylonians and the Edomites cruelly mistreated God's people.

Since the days of conflict between Jacob, who was also called 'Israel' and fathered the Israelite nation, and his brother Esau, the father of the Edomites, there has always been conflict between Edom and Israel. Edom supported Babylon's razing Jerusalem to the ground. They both were happy to dash young children '*against the rock*'. The psalmist warns his cruel foes that they will be conquered and cruelly overrun, too. They were, just as God predicted it (Obadiah 1:8-21, Jeremiah 49:7-12).

Psalm 138—Our LORD over all 'gods'

A Psalm of David.
[1]I will praise You with my whole heart;
Before the gods I will sing praises to You.
[2]I will worship toward Your holy temple,
And praise Your name
For Your lovingkindness and Your truth;
For You have magnified Your word above all Your name.
[3]In the day when I cried out, You answered me,
And made me bold with strength in my soul.

[4]All the kings of the earth shall praise You, O LORD,
When they hear the words of Your mouth.
[5]Yes, they shall sing of the ways of the LORD,
For great is the glory of the LORD.
[6]Though the LORD is on high,
Yet He regards the lowly;
But the proud He knows from afar.

[7]Though I walk in the midst of trouble, You will revive me;
You will stretch out Your hand
Against the wrath of my enemies,
And Your right hand will save me.
[8]The LORD will perfect that which concerns me;
Your mercy, O LORD, endures forever;
Do not forsake the works of Your hands.

(VERSES 1-3) This psalm of David combines so many helpful truths and principles we find throughout the psalms. He applies them to his current situation. God's truths are never just to be looked at as an antique collector looks through an antique shop window. They are for us to apply as we live for the Lord Jesus Christ. They bless, rebuke, challenge and lead us, as well as lead those to Christ who have not yet turned from their sins and trusted in our crucified, risen, and ever-living Lord.

David's commitment shines out through all this. He is determined to praise the LORD with his *'whole heart'*. He shuns the petty 'gods' of his world, just as we must shun the 'gods' of our world: materialism, false religion, ungodly living, wrong views of sex and behaviour, lust for entertainment—we could go on and on. All are nothing compared to knowing and following the Lord Jesus Christ.

> *'Let this mind be in you which was also in Christ Jesus, who, being in the form of God, did not consider it robbery to be*

> *equal with God, but made Himself of no reputation, taking the form of a bondservant, and coming in the likeness of men.*
> *And being found in appearance as a man, He humbled Himself and became obedient to the point of death, even the death of the cross. Therefore God also has highly exalted Him and given Him the name which is above every name, that at the name of Jesus every knee should bow, of those in heaven, and of those on earth, and of those under the earth, and that every tongue should confess that Jesus Christ is Lord, to the glory of God the Father.'*
> (Philippians 2:5-11).

When you realise that Jesus' *'death of the cross'* was to bear God's punishment and wrath on your sins, it is mind blowing. When you then think about His resurrection from the dead and His risen life, by which through the Holy Spirit He enters the lives of those who trust Him, you become lost for words! David praised God, looking towards Zion's temple. We just look to Jesus. He answers us, just as He answered David. May He make us *'bold with strength in my soul'* too, in living for Jesus and making Him known.

(VERSES 4-5) We can understand why King David wants all mere human kings to hear God's Word, praise Him, sing of His ways, and realise His glory. It far exceeds his and their reigns in quality, amount, and time span.

(VERSE 6) Our glorious and exalted LORD on high is not attracted by man's pomp and pride. He looks for sinners who admit they need God's mercy, grace, pardon and help. The way 'up' is 'down'. Do you recall this encouraging prayer which the Lord Jesus Christ emphasised? *'And the tax collector, standing afar off, would not so much as raise his eyes to heaven, but beat his breast, saying, "God, be merciful to me a sinner!" I tell you, this man went down to his house justified rather than the other; for everyone who exalts himself will be humbled, and he who humbles himself will be exalted'* (Luke 18:13). Jesus said that this sinner's prayer was answered by God.

(VERSES 7-8) David found that God revived and saved him *'in the midst of trouble'* and even when *'the wrath of* [his] *enemies'* was arrayed against him, with serious risk to his life. God's loving mercy and purposes for His servant never faltered. The same is true for you if you know and follow the Lord Jesus. Please read Romans 8:28 and 37. Note from Romans 8:37 that God does not always deliver us by taking out of such adverse circumstances but rather that it is *'in all these things we are more than conquerors through Him who loved us'*.

Psalm 139—'Search me, O God'

For the Chief Musician. A Psalm of David.
1O LORD, You have searched me and known me.
2You know my sitting down and my rising up;
You understand my thought afar off.
3You comprehend my path and my lying down,
And are acquainted with all my ways.
4For there is not a word on my tongue,
But behold, O LORD, You know it altogether.
5You have hedged me behind and before,
And laid Your hand upon me.
6Such knowledge is too wonderful for me;
It is high, I cannot attain it.

7Where can I go from Your Spirit?
Or where can I flee from Your presence?
8If I ascend into heaven, You are there;
If I make my bed in hell, behold, You are there.
9If I take the wings of the morning,
And dwell in the uttermost parts of the sea,
10Even there Your hand shall lead me,
And Your right hand shall hold me.
11If I say, "Surely the darkness shall fall on me,"
Even the night shall be light about me;
12Indeed, the darkness shall not hide from You,
But the night shines as the day;
The darkness and the light are both alike to You.

13For You formed my inward parts;
You covered me in my mother's womb.
14I will praise You, for I am fearfully and wonderfully made;
Marvelous are Your works,
And that my soul knows very well.
15My frame was not hidden from You,
When I was made in secret,
And skillfully wrought in the lowest parts of the earth.
16Your eyes saw my substance, being yet unformed.
And in Your book they all were written,
The days fashioned for me,
When as yet there were none of them.

17How precious also are Your thoughts to me, O God!
How great is the sum of them!
18If I should count them, they would be more in number than the sand;
When I awake, I am still with You.

19Oh, that You would slay the wicked, O God!
Depart from me, therefore, you bloodthirsty men.
20For they speak against You wickedly;
Your enemies take Your name in vain.

21 Do I not hate them, O LORD, who hate You?
And do I not loathe those who rise up against You?
22 I hate them with perfect hatred;
I count them my enemies.

23 Search me, O God, and know my heart;
Try me, and know my anxieties;
24 And see if there is any wicked way in me,
And lead me in the way everlasting.

(VERSES 1-6) The LORD is 'omniscient' ('all-knowing'). God searches David and knows all about him: where he sits and rises, his thoughts, where he goes and sleeps, and what he does and says. God is before and behind him, like a hedge. God's hand is on David, but this is too *'wonderful'* and too *'high'* for David to grasp.

(VERSES 7-10) By His Spirit, God is everywhere. David cannot flee from Him. Whether high or deep, however early in the day, wherever he goes even *'in the uttermost parts of the sea'*, God's guiding and holding hand is on and with David.

(VERSES 11-12) Darkness and light are alike to God. He sees His servant all the time.

(VERSES 13-16) God even knew David in his mother's womb and *'formed his inward parts'*. That is why each baby is *'fearfully and wonderfully made'* and part of what God has *'wonderfully made'*, though unseen, from conception. God even specifically fashions all our days of life *'when as yet there were none of them'*. A foetus is not just a *'product of conception'* but he or she is already a human being, precious to God. He or she should be precious to us, too.

(VERSES 17-18) God's thoughts towards all people He has created, from the womb onwards, are *'precious'* and *'more in number than'* the sum of all the world's grains of sand. God is personally always present with David, and now with each sinner who trusts in the Lord Jesus.

(VERSES 19-22) David loves God so much that, by comparison, he hates all whose *'bloodthirsty'* and sinful conduct and words show they hate God and rebel against Him. David counts God's enemies as his.

(VERSES 23-24) David wants God to search, know, and test his heart and life. He asks God to remove from him both anxiety and anything offensive and lead him in God's everlasting way. Because

Jesus bore your sins and their penalty on the cross, He can remove your sins from God's sight and from you, and you, too, can have your heart cleansed each day through the precious shed blood of Jesus.

If you have not done so yet, please open your life now to the risen Lord Jesus: repent and receive Him.

Psalm 140—Praying it through

To the Chief Musician. A Psalm of David.
1Deliver me, O LORD, from evil men;
Preserve me from violent men,
2Who plan evil things in their hearts;
They continually gather together for war.
3They sharpen their tongues like a serpent;
The poison of asps is under their lips. Selah

4Keep me, O LORD, from the hands of the wicked;
Preserve me from violent men,
Who have purposed to make my steps stumble.
5The proud have hidden a snare for me, and cords;
They have spread a net by the wayside;
They have set traps for me. Selah

6I said to the LORD: "You are my God;
Hear the voice of my supplications, O LORD.
7O God the Lord, the strength of my salvation,
You have covered my head in the day of battle.
8Do not grant, O LORD, the desires of the wicked;
Do not further his wicked scheme,
Lest they be exalted. Selah

9"As for the head of those who surround me,
Let the evil of their lips cover them;
10Let burning coals fall upon them;
Let them be cast into the fire,
Into deep pits, that they rise not up again.
11Let not a slanderer be established in the earth;
Let evil hunt the violent man to overthrow him."

12I know that the LORD will maintain
The cause of the afflicted,
And justice for the poor.
13Surely the righteous shall give thanks to Your name;
The upright shall dwell in Your presence.

(VERSES 1-3) When David prays, he gets straight to the heart of his prayer. A young child in need talks like that to his parents. It is good to remember to pray like that. David starts this psalm with two requests: one is for rescue; the other is for protection. The good news of the Lord Jesus Christ deals with both those very important matters: rescue and protective preservation for all who trust Him. We are, by nature, sinners who cannot do right consistently or continually. We are on the broad road to a lost and eternal place of destruction (Matthew 7:13-14). We cannot conquer the sin in us or around us, or the malicious power of the devil. We cannot save ourselves. We need to be rescued from sin, death and Hell just as a drowning man who cannot swim needs to be rescued from the rough sea engulfing him. David had to face men of violence, evil planning, daily warfare, and evil lips and mouths that were as sharp as a serpent's and poisoned their hearers about him. God rescued David. The Lord Jesus is our Rescuer. Never forget that as '*the Son of Man* [He] *has come to seek and to save what was lost' (Luke 19:10).* He lived a perfect life without any sign, suggestion or hint of sin. His perfect body bore God the Father's wrath against us as the penalty for our sins. He died and rose again. All who now turn from sin and trust Him receive God's pardon and eternal life. He rescues us from Hell, for Heaven. He is with us to keep and help us walk on His narrow but blessed way. He is our Deliverer. He is also our protecting Preserver. The Lord now protects, guards and guides us spiritually, just as He protected David then from his vicious foes.

(VERSES 4-11) Having laid all this before God in prayer, David faces the fact that he has strong and able enemies. That very fact keeps him trusting the Lord, because he has insufficient strength of his own to win.

It is the same for us in our spiritual battles. We are overwhelmed, but God is with us. We sometimes are opposed by people like those who work, conspire and plan to trap and bring down David. David reminds God that He is his God. David turns all their opposition into specific prayers to sustain and help him. He asks God to defeat his enemies in physical ways. We must pray for His help spiritually. His emphasis is that his foes be judged and removed. Our attitude to any who oppose us is to ask God to save and bless them, so that they will come to love the Lord. Only Jesus Christ can do that. That has the side effect of protecting us, too. I remember once being threatened by the tough father of a converted teenage girl in our Young Life group, not because I had done anything wrong but because of jealousy about the influence that the gospel was having in her life. As he was an expert in unarmed combat, I realised the threat could be real. (He has also expressed himself violently before to someone else.) We prayed for him. I think it was two days later he called me in a friendly manner and told me he had come to Christ. I was thrilled for him, and not a little relieved for myself!

(VERSES 12-13) Having shared his needs and his heart in prayer with the God who loves him, David's confidence in God and in God's character and His actions rises to the top in David's prayer priorities. The *'cause of the afflicted'* and God's *'justice for the poor'* will therefore prevail. All counted *'righteous'* and *'upright'* by God will praise Him and *'dwell in* [God's] *presence'* eternally. That also includes sinners made right with God through faith in the Lord Jesus Christ. His blood cleanses away their sins, and His spotless and perfect righteousness is counted as theirs. When? At the moment that they turn from sin and ask Him into their lives to forgive and bless them and direct them in the future.

Psalm 141—What makes a man of God?

A Psalm of David.
1 LORD, I cry out to You;
Make haste to me!
Give ear to my voice when I cry out to You.
2 Let my prayer be set before You as incense,
The lifting up of my hands as the evening sacrifice.

3 Set a guard, O LORD, over my mouth;
Keep watch over the door of my lips.
4 Do not incline my heart to any evil thing,
To practice wicked works
With men who work iniquity;
And do not let me eat of their delicacies.

5 Let the righteous strike me;
It shall be a kindness.
And let him rebuke me;
It shall be as excellent oil;
Let my head not refuse it.

For still my prayer is against the deeds of the wicked.
6 Their judges are overthrown by the sides of the cliff,
And they hear my words, for they are sweet.
7 Our bones are scattered at the mouth of the grave,
As when one plows and breaks up the earth.

8 But my eyes are upon You, O God the LORD;
In You I take refuge;
Do not leave my soul destitute.
9 Keep me from the snares they have laid for me,
And from the traps of the workers of iniquity.
10 Let the wicked fall into their own nets,
While I escape safely.

(VERSES 1-2) David's prayer is not just *'LORD, I cry out to You'*, but *'O LORD, I cry out to you.'* Hundreds of prayers in the Psalms use *'O'*. It reveals the *heart* of the one praying. We must pray from the heart. David now starts praying urgently about his troubles and ends peacefully. He focuses on God. We must focus on God when we pray. David asks God to *'make haste'* to him, and to regard his prayer like the sweet scent of incense used in Old Testament worship, and accept it as He accepts the temple sacrifice, each evening.

(VERSES 3-4) Next, we see that David is a real man of God. We know he is a sinner and has fallen badly in the past. But we also know that God heard his prayer of genuine repentance, and forgave, cleansed, restored and revived him spiritually. Read Psalm 51 to see how he prayed. Please do not think that because you are a big sinner, perhaps with very wrong things in your past, that you cannot become a man of God. By God's grace you can. Every man or woman of God was a lost sinner, saved by God, when he or she repented and asked for God's forgiveness. That is the very reason why the only Man who never sinned, the Lord Jesus Christ, the 'God-Man', died on the cross of Calvary for you and rose again to be your Lord and Saviour. In His death He carried all your sins and paid for them as He hung there, willing to be punished by God the Father in your place for those sins. There is no punishment left for those who turn from settling for sin in their lives, repent and receive the risen, living Lord Jesus in their hearts. They must then stay close to Him. They grow spiritually each day by reading God's Word, the Bible, and by praying personally to Him. They are much helped by meeting up with other *'born-again'* sinners each week. Each Sunday—the Lord's Day—they meet with other Christians, in a church or fellowship, to worship God and hear His Word preached. During the week, they gather for Bible study and prayer. That is how a man or woman of God grows. David seeks to be a man of God, so he asks God to *'guard'* his mouth and *'keep watch'* over his lips. He wants to avoid his heart being inclined *'to any evil thing'* or to *'practise wicked works'*. He will avoid and shun joining in the pleasures of *'men who work iniquity'*. Today, we do need to meet with and get to know other sinners to witness to them. But do not get *too* close to those intent on evil, whose wrong living can lead you astray. We should meet with them, love them for Christ's sake, show forth Jesus by life and by lip, but not get too close to them in their pastimes, pleasures and ambitions, here summarised in principle by the phrase *'And do not let me eat of their delicacies.'*

(VERSES 5-7) There is a striking comparison that David now gives between being rebuked by *'the righteous'*—meaning someone who knows God, having been counted as righteous through repentance and faith in the Lord—and being opposed by *'the wicked'*. It can be a blessing from the Holy Spirit if a keen brother in Christ rebukes you for something wrong. (It can seem hard at the time!) Such exhortation often helps you to confess your sins and know God's loving pardon and cleansing in your daily life with Christ. God will deal with and judge those who wickedly oppose you, as He will for any sin they do unless that person repents, turns to Christ, and so is forgiven.

(VERSES 8-10) David ends by continuing to look to God. He addresses God as '*O God the LORD*'. Our *Sovereign* LORD is in full control. The word 'Lord' (not in block capitals) can mean the same thing, so you understand what '*Jesus is Lord*' (see 1 Corinthians 12:3) says about our Saviour! The word '*LORD*', (in block capitals) is where God is called '*Jehovah*' or '*Jahweh*' in our Bibles. Our Three-in-One God is both *Lord* and *LORD*! Like David, if you '*take refuge*' in the Lord, you conquer death, Hell, and avoid the enemy's snares set to trap you. You will pass by them safely by daily keeping close to the Lord.

Psalm 142—With God in the cave

A Contemplation of David. A Prayer when he was in the cave.
1I cry out to the LORD with my voice;
With my voice to the LORD I make my supplication.
2I pour out my complaint before Him;
I declare before Him my trouble.

3When my spirit was overwhelmed within me,
Then You knew my path.
In the way in which I walk
They have secretly set a snare for me.
4Look on my right hand and see,
For there is no one who acknowledges me;
Refuge has failed me;
No one cares for my soul.

5I cried out to You, O LORD:
I said, "You are my refuge,
My portion in the land of the living.
6Attend to my cry,
For I am brought very low;
Deliver me from my persecutors,
For they are stronger than I.
7Bring my soul out of prison,
That I may praise Your name;
The righteous shall surround me,
For You shall deal bountifully with me."

(VERSES 1-2) This prayer is similar to some of David's other prayers in the psalms he writes. He often starts with urgent prayer because of some testing problem he faces. He works through the situation in prayer until he arrives at God. That always makes a big difference to David. Like him, we should focus on God when we pray. Psalm 142 starts with his crying out to the LORD. His *'supplication'* seems to have been out loud to God. David tells God that he will *'pour out'* his *'complaint before Him'* and then share his *'trouble'* with his Lord. It is far wiser to share what is on his mind with God first, than to be worried or fearful or discuss it with other people before he has made it known to his Lord. We need to have *God* first as our aim. The apostle Peter wrote, in 1 Peter 5:7, that you should be *'casting all your care on Him* [the Lord] *for He cares for you'*. That is what God the Father wants His *'born-again'* children to do. If God the Son is your Saviour, God the Father is your father, and God the Holy Spirit is your Helper, you have every reason to do that.

(VERSES 3-4) David shares with God why he knows he needs His help and support. He speaks in general about how God can help, but he has King Saul's opposition in mind. He helps His disciples when they need it. David needs His help when:

- his '*spirit was overwhelmed within* [him]'.
- His foes '*secretly set a snare for him*' to trap him.
- '*no one*' (except God) 'acknowledges' him or '*cares for* [his] *soul*'.
- he has no '*refuge*' (except God).

David's specific troubling problem is referred to in the title: '*A Prayer when he* [David] *was in the cave.*' David continues to hide in Adullam's cave with a growing group of seeming misfits, but whom God will enable David to mould into his army of 'mighty men' (1 Samuel 22:1-2).

David now hides from King Saul who, with his national forces, hunts David to kill him (1 Samuel 19:1). It seems a question of time before David is found and killed. God has other ideas. But David might well feel faint, trapped, relatively alone, and with no refuge except God. You may never be in a situation like David's, but if you know the Lord Jesus Christ, remember that, if your Adullam's *cave* experience causes you to worry, fear or despair, Jesus promises all those who trust Him that God has said, 'I will never leave you nor forsake you' (Hebrews 13:5). He will never let you down. Keep close to Him each day.

(VERSES 5-7) In this weak and vulnerable position, David now focuses afresh on God. See how he relates to God. Learn for yourself how to trust and follow Jesus when the pressure is on you. David cries out, '*O LORD*' again. He reminds himself that God *is* his '*refuge*'. The Lord Jesus Christ died on the cross in our place to bear our sins and their penalty, rose again, and lives today. He is our '*refuge*' if we turn from sin to receive Him into our lives. God is David's '*portion in the land of the living*'. The LORD is also all we need. And we are in '*the land of the living*' spiritually and eternally, as well as physically. In his low state, David asks God to answer him. He asks to be rescued and freed from his '*prison*' in that cave. He is confident that he will meet with other believers again, and that God '*shall deal bountifully with* [him]'. God does all that for him! He will do it for you as well, through Christ.

Psalm 143—How to pray under pressure

A Psalm of David.
[1]Hear my prayer, O LORD,
Give ear to my supplications!
In Your faithfulness answer me,
And in Your righteousness.
[2]Do not enter into judgment with Your servant,
For in Your sight no one living is righteous.

[3]For the enemy has persecuted my soul;
He has crushed my life to the ground;
He has made me dwell in darkness,
Like those who have long been dead.
[4]Therefore my spirit is overwhelmed within me;
My heart within me is distressed.

[5]I remember the days of old;
I meditate on all Your works;
I muse on the work of Your hands.
[6]I spread out my hands to You;
My soul longs for You like a thirsty land. Selah

[7]Answer me speedily, O LORD;
My spirit fails!
Do not hide Your face from me,
Lest I be like those who go down into the pit.
[8]Cause me to hear Your lovingkindness in the morning,
For in You do I trust;
Cause me to know the way in which I should walk,
For I lift up my soul to You.

[9]Deliver me, O LORD, from my enemies;
In You I take shelter.
[10]Teach me to do Your will,
For You are my God;
Your Spirit is good.
Lead me in the land of uprightness.

[11]Revive me, O LORD, for Your name's sake!
For Your righteousness' sake bring my soul out of trouble.
[12]In Your mercy cut off my enemies,
And destroy all those who afflict my soul;
For I am Your servant.

(VERSES 1-2) Some psalms are 'linear' and some 'circular' in content: the 'linear' ones go down a list of topics; the 'circular' ones keep returning to the same topics. Some psalms blend them both together. Such a blend reminds us to be ordered in our thinking before God and to cover all the ground, but also makes sure we do not just go through a 'to do' list without our hearts being in it. Psalm 142 is linear; Psalm 143 is more circular. It starts with clear gospel principles: David cries for God to listen to his *'supplications'*. He seeks God's *'faithfulness' and 'righteousness'* for his *relief'*; he wants to avoid *'judgment'*; he admits he is not *'righteous'* before God. We are not *'righteous'* because of our defiling sin. We deserve God's *'judgment'* for that sin. But *relief* from God's wrathful judgment is ours if we turn our back on our sin, thank Jesus for taking our *'judgment'* in His own body on the cross where He died in our place, and trust solely in Christ. When the Lord forgives our sin, He credits us with God's perfect *'righteousness'*. His *'faithfulness'* is shown in how He always answers any sinner's prayer to come to Christ. Acts 2:21 says, *'whoever calls on the name of the Lord shall be saved.'*

(VERSES 3-4) As in Psalm 142, David is suffering from his enemy's continuous persecution which causes him at times to *'dwell in darkness'*, *'grow faint'* in spirit, and be *'crushed'* and *'overwhelmed within' himself'*. He is *'distressed'* in his *'heart'*. He is right to be open with God, even though God's light, strength, and peaceful joy are his if he trusts in and looks to the Lord. We, too, need be honest with God about our state and our needs, but still to trust Him fully.

(VERSES 5-6) David looks back to all his unchanging God has already done for him. He prays and thirsts for God. Recalling His faithfulness and thirsting for Him are vital in our walk with God and spiritual warfare.

(VERSES 7-12) These last six verses again go through David's prayers, weakness, trust, enemies, requests, commitment, and remembering who God is. At school I was taught that a verb is a *doing word.* We close our thoughts on Psalm 143 by seeing what David prays for God to *do for him*:

- *'Answer me speedily.'*
- *'Do not hide Your face from me.'*
- *'Cause me to hear Your loving kindness in the morning.'*
- *'Cause me to know the way in which I should walk.'*
- *'Deliver me. . . from my enemies.'*

- *'Teach me to do Your will.'*
- *'Lead me in the land of uprightness.'*
- *'Revive me.'*
- *'Bring my soul out of trouble.'*
- *'Cut off my enemies.'*
- *'Destroy all those who afflict my soul.'*

The Lord Jesus not only saves sinners from Hell to welcome them in Heaven; He helps us *each day*. He is with us *now* to bless us. We can pray to Him with great confidence. Bear in mind, as we have noted before in the Psalms, that as Christians we need God's help and strength to fight against our spiritual enemies—the world, the flesh and the devil.

Psalm 144—God's character and acts

A Psalm of David.
1Blessed be the LORD my Rock,
Who trains my hands for war,
And my fingers for battle—
2My lovingkindness and my fortress,
My high tower and my deliverer,
My shield and the One in whom I take refuge,
Who subdues my people under me.

3LORD, what is man, that You take knowledge of him?
Or the son of man, that You are mindful of him?
4Man is like a breath;
His days are like a passing shadow.

5Bow down Your heavens, O LORD, and come down;
Touch the mountains, and they shall smoke.
6Flash forth lightning and scatter them;
Shoot out Your arrows and destroy them.
7Stretch out Your hand from above;
Rescue me and deliver me out of great waters,
From the hand of foreigners,
8Whose mouth speaks lying words,
And whose right hand is a right hand of falsehood.

9I will sing a new song to You, O God;
On a harp of ten strings I will sing praises to You,
10The One who gives salvation to kings,
Who delivers David His servant
From the deadly sword.

11Rescue me and deliver me from the hand of foreigners,
Whose mouth speaks lying words,
And whose right hand is a right hand of falsehood—
12That our sons may be as plants grown up in their youth;
That our daughters may be as pillars,
Sculptured in palace style;
13That our barns may be full,
Supplying all kinds of produce;
That our sheep may bring forth thousands
And ten thousands in our fields;
14That our oxen may be well laden;
That there be no breaking in or going out;
That there be no outcry in our streets.
15Happy are the people who are in such a state;
Happy are the people whose God is the LORD!

❖

(VERSES 1-2) David begins this psalm with the word '*blessed*', which is a good way to begin anything directed at God. He blesses God for *eight* things *He is*, and *three* things *He does*. Although God does what He does because He is who He is, it is good to praise Him for His character before you praise Him for His acts, even though one is bound to lead to the other. So here are *eight* aspects of *God Himself* that cause David to praise Him.

The LORD God is David's:

- *Rock;*
- *Lovingkindness;*
- *Fortress;*
- *High tower;*
- *Deliverer;*
- *Shield;*
- *Refuge;*
- *Subduer of David's people under him.*

Here are the *three* ways that God acts to bless and help David:

- God trains him for warfare which he must conduct as the king and army commander of a nation which has to fight against real enemies.
- God gives David refuge through being his Fortress, High tower, Deliverer, Shield, and Refuge.
- God subdues people under King David.

If you repent of sin and trust in the now-risen Jesus, through His substitutionary death on the cross when He bore your sins and penalty for them, all of the above things are true of Him for your spiritual blessing. You then discover Jesus as *the One who fulfils all of the eight and three points listed above.* Through the Bible truth, the help of the Holy Spirit, and your daily and weekly drawing close to God, He trains you for the spiritual warfare you will face against the world, the flesh and the devil.

(VERSES 3-4) Human life is short. Like a '*breath*' or a passing '*shadow*', life passes very quickly. Yet God cares for and thinks about us. In Christ He became a man to die for us so we can trust in Him and be saved.

(VERSES 5-8) David asks God to intervene from Heaven to deliver and rescue him from the lies and deceit of foreign foes. We must seek His help in our spiritual battles against our foes.

(VERSES 9-10) David plans to praise God in a new song for victory, '*salvation*' and deliverance He gives David from the '*deadly sword*'. We should thank and praise Him often for saving us.

(VERSES 11-15) David prays again. He asks for deliverance from '*foreigners*', from liars, and from those who promote '*falsehood*'. He is so blessed by God's saving him. There is no captivity, crying or distress. Growing sons and daughters, full barns of provisions, and increasing livestock (both sheep and oxen) all show that the Lord is on His people's side. That is true for us, too, in trusting Jesus. We are doubly blessed and '*happy*', because we are people whose '*God is the LORD*'.

Psalm 145—Praise God because. . .

A Praise of David.
1I will extol You, my God, O King;
And I will bless Your name forever and ever.
2Every day I will bless You,
And I will praise Your name forever and ever.
3Great is the LORD, and greatly to be praised;
And His greatness is unsearchable.

4One generation shall praise Your works to another,
And shall declare Your mighty acts.
5I will meditate on the glorious splendor of Your majesty,
And on Your wondrous works.
6Men shall speak of the might of Your awesome acts,
And I will declare Your greatness.
7They shall utter the memory of Your great goodness,
And shall sing of Your righteousness.

8The LORD is gracious and full of compassion,
Slow to anger and great in mercy.
9The LORD is good to all,
And His tender mercies are over all His works.

10All Your works shall praise You, O LORD,
And Your saints shall bless You.
11They shall speak of the glory of Your kingdom,
And talk of Your power,
12To make known to the sons of men His mighty acts,
And the glorious majesty of His kingdom.
13Your kingdom is an everlasting kingdom,
And Your dominion endures throughout all generations.

14The LORD upholds all who fall,
And raises up all who are bowed down.
15The eyes of all look expectantly to You,
And You give them their food in due season.
16You open Your hand
And satisfy the desire of every living thing.

17The LORD is righteous in all His ways,
Gracious in all His works.
18The LORD is near to all who call upon Him,
To all who call upon Him in truth.
19He will fulfill the desire of those who fear Him;
He also will hear their cry and save them.
20The LORD preserves all who love Him,
But all the wicked He will destroy.
21My mouth shall speak the praise of the LORD,
And all flesh shall bless His holy name
Forever and ever.

(VERSES 1-2) David's *psalm of praise* paves the way for the next and last five praise psalms in the book of Psalms. It is 'acrostic', meaning that each verse (verse 13 consisting of *two* combined verses) begins with a new letter of the Hebrew alphabet, all in Hebrew alphabetical order.

David expresses his intention to *'extol' 'my God, O King'*, and to *'bless'* God's *'name'* both *'every day'* and *'forever and ever'*. If you know Jesus as the Saviour who bled and died for you to bear your sins and penalty for your sins, and as the Lord who rose up from the grave, you will have no problem in praising Him for eternity in Heaven. No sin will be there to hinder you and you will be with the glorified Lord Jesus Christ for ever. To discipline yourself to praise Him every day before death is not easy at times, especially if you are going through hard times. But real praise comes from a willing heart, not from emotion. With God's help, you can praise Him daily for who He is and all He has done. This can occur only if you repent of sin and receive Jesus in your heart by faith.

David teaches we ought to praise our loving Lord because of His qualities shown in the remaining verses of this psalm, as follows:

(VERSES 3-7) . . . ongoing and *'unsearchable'* greatness, shown in His *'mighty', 'wondrous', and 'awesome' 'acts'*, and revealing the *'glorious splendor of* [His] *majesty'*, His *'might'*, His *'great goodness'* and His *'righteousness' which are a good reason to 'sing' about Him.*

(VERSES 8-13) . . . His *'graciousness'* and fulness of *'compassion'*; slowness *'to anger'* and greatness in *'mercy'*; goodness *'to all'* and tenderness in His *'mercy'*; His praising *'saints'* (saved and separated people) *'blessing'* Him and telling others of His glorious and majestic *'everlasting kingdom'* of *'splendor', His 'power'* and His enduring *'dominion'* over and *'throughout all generations'*.

(VERSES 14-16) . . . upholding and uplifting help to all who fall and are 'bowed down'; generous supplying and satisfying the needs and *'desires of every living thing'*, including food.

(VERSES 17-20) . . . gracious righteousness *'in all His works'*; nearness to *'all who call on Him in truth'*; fulfilling of desires and hearing the cries of God-fearing people; saving those who do cry to Him; preserving all His loved ones; destruction of *'all the wicked'* who do not repent and trust in Him.

God is the God of amazing love and grace. But He is also holy and hates sin. His love caused Him to send Jesus into the world to save sinners (John 3:16, 1 Timothy 1:15). But unrepentant sinners remain lost. Their unforgiven sin excludes them from Heaven, because *'Nothing impure will enter it'* (Revelation 21:8, 27). John 3:36 says that *'the wrath of God abides'* on unforgiven sinners. They must turn from their sin and believe wholeheartedly on the Lord Jesus Christ.

(VERSES 21) David ends by promising to *'speak in praise of the LORD'*. He has confidence that *'all flesh shall bless His holy name forever and ever'*. That obviously speaks of all Christians because they have survived God's judgment on sin, through faith in Christ crucified and risen again.

Psalm 146—Hallelujah: Praise the LORD

[1]Praise the LORD!

Praise the LORD, O my soul!
[2]While I live I will praise the LORD;
I will sing praises to my God while I have my being.

[3]Do not put your trust in princes,
Nor in a son of man, in whom there is no help.
[4]His spirit departs, he returns to his earth;
In that very day his plans perish.

[5]Happy is he who has the God of Jacob for his help,
Whose hope is in the LORD his God,
[6]Who made heaven and earth,
The sea, and all that is in them;
Who keeps truth forever,
[7]Who executes justice for the oppressed,
Who gives food to the hungry.
The LORD gives freedom to the prisoners.

[8]The LORD opens the eyes of the blind;
The LORD raises those who are bowed down;
The LORD loves the righteous.
[9]The LORD watches over the strangers;
He relieves the fatherless and widow;
But the way of the wicked He turns upside down.

[10]The LORD shall reign forever—
Your God, O Zion, to all generations.

Praise the LORD!

(VERSES 1-2) We now begin the last five psalms with the words, '*Praise the LORD.*' Each of the five psalms starts and finishes with '*Praise the LORD*' and repeats it often. The word '*praise*' comes 540 times in the Bible, 207 times in Psalms, and 50 times in 61 verses of the last five psalms. '*Praise the LORD*' translates the Hebrew '*Hallelu Jah*'. As one word, '*Hallelujah*', it comes only in Revelation, where it is used 4 times. '*Halle*' means '*Praise*', and '*Jah*' means '*Jehovah*' or '*Jahweh*', which the NKJV presents as '*LORD*'. If the Lord Jesus Christ, who is Jehovah and Man, is your Saviour, you have much to praise God for. He died in your place on the cross to be punished for your sins. He rose again. He ascended into Heaven. He reigns there but will come back again in power and glory. He dwells in your heart if you have repented and trusted in Him as your Lord and Saviour. Every Christian and non-Christian should praise God for 'common grace' such as, food, family, friends, health and daily blessings. We lose some of those in life, especially as we get older. If you know Jesus, you will never lose Him! So, the psalmist proclaims that, like David in Psalm 145, he will *'praise the LORD'* all his life and sing that praise *'while I have my being'*—in other words, *as long as he lives*. Ask God to make you become like that. It will change you. When praising God, you do not sulk or grumble. The real blessing is that, because God gives us eternal life when we trust in Jesus, that means we will never stop praising the LORD, and never be tired of doing so in Heaven!

(VERSES 3-4) Those who trust the LORD praise Him. He is worthy of your trust. Don't trust in any man *('a son of man, in whom there is no help')* even the most influential men (*'princes'*). They will die, but God is everlasting and unchanging.

(VERSES 5-9) The *'God of Jacob'* (father of the twelve tribes of Israel but man who had many ups and downs in his inconsistent life) is the Christian's God and *'help'* too. Our certain *'hope'* is in Him, the great Creator of heaven, earth, sea, and all creatures. He *'keeps truth forever'* which means we can always rely totally on what He says through His Word, the Bible. He *'executes justice for the oppressed'*, feeds *'the hungry'*, gives prisoners *'freedom'*, *'opens the eyes of the blind'*, *'raises those who are bowed down'* and *'loves the righteous'*. All these were true of Jesus coming as Messiah. They are also true spiritually for every sinner who trusts in Jesus and so becomes *'born-again.'* Just think about it and note that a person who truly believes in the Lord Jesus Christ:

- *Trusts* in no one else but Jesus, who always helps him.
- Has that *certain* hope of Heaven.
- Finds that Jesus' Word is *always true*.
- Is *upheld* when oppressed.
- *Is fed spiritually* from the Bible, as well as physically by food God provides.
- Is *set free* from besetting sins by faith in Christ.
- Receives spiritual *sight* (*understanding*) when he is *'born-again'*.
- Is *lifted from guilt* and bondage to sins into God's peace.

- Is *counted as righteous* because Jesus' blood cleans him from sin, and Jesus' righteousness counts as his.

Note that a Christian must care for foreigners, strangers, fatherless and widows, as God does. They all need to trust Jesus. A Christian also needs to encourage the '*wicked*' to repent from his sin, receive Jesus in his heart, and be saved.

(VERSE 10) The psalm ends with '*Praise the LORD*', having assured Zion of God's eternal reign 'to *all generations*'. Zion's temple is the worship centre for Israel. Our triune God—Father, Son and Holy Spirit—reigns in the hearts of all '*born-again*' sinners, and then for ever in Heaven.

Psalm 147–Keep on praising the LORD

1Praise the LORD!
For it is good to sing praises to our God;
For it is pleasant, and praise is beautiful.

2The LORD builds up Jerusalem;
He gathers together the outcasts of Israel.
3He heals the brokenhearted
And binds up their wounds.
4He counts the number of the stars;
He calls them all by name.
5Great is our Lord, and mighty in power;
His understanding is infinite.
6The LORD lifts up the humble;
He casts the wicked down to the ground.

7Sing to the LORD with thanksgiving;
Sing praises on the harp to our God,
8Who covers the heavens with clouds,
Who prepares rain for the earth,
Who makes grass to grow on the mountains.
9He gives to the beast its food,
And to the young ravens that cry.

10He does not delight in the strength of the horse;
He takes no pleasure in the legs of a man.
11The LORD takes pleasure in those who fear Him,
In those who hope in His mercy.

12Praise the LORD, O Jerusalem!
Praise your God, O Zion!
13For He has strengthened the bars of your gates;
He has blessed your children within you.
14He makes peace in your borders,
And fills you with the finest wheat.

15He sends out His command to the earth;
His word runs very swiftly.
16He gives snow like wool;
He scatters the frost like ashes;
17He casts out His hail like morsels;
Who can stand before His cold?
18He sends out His word and melts them;
He causes His wind to blow, and the waters flow.

19He declares His word to Jacob,
His statutes and His judgments to Israel.
20He has not dealt thus with any nation;
And as for His judgments, they have not known them.

Praise the LORD!

(VERSE 1) We continue with God's plan that we should *'praise the LORD'* in this psalm. The psalmist gives us reasons to praise God. Some underline the reasons we have already considered, and some give a new emphasis. We need to remember that to go on thanking God for the same things is always very good. At the same time, we should be looking for new things we have experienced and blessings we have received which cause us to thank and praise Him. Even the morning I wrote this, I was tempted to look at God through the lens of some problems rather than look at those problems through God, and I decided to praise Him aloud for some of the many things in which God has blessed and led me personally. It is always helpful to do that, and He blessed and helped me today and helped me to serve Him in doing a task which was demanding. I praise Him for that! Praise always breeds more praise, whether with other Christians or solo. The psalmist starts with a new explanation of why to praise God. *It is 'good to sing praises to our God'.* It must always be '*good*' to do good! He then adds in doing that we will find that it is '*pleasant and praise is beautiful*'. Something '*pleasant*' and '*beautiful*' pleases us, as well as God! It *pleases* God to hear it, it *pleases* you to do it, and it *pleases* others to join together with you, whether in twos and threes, or in larger numbers. Try it and see! Of course, it is not until you connect with God as your loving Father in Heaven that this takes on special meaning. You become a child of God by receiving the Lord Jesus Christ in your heart through the Holy Spirit (John 1:12) when you see that Jesus died on the cross to take your sins and pay the penalty for them with His own precious blood. Then you ask God to forgive you for those sins, turn your back on them, and receive Christ into your heart as your personal Lord and Saviour.

(VERSES 2-20) What is on the psalmist's 'praise agenda' for praising God?

- He restores Jerusalem and its exiles.
- He heals the broken-hearted and deals with their wounds.
- He numbers and names each star.
- He is great, mightily powerful, and his understanding is infinite.
- He sustains humble people.

- He casts down the wicked who do not repent.
- He provides water and food to cattle.
- He delights when we fear Him.
- He delights when we hope in Him and in His mercy.
- He secures and satisfies Jerusalem with peace, blesses its children, and provides '*the finest of wheat*'.
- He is in control of even harsh winter weather and still supplies water.
- He reveals Himself to Israel by the Scripture and to no other nation.

In the Old and New Testaments (the Bible) God has also done that, too. It often applies physically to all kinds of people, and always applies spiritually to those who know God through the Lord Jesus Christ. So do read through the psalm again and please '*praise the LORD!*' Will you do that?

Psalm 148—From Heaven to Earth to mankind

1Praise the LORD!

Praise the LORD from the heavens;
Praise Him in the heights!
2Praise Him, all His angels;
Praise Him, all His hosts!
3Praise Him, sun and moon;
Praise Him, all you stars of light!
4Praise Him, you heavens of heavens,
And you waters above the heavens!

5Let them praise the name of the LORD,
For He commanded and they were created.
6He also established them forever and ever;
He made a decree which shall not pass away.

7Praise the LORD from the earth,
You great sea creatures and all the depths;
8Fire and hail, snow and clouds;
Stormy wind, fulfilling His word;
9Mountains and all hills;
Fruitful trees and all cedars;
10Beasts and all cattle;
Creeping things and flying fowl;
11Kings of the earth and all peoples;
Princes and all judges of the earth;
12Both young men and maidens;
Old men and children.

13Let them praise the name of the LORD,
For His name alone is exalted;
His glory is above the earth and heaven.
14And He has exalted the horn of His people,
The praise of all His saints—
Of the children of Israel,
A people near to Him.

Praise the LORD!

(VERSES 1-6) This psalm starts with *'Praise the LORD from the heavens.'* The word 'heaven' has three meanings. First, the ultimate, eternal, and perfect Heaven is pictured in Revelation 21, and referred to there as the *'new Heaven'* or the *'new Jerusalem'*. It is home to *'all His angels'*, also called *'all His hosts'*. (Some rebelled and were cast out of Heaven.) This Heaven is the first one in the 'choir' bidden to *'praise Him'*. Our Three-in-One God reigns over everyone and everything for ever and deserves their praise. It is where saved sinners are with Christ for ever and join in Heaven's praise of Jesus with the words *'Worthy is the Lamb who was slain to receive power and riches and wisdom and strength and honor and glory and blessing!'* (Revelation 5:12). Like sinners now, they are 'saved' only because the blood of Jesus was shed for them as He bore their sins and judgment on Calvary's cross in their place. The second 'heaven' is the home of the *'sun and moon'* and *' stars of light',* which we loosely call 'space'. Then there is the third heaven where aeroplanes now fly, and where clouds billow and rain falls. Genesis chapter 1 tells us how, by His Word, God created in an instant and set in place permanently these vast and seemingly timeless second and third types of heavens. These created heavens join the praise 'choir' and are urged, poetically, to *'praise Him'.*

(VERSES 7-10) After the heavens we now *'praise the LORD'* from Planet Earth. Again poetically, all creation, including all living creatures, are bidden to *'praise the LORD'*. As in the case of the heavens, they already cause open observers to find the urge to praise God arising within them. We do need to consider carefully all God's design, beauty and power in His Creation, and praise Him for all that even when we feel no inner urge to do so. Here are examinable facts. This varied choir of poetic worshippers includes the *'great sea creatures'*, the ocean, cold and stormy conditions, mountains and hills. They all make thinking men and women aware of God's power and design. I remember, even before I came to know Christ, that feeling of "There must be a God" just by gazing around from the top of Ilkley Moor in my native Yorkshire. Cedars and fruit trees, which represent what God grows in His earth, are joined by animals, both wild and domestic ('cattle'), *'creeping things and flying fowl'.* (I assume the birds form the treble section of this great *choir*!) But all these are relatively few examples of God's amazing, miraculous and very varied Creation.

(VERSES 11-13) Now we focus on man, God's steward who oversees creation. God commands mankind to *'praise the name of the LORD, for His name alone is exalted; His splendor is above the earth and the heavens.'* Only man, a spiritual and thinking being, can grasp logic like that. But which kind of men are now commanded, not merely recommended, to praise God? In one word, *'everyone'*—young and old, men and women, and children. This universal command is for men and women of influence and *'all peoples.'* This includes *'kings'*, *'princes'*, *'judges'* and everyone else, no matter who they are or where their people groups are centred. Now God *'commands all people everywhere to repent'* (Acts 17:30). No exceptions exist: *'all people everywhere'*. Psalm 72:11 says, *'Yes, all kings shall fall down before Him; All nations shall serve Him.'*

(VERSE 14) All the world's people must *'praise the LORD'*, but we close by focusing on the few who really want to *'praise the LORD'*. It is music in their ears and produces a joyful and willing response. These men and women are *'His people'* who are *'all His saints'* (set apart) for the Lord. Israel was in mind when this psalm was written. Now, it refers to all repentant sinners who receive Christ as Lord and Saviour. Such people then form part of God's universal church. They should seek to join a local church of *'born-again'* sinners. *'Horn'* points to strength: God makes believers strong in Christ by praising God together, including you, if you trust and *'praise the LORD'*.

Psalm 149—The praise of the saints

1Praise the LORD!

Sing to the LORD a new song,
And His praise in the assembly of saints.

2Let Israel rejoice in their Maker;
Let the children of Zion be joyful in their King.
3Let them praise His name with the dance;
Let them sing praises to Him with the timbrel and harp.
4For the LORD takes pleasure in His people;
He will beautify the humble with salvation.

5Let the saints be joyful in glory;
Let them sing aloud on their beds.
6Let the high praises of God be in their mouth,
And a two-edged sword in their hand,
7To execute vengeance on the nations,
And punishments on the peoples;
8To bind their kings with chains,
And their nobles with fetters of iron;
9To execute on them the written judgment—
This honor have all His saints.

Praise the LORD!

(VERSE 1) The psalmist does not explain his immediate reason for calling for praise. It involves dedicated Israelites who could be celebrating a military victory. It seems that *both* spontaneous *and* organised praise are in mind.

The first call is to *'Sing to the LORD'* a *'new song'*. The *'new song'* may invite informal praise *'to the LORD'*. No temple then, or church service now, is needed to sing praise to God. One good friend of mine sang hymns in his bath! He said it was 'One in the eye for the devil, and one in the ear for the neighbour.' I am not sure what his neighbour thought! We should praise God on our own *and* with others, in both off-the-cuff and organised situations. One hymn teaches that, if you have received the new birth in Christ, you have a new song in your heart. 2 Corinthians 5:17 says, *'If anyone is in Christ, he is a new creation; old things have passed away behold all things have become new.'* You become *'born-again'* when you admit your sins to God with shame, turn from them, ask God to forgive you, believe that on the cross Jesus died for you as He suffered the penalty for your sins in your place, and trust Him with all your heart. By the Holy Spirit, He enters your heart to dwell there as your Saviour, Lord and God.

The second call is to an organised time of singing *'His praise in the assembly of the saints'.* Do this each Sunday, the Christian Sabbath, and during the week. '*Saints'* are people set apart for God. Israel, the Old Testament *'saints'*, worshipped God focused on the temple at Zion in Jerusalem. Today, all who trust in Jesus as Lord and Saviour are God's *'saints'. They* praise Him now and will do in Heaven with others, after they die. Are you a *'saint'*? This is a way to ask, 'Do you know Jesus as your Saviour?' If so, you are a *'saint'* you belong to Him!

(VERSES 2-3) God's saints of all times can *'rejoice'*, *'be joyful in their King'* and *'praise'* God with enthusiasm and with (or without) music! At school I *played* the *tambourine* (similar to *'timbrel'*) in singing lessons. I enjoyed that; it was loud and joyful, and I needed no sense of music to do it. I am not musical, but I do love the melody and sound of the *'harp'.* Praising God needs *both* joyful and loud singers, *and* melodious music and songs. God looks at our hearts, not at our musical abilities. But He will use any musical ability you have for His glory, if your heart is right.

(VERSES 4-6) God *'takes pleasure in His people'*, namely the *'saints'* who praise Him. They are *'humble'* and are saved by God. They will 'be *joyful'* and *'sing aloud'* anywhere, even *'on their beds'.* God's praise is *'in their mouth'*. A weapon of war, *'a double-edged sword* [is] *in their hands'.* Believers in Jesus have a *'sword'*, the Word of God (the Bible), for *spiritual* warfare. Hebrews 4:12 says, *'The word of God is living and powerful and sharper than any two-edged sword.'* It cuts you off from sin and judgment. With it you fight Satan. It frees others by applying gospel truth in *'the word of God'*.

(VERSES 7-9) Israel fights *physical* wars with metal swords against human foes. God judges ungodly nations through them. They capture enemy rulers and leaders to carry out God's sentence on them. *'Born-again'* sinners (for that is what real Christians are) fight *spiritual* wars against the world, the flesh and the devil. Do that with God's praise in your heart and mouth. Always remember: *'Praise the LORD!'*

Psalm 150–Final thoughts on praising God

[1]Praise the LORD!

Praise God in His sanctuary;
Praise Him in His mighty firmament!

[2]Praise Him for His mighty acts;
Praise Him according to His excellent greatness!

[3]Praise Him with the sound of the trumpet;
Praise Him with the lute and harp!
[4]Praise Him with the timbrel and dance;
Praise Him with stringed instruments and flutes!
[5]Praise Him with loud cymbals;
Praise Him with clashing cymbals!

[6]Let everything that has breath praise the LORD.

Praise the LORD!

(VERSES 1-2) I am starting this last psalm in the book of Psalms with a confession! After spending many hours writing and recording the psalms, I was looking forward to the last five because I thought I could do them quickly and 'polish off the job'. That was a wrong attitude, and I have repented of it and asked God's forgiveness. The truth is that God has blessed me so much by the fact that I should be praising Him at all times and in all situations, because He is worthy of it, and not only because of all the wonderful things He has done for me in history and in my life since I trusted in Jesus. I have been challenged and greatly helped by that thought, and I praise God for that. To think on this short psalm of just six verses, I am using a 'Question and Answer' ('*Q*' and '*A*') approach for each verse. Here we go:

(VERSE 1) *Question: Whom should we praise? Answer: 'The LORD'* who is God.'

To praise and worship anyone but God would break the first commandment (Exodus 20:2-3).

Question: Where should we praise Him? Answer: 'In His sanctuary.'

Israel praised God in Zion's temple; saved sinners praise Him from clean and renewed hearts and dedicated bodies (Romans 12:1-2). Heaven is our eternal '*sanctuary*' in Christ. Two created 'mighty heavens'—space and sky—show the need to praise the Creator.

(VERSE 2) *Question: What else do we praise Him for? Answer: 'His mighty acts'*; and *'His excellent greatness.'*

In short, His acts and character.

(VERSES 3-5) *Question: What musical instruments should we use to praise Him? Answer:* Wind, stringed and percussion instruments, such as:

- *'the trumpet'*
- *'the lute and harp'*
- *'timbrel*
- *'strings and flute'*
- *'cymbals'*—some *'clashing'*

Question: What should be our attitude in praise? Answer: With enthusiasm and energy, when fitting. The occasional Old Testament *'dancing'* was not smoochy or sexy, or wild like disco fever or rock 'n' roll, or like ballroom dancing; it was similar to folk dancing or that done by Morris Dancers. Each dance would have a clear meaning to help Israel worship and praise God. It was not a worldly intrusion.

(VERSE 6) *Question: Who must 'praise the LORD'? Answer: 'Everything that has breath.'* Think back to Psalm 148. All living things—animals, birds and aquatic beings that God the Creator made, are to 'praise Him'. For them, that praise is 'poetic'. It reminds *us* to praise God for *their* beauty, design, strength, power, and abilities which demand and show forth that there is an almighty and divine Creator/Designer.

But as *all* humans have *'breath'*, they *all* are commanded to *'praise Him'*, whether high or lowly, male or female, young or old, and of all skin colours and races. It includes *all* the world's kings, rulers, and the most powerful and influential people in all the world. *All* nations are commanded *'to praise the LORD'*. Not to *'praise the LORD'* is a huge sin against God. It will be judged and punished eternally, with all other sins (Hebrews 9:27, Romans 1:18).

Closing thought on Psalm 150 and on all the psalms

On that great day of judgment, all sinners will be judged, except those who have repented of their sins and bowed their hearts and beings to the Lord Jesus Christ. They will be forgiven for their sins and be saved in Heaven. Hell awaits unrepentant sinners. Jesus took Hell's judgment for us on the cross so that all who trust in Him will avoid Hell and enjoy Heaven for ever. Jesus' arms were nailed open there, when He shed His blood for sinners. Today His arms are open to forgive all, but only if they come to Him in repentance. Have *you* turned to Him with all your heart? If not, please do it now. You will then have eternal reasons to gratefully '*praise the LORD*'.

Printed in Great Britain
by Amazon